Administration of
National Economic Control

THE MACMILLAN COMPANY
NEW YORK · CHICAGO
DALLAS · ATLANTA · SAN FRANCISCO

**THE MACMILLAN COMPANY
OF CANADA, LIMITED**
TORONTO

Administration of National Economic Control

EMMETTE S. REDFORD
Professor of Government
The University of Texas

New York
THE MACMILLAN COMPANY

Preface

The multiplication of agencies to administer government's economic controls has led to a vast amount of writing on the legal, administrative, and economic aspects of their work. Yet there is no comprehensive discussion of the administrative system which has been developed for control of economic activities and of the problems of an administrative nature which arise in such control.

In other fields, such as education, health, and welfare, numerous books have treated all aspects and problems of administration relating to the particular function. These books on program administration in separate fields have served real needs, for only in part are the problems of administration the same for all functions. In economic control, as in these other functions, there are some features and problems of administration which are peculiar to the particular field of activity and other features and problems which are common to all fields of administration.

The aim of this book is to show the features of the administrative system in use in economic control and the approaches which have been or may be effective in meeting the crucial problems of administration. It is the author's conviction, however, that there have been errors—dangerous errors—in past thinking on this problem of administering economic controls because of the failure to understand the nature of administration and of administrative operations. This volume also, therefore, gives as much attention to general aspects of administration as is required for understanding of the particular problems with which it deals.

The writing of a book of this type is difficult. The materials are scattered. The experience of agencies has not been adequately recorded. The separate behavior patterns in the several agencies cannot be fully grasped by one who has not been immersed in their operations. Inevitably, a general analysis must be based upon the available materials and cannot give sufficient attention to those areas where publication has been meager. The author had four years of experience in the Office of Price Administration during World War II, and hence has been able to use many illustrations from the work of this agency with complete assurance that he was offering a true picture of actual behavior in an administrative organization.

Early in the development of the material it was found to be infeasible to include both national and state experience. Publication on economic control in the several states is limited, and the settings in which control is exercised vary considerably. There were advantages also in concentrating on the problem at the national level.

I am deeply indebted to many friends who so generously provided help. Professor Harvey C. Mansfield painstakingly read the entire book and gave me many suggestions for improvement. Dean Paul H. Appleby read the volume and gave me encouragement in bringing it to its final form. My colleague, Professor J. Alton Burdine, has patiently given assistance on many sections of the book. Colleagues from the School of Law, namely, Dean Page Keeton, Professor Gray Thoron, and Professor Parker C. Fielder, and Professor Clarence Ayres of the Department of Economics, read parts of the manuscript. Professor Roscoe C. Martin and Mr. Eddins A. Lipscomb, Hearing Examiner in the Federal Trade Commission, read chapters. All of these gave me their suggestions; the author has, of course, decided upon the use of these suggestions and the defects are therefore, assuredly, his own responsibility.

To the University of Texas I am grateful for special grants for student aid and typing costs and for a research leave for one semester to complete the book.

Emmette S. Redford

Contents

Table of Cases

xiii

Administration of
National Economic Control

Chapter I

Introduction

This is an age of administration. In business corporations, labor unions, trade associations, benevolent organizations, and government the talent of men is laid to the task of organizing means for achieving objectives, of harnessing things and directing men, of programming operations and systematizing procedures—in short, of getting jobs done through the continuous and coordinated efforts of men. In the vast spread of social organizations, administrative organization and process have become central features of man's effort to be the master of his future.

The development is reflected in the concepts of current thought. In an earlier day men thought in terms of market controls, a self-regulating economic system, individual enterprise, laissez faire, and judicial supremacy. Today, we hear also of administered prices, social control, the managerial society, the administrative state, administrative legislation, administrative adjudication, and a science of administration.

The goal of administration is to get jobs done. In public affairs this raises many troublesome questions. What are the conditions of success? What kinds of authority must be given to administrative agencies? What is and what should be their relation to legislatures, chief executives, and the courts? Are adequate tools available for administrative agencies? Can they be given sufficient strength to at-

1

tain public objectives? By what means can the supremacy of the public interest be best maintained in administrative action? Can energy and flexibility be achieved in administrative institutions? Can the necessary degree of coordination of separate units of administrative organization be achieved? Can the representatives of the people maintain control over the conduct of public affairs?

In no other area are these problems so complex and so difficult as in that of public administrative action affecting the conduct of economic affairs by private, i. e., non-governmental, agents. The basic structure of economic activity is complex and day-to-day operations extend to myriad and shifting details. The administrative structure of the state must come to grips with things as they are and as they may be; technical knowledge and broad grasp are essentials of effective performance. Moreover, a dual system is created in which public authorities stand above private management to restrain or direct its action. The state action may appear to be an alien force to those who are conducting economic operations; on the other hand, it may merely reflect the particularistic desires of such groups. In either case ineffectiveness may be the result: in the former, because of the resistance or evasion of those presumably subject to public authority; in the latter, because the administrative agency lacks the vigor and independence necessary for protection of the general interests of society. Finally, in government action toward economic affairs the effects of action in particular areas on other areas and on the economy as a whole are often of great significance. The problem of coordination of administrative units fuses into a larger problem: can administration in particular agencies be brought into a sufficient measure of accord with over-all economic objectives and contribute to the successful operation of the economic system?

There is, moreover, no field of domestic policy in which the effectiveness of administrative action is more significant to Mr. Citizen. Notwithstanding the differences of opinion concerning the proper scope for public action and the proper approaches in policy, there would undoubtedly be general agreement that government has entered and will remain in the field of economic control. It will also be admitted, generally we believe, that there are periods in which the very safety of the nation may depend upon the effectiveness of public economic controls.

The problems presented in this field are significant for two reasons. First, since public administrative controls must be or will be established or maintained in many areas, effectiveness in their exercise is a desirable public objective. Second, decision on what should be done through public control of private economic action, as distinct from uncontrolled private action on the one hand, or from direct government supply of commodities and economic services on the other, is affected in some degree by judgments on the chances for effectiveness in public control.

Since the passage of the National Bank Act in 1863 there has evolved an extensive system of controls by national administrative agencies over the conduct of economic affairs by non-governmental persons. Along with this there has been an expansion and diversification of administrative methods, and a period of experience in use of administrative controls. Moreover, the experience has revealed the nature of administrative controls and the techniques available, some of the essentials for effective performance, and some of the problems which will be encountered in the future. The understanding of the future and of its problems is possible only against the background of what has emerged and what has been revealed by experience.

The developed pattern of national administrative action in the field of economic controls is not fully described in any existing book. It is probably impossible to encompass so large and complicated a task in a single volume. Nevertheless, there should be value—to students of public administration, of administrative law, and of economic controls—in a summary of the basic features of the existing system and a discussion of some major problems. This is the task undertaken in this volume.

Two initial questions arise: What precisely is the area to be covered? What approach will be used?

The area can be identified by some brief explanations and restrictive definitions. First, this book deals with the administrative aspects of public economic controls. Except for one brief chapter (Chapter II), it avoids discussion of the substance of public action, even when such action is taken through administrative agents. It centers on the methodology of government, on the mechanics of public action, on the institutional framework within which substantive action is taken. It assumes a position of neutrality as to what government should do and seeks only to explain the mechanism of control and to indicate some of the essentials for effectiveness of government in performance of whatever functions it assumes.

Moreover, this book makes no attempt to measure the impact of administrative control on the economy and the happiness and freedom of man.[1] It deals only with the *operation of a system of administration* as it is and as it may be. Except for suggestive comments in a brief concluding chapter it does not face up to the question as to whether the system can move mountains, and if so beneficently, or whether, even with maximum improvement, it can only shift a bit of soil from place to place. It assumes, however, that the weight of the impact on the economy is in part dependent upon the type of mechanism which exists and that when men have chosen to use government for attainment of policy objectives they must be interested in the search for methods which will yield greatest results, insofar of course as these do not conflict with their fundamental ideals.

The word *administration*—used interchangeably herein with the terms *administrative arm, administrative process*, and *administrative action*—refers to all decision or action which is not taken in the judicial system and which is not part of the highest level of policy decision. The judicial system must be understood, however, to include all regular or special, constitutional or legislative courts, that is, all agencies whose functions are entirely or almost exclusively judicial in nature.

The foregoing statement on the meaning of administration allows discussion of the whole of an evolved process of government

---

[1] On the latter problem see the argument of Friedrich A. Hayek, *The Road to Serfdom* (Chicago, 1944) and the answers of Herman Finer, *Road to Reaction* (Boston, 1945) and Barbara Wootton, *Freedom under Planning* (Chapel Hill, 1945).

without limitation by restrictive differentiations in past concepts. Students of public administration have for two generations drawn a distinction between politics and administration. Professor Goodnow succinctly stated the distinction: "Politics has to do with policies or expressions of the state will. Administration has to do with the execution of these policies." [2] On the other hand, realistic students have seen that there is no line separating the two major functions of making and executing policy. Thus, Professor Friedrich has said: "Public policy, to put it flatly, is a continuous process, the formation of which is inseparable from its execution. Public policy is being formed as it is being executed, and it is likewise being executed as it is being formed." [3] Government is a stream, a "continuum," as Appleby has said,[4] of policy making and action. The really significant fact is that the function of government is carried through a succession of levels of decision and action. What is a policy decision to those at one level of authority, because they have discretion to make it, or must seek higher authority to get it, is a matter of administration to those at higher levels who have conferred on subordinates the discretion to make it.

Yet all is not administration. Every translation of the demands of political superiors into concrete policy is not administration. Congress is not administering when it performs this function for the electorate. Some part of what the President and his political aides and subordinates do is likewise nonadministrative. A general guide for differentiation of these non-administrative functions of Congress and the President and his aides is at hand. When the President made a decision during World War II under the grant of power by Congress in the Second War Powers Act to allocate scarce "material or facilities," he was acting as an administrative agent of Congress. When, on the other hand, President Washington issued the Neu-

---

[2] Frank J. Goodnow, *Principles of the Administrative Law of the United States* (New York and London, 1905), 6. See also by the same author, *Politics and Administration* (New York, 1900), and Woodrow Wilson's essay, "The Study of Administration," *Political Science Quarterly*, II, 197-222 (1887).

[3] C. J. Friedrich and Edward S. Mason, *Public Policy*, 6. Copyright 1940 by the President and Fellows of Harvard College.

[4] Paul H. Appleby, *Policy and Administration* (University, Ala., 1949), 15. For elaboration of the point of view stated above, see my Chapter IV.

trality Proclamation, he made (1) as an independent officer and not as an agent of Congress (2) an *initial* policy decision which set the basis for future decision and action. There is, in other words, an area in which the basic undertakings and the initial guiding points of policy are or should be determined, and beyond this is administration—a function in general of going forward with policy elaboration and execution. The breaking point in the executive branch of government is not always clear. To define an area of study, however, it is enough to say that, in general, administration includes all the work of the branches of government except that done in Congress, the courts, and some of the work done by the President and his political aides and subordinates.[5]

The description of administrative action and of administration given here, although familiar to professional students of public administration, is broader than that given by some authorities. The Supreme Court of the United States, speaking through Justice Sutherland in Rathbun *v.* United States, distinguished between "purely executive officers" and an "administrative body," on the one hand, and "quasi-legislative and quasi-judicial bodies," on the other.[6] Following the same line, the Attorney General's Committee on Administrative Procedure said that it "regarded as the distinguishing feature of an 'administrative agency' the power to determine, either by rule or by decision, private rights and obligations."[7] It discussed the "advantages of administration as compared with

[5] Compare Appleby, *ibid.*, p. 25, where it is stated that "Most presidential policy making" is on the administrative level, and pp. 29-30, where it is said that "the eighth [process of government] is the administrative or executive process, involving everything done by agencies other than the legislative and judicial ones."

Our concluding sentence in the text denotes a structural focus for study. It is recognized, of course, that some work which is administrative is done in Congress and also in the courts, that there is an over-all problem of administering the work of Congress and the courts, and that in large measure the judicial system is only a specialized system of administration. Some day some one studying public administration may enlarge the literature of the field by absorbing the judicial process into a larger discussion of all the ways in which society may administer its affairs. We are more humble and stick to the process revealed in a so-called administrative arm. After all, the cake has to be cut in some way.

[6] 294 U. S. 602 (1935).

[7] *Final Report of the Attorney General's Committee on Administrative Procedure* (Washington, 1941), 7.

executive action," contrasting the "administrative process" with the use of "ordinary executive officers," an "administrative tribunal" with "executive officers charged with acting substantially as officers of business enterprises act," and "administrative adjudication" with "fluid executive action." [8] The Passport Division of the Department of State, the expenditure of public funds, and the Works Progress Administration were given as examples of executive or non-administrative action.[9]

Whether these distinctions have some value in defining an area of study for lawyers, or for constitutional interpretation, need not concern us here. We urge, however, that the limited use of the term "administration" cannot be accepted by the student of the subject, who must insist that his study has encompassed and must continue to encompass more because of the purpose and nature of administration. It deals with more than "private rights and obligations"; it deals also and most significantly with public interests. It deals with all the ways by which public jobs are done. Thus, it includes the detailed work of the Passport Division, the use of public expenditures in carrying out public objectives, and the work of the former Works Progress Administration. It includes also management of enterprises and the administrative decision which cannot be likened to a rule or a judicial decision, as in the decision of the Federal Reserve Board to expand its open-market negotiations.

This practical, as distinguished from the legal, concept of public administration provides the most significant basis of analysis. It enables attention to be fixed upon all the ways public jobs are done, rather than on those only which resemble the ways of legislatures and courts.

The word *control* is used herein in a broad sense to include every decision or action which seeks to limit or set the conditions under which private enterprise shall be conducted or to determine or influence the direction of private economic endeavor. The control may be exercised over a segment of the economy, as when railroads are regulated or safety standards are enforced in mines. Or the

[8] *Ibid.*, 11.
[9] *Idem.*

control may aim toward governing the conditions of the economy as a whole, as when anti-trust laws seek to maintain a free market or when credit is regulated and government's fiscal powers are used to prevent or mitigate cyclical fluctuations in the economy.

In the broad sense in which we have defined control, it may include some activities which appear to be of a service nature. It is true, of course, that control may normally be distinguished from service, whether the latter is rendered for a charge—as in loans and sales by government, or in the form of benefits—as in consular services, highways, and education. On the other hand, service is often, as Freund said, a "vehicle of control";[10] service to one economic group may be control of another; service is intertwined with control in the larger patterns of governmental action; and there is really no clear line of distinction.[11] It is possible, nevertheless, and this is all that is important here, to discuss the control aspects of government action.

By the term *economic control* the discussion here is limited to the activities of government directly related to the supply of commodities or services for business rather than charitable or welfare objectives. The distinction is subject to objection, either on the ground that there is overlapping of the two purposes, or that all government activities have significance in the economic order; but the point made in the distinction is sufficient, nevertheless, to establish the rough outlines for a field of analysis.[12]

By concentrating on the economic area and on economic control we are able to exclude from our discussion public administrative action in the following fields: (1) personal benefactions—e.g., veterans benefits, relief, old age benefits; (2) controls over personal

---

[10] Ernst Freund, *Administrative Powers over Persons and Property* (Chicago, 1928), 8.

[11] Note also A. W. Macmahon's statement regarding cooperation between government and groups: "Already collaboration has progressed so far that it is difficult to draw a line between governmental functions of restraint and of service." *Boards, Advisory, Encyclopedia of the Social Sciences,* II (1930), 610. See my Chapter XI.

[12] The word *national* in our title needs no explanation. Occasional references will be made to state or local control, but the discussion would have been too complex if extended generally to these areas.

life—e.g., aliens, selective service; (3) proprietary (public lands, parks, etc.) and fiscal (taxing and borrowing) functions; (4) institutional social services, as through hospitals and corrective institutions; (5) institutional service in the economic area, as through administrative units selling power or loaning money, except in so far as these form a part of a larger system of control; and (6) national action which is largely completed through the action of other governments, as in highways, forest protection, and education.

Limitation of discussion to control of private economic activity does not mean that such activity may not be affected by government action in the other areas listed above. Nor does it mean that there is no common core of administrative method in all the areas of public administration. On the contrary, much that is said about public administration in economic control is applicable to all or several of the other areas. In fact, half of this book is descriptive of a broader field than economic control. Nevertheless, there are some differences, either in the methods, or the problems, or in the setting in which administrative action is taken. For continuity and unity of presentation, a focus is needed in any functional study. Moreover, the area selected has distinctive significance in the public discussion of our day.

By focusing attention on administrative action in the area of economic control we are able to choose an approach which we believe is now needed in the study of public administration. This subject, it may be said, can be studied as a problem of institutional management. As such, it deals with factors of organization, finance, personnel, and materials, in short with "the management of men and materials in the accomplishment of the purposes of the state." [13] Attention in such a study is focused largely on internal structure and operations, albeit with recognition that the mechanism must function toward public objectives.

[13] Leonard D. White, *Introduction to the Study of Public Administration* (rev. ed., New York, 1939), 6. For discussion of various approaches in the study of public administration, see M. E. Dimock's "The Meaning and Scope of Public Administration," in J. M. Gaus, L. D. White, and M. E. Dimock, *The Frontiers of Public Administration* (Chicago, 1936), Chapter I.

Or public administration may be studied as a phase of the legal framework, as a part of the system for the development and application of law. As such, it deals with the powers of administrative agents and with the legal requirements concerning their procedure. Attention is focused on legislative standards, judicial review, and functions or processes which seem to be similar in some respects to those of courts.

There is yet another and broader approach to the study of public administration. It may be studied as a system of decision and action for getting government jobs done. As such, it deals not only with internal or management aspects but also with the varied instruments, techniques or methods of carrying the program of government to the people, with the unfolding of the process of government from the centers of political power and decision to the fingertips of action. It deals not alone with the legal process but also with all the practical techniques for getting jobs done and getting them accepted by the public. It considers functioning mechanism and administrative power as instrumentality and turns a large measure of attention outward to the flow of action toward the citizen.

In this last approach study is extended to all aspects of getting jobs done which have been entrusted to administrative agents. In each field, whether it be highway development and maintenance, health protection, regulation of business, or other field of administrative action, the success of the doers of public jobs will depend upon a variety of factors. Many of these are encompassed in a study of management and law set in a broad perspective where they are considered as tools for use in achieving public purposes. Others relate to such varied problems as choice of techniques, keeping the public interest dominant, planning and development of policy, and compliance with programs.

This functional approach motivates the present analysis. Without denial of the importance of study of management techniques as such, or of administration as part of the legal framework, the questions on which attention is focused in this volume are: what techniques are available and what problems of structure and operation

are faced in the effort to control private economic activity through
public administrative agencies?

In such an analysis one is aided by the many studies of particular aspects of the subject. There have been a number of exhaustive studies of the work of particular agencies, such as those of
Sharfman on the Interstate Commerce Commission, Henderson on
the Federal Trade Commission, Patterson on the Insurance Commissioner, Dodd on the Workmen's Compensation Commission,
Gaus and Wolcott on the Department of Agriculture,[14] and the recent historical studies of the control agencies during World War II;
there have been studies of particular types of administrative
problems, such as those of Herring on administrative personnel,
Herring and Leiserson on the relations between administrative
agencies and interest groups, and those of Cushman, Fesler, and
the Hoover Commission on the independent commission;[15] there has
been an increasing flow of studies on administrative powers and
procedure, including the monumental study of the Attorney General's Committee on Administrative Procedure;[16] and the various
studies on policy development in particular areas, such as transportation, utilities, labor and monopolistic practices, and also those on

[14] I. L. Sharfman, *The Interstate Commerce Commission* (New York, 1931 to
1937), Vols. I, II, III-A, III-B, and IV; Gerald C. Henderson, *The Federal Trade
Commission* (New Haven, 1925); Edwin Wilhite Patterson, *The Insurance Commissioner in the United States, A Study in Administrative Law and Practice*
(Cambridge, 1927); Walter F. Dodd, *Administration of Workmen's Compensation* (New York, 1936); John M. Gaus and Leon M. Wolcott, *Public Administration and the United States Department of Agriculture* (Chicago, 1940).

[15] E. Pendleton Herring, *Federal Commissioners: A Study of Their Careers
and Qualifications* (Cambridge, 1936); E. Pendleton Herring, *Public Administration and the Public Interest* (New York and London, 1936); Avery Leiserson,
Administrative Regulation: A Study in Representation of Interests (Chicago,
1942); Robert E. Cushman, *The Independent Regulatory Commissions* (New
York, London, and Toronto, 1941); James W. Fesler, *The Independence of
State Regulatory Agencies* (Chicago, 1942); Commission on Organization of
the Executive Branch of the Government, *Regulatory Commissions* (Washington, 1949), and Task Force of the Commission, *Regulatory Commissions*
(Washington, 1949).

[16] *Final Report of the Attorney General's Committee on Administrative Procedure* (Washington, 1941) and printed as Sen. Doc. 8, 77th Cong., 1st Sess.,
1941; and the monographs on separate agencies printed in Sen. Doc. 186, 76th
Cong., 3d Sess., 1940, and Sen. Doc. 10, 77th Cong., 1st Sess., 1941.

public administration, have given attention to administrative problems arising in the control of the economic system.

It is our hope that an over-all analysis in a single place of the national administrative system as related to control of men's economic activities will be a useful complement to the specialized studies in the field. The discussion goes through three phases: the next three chapters explain the nature and present position of administration in economic control, the following four chapters analyze tools and techniques available for administrative control, and the last four chapters deal with key problems of a very broad nature.

Chapter II

Administration As a Phase
of Economic Policy

Administration is method. The study of administration
is the study of means of getting jobs done. But method cannot be
understood apart from substance or content of programs. This chapter seeks, therefore, to draw from the tangled skein of economic
legislation the basic directions of public action; discussion of these
will reveal, in part, the task of administration.

TYPES OF GOVERNMENT ACTIVITY

There are six distinguishable, though overlapping, types of public
activity relating to the satisfaction of men's wants. These are government service, maintenance of a general framework, maintenance
of standards, industry management, functional management, and
economy management.[1] These several types of activity are separately discussed, not for the purpose of classification, but as a

[1] Compare M. E. Dimock, *Business and Government* (New York, 1949), 7,
where the "four principal functions relative to the economy" are listed as assistance, regulation, operation of economic services, and planning and stabilization; and Merle Fainsod and Lincoln Gordon, *Government and the American
Economy* (rev. ed., 1948), where government functions are discussed under the
headings of promotion, regulation, and public enterprise and conservation.

means of showing the total scope, variety, and general trends in government activity.

Government service is extensive and varied. There are services rendered to the community generally, such as protection of health and provision of educational and recreational facilities. There are other services which are particularly significant as aids to production and distribution, such as enforcement of contracts, protection of property, construction of roads and waterways, maintenance of foreign consular services, distribution of economic data, supply of monetary mechanisms, loans to industry, and benefit payments to agriculture. There are services which are rendered free of charge; others, such as sale of utility service and loan of money, are rendered on the pattern of economic enterprise for a charge.

Government service is extensively intertwined with the so-called system of private enterprise. It fills gaps left by private enterprise. It supports private enterprise in so many ways that the latter could not be conducted without it. It may influence the direction of private economic action, as when loans to industry, the protective safeguards of a tariff, or internal improvements (roads, canals, river developments, etc.) stimulate or deflect the private entrepreneur into new fields of activity.

The second type of public activity is the maintenance of a general framework, or set of social arrangements, within which private enterprise shall operate. Illustrative are recent developments in the field of labor. American industry now operates within the framework of government-prescribed systems of workmen's compensation, unemployment insurance, old-age and survivor's insurance, collective bargaining, and conciliation of labor disputes. Another illustration is the Sherman Anti-Trust Act: by placing limits upon freedom of contract and combination it sought to insure that business should be conducted in a free market. Other examples of the effect of public action on the framework within which economic enterprise is conducted may be cited: rules of property and contract, nineteenth century land and twentieth century conservation policies, rules concerning issuance of corporate charters and the conduct of corporate business.

Third, public action may govern the standards under which private enterprise operates. Long before the rise of modern regulation judicial decisions set standards of fair competition and (as in common callings) standards of fair dealing with the public. At the close of the nineteenth century there was a great expansion of legislative acts designed to protect health, morals, and safety; in this century there has been a further growth of such legislation but also a tendency to prescribe standards with purely economic objectives. Among the federal statutes passed with the objective of maintaining a standard of conduct are the Federal Trade Commission Act, the unfair practices provisions of the National Labor Relations Act, the Walsh-Healey Act, and the Federal Food, Drug, and Cosmetic Act; in addition, most of the national acts providing for regulation of particular industries include provisions setting standards of conduct. The various states and municipalities have also passed much legislation of this type.

A fourth type of public activity is the regulation of particular industries. Oftentimes such regulation has aimed, at least initially, only toward the maintenance of standards of conduct, and the method of control has been negative, consisting mainly of prohibition of certain types of action. Normally in these days the control tends to be positive and takes the form of public consent or direction on matters of managerial discretion. Public agencies make judgments continuously on the proper organization, policies, and management of particular industries. The general objective is the positive one of pointing the conduct of an industry toward desired public objectives.[2]

Our courts have sometimes drawn a distinction between regulation and management. The Supreme Court of the United States once said: "It must never be forgotten that while the state may regulate with a view to enforcing reasonable rates and charges, it is not the owner of the property of public utility companies, and it is not clothed with the general power of management incident to

---

[2] Landis has forcibly emphasized the broader purpose in regulation. He described the function of one type of agency as being the maintenance of the "economic health" or "economic well-being" of an industry. James M. Landis, *The Administrative Process*, 11-16. Copyright 1938 by Yale University Press.

ownership." [3] Regardless of whatever legal significance may still rest in this distinction between regulation and management, it is nevertheless necessary to recognize that, incident to the exercise of sovereignty, there has developed a system which has been aptly described as "policy and managerial regulation." [4] In this type of regulation, government has become in a sense a board of directors for particular industries, carrying a kind of holding company responsibility for the functioning of each of a number of selected industries. For brevity, and for distinction from the fifth type of control, it may be called industry management.

The broader objective in public control may be illustrated by reference to railroad regulation. Regulation first came as a result of popular demand for correction of abuses and the chief aim of public control was to prevent unfair and discriminatory charges. But in the Transportation Act of 1920 the objective became the positive one of maintaining an adequate transportation system. Thereafter, public control was centered "upon the guidance and supervision of the industry as a whole" and extended to almost every aspect of railroad organization and policy. Not only rates, but service, finance, and railroad organization were to be controlled for the purpose of insuring the "health" of the industry and the "discharge of its responsibilities" to the public. [5]

"Policy and managerial" regulation has been extended to a large

[3] State of Missouri *ex rel.* Southwestern Bell Telephone Co. *v.* Public Service Commission of Missouri, 262 U. S. 276, 288 (1923).

Compare the following statement of Justice Brewer: "It must be remembered that railroads are the private property of their owners; that while from the public character of the work in which they are engaged the public has the power to prescribe rules for securing faithful and efficient service and equality between shippers and communities, yet in no proper sense is the public a general manager." Opinion of the Supreme Court in I.C.C. *v.* Chicago G.W. Ry. Co., 209 U. S. 108, 118-119 (1908).

[4] The term was used by F. F. Blachly and Miriam E. Oatman in their *Federal Regulatory Action and Control* (Washington, 1940). See their discussion at pages 18-25. Of particular interest is their list of the chief functions of management and the discussion showing that in railroad regulation the government exercises control over each function. They conclude: "In other words, government management has, in the transportation field especially, and in several others notably, to a very appreciable extent supplanted private management." P. 23.

[5] James M. Landis, *The Administrative Process*, 15. Copyright 1938 by Yale University Press.

number of industries. State control of household utilities, and later
national control, has paralleled railroad regulation in its breadth and
intensity. The broad controls over finance, facilities, and service
cannot be explained realistically in terms merely of correction of
abuses or maintenance of standards of conduct. Banking and insurance have long been subjected to specific controls designed to
insure solvency and adequate discharge of public responsibilities.[6]
State oil control measures have gone further than mere maintenance of standards. Decisions on well spacing and rate of production
are made in terms of positive public objectives, namely, conservation, stabilization, and protection of correlative rights of owners.
New Deal legislation carried the assumption of responsibility for
the well-being and proper conduct of particular industries into
new fields: stock exchanges, utility holding companies, agriculture,
coal, and others; and the necessities of World War II led to temporary expansions of this type of control.

Control of economic enterprise in wartime and reconversion
points to a fifth type of government activity which may be called
functional management. In this type of action government exercises controls comparable to those in industry management but the
controls are over particular economic functions or types of policy
decisions rather than over particular industries. Thus, during the
war, productive effort was coordinated through the War Production
Board, manpower uses were controlled by a War Manpower Commission, wages by a War Labor Board, and prices by an Office of
Price Administration. The controls were different from mere maintenance of standards or general framework; here again government
was engaged in "policy and managerial regulation." Decisions formerly made by private management and boards of directors were
made by government as a kind of super-holding company.

The objectives of government in managerial regulation may ex-

---

[6] The position of the Federal Reserve Board is especially emphasized in the
following statement: "The Federal Reserve Board, however, was essentially a
managerial agency actually sharing in the direction of banking operations, exercising no quasi-judicial duties, and settling no disputes." Cushman, The Independent Regulatory Commissions, 146. Copyright 1941 by Oxford University
Press, Inc.

tend beyond the control of industries or particular functions to the efficient functioning of the economy as a whole. To the extent that this is true, government embarks on a sixth type of activity which may be called economy management.

It may be said that government is engaged in economy management to the extent to which it accepts responsibility for continuing adjustment of its policies in order that public objectives concerning the functioning of the productive and distributive mechanism as a whole may be attained. It is distinguishable from maintenance of standards, industry and functional management by the breadth of its objectives, from service activities by its control objective, and from maintenance of framework by the factor of continuous adjustment of policy. It is distinguishable from all of these in that they may all be used as parts of a larger program of economy management.

Economy management may reflect varying purposes. During the war the activities of government toward the economy were all affected by the dominant objective of increasing the production of needed war materials and supplies, and to a lesser extent various types of activities were correlated with the stabilization objective. After the war the Employment Act set the objective of maintenance of maximum employment, production, and purchasing power.[7] Since the great depression the idea has developed that a basic function of government in the economy of the future is planning and stabilization.

Planning is a word of many meanings. To some it means a blueprint for the future; to others it means only foresight, and action in accord with the forward look. To some it means detailed controls of price and production, to others it means the use of the fiscal and credit policies of the government for regulation of the economy as a whole. To some it means government responsibility to take whatever action is necessary to insure that the economic system operates efficiently, to others it means only that the government should correlate whatever functions it undertakes toward desired over-all objectives. The word stabilization likewise carries diverse

[7] February 20, 1946, 60 U. S. Stat. at Large, 23.

connotations. Generally, however, when used in connection with the concept of planning, it means only that the violence of fluctuations in the economy shall be moderated.

Some measure of economy management by government in the future is inevitable. No political party and no Administration can avoid response to the political demand that government try to plan its action so that there will be mitigation of economic depression, jobs for all or nearly all, and an acceptable level of purchasing power for the various groups in the population. To an extent, the other types of government activity outlined above will be geared to these broader objectives.

Nevertheless, each of the other types of government activity will have a distinct and separable significance. Government's purposes are multiple and diverse; it initiates programs to relieve stresses or meet demands in particular segments of the economy or to meet general objectives extending to the whole economy. All of the types of public activity we have distinguished, separately and jointly, fix the nature of the present and future task of public administration.

ADMINISTRATIVE CONSEQUENCES

The developments in government action discussed in the preceding section have had material effects upon the breadth, intensity, nature, and ramifications of administrative action.

First, administrative action is the normal method of getting the various jobs done. Some standards and some elements in the general framework have been maintained by private action in the courts, but even in these types of activities statutes usually now provide for administrative action. Service activities call automatically for administrative agencies; and where industry management, functional management, or economy management are adopted as government approaches administrative action is likewise always the essential method of performance.

Second, the developments in government service and control have led, not only to the multiplication of administrative activities, but also to a growth in the intimacy, normality, and density of the action taken through public administrative channels. By intimacy we refer to the degree of penetration of public controls and service toward the central core of private managerial responsibility. By normality we refer to the fact that public administrative action may not be merely intermittent, occasional, or unusual, but often becomes an established element in economic operations. By density we mean the total amount of administrative regulation and service for a given unit or field of economic enterprise.

The intimacy, normality, and density of the administrative impact may increase as the result of the extensions of policy along any of the lines heretofore discussed in this chapter. They are likely to become more apparent, and be most consciously felt, when standards are extended, or elements of industry management or functional management are imposed. The density of the administrative impact is, however, a result of the cumulative effect of diverse types of government action. The final result is that public administrative action either encompasses a large proportion of the decisions which have according to traditional theory inhered in private management or delimits business management's area of free choice. Thus, a banker may find that his credit decisions are limited by the cumulative effect of decisions of the Comptroller of the Currency, Federal Deposit Insurance Corporation, Federal Reserve Board, Reconstruction Finance Corporation, and perhaps other agencies; that his credit opportunities are also affected by government credit or insurance programs in agriculture, housing and other fields; and that his employment policies are hedged in by administrative application of numerous laws for the protection of labor. The resulting system cannot realistically be described as exclusively one of private management or public management; it is indeed a mixture of private enterprise and public controls, with the public participation being carried continuously by administrative agencies.

Third, the system of administrative action which has been developed for carrying out the various types of governmental programs is exceedingly complex. It is more complex than the judicial or legislative process in government or the managerial process in business because it has had to provide means of doing many different types of government jobs. Thus, the techniques for maintaining standards may differ from those used in regulation of industries; the methods used in industry or functional management may include a variety of approaches and techniques used in traditional law enforcement procedures and in business management; and the processes of service agencies will differ from those of regulatory agencies.

Fourth, one effect of the varied approaches is to lead to patterns of administrative action in which there are new combinations of legal technique and discretionary operation. The essence of public action increasingly becomes policy and management rather then mere application of legal rules; the approach is often more similar to that of a board of directors in a private enterprise than to that of law enforcement and judicial organs. To be effective the control and service must be readily adjustable to changing circumstances and objectives. It often becomes "fluid," flexible, or even pragmatic. Whether it is the Federal Reserve Board gauging its open-market operations to larger objectives, the Interstate Commerce Commission deciding whether a raise in rates will yield more returns to railroads,[8] or an Office of Price Stabilization determining which methods of obtaining public compliance will work most effectively, the pattern is one in which men measure prospective results against present objectives, as in business enterprise. Such a system may strain or escape from traditional legal approaches which have been used in simpler systems of control. Law and management have thus received a new challenge to find a *modus operandi*.

Fifth, the extension of government action along the lines outlined above has given rise to a many-sided set of administrative relationships. Jobs have to be done within a complex of political, legal, economic, and interagency influences and controls. The agency of control and service operates under political directive, influence, and control, and under the necessity of obtaining continuing political support. It operates likewise within a framework of legal order, enforced in part by judicial decision. It gets support,

[8] See pages 69–73 for discussion of the objectives in railroad rate making.

resistance, or myriad pressures from the affected economic groups. Its work is intertwined with that of other agencies carrying overlapping, parallel, or conflicting objectives; and its administration of particular tasks may need to be adjusted to the dominant purposes of the government as a whole. These various factors complicate the task of the public administrative agencies carrying the diverse government programs to the people.

Sixth, one particular type of relationship has become more complex and difficult as the result of the expansion of government activities and the rise of the concept and purpose of planning and stabilization. This is the relation between the separate units of administration and the top structure of the government. National administration has not been closely integrated in the area of economic control, where the independent commission has been used extensively, though by no means exclusively. This area of economic control is one where the issue of integration or disintegration is particularly significant in our national administration.

Finally, in spite of the diversity of government approaches and the complexity of the system of administrative action which has arisen, certain patterns of administrative action have developed and the main outlines of a new institutional system are being revealed. The patterns have resulted from the sharing of experience from one agency to another, the tendency of framers of statutes to borrow from earlier statutes, and the setting of lines of possible action by judicial decision. The particular patterns fit into a larger institutional system, which may be called variously the administrative process, administrative action, or the administrative arm. The patterns are like blocks fitted together in a larger structure. The blocks do not fit together neatly, but this is true of most social arrangements. What is significant is that there are certain areas of uniformity in the process of administrative regulation and service —that there is a certain unity revealed in the institutional system which has been evolving. Moreover, there are key problems which arise here and there or throughout the whole or major parts of the field of government's economic action. These are mainly problems of choice of technique, of interrelationship, of responsibility, and of impact on men and economic operations.

One purpose of the succeeding chapters is to unfold the institutional system and to show the main elements of diversity and generality in the system. The second purpose is to thrust the key problems into clear focus and here and there to suggest some possible solutions.

Chapter III

The Nature and Causes

of Administrative Action

In the previous chapter we noted the development of administration as a phase of economic policy. In this chapter it is appropriate to begin discussion of administration as a phase of government.[1] In governmental processes what is distinctive about administration? What is its place in the evolution of government functions? And why has administration become so large a part of government?

THE NATURE OF ADMINISTRATION

The answer to the first question may be given, in part, by reference to purpose, function, organization, and process.

a. One pervasive and dominant purpose stands behind much of the work of administrative agencies. That purpose is to go forward with the tasks of government prescribed in the political centers. Although administration is ofttimes only a framework for disposing of mechanical tasks, or is passive, or moves intermittently, it is in the large and in the main the conveyor line for the positive and continuing impulses of governmental activity.

[1] The subject will be continued in Chapter IV on "Program Development by Administration."

This purpose of positive and continuous effort sharply distinguishes action in the administrative arm from that in the judicial and legislative branches. The purpose of the judicial system has been to provide a method of decision on particularized claims of existing right, interest, or duty when presented in the form of cases. This function is performed through a set of "waiting tribunals." The courts wait for the initiative of private parties, acting under a system of self-help, or for the action of other governmental organs. The primary purpose of legislative action, on the other hand, has come to be the direct prescription in the form of law of a policy which operates prospectively to determine, or provide a basis for determining, claims of right or interest, or to establish a framework in which private or public action is to be taken.[2] So the judiciary applies a policy, but only sporadically as it gets cases; while the legislature declares a policy which it cannot by itself put into effect. But while the judiciary waits and the legislature declares, the administration works continuously to get a job done, formulating its policy as it goes. The growth of public

[2] Although our distinction at this point is between the work done by *organs* of government, the following definitions of *function* may be compared. "Legislation is the creation by the state of a right (including an authority, a privilege or an immunity), duty, or status not dependent on the existence of a previous right, duty, or status." "Adjudication is the imposition of a specific duty *in personam*, or of a liability, or the granting of a right or status which is dependent on a previous right or duty, in that it is imposed by way of giving effect to a right or duty determined to exist or to have existed, or by way of redress or punishment for its violation." Frederick Green, "Separation of Governmental Powers," *Yale Law Journal*, XXIX, 369, 373-374 (1920).

Our definition of the purpose of legislatures is broader than Green's definition of legislation. It emphasizes the varying purposes which inhere in modern legislation. Legislation may create and fix rights (as in provisions in the National Labor Relations Act defining unfair labor practices), or lay a basis for determination of claims of right or interest (as in the laying of guides for grant of certificates of public convenience and necessity), or give a framework within which private action is to be taken (as in the requirement of submittal of a prospectus before securities are sold through channels subject to national control), or within which public action is to be taken (as in the two previous examples, or, more recognizably, in delegations to the Federal Reserve Board of power to set discount rates or the President to effect alterations in tariff rates). For a court case dealing with legislation which created no private rights but only a framework for public decision see Perkins *v.* Lukens Steel Co. (interpreting the Public Contracts Act of 1936), 310 U. S. 113 (1940).

For further discussion of the nature of a legislative act, see page 98.

administration occurs with the expansion of government beyond the arbitral function, exercised traditionally through the judiciary, and the prescriptive function, carried initially through the legislature. The growth signifies the assumption by government of the responsibility for advancing, promoting, or defending by *positive* and *continuous* effort the general or special interests which government policy represents.

b. In function, administration shows a diversity of activities and flexibility in their combination. It includes, first, a host of routine functions. Examples are the functions of recording (as deeds, births and deaths, wages earned), of compiling data (for the use of governmental officials or distribution to the public), of inspecting (as dairy premises, railway locomotives, meat packing establishments), of maintenance of buildings and operation of physical equipment. It involves, second, the performance of "law-exerting" functions. The police and prosecutory functions are old and familiar examples, but modern administration shows many and varied forms of such activity. Included therein are the many orders of regulatory agencies requiring or prohibiting action. Third, it involves "consent-granting" (licenses, privileges, etc.). Fourth, it calls for management functions, such as the management of publicly-operated utility systems or credit institutions. Finally, it involves almost any combination or fusion of these types of action.

This final category reveals that public administration is more than diversity. If it is many-sided in its reflections, it also represents a combination of approaches in getting public jobs done. Two examples will illustrate this combination.

The first is traffic flow. A policeman stands at a street intersection alternately giving go and stop signals. He is a little Napoleon on the spot giving orders that are, in fact, as conclusive as a court order to pay a fine. Back of him stands an enveloping system. In offices men sit with traffic charts, with statistics showing the movement of people across intersectional points, planning the flow of vehicles and pedestrians. In other places men are giving tests and issuing or denying licenses to operators of motor vehicles. Elsewhere men are telling citizens to tear up traffic tickets or to report to a municipal court, and back of that is a policy of leniency or strictness unknown in most cases to the letter of city ordinances. Still elsewhere men are planning, building, maintaining a system of public property—the public streets. The whole is a network in which routine, orders, licenses are but parts of broader programs in motion.

The example is outside the economic field. But it may be necessary to draw an illustration occasionally from outside that field to reveal that regulation by men, discretionary orders, and planning and management are universal attributes of government in movement. But this is by the side; our point here is that administration is diversity because many techniques must be chosen in order to get public jobs done.

Another example—taken from the economic area—is radio regulation in the Federal Communications Commission. Applications for licenses are being sent through a chain of offices in Washington: to a secretarial office for checking on form; to the Bureaus of Engineering, Accounting, and Law for substantive review; and finally to the Commission. Monitoring stations and a field engineering staff are constantly maintaining "ether traffic control" over broadcasting stations. The Commission, aided by experts scattered through its staff, is considering the revision of the allocation of wave lengths to various purposes. Complaints are being received and sifted by subordinates; quasi-judicial hearings are being held in a hearing division; and judgments on granting, suspending, revoking licenses are being made by the Commission, assisted by its staff. Investigations are being conducted, rules having the force of law are being made. Plans are being made for international conferences and agreements. Activities of stations engaged in experimental activities are being studied. All of these activities form a part of a complex but coordinated program.

c. An institutional fabric is indicated in these examples. Its features are organization and process.

As for organization, there are three outstanding characteristics of the institutional fabric. The first is specialization. The continuing tasks of government are assigned to special agencies. Radio regulation or traffic control becomes the responsibility of one or more agencies. In addition, there is specialization of tasks within the agencies. In radio regulation the engineer, the lawyer, and other types of personnel handle particular parts of the whole job. The second characteristic is hierarchy. Authority descends and responsibility ascends through one or more chains of contact. Directions flow downward and problems and proposed solutions rise upward. Through hierarchy unity and common purpose are maintained. Coherence within and unity in external impact are achieved in spite of specialization. The third characteristic is cross-servicing and lateral cooperation. Within administrative organization contact is crosswise as well as upward and downward. Parallel departments, commissions, or bureaus, or groups of specialists within these, work together on related activities.

These organizational features point toward the essence of the administrative *process*. In organizations of considerable size, allocation of duties necessitates the combining of specialized activities in patterns that fix detailed responsibilities and also make possible group collaboration toward a common goal. *The administrative process becomes one in which decision or action is the result of the complementary contributions of units with different competences.* Thus, in OPA, for a typical example, a decision on a price might have been the result of the complementary contributions of economists, accountants, attorneys, industry specialists, advisory committees, and many others. Each was to bring a different element of competence to the decisional center. Whether the final decision was in one man's name or in that of an organization, the process was unavoidably institutional.[3]

d. One attribute of administrative organization and process is now thrown in focus. This is the factor of relatedness. Things are combined or correlated either in relation to the specific tasks to be performed or to the broad purposes to be attained. In the examples cited above from OPA and radio regulation, process linked the activities and competences of separate groups in getting spe-

[3] For further discussion of this feature of administration and its implications in administrative operations see pages 181-182, 199-209, 211-214.

cific jobs done. In radio regulation, where many different types of function are performed, there is an implicit assumption that the many parts of the regulatory process are related, nevertheless, to the broad purpose of developing and regulating radio communication and hence that this relatedness calls for a unified approach through a single agency. As for traffic control, separate aspects of the public system are related to other public objectives and hence the total operation calls for action in police, public works, and other departments. In all of these, nevertheless, things are combined through organization and process on the basis of their joint relation to the ends in view.

Since in some degree all things are related, guides are needed for determining the relationships to be recognized as dominant. Activities may be combined according to major purpose (safeguarding public health, fire protection, regulation of insurance), type of skill (printing, legal advice), clientele (Indians, aliens, agriculturists), area (T.V.A.), or common knowledge available (employment service and unemployment compensation offices).[4] But two things are significant: First, in public administration activities are put together in units of organization or they are pulled together through working processes because of their relationships to tasks to be performed and goals to be attained, and this characterizes administration from bottom working unit to top coordinating process; second, no single rule for drawing together the complementary efforts of separate groups exists, but rather there must be a constant search for the best methods of organization and process in order that public objectives may be attained.

e. These then are the attributes of the administrative process: responsibility for continuous action toward attainment of public objectives; use of varied approaches and techniques; and complementary and coordinated effort of specialized groups of men having responsibilities related to common tasks and goals.

[4] For fuller analysis see Schuyler C. Wallace, *Federal Departmentalization: A Critique of Theories of Organization* (New York, 1941), 91-146; L. Gulick and L. Urwick, eds., *Papers on the Science of Administration* (New York, 1937), 21-30; George C. S. Benson, "Internal Administration Organization," *Public Administration Review*, I, 474-484 (1941).

ADMINISTRATION AND THE TRIPARTITE THEORY OF FUNCTION

American constitutions have restated and institutionalized the theory of major functions announced by Montesquieu in his chapter on English government in *The Spirit of the Laws* in 1748. According to this theory there are three inherently different functions of government—the legislative, the executive, and the judicial. How does the function of administration mesh with this tripartite theory? Or does it?

Montesquieu's theory grew out of a look backward in England. It summarized institutional development in England up to a turning point in its history. Parliament arose, the theory of sovereignty developed, and Parliament in 1688 took unto itself this sovereignty or law-making function. This development was recorded by Locke in his Second Treatise. Meanwhile, an early aspect of royal business was separately organized in courts, the judges "waxed strong," they and the rest of the legal fraternity developed a sense of separateness, and finally in 1701 their independence was safeguarded in the act which withdrew the right of the crown to remove judges. Montesquieu could then state the idea of the separateness of the judicial function.[5]

In part, then, public administration is a residuum of crown functions not taken away. In the development of modern states the judicial and legislative methods of finding or applying solutions for social problems tended to be differentiated and segregated in separate organs. Moreover, certain types of action, involving the representation of the state as a whole, such as the conduct of foreign affairs, and the extradition of criminals, were given to or retained by the chief executive. Remaining functions rested in numerous organs not clearly distinguishable from each other but exercising a variety of functions by a variety of methods. Some like

[5] For American origins of the separation of powers see Benjamin F. Wright, Jr., "The Origin of the Separation of Powers in America," *Economica*, XIII, 169-85 (May, 1933); Malcolm Sharp, "The Classical American Doctrine of the Separation of Powers," *University of Chicago Law Review*, II, 385-436 (April, 1935).

the justice of the peace would defy description in terms of modern distinctions; others like the British Board of Trade and Postoffice constituted the remaining core of administration, as we would choose terms today.

To an even larger extent, however, today's administrative action is a later growth. In the United States, at least, the administrative system as we see it today, particularly in the economic area and at the national level, is the result of developments of the last 100 years. As the nature of governmental responsibilities has changed, administration has expanded and has tended to become the core of government. It has come to encompass a larger part of the total stream of government.

This is revealed, first, in the redistribution of governmental functions. Activities once regarded as appropriate for the legislative and judicial arms of government have been committed to administrative organs. Rate determinations were originally made by the judiciary under common law rules, later made by legislatures, and finally rate determination became a function of the administrative arm. Protection of security buyers was once a function of the judiciary under the common law doctrine of deceit; it has now become primarily a function of national and state administrative agencies. The granting of charters of incorporation was once done by special act of legislatures, is now done through the administrative process.

The expansion of administration is revealed also in the change in locus and span of administrative action. In certain situations administrative action is withheld until after a judicial decision has been rendered on a particularized situation. Private parties bring an action and present the evidence; an administrative officer enters the picture only to record or enforce a judgment of the court. In such cases the administrative is not a separate system of action but is merely an auxiliary to the judicial system of action. The relationship between administrative and judicial action may be modified to provide for administrative aid to the courts in the process of decision, as where a parole officer or social worker intervenes in a case or the Interstate Commerce Commission approves a railroad reorganization in bankruptcy proceedings. Normally, however, legislative provision for new social policies is accompanied by arrangements for intervention of the administrative arm at an earlier stage and in a more comprehensive manner. Typically, administrative action is either intermediary between legislative and judicial action, or—what is more typical—it picks up a part of the policy-making function and carries through to the final completion of the separate applications of policy. In the total stream of government, administrative action begins early and remains to the end.

In the course of this broad span administrative action "presents an assemblage of rights normally exercisable by the government as a while." [6]

One part of the change is the increasing delegation of legislative power to administrative agencies. It may be "softened by a *quasi,*" as one justice has said;[7] it may be called "administrative detail";[8] it may be asserted that the powers delegated are not "strictly and exclusively legislative";[9] but these are judicial fictions. Any careful observer knows that commissions, departments, and bureaus are making law. They have become subordinate legislative organs.[10] The term "administrative legislation" aptly describes the continuation of the legislative process in administration. The growth of administrative legislation is so generally recognized that the point needs no further discussion.

[6] Landis, *The Administrative Process,* 15. Copyright 1938 by Yale University Press.

[7] Justice Holmes, dissenting in Springer *v.* Government of the Philippine Islands, 277 U. S. 189, 210 (1928).

[8] As in U. S. *v.* Grimaud, 220 U. S. 506, 516 (1911).

[9] The words were first used by Chief Justice Marshall in Wayman *v.* Southard, 10 Wheat. 1, 42 (1825). The fiction that agencies only put in details also comes from the same case, for it was here that Marshall used the term "fill up the details." P. 42.

[10] "The administration today is thus a great deal more than a mere machine for the application of law. To an increasing extent it has become a creator of law; in this sense and within the limits of their respective competences, the administrative departments and agencies resemble a group of special legislative bodies." F. F. Blachly and M. E. Oatman, *Administrative Legislation and Adjudication* (The Brookings Institution, Washington, 1934), 4. Quoted with consent of The Brookings Institution, publisher.

Likewise, adjudicatory decisions are made by agencies called administrative. This too is generally recognized. Yet there is danger that the fact will be accepted without appreciation of differences between administrative and judicial functions. It is misleading to refer to administrative adjudication without taking account of the variety of types of administrative decision and of the relation of adjudicatory decisions within administration to the larger process of government of which they are a part. In other words, the old conceptualism of three distinct functions breaks down before the variety and unity of the administrative process.

The conceptualism itself is not simple, except in its most dogmatic form, namely, that every governmental action must be classifiable under one, and only one, of the three functions. The difficulties of such dogmatism are apparent when we consider what is meant by adjudication and what the agencies of government do. In its most complete sense, an adjudicatory decision is one which meets the requirements for a "case or controversy" such as may be decided in a constitutional court of the United States. Essentially, this means that there must be a controversy between parties on a matter of legal right or interest on which a judgment may operate in a concrete and binding way. Conversely, certain types of functions are said not to be judicial because preliminary (not finally binding), or executive or administrative, or legislative, in nature. The tests for these distinctions have not always been clear, but decision has normally been regarded as judicial in nature if there was a threat (which was not too remote or indefinite) to a legal right and the setting was appropriate for the exercise of the judicial function. Parallel to these ideas about adjudication as a function has been the idea that adjudication is a process of determining disputed questions, i.e., a process in which decision is by an impartial tribunal, after a hearing, and is based upon the application of law to facts presented by the parties to the dispute.[11]

[11] The Committee on Ministers' Powers in Great Britain gave the following description:

"A true judicial decision presupposes an existing dispute between two or more parties, and then involves four requisites:—

"(1) The presentation (not necessarily oral) of their case by the parties to

The complexity of administration is revealed as these elements of conceptualism are measured against its segments. In certain types of administrative decisions the adjudicatory aspects are fully revealed. One is where, as in workmen's compensation cases and cases brought by shippers for reparation from carriers for excess past charges, two private parties stand before an administrative agency for determination of their rights. A second is where a private citizen tests the action of an administrative officer before an appellate administrative body.[12] In both cases, the substance of a "case or controversy" may exist. There is the joinder of parties on a matter of right or interest on which a judgment may operate concretely.

In a third type of case the adjudicatory aspect is equally apparent but adjudication is combined with law-enforcing functions. Thus, the Federal Trade Commission and certain other agencies may bring charges of violation of law against an individual or corporation. An adversary relationship between government and private party is established and a decision is made after a hearing on the question of guilt. The adjudicatory and law-enforcing functions may be vested in separate agencies or they may, as in the Federal Trade Commission, be combined in the same agency.

It is easy to compare any of the foregoing types of cases with a pure judicial decision such as courts habitually make. In a fourth type of case administration performs functions dissimilar to usual court functions, but *an element of adjudication* appears in that there is an acquired legal right in a private party. Included in

---

the dispute; (2) if the dispute between them is a question of fact, the ascertainment of the fact by means of evidence adduced by the parties to the dispute and often with the assistance of argument by or on behalf of the parties on the evidence; (3) if the dispute between them is a question of law, the submission of legal argument by the parties; and (4) a decision which disposes of the whole matter by a finding upon the facts in dispute and an application of the law of the land to the facts so found, including where required a ruling upon any disputed question of law." Cmd. 4060 (1932), 73.

[12] A summary of such cases was given by Frederick F. Blachly in his "Working Papers on Administrative Adjudication," printed for the Senate Committee on the Judiciary, 75th Cong., 3rd Sess., 1938. The "Working Papers" may be found in Kenneth C. Sears, *Cases and Materials on Administrative Law* (St. Paul, 1938), Appendix I.

this type is the legislative proceeding in which existing rights must be considered in the fixing of a rule of future applicability. The familiar example is rate making for utilities.[13] A similar case is the allocation of production quotas in the oil industry. Included also in the fourth type of case is action regarding licenses or other permits where the individual has recognized legal rights. Revocation of professional licenses, or even action on a request for a license in certain cases, is a familiar example. Another example is the application for a permit to drill an oil well on property owned by the petitioner, for the petition is based on a recognized property right in subsurface deposits.

In these cases the judicial element is imbedded in other phases of the governmental process. Moreover, the judicial element may be attenuated. Sometimes there is no clear joinder of adversaries. And the administrative decision may be made, as in the case of oil production quotas or the permit to drill an oil well, in the light of such complex and varied guides of public policy that the right of the individual may become little, if anything, more than a right to have his case fairly considered in relation to similar grants to other parties.

In other types of cases the earmarks of adjudication either vanish or become even less distinct. First, the judicial element is entirely missing in most rule making. Thus, in decisions on bank discount rates or margin requirements for traders in stocks the administrative decision may be made on public considerations exclusively, i.e., without limitation of preexisting rights as in rate making for utilities. Second, there is the expanding area in which the individual receives some benefit from government, either on the basis of his petition or through administrative notice. We may re-

---

[13] E.g., Interstate Commerce Commission v. Louisville and Nashville R. Co., 227 U. S. 88, where the Supreme Court held that an order of the I.C.C. setting aside a rate was "quasi-judicial" in nature; Morgan v. U. S., 298 U. S. 468 (1936), where the Supreme Court said in regard to the fixing of future stockyards rates that "while the order is legislative and gives to the proceeding its distinctive character," "the making of an order supported by such findings, has a quality resembling that of a judicial proceeding." See our further discussion at pages 38, 97, and John Dickinson, *Administrative Justice and the Supremacy of Law* (Cambridge, Mass., 1927), 16-20.

fer to such varied cases as the permit to graze stock on government land, the agricultural benefit payment, the old-age pension or veteran's payment, the granting of loans, government contracts, or tax amortization certificates. In such cases there is no preexisting right; rather, any individual right rests on statute, administrative regulation, or agency policy. In some of these cases, viz. loans, contracts, and tax amortization certificates, the scope for agency dicretion in the application of policy can be so broad as to deny the judicial nature of the proceeding. In some the right of the individual which may be asserted in agency proceedings may be nothing more than a right not to be treated in an arbitrary or discriminatory manner. Also, multitudes of decisions may be made in these several types of situations without any joinder of parties or contest of disputed issues such as exists in court cases. They are made on application of individuals, or by negotiation, or by administrative calculation of benefits and notice to individuals, or by other methods distinctly different from traditional adjudication.

It is evident—without analysis of further variations—that administrative decisions are too diversified in nature to fit the strict categories of the past. This diversity has resulted in a tendency among legal students of administration to seek a frame of reference which was more inclusive than the conceptualism which surrounded court adjudication. The term "administrative adjudication" has been used broadly to include all decisions on applying law or policy to particular fact situations or, differently stated, all decisions applicable to private parties except rule making.

This broader concept is acceptable only if two other aspects of administration are not overlooked. The first is the variety of techniques of procedure which must be allowable. Within administration empirical considerations may override conceptual tests. On the one hand, elements of judicial procedure may sometimes be incorporated into the process of making general rules of future applicability, merely because elements of the judicial process of gathering and testing facts are useful in other phases of human behavior. On the other hand, practical considerations may lead to avoidance of judicial procedure even where the function appears to be adjudicatory. O.P.A. referred to all decisions on grants of rations (except mass distributions) as "adjudication" and distinguished these from the operations of clerks, but it necessarily handled these grants through application and occasional conference rather than through adjudicatory procedure; even appeals were determined on the basis of facts on a written record.[14] In the Federal Trade Commission the function of deciding on a charge of violation of law is clearly adjudicatory but the agency tries to settle a large proportion of cases without any adjudicatory process. One test of good administration is ability to select and combine operating or procedural techniques according to the practical requirements of its particular forms of action.

The other aspect to be borne in mind is that organization is used to provide unity, coherence, and direction in the affairs of government. As a result the whole variety of functional distinctions and procedural possibilities become, in part, internal questions of administration. All types of functions are performed within a unified structure and all types of procedure are used, somewhere or other, in the flow of government from legislature to people.

It is clear that there is much mixture of government functions and processes in administration. It may not be useful to argue whether many things are judicial in nature and when done by administrative agencies should be called administrative adjudication, or whether they are primarily executive, or administrative, or legislative and when done through process similar in some respects to those of courts should be called judicialized administration.[15] What is significant is that, on the one hand, the legal tests for classification as adjudication—is there a legal right? is there conflict of adversaries? is there a legally enforceable decision?—have broken down or lost some of their significance; and, on the other

---

[14] On adjudication in rationing see the author's *Field Administration of Wartime Rationing* (Washington, 1947), Chapter VI.

[15] Might the same term be applied to court adjudication? Note the following: "Judicial administration, as Sir Josiah Stamp points out, is merely a specialized form of general administration which 'has acquired an air of detachment.'" W. A. Robson, *Justice and Administrative Law: A Study of the British Constitution* (London, 1928), 11.

hand, that things which functionally or procelurally are more or less comparable to things done in the judicial arm have been placed *in a different institutional system where relatedness to broader purpose leads to combination with other administrative functions.*

What is occurring is that the functions and processes of government—however defined—are being unified in administration. In rate making we can even refer to judicialized administrative legislation—the courts say the function is legislative,[16] it is most frequently done by administrative agencies, but elements of judicial procedure are incorporated in the process.[17] This is an extreme manifestation of a definite tendency. The tendency is further revealed in the frequent foreshortening of the law-enforcing and law-deciding functions in one agency. The same agency becomes responsible for positive action in finding cases where the law should be applied and for making a decision applying the law. The tendency is shown in the judicialization of some traditionally administrative processes, as in the requirement (by judicial decision or legislative enactment) of notice and hearing in some licensing proceedings. The tendency is also shown in the combination in the same agency (e.g., the Social Security Administration), first of specialized groups of persons who make thousands of decisions on individual rights or benefits by non-judicial methods, and second, of other specialized groups who hear cases on appeal with or without some element of a hearing such as inheres in adjudicatory process. The trend is further exemplified in the choice allowed to many agencies between legislative or judicial methods of finding solutions for problems: they may make advance, general rules or may work out a public policy through the decision of particular cases. Above all, the trend is exemplified in a larger movement of which

[16] E.g., I.C.C. *v.* Cincinnati, New Orleans, and Texas Pacific R. Co., 167 U. S. 479 (1897); Prentis *v.* Atlantic Coast Line Co., 211 U. S. 210, particularly at p. 226 (1908); Louisville and Nashville R. Co. *v.* Garrett, 231 U. S. 298, 305 1913); Morgan *v.* U. S., 298 U. S. 468 (1936).

[17] This is, of course, only one way of putting it, for the courts have said the function itself has a judicial element. See footnote 13 on page 35.

these things are only internal reflections—the establishment of organizational structures which can draw their methodology from the total offerings of managerial, legal, and political processes.

Recently, Congress passed the Administrative Procedure Act.[18] In spite (or, perhaps indeed, because) of all the effort toward definition and simplification of administrative processes which preceded the Act, it yet shows final recognition of the diversity and complexity of administrative processes. True, it defines "adjudication" broadly to include "agency process" for any "final disposition" except rule making.[19] But the main procedural requirements relating to adjudication set forth in the Act extend only to those cases where statute requires determination on the record after opportunity for an agency hearing. And the requirements are riddled by many exceptions. Moreover, the act leaves untouched administrative technique for planning the job to be done, selection of areas of effort, use of organization and process to get jobs done without judicial process, and extra-legal methods of getting people to accept administrative decisions. Administration, it is manifest, includes adjudication and rule making but only as parts of a larger process of government.

The Act also accepted the mixture of functions in the same agency and the combination of legislative and judicial functions with the rest of the administrative process. True, it provides for some separation of clearly defined judicial functions and personnel inside the agencies and may even carry this further than consists with the effective use of organization to get jobs done. But the act sought only regularization, not destruction, of an institutional fabric in which diverse but related functions are unified by organization and process.[20]

In conclusion, it may be said that modern government is more

[18] June 11, 1946. 60 *U. S. Stat. at Large*, 237, 5 U.S.C.A. 1001.

[19] Section 2 (d): " 'Order' means the whole or any part of the final disposition (whether affirmative, negative, or injunctive, or declaratory in form) of any agency in any matter other than rule making but including licensing. 'Adjudication' means agency process for the formulation of an order." The Administrative Procedure Act is discussed further in Chapter VIII.

[20] For further discussion of the Act, see pages 211-214.

complex than the traditional statements of the classic tripartite division.[21] Most of the complexities have resulted from the growth of administration. Through it, in the main, the varied activities of government are carried out. In large part the legislature's function is related to administration and through administration the citizen is reached; the legislature's function is direction and correction of administration.[22] In the newer areas of public policy, the judiciary's function is also related to administration; the administration decides and the judiciary's functions tend to be corrective only. The business of government is continuing and all related aspects of continuing jobs tend to be placed in a complex institutional pattern called administration.

[21] In Cushman's *The Independent Regulatory Commissions* the confusion concerning types of functions exercised by the regulatory commissions is patently revealed on page after page of the discussion. For example, Cushman notes that the I.C.C. has been described as "in essence a judicial tribunal," "an administrative body," "the arm of Congress," "an executive body," "a purely administrative body," "wholly legislative," having "only executive power." P. 418. These designations were often only instances of the use of conceptualism as tool of advocacy: "In 1906, to meet the charge that legislative or judicial powers were being delegated to it, the administrative or executive character of the commission was strongly stressed. When in 1910 there was fear of subordinating the commission to an executive department under the provision requiring the Attorney General to defend commission orders before the Commerce Court, emphasis was laid upon the legislative character of the commission and the fact that it was an 'arm of Congress.' In 1920, with vast administrative and managerial responsibilities about to be conferred upon it, the judicial nature of the commission was emphasized." P. 129. Cushman concludes: "Nothing seems clearer from a study of this whole problem than the futility of trying to apply to the vitally important development of the last fifty years any rigid concepts drawn from the doctrine of the separation of powers." P. 445. Robert E. Cushman, *The Independent Regulatory Commissions*. Copyright 1941 by Oxford University Press, Inc.

Compare the following conclusion from Edwin W. Patterson, *The Insurance Commissioner in the United States* (Harvard University Press, Cambridge, 1927), 5: "We may as well recognize that sometimes the insurance commissioner is an official clerk, sometimes he is a judge, sometimes he is a law-giver, and sometimes he is both prosecuting attorney and hangman. He is partly executive, partly judicial, and partly legislative; and yet he is not confined within any of these categories. I defy anyone to tell me when he stops legislating and begins to judge, or when he stops judging and begins to execute."

[22] For further discussion of this development see pages 348-360.

CAUSES OF GROWTH IN ADMINISTRATIVE ACTION

The most significant recent governmental development in this country has been the growth in administrative action.[23] In one field after another special administrative agencies have been established and given extensive authorities. Why has this expansion occurred?

Many have explained this development by reciting the inadequacies of other methods. Thus, one eminent author has said, "The administrative process is, in essence, our generation's answer to the inadequacy of the judicial and legislative processes.[24] This, it seems to the author, is a negative statement of a tremendous half-truth. As for the negative nature of the statement, it may be said that the rise of the administrative arm might be explained in terms of the positive advantages of new methods. It is probably true that the adoption of new methods is most frequently motivated by realization of the inadequacies of old methods; but it may be true also that consideration of the possible advantages of alternatives has weight in men's judgments, particularly after the example of new methods is presented in a number of cases. As for the fractional nature of the statement, it may be said that it overlooks the fact that administrative growth has occurred in the main because government policy has expanded and as a result of the expansion *public work has to be done which is different from that for which legislative and judicial organs were created.*

A simple analogy may illustrate the difficulties of single explanations. A parent may send his boy to a medical specialist because the general practitioner has failed or because he has decided that the ailment was of a type where the specialist could offer advantages, but a parent would never say that he had sent his boy to school because of the deficiencies of the medical practitioner. Likewise,

---

[23] We dislike using the word "action" instead of the term "decision and action" but do so repeatedly for brevity only.

[24] From page 46 of James M. Landis, *The Administrative Process.* Copyright 1938 by Yale University Press.

the Federal Trade Commission may have been established because of deficiencies revealed in old methods or, in part, because of belief in the advantages of specialized action by a new tribunal; but the use of administrative agencies in bank examinations, the open-market negotiations of the Federal Reserve Board, the loaning of money by the R.F.C., or the granting of agricultural benefits or of certificates of public convenience and necessity, cannot be explained realistically by reference to the inadequacies of the general practitioners in courts and legislatures. What would seen naïve in a parent's explanation is possible in learned literature only because administration is defined as something less than the whole of the process—i..e., as including only work which can be likened to that of courts and legislatures, or because writers are so accustomed to looking at legislatures and courts that they cannot see that administration has its own distinct quality.[25]

Although a full explanation of the growth of administration would necessitate an examination of the special factors in each field in which administrative action has developed, the core of general cause may be found in the trends in government policy. In large part the growth of administration is merely a corollary of the trend toward establishment of public policies or mechanisms through which the common interests of men may be safeguarded or advanced. If one looks behind the various forms of public action discussed in the preceding chapter he sees an increasing tendency to supplement individual action with collective action for the protection or promotion of common interests, both within government and without. Increasingly, organized institutional action is substituted for or supplements individual self-help in the

[25] The concluding sentence as well as the preceding comments are written in protest against a habit of thought rather than against the isolated statement of an individual. Landis, like many others, has sought to explain the administrative process by looking at the work of particular types of agencies, excluding others which did not fit the selected patterns. On the other hand, he has—in spite of the quoted statement—done more perhaps than anyone else to show that *even in the areas selected for his discussion* administration has qualities which are quite different from those of legislatures and courts. See *The Administrative Process*, Chapter I, *passim.* The author's own debt to Landis' writings is reflected in more places in this chapter than can be indicated by specific references.

many areas in which demands for government action arise. In-creasingly, the particular problems of men are met through gen-eral solutions. There is a tendency—reluctantly accepted perhaps but existent nevertheless—to seek for the solution of problems by development of a social policy or a general framework for public action.[26]

It is this change which has, in large part, accounted for the con-siderable replacement of courts by legislatures as agents for the development of public policy. Courts arose in an individualistic pattern in which each man protected himself through self-help and the elements of social policy were pricked out under the contest of individuals. Legislatures have developed as media through which men may cut straight through to an advance decision which has the effect of resolving a social problem and establishing a frame-work within which common interests can be protected.

The corollary to this change is public administration. This re-sults from the fact that the framework of public policy adopted by the political organs cannot be realized in practice without the con-tinuing positive effort afforded by administrative agencies. This has become so generally recognized that an almost universal ques-tion faced in consideration of new legislation is: by whom and by what methods will the program be administered?

Examples will illustrate the trend toward general solutions and the accompanying provision for institutional effort. In rate making all elements of a complex situation are resolved in an advance deci-sion. Under the common law, a party could bring action in the courts in case of an excess charge. Not only did such a form of procedure place the burden of protecting a group on one or a limited number of parties, but it was an unsatisfactory method of considering the general rate problem. As a consequence, advance determination of general rate schedules has become a customary form of action. Protection against fraudulent sales of securities formerly depended on individual, private suit under the law of

[26] The point we are making has practical importance. The development of administration could not be materially checked by legislative and judicial re-form; this result could be achieved only by stopping the trend of legislation.

deceit; today a new framework of public action has been established in which the interests of all investors are protected through the efforts of a central organ of examination and action. Likewise, protection against false advertising by sellers of goods is now achieved in some measure by the general system of examination of advertising copy by the staff of the Federal Trade Commission. Or again, protection of the bank depositor has been sought through a general system of bank examinations and insurance of bank deposits.

This trend is even more apparent if one looks at the managerial aspects of public control and service. Industry, functional, and economy management reflect the search for broadly inclusive policies,[27] and produce administration as inevitably as public education produces schools.

The growth of administration with the modern trend of policy is due to the fact that the very things which characterize administration are required for effectuation of policy. Somebody must keep working on the tasks undertaken. Continuity is essential. Tasks recur daily, continuous oversight is required, policy adaptations must be made. Also, public effort must be positive if it is to be an effective substitute or supplement for individual self-help.

Another factor is the tremendous size of public undertakings. This is revealed sometimes in the magnitude of particular decisions. A rate-making proceeding may involve research and study by a sizable staff for a considerable period, and even the use of accumulated information from the experience in earlier cases. It is revealed also in the huge volume of decisions or actions.[28] It is re-

[27] *Supra,* pages 15-19.

[28] For a summary of volume of some agencies, see *Final Report of the Attorney General's Committee on Administrative Procedure* (Washington, D. C., 1941), 314-326. Note this one example on one-year case loads: "Thus the Treasury alone decided more cases than all the Federal constitutional and legislative courts. In fact, the Treasury Department had far more intradepartmental appeals than the number of federal civil cases brought before, or decided by, all of the federal courts—the comparative number being 92,185 cases on administrative appeal in the Treasury as compared with 16,669 federal civil cases decided by the constitutional courts and 20,642 such cases decided by both the constitutional and legislative courts." Col. O. R. McGuire, "Judicial Reviews of Administrative Decisions," *Georgetown Law Journal,* XXVI, 574-605, at p. 577 (1938).

vealed in addition in the great mass of detailed work and of records which must be maintained.

As the Attorney General's Committee on Administrative Procedure pointed out, there is a "need for organization to dispose of volume of business and to provide the necessary records," [29] And the demands of volume and magnitude are clear: specialization, delegation, and cross-servicing. Size of jobs magnifies the institutional framework described earlier in this chapter. Size of public undertakings makes for a large administrative center in the state.

Still another factor should be noted. Administration has been a flexible and evolving process which provided methods by which the varied public undertakings could be carried forward. It offers, for example, the licensing technique, under which advance check is possible. It offers an institutional process under which a multitude of particulars can be examined and action taken on the limited group on which action is required. It offers many approaches in procedure: the inspection of premises, the examination of books, the conference table, and the variations of formal legal procedure. It offers an opportunity for managerial discretion, for adaptation of policy to particulars, and for continuous development of policy itself. And it offers, after a time, a set of organizational entities which can take on new tasks as these are outlined by the legislature.

What we have said relates to the existence of administration. Its placement is another question.

As modern legislative policy has unfolded, legislatures and courts have recognized that they should not try to carry responsibilities which were unsuited to their essential functions.

This is revealed in the tendency of legislatures to shed decision on recurring particulars. More and more, legislative action on special cases has given way to general statutes applied by administrative action. The transfer of the granting of corporate charters from legislatures to administration may be cited as an example. The trend was patently revealed in banking legislation. As the legislatures accepted the principles of "free banking" they passed the function of granting permits for banking privileges to admin-

[29] *Final Report,* 17.

istrative agents. The trend toward legislative relinquishment of recurring tasks has continued right up to the Legislative Reoganiza-
tion Act of 1946, in which settlement of small tortious claims
against the United States government and consent for construction
of bridges over navigable waters were made administrative responsibilities.[30]

Equally significant has been the yielding of supervisory responsibilities. Roughly in the half-century following 1840 the states
moved in railroad legislation from special legislation to general
laws with legislative supervision—sometimes with the help of commissions set up to help with special *ad hoc* situations, then to permanent advisory administrative commissions, and finally to the authoritative regulatory commission. The same trend from legislative to
administrative action occurred in regulation of utilities, beginning
near the end of the century. By the twentieth century the continuing
nature of the tasks in economic control had become sufficiently clear
that legislative bodies almost automatically created agencies of administration as new programs of control were initiated. Two things
seemed to be apparent: first, that control and service required continuous supervision; and second, that this was a different type of
function from that for which legislatures were organized.

The federal courts have likewise recognized that there were administrative functions which they should not try to exercise. Self-
limitation by the courts to things judicial in nature has helped to
create the vacuum in which administrative action has arisen. The
Supreme Court of the United States has said that its jurisdiction
is by Article III of the Constitution "limited to cases and controversies in such form that the judicial power is capable of acting on
them and does not extend . . . to the administrative or legislative issues or controversies." [31] The effect of judicial construction of
Article III has been to restrict the constitutional courts in many

[30] Titles IV and V, 60 *U. S. Stat. at Large*, 812, 842-849.
[31] Keller *v.* Potomac Electric Power Co., 261 U. S. 428 (1923). For general
discussion see W. G. Katz, "Federal Legislative Courts," *Harvard Law Review*,
XLIII, 894 (1930), and the summary on "The Jurisdiction of Constitutional
Courts" in F. F. Blachly and Miriam E. Oatman, *Federal Regulatory Action and
Control* (Washington, D. C., 1940), 333-338.

areas of social control and service to review of action taken by special agencies. By refusing to dilute their own jurisdiction, the courts have, in many areas, been placed outside the main stream of government action and assumed only a corrective rôle. For example, the Supreme Court, holding that rate making was a legislative function, has refused to take jurisdiction to determine the rate of charge but will decide only whether the rates prescribed by legislatures, administrative organs, or special "legislative" courts conform to statutory and judicial standards.[32] What has been held with respect to rate making is, of course, obvious with respect to granting of licenses, inspection of factories, classification of grains, payment of agricultural benefits, loaning of money, and conducting open-market negotiations: these are not the types of functions for which the judicial arm was established.

In the main, then, the administrative arm has grown because the attempt to find general and advance solutions has led to the need for organization which can maintain continuous supervision, handle a huge load of work, and carry a variety of tasks; and because legislatures and courts recognized that these things were functionally distinct from their own essential duties.

This, however, is not the whole story. The administrative arm has come to encompass some things which are legislative and judicial in nature. For this it would appear that there are two types of explanation.

First, in these areas the inadequacies of old or the comparative advantages of new methods are significant factors. Legislatures are now forced by a variety of factors to legislate in broad terms and leave the further task of legislation to subordinate, administrative organs. Port has summarized the chief of these factors as urgency, lack of time, technicality, and need for experimentation;[33]

---

[32] Keller v. Potomac Electric Power Co., 261 U. S. 428 (1923).

[33] F. J. Port, *Administrative Law* (London and New York, 1929), 137-146. See also C. K. Allen, *Bureaucracy Triumphant* (London, 1931), 82-86. Allen points out that Lord Chief Justice Hewart in *The New Despotism* (New York, 1929), 8 and 159, found a deeper and more insidious reason: "deep-seated official conviction . . . that this, when all is said and done, is the best and most scientific way of ruling the country"; "manifestly the offspring of a well-thought-

to these the author would add need for adaptation to particulars and continuity, for even the process of legislation now requires flexible and continuous procedure.

As for judicial activities, the administrative process has provided opportunities for escape from many of the limitations of courts. It has provided an opportunity to match the complexity of economic situations with specialized jurisdictions. Whereas courts have normally been organs of general jurisdiction and judges, as Dean Landis has said, are "jacks-of-all-justice," specialized administrative agencies, immersed in continuous control, may acquire a "skilled discretion" in functional areas. It has provided an opportunity to escape from the lack of uniformity which comes from initial consideration of complex fact situations by a scattered body of tribunals. It has offered an opportunity to escape from formalized, expensive and lengthy procedure; [34] it has provided alternatives to

---

out plan, the object and the effect of which are to clothe the department with despotic powers." Many American legalists and votaries of noninterference by government share these sentiments of the English justice. The English Committee on Ministers' Powers reported, however, that there was not "the smallest shred of evidence" that the increase in the power of English departments to issue orders was due to an attempt of the Civil Service to aggrandize itself. See the Report of the Committee on Ministers Powers, Cmd. 4060 (1932), 59. Note also the comments on page 7 of the report.

[34] In connection with some of the deficiencies of the courts discussed in the text, note the following conclusion by a careful scholar:

"Where attempted in the United States, it may safely be said that court administration of workmen's compensation has failed. This has not been because of inefficiency in the courts, but the judicial machinery is not, and cannot be adapted to the new problems of administration presented by the system of workmen's compensation. The judicial function is primarily that of settling controversies between parties equal before the law. The principle of liability without fault of itself assumes an inequality between the parties, and this inequality is accentuated by the fact that in the great bulk of compensation proceedings the employer-employee relationship has given way to a relationship between the employee on the one side and the insurance company carrying the employer's insurance risk on the other. Moreover, workmen's compensation proceeds upon an assumption of equality of treatment of similar injuries whether a claim be contested or uncontested, and no machinery now exists in this country for the correlation of the activities of various courts so as to produce such equality. Any effort to set up such machinery would lead to delay and expense equally as great as under the displaced system of common law liability. And the essential purpose of compensation is not only equality of payment, but promptness and reduced expense to the injured workmen. In addition, workmen's compensation, if properly administered, presents many problems of conthe modern trappings erected on medieval trial by battle technique in the various forms of institutional research and fact-finding. Of special significance are the means provided for handling the great bulk of cases without judicialized procedures.[35] And it has provided an opportunity to infuse new viewpoints in the administration of justice. Whereas the judge has been accustomed to thinking in terms of private or particular interests—a habit of mind which has been fostered by the nature of the judicial process, the ideology of *laissez faire,* and the individualistic traditions of the common law,[36] the administrator may concentrate attention on development of social policy and attempt a new adjustment of particular and general interests. Finally, the growth of administration has provided a chance to escape from the inexpertness of juries, the unpredictability and lack of uniformity of their decisions, and the protective procedures devised to fit the system of decision by persons inexpert in careful fact evaluation.

The other explanation for administrative legislation and administrative adjudication is that these are related to other aspects of the regulatory process. They appear to be, in instances at least, incidents of a larger process of carrying forward the task of government.

---

tinuous supervision for which the courts are ill adapted. Judicial machinery, even though properly adapted to the settlement of private controversies, cannot, at the same time, meet the entirely different needs of an efficient system of workmen's compensation."—Walter F. Dodd, *Administration of Workmen's Compensation,* 98-99. Copyright 1936 by The Commonwealth Fund.

[35] See pages 182-187.

[36] See Roscoe Pound, *The Spirit of the Common Law* (Boston, 1921).

"Most of the common law has developed in that atmosphere of indifferent neutrality which has enabled courts to be impartial, but also keeps them out of touch with vital needs. When interests are litigated in particular cases, they not only appear as scattered and isolated interests, but their social incidence is obscured by the adventitious personal factors which color every controversy. If policy means the conscious favoring of social above particular interests, the common law must be charged with having too little policy." Ernst Freund, *Standards of American Legislation* (University of Chicago Press, Chicago, 1917), 48.

"Social interests cannot be secured, or a social policy effected by the application of abstract principles of justice, as between man and man." William A. Robson, *Justice and Administrative Law, A Study of the British Constitution* (London, 1928), 252.

As for administrative legislation, it may be said that this is a continuing process and that extension and refinement of rules of public policy grow out of the process of trying to move forward with public jobs. Administrative adjudication (or judicialized administration) grows out of administration in many ways. It is, for example, sometimes the last step in a process of investigating, sifting, determining a probable violation, and testing this midway decision. This is true of such agencies as the Federal Trade Commission which investigates many complaints, examines much advertising copy, and initiates many investigations. These are followed by dismissals or agreements of parties to desist from alleged practices; the remaining cases move on to trial of the facts. It is, in other instances, only a formal procedure for handling a few of the many cases normally handled by informal, or even routine, procedures. Thousands, or multiples of thousands, of decisions may be made in day-to-day administration; and an occasional one set, either on petition or on the initiative of the administration, for formal or informal hearing process.

It would not be appropriate at this point to attempt a discussion of the question of whether this process of combining related functions in unified organizations has been carried too far. The next chapter analyzes more fully the problem of administrative participation in policy making. A later chapter analyzes the proposals for separating the judicial from other functions of administrative agencies.[37] It is sufficient at this point to say that, in the past, legislative bodies have seemed to move instinctively toward decision in favor of a form of organization in which all aspects of particular programs are combined in a single agency; as Landis has shown, the "triadic" concept of the separation of powers has been giving way to the industrial "analogue" in which the job to be performed, rather than the type of function, is the clue to organization.[38]

[37] Chapter X.
[38] James M. Landis, *The Administrative Process*, particularly 10-12. Copyright 1938 by Yale University Press.

SUMMARY

Administration provides the opportunity for positive, continuous action toward attainment of public objectives. It is a broad tent under which many types of action may be located. It is organization and process for getting jobs done. It is, to an extent, a residuum; but it is, to a much greater extent, a growth. It has comprised an increasing part of the task of government, including things more or less similar to the functions of legislatures and courts, but primarily including things which were different. It has arisen, in the main, because the public, in search for general and advance solutions for social problems, has undertaken tasks which call unavoidably for continuous and positive process, organization capable of handling a huge volume of work, and a framework for getting many types of jobs done; but also because of the inadequacies of legislative and judicial arms for the full task of government—and the comparative advantages of administrative action; and finally because the functions of subordinate legislation and adjudication of particulars have become part and parcel of the larger task of government.

Chapter IV

Program Development by Administration

In Chapter I we noted that there was no clear line separating the function of policy making, traditionally regarded as the area of "politics," and that of execution, traditionally defined as the area of administration. We now turn to an analysis of the general extent and methods of administrative participation in shaping the substance or content of program. Three topics are discussed: first, the nature and limitations of statutory directives; second, the development of program within administration; and third, the development of program through the collaboration of administrative agencies with the Congress.[1] The discussion will start with legal and formal aspects and move toward the practical issues raised by administrative participation in policy development.

STATUTORY DIRECTIVES TO ADMINISTRATORS

Administrative responsibility begins with a directive.[2] The directive may come from Congress, the President, or a higher administrative authority. It is customarily formalized in a statute or admin-

---

[1] Succeeding chapters, dealing with the tools and techniques of administration, will supplement the present chapter in that they will reveal the various ways in which choice and use of method affect the development of program.

[2] The term is used in a broad sense. Delegations may appear to be either directives or authorizations. But an authorization is only a directive to exercise discretion as to whether and what action shall be taken and carries an implied directive to act under some contingency.

istrative order.[3] Particularly significant are statutory directives and only these are discussed in this section.

Directives commit responsibility for areas of action and decision; they may also tell how and within what limits the responsibility is to be exercised. A directive may include (1) a statement of purpose; (2) a statement of subjects on which action may be taken; (3) a prescription of standards or guides to govern action on the stated subjects; (4) a group of restrictions on scope or exercise of the delegation; and (5) a set of requirements on administrative methods, extending perhaps to organization, techniques of application, and procedural processes. The first four and sometimes the fifth comprise the guides to administrators on the substance of their programs.

A single directive may contain all five of the elements listed. This was true, for example, of the Emergency Price Control Act of 1942,[4] which was carefully framed after a period of experience in price regulation. Other directives, the Second War Powers Act for example, may contain much less. Some statutes begin with a kind of preamble which states the purpose. It may be called variously, as "Purposes" in the Price Control Act, "Declaration of Policy" in the Merchant Marine Act of 1936,[5] "Findings and Declaration of Policy" in the Fair Labor Standards Act of 1938,[6] or "Necessity for Control of Holding Companies" in the Public Utility Holding Company Act of 1935.[7] On the other hand, the statement of purpose may be missing, as in the Securities Act of 1933.[8] The Supreme Court has held that the constitutional principles forbidding delegation of legislative power will be violated if the subject is not named

---

[3] The function of statutes changes as administration develops. They become relatively more significant as directives to administration and less complete as definitions of specific rights or obligations of individuals. Even when statutory prescription is largely in the form of stated prohibitions of private action, as in the Securities Exchange Act, the prohibitions become meaningful because of the directives to an administrative agency.

[4] 56 *U. S. Stat. at Large*, 23.

[5] 49 *U. S. Stat. at Large*, 1985.

[6] 52 *U. S. Stat. at Large*, 1060.

[7] 49 *U. S. Stat. at Large*, 803.

[8] 48 *U. S. Stat. at Large*, 74.

in a statutory delegation.[9] The statutory directive will, therefore, indicate that it is rates, prices,[10] securities, or other subject which is regulated. It is a constitutional principle, also, that the statute must contain some standard, guide, or "intelligible principle" on which action may be based.[11] It may be, however, that this can be found in the general statement of purpose, if this exists.[12] Statutes usually contain some exemptions or other limitations, and some prescription of organization and method. The Emergency Price Control Act, for example, included a considerable amount of both. On the other hand, the grant to the President of authority to allocate scarce materials and facilities in the Second War Powers Act was free from restrictions on the judgment of the President, either as to policy or organization and methods.[13]

Directives may be multiplied. The I.C.C., for example, has derived its functions from directives in a succession of laws which have extended the subjects of regulation and the authority of the Commission over these. They may come in varied forms, as in a basic statute, amendatory statutes, or riders on appropriation bills. They may even come in an extralegal and informal way but with unmistakable force nevertheless, as when a powerful Congressional committee supplements or conditions the legal and formal directive with suggestions or criticism concerning action taken or to be taken in an agency.[14]

An agency may have the advantage of continuity and dependability in its directives. Or it may be held under continuing uncer-

[9] A. L. A. Schechter Poultry Corporation v. U. S., 295 U. S. 495 (1935).

[10] In upholding the Agricultural Marketing Agreement Act of 1937 in U. S. v. Rock Royal Coöperative, Inc., 307 U. S. 533 (1939) the Supreme Court took note of the fact that the statute did not leave the Secretary of Agriculture "freedom of choice as to the commodities" which might be covered by an order (p. 576), but in Kakus v. U. S. 321, U. S. 414 (1944), the Emergency Price Control Act of 1942, which allowed control to reach commodities generally, was upheld.

[11] The term "intelligible principle" was used by Chief Justice Taft in J. W. Hampton, Jr., and Co. v. U. S., 276 U. S. 394, 409 (1928).

[12] See Panama Refining Co. v. Ryan, 293 U. S. 388 (1935), for an example of judicial search in the "declaration of policy" for a standard.

[13] 56 U. S. Stat. at Large, 176, March 27, 1942, amending Act of May 31, 1941, 55 U. S. Stat. at Large, 236.

[14] See pages 348-354 for discussion of the manifold ways in which the Congress influences or directs administration.

tainty, as was the case with the Federal Radio Commission[15] and O.P.A., both of which operated under short-run statutes and the threat of deflection of program by modification of statutory authorization. An agency gains its greatest opportunity for program development when its directive is dependable.

The most significant aspect of statutory directives is the extent of discretion left to administrators in program development. Some directives are specific. The Fair Labor Standards Act with its prescription of figures for minimum wages and maximum hours, and with its statement of coverage and exemptions, makes the administrative an enforcement authority and reserves program adjustment to the Congress.[16] So too with the income tax and immigration laws; and so it used to be with the tariff. Statutes can frequently add specificity as experience is gained. Thus, the Railway Labor Act of 1926 contained a general provision inhibiting employer interference with labor organization,[17] but the National Labor Relations Act of 1935 could follow general provision with enumeration of specific acts which constituted unfair labor practices.[18] The Emergency Price Control Act in its postwar extensions was far more specific than in its original form.[19]

Generality is, however, the characteristic of much economic legislation. Sharfman emphasizes this with respect to "legislative mandates" to the I.C.C.[20]

[15] See E. Pendleton Herring, *Public Administration and the Public Interest* (New York, 1936), Chapter X.

[16] 52 *U. S. Stat. at Large,* 1060. The opportunity for administrative participation in developing program substance ended when the one-time 40 cent minimum came to apply automatically to all industries under the act.

[17] Section 2, 44 *U. S. Stat. at Large,* Part II, 576, 578.

[18] Section 8, 49 *U. S. Stat. at Large,* 449, 452.

[19] Speaking of writing standards into legislation after a period of administrative discretion, Charles S. Hyneman concludes: "This is the history of a great part of our legislation. In the initial period of regulation, Congress is forced to abdicate to the administrator for the extension of policy beyond the statement of general purposes. As time passes and administrative experience is examined, Congress is able to incorporate into statute the policies formulated and pursued by the administrative department." *Bureaucracy in a Democracy,* 88-89. Copyright 1950 by Harper & Brothers.

[20] *The Interstate Commerce Commission,* II, 358. Copyright 1931 by The Commonwealth Fund. See pages 357-367 of the volume cited for a full discussion of legislative mandates.

The Commission has been authorized to act in various situations "at its discretion," "whenever deemed by it to be necessary or desirable in the public interest," "in such manner and by such means as it shall deem proper," when "not inconsistent with the public interest," if it "finds the public interest will be promoted," in such a way "as in its judgment the convenience and necessity may require" or "as in its judgment the public interest demands," "if it sees fit," and the like. . . . This approach is typical of the Commission's powers of control in all of the major segments of the field—in matters of finance and management, service and facilities, rates and charges.

Similar summaries could be taken from other big regulatory statutes. Note may be taken, for illustration, of the grant of authority to the N.L.R.B. in 1935 to determine the unit of collective bargaining "in order to insure to employees the full benefit of their right to self-organization and to collective bargaining, and otherwise to effectuate the policies of this Act," [21] to the Federal Reserve Board to set margin requirements for security purchases "For the purpose of preventing the excessive use of credit for the purchase or carrying of securities," [22] to the Securities and Exchange Commission to make certain rules and regulations "as it deems necessary or appropriate in the public interest or for the protection of investors," [23] and to O.P.A. to set prices which were "generally fair and equitable and will effectuate the purposes of this Act." [24]

Sometimes the courts will determine the content of general statutory provisions, as in the case of the words "unfair methods of competition" in the Federal Trade Commission Act,[25] or of the words "fair," "just," or "reasonable" in utility legislation. But in recent years the administrative authority to fill in the program content of general laws has grown. Either the decision is obviously

[21] Section 9 (b), 49 *U. S. Stat. at Large,* 449, 453.
[22] Securities Exchange Act of 1934, Sec. 7 (a), 48 *U. S. Stat. at Large,* 881, 886.
[23] Securities Exchange Act of 1934, Section 11 (a), 48 *U. S. Stat. at Large,* 881, 891.
[24] 56 *U. S. Stat. at Large,* 23, 24.
[25] In Federal Trade Commission *v.* Gratz, 253 U. S. 421, 427 (1920), the Supreme Court said: "The words 'unfair method of competition' are not defined by statute and their exact meaning is in dispute. It is for the courts, not the commission, ultimately to determine as a matter of law what they include."

managerial and discretionary, as in banking and currency control, or the courts let administrative judgment stand because of technicality or other reasons.[26]

Directives to administration may carry multiple standards. Thus, the Interstate Commerce Commission's decision in one type of case has been dependent upon a showing "that neither public nor private interests will be adversely affected," in another that relief "will be in the interest of better service to the public, or economy in operation, and will not unduly restrain competition."[27] The best illustration in Supreme Court decisions is Yakus v. U. S.[28] where the standards for fixing prices in the Emergency Price Control Act as amended were held to be sufficient. There were really three levels of guides in the Act. First, it stated a number of purposes, all related to the effects of inflation on the economy and the war program. Second, it stated a general guide to the Administrator. Whenever in his judgment prices "have risen or threaten to rise to an extent or in a manner inconsistent with the purposes" of the Act, he could fix such prices as "in his judgment will be *generally fair and equitable and will effectuate the purposes*" of the Act (my italics). Third, it contained subsidiary guides: "due consideration to the prices prevailing between October 1 and 15, 1941,"[29] or to the nearest two-week period if these dates were not representative of prevailing market prices, and "adjustments for such relevant factors as he may determine and deem to be of general applicability. . . ." So the Administrator could raise a price ceiling to insure equity or stimulate production, or he could refuse to do so in the name of stabilization; and either way he followed a Congressional directive.

Another example may be cited from a peacetime statute for a permanent program. The Civil Aeronautics Act of 1938 contained guides for issuance of air route certificates. The standard of "public

[26] See Chapter XI.

[27] Sharfman, *The Interstate Commerce Commission*, II, 359. Copyright 1931 by The Commonwealth Fund. The term "public interest" itself is, in the words of Justice Frankfurter, "a texture of multiple strands." Federal Power Commission v. Hope Natural Gas Co., 320 U. S. 591, 627 (1944).

[28] 321 U. S. 414 (1944).

[29] These date guides were affected by amendments in an act of October 2, 1942.

convenience and necessity" is stated in the section dealing specifically with certificates. In addition, however, the declaration of policy directs the C.A.A. to consider "among other things, as being in
the public interest, and in accordance with the public convenience
and necessity" six factors in judgment. Among these are the "encouragement and development of an air-transportation system" and
"competition to the extent necessary to assure the sound development of an air-transportation system. . . ." In another section
C.A.A. is directed to grant new certificates for additional mail service if "required by the public convenience and necessity." [30] To implement any policy developed under these directives the C.A.B.
may assume the payment by the government of air mail subsidies,
exercising broad discretion both as to the amount and period
of payment.[31] These directives, it appears, are as general and as
multiple as those in the Emergency Price Control Act.

Directives may carry standards which call quite obviously for reconciliation of opposed objectives. In U. S. v. Rock Royal Co-opera-
tive, Inc.,[32] the Supreme Court upheld, against the charge of invalid
delegation of legislative powers, an authorization to the Secretary of
Agriculture to issue marketing orders. The basic guide was a directive to provide parity prices to producers, but for consumer protection the Secretary was to move for "gradual correction of the
current level at as rapid a rate as the Secretary of Agriculture
deems to be in the public interest and feasible in view of the current consumptive demand in domestic and foreign markets." As
Justice Roberts said in a dissent in a companion case the Secretary
was "to form a judgment by balancing a price-raising policy against
a consumer-protection policy according to his views of feasibility
and public interest." [33] Another example of opposed objectives in
statutes is the directive to the I.C.C. to consider in rate making the
need of the railways for revenue and the effect the rates may have

[30] See Title I, Section 2, Title IV, Sections 401 (d) (1) and 401 (n), 52 U. S.
Stat. at Large, 973, at pages 980, 987, and 990.
[31] See the comments of James M. Landis, "Air Routes under the Civil Aeronautics Act," The Journal of Air Law and Commerce, XV, 295-302 (Summer,
1948).
[32] 307 U. S. 533 (1939).
[33] H. P. Hood and Sons, Inc., v. U. S., 307 U. S. 588, 605.

on "movement of traffic." [34] Since high rates are designed to bring revenue and low rates encourage more "movement of traffic" on railroads, this is forming a judgment by balancing a high-rate policy and a low-rate policy.[35]

The appearance of definiteness in a statutory provision may be deceptive. The Tariff Act of 1922 seemed to give a definite guide. The President would "equalize" "costs of production" at home and abroad within the limits allowed in the Act.[36] But the conclusion that "the ascertainment of *actual* costs of production is in many instances a physical impossibility" (author's emphasis) is heavily substantiated.[37] Moreover, "the Tariff Commission was able in a period of thirty months, to investigate only about three-tenths of one per cent of the commodities covered by the act." [38] Where was. the guide to the Tariff Commission on selection of articles to be investigated?[39] The rule of "annual . . . fair return upon the aggregate value" in the Transportation Act of 1920 turned out to be a rule which could not be applied at all.[40] The base period dates of October 1-15, 1941 in the Emergency Price Control Act and September 15, 1942 in the amendments of October, 1942[41] were often not controlling because of the sheer impossibility of rolling prices down to the base-period level; increasingly, the rule "generally fair and

[34] 48 *U. S. Stat. at Large,* 211, 220.

[35] For further discussion, see pages 69-73.

[36] 42 *U. S. Stat. at Large,* 858, 941-42.

[37] The conclusion is that of John Day Larkin in *The President's Control of the Tariff* (Cambridge, 1936), 71. He carefully substantiates the conclusion at pages 114-150. Compare E. E. Schattschneider's statement "that the costs formula is worked out so badly in practice that it can be made to mean almost anything." *Politics, Pressures, and the Tariff* (New York, 1935), 9. And see the references cited by Herring, *Public Administration and the Public Interest,* footnote at pages 94-95.

[38] Schattschneider, *op cit.,* 25.

[39] "Cost-of-production investigations were undertaken at the behest of commercial interests acting through the President and the Senate." E. Pendleton Herring, *Public Administration and the Public Interest,* 97. Copyright 1936 by McGraw-Hill Book Company, Inc. After amendments in 1930 required that investigations should be made on the request of the President or motion of either house of Congress, the big majority of the investigations were made as a result of such requests or motions. See Herring, *Ibid.,* 102-103, and the sources cited there.

[40] *Infra,* pages 69-70.

[41] 56 *U. S. Stat. at Large,*

equitable" became the only significant guide for non-agricultural prices. Does it not appear that in the complicated task of economic regulation generality of directive may often be the only practicable course? [42]

In the past this problem of generality of directives has been regarded as one for the courts. The Supreme Court accepted the principle that Congress could not delegate legislative power to the President as one "universally recognized as vital to the integrity and maintenance of the system of government ordained by the Constitution." [43] But it has also proclaimed relative to this issue of delegation that "The Constitution . . . does not demand the impossible or the impracticable." [44] Hence, legislative power can be delegated to executive agents or independent commissions "when it is necessary to do so in order to achieve the results which it [Congress] desires." [45]

---

[42] The case "illustrates the wisdom of the legislature in prescribing as the sole standard of maximum rates that they shall be reasonable. Any other standard, unless 'a mere generality,' would surely be challenged as arbitrary." Chief Justice Cullen, referring to an earlier rate case in Trustees of Village of Saratoga Springs v. Saratoga Gas, Electric Light and Power Company, 83 N. E. 693, 700 (1908).

[43] Field v. Clark, 143 U. S. 649, 692 (1892). Is there a difference between delegation to the President and to executive departments and independent commissions? Apparently, the rules relate to what Congress may pass to another, and are not affected by the character of the agent. There may be some difference where the President also has powers from the Constitution, as in foreign affairs.

The doctrine that legislative power cannot be delegated is part of a political tradition which channeled through Locke. Second Treatise on Civil Government, Chapter XI. It had support from a legal doctrine coming, it appears, from the printed text of Bracton's De Legibus down through Story and Kent who interpreted the maxim of the common law: "Delegata potestas non potest delegari," for the law of agency. See Patrick Duff and Horace E. Whiteside, "Delegata Potestas non Potest Delegari: a Maxim of American Constitutional Law," Cornell Law Quarterly, XIV, 168 (1929).

[44] Yakus v. U. S., 321 U. S. 414, 424.

[45] E. S. Corwin, The President: Office and Powers (New York, 1940), 119, interpreting the Supreme Court's language in Buttfield v. Stranahan, 192 U. S. 471 (1904).

The Constitution does not prohibit delegation; on the contrary, reasonable delegation would seem to be justified under the "necessary and proper" clause. Speaking of Chief Justice White's opinion in Clark Distilling Co. v. West Maryland R. R.—re delegation of Congress' power to the states—242 U. S. 311 (1917), E. S. Corwin says, "It thus becomes assimilated to the 'necessary and proper' clause, and Congress is enabled to delegate its powers whenever it is necessary and proper to do so in order to exercise them effectively." Twilight of the Supreme Court (New Haven, 1934), 144-145. Necessity, or differently

The legal link between the doctrine that legislative power cannot be delegated and the practical fact that it can is that there must be a guide to the administration. But this is a slender link. After the decisions in 1935 holding invalid two delegations because administrative discretion was not "confined" within proper boundaries,[46] the Supreme Court accepted guides for administrators which were as general as any advocate of program flexibility could reasonably urge.[47] This, it appears, is no longer a judicial problem of significance.

It should now be recognized that statutory directives to administration are primarily a problem of legislative science and inclination. The legislator and his aides are under a challenge to reconcile constitutional ideal with program necessity. On the one hand, they need to keep in mind the constitutional delegation to the Congress and the fact that in the evolved democracy of the nation the Congress and its collaborator in legislation—the President—are the representative organs of the government. On the other hand, legislators have to consider need for elaboration of program in the process of its administration and need for adjustment to varying circumstances. Under these opposed constraints, legislative science seeks a standard which guides and confines but does not impair.[48]

---

stated, the test of practicality, has now overridden strict constitutional theory in the line of Supreme Court cases.

[46] A. L. A. Schechter Poultry Corp. et al. v. U. S., 295 U. S. 495 (1935), Panama Refining Co. v. Ryan, 293 U. S. 388 (1935).

[47] That two of the leading cases relate to a war situation (Yakus v. U. S.) and to foreign relations (U. S. v. Curtiss-Wright Export Corp. et al., 299 U. S. 304, 1936) does not appear to be significant. Foreign affairs, cold or hot wars, and domestic emergencies may be more characteristic of the future than what some of us once thought was "normalcy." What is important is that the Supreme Court upholds whatever delegation is needed in order to accomplish lawful purposes.

[48] On the responsibility of Congress, see Hyneman, op. cit., particularly Chapter 5 titled "Giving the Bureaucracy Its Job." Hyneman writes as follows: "First, and fundamental, is the rule that Congress should specify in the statute every guide, every condition, every statement of principle, that it knows in advance it wants to have applied in the situations that are expected to arise." P. 81. But Hyneman writes also that "Congress should not define and describe a governmental undertaking in such detail that administrative officials are rendered incapable of achieving the major objectives toward which legislation is directed." P. 85. Charles S. Hyneman, Bureaucracy in a Democracy. Copyright 1950 by Harper & Brothers.

The task involves purposes, economic insight, and draftsmanship. What are the objectives of public policy? In what ways will present conditions yield to public action? What conditions or contingencies of the future may be anticipated? What language joins purpose with conditions as they are and with prediction of things as they may be and yet leaves flexibility for the unpredictable?

The search may be difficult because of the conflict of purposes. An operating compromise or a "dilatory compromise" [49] may result. The former provides for administration a compromise statement under which it must operate, the latter leaves the question at issue open. It may remain open or it may be that the administration will be forced to resolve problems on which legislators could not agree, and so "passed the buck."

The search may be difficult also because of the complexity of economic factors or the futility of prediction. In such cases legislative science may encompass less in statutory language than meets the ideals of representative government. But in part the task of legislative science is to recognize its limitations and to create mechanism in which delegates may tackle problems at the point where standard expires.

The important need is that *purpose and the will to action be matched with insight and vision on the function of standard and discretion in particular programs.* As new proposals for economic action are advanced, the problem of implementation in legislation becomes important. It is easy in moments of crisis to propose that a general policy of public arbitration be substituted for collective bargaining on the terms of the wage agreement; but what standards would be used? A few cases might be settled without standards but if public settlement were adopted for all stoppages which produced "emergencies" in "key" industries the necessity for development of standards would be inescapable. Could the Congress frame a formula —like parity in agricultural pricing and cost equalization in tariff change? Or would it fall back on such a phrase as "fair and equi-

---

[49] This useful term is recalled from Professor C. J. Friedrich's class lectures two decades ago.

table" and leave an administrative agency with the hottest problem in the imagination of man? [50]

Similar questions arise in proposals for administrative decision on industry organization and policies. From the time of President Theodore Roosevelt men have shrunk from delegation of power to administration to distinguish between "good" and "bad" combinations because they saw before them no satisfactory standards for distinction. But the same questions keep arising as antitrust is used as a weapon for reorganization of industries.[51] Can Congress contribute any guides or must the whole discretion rest in the Department of Justice and the courts? And similar questions arise on proposals that government try to exercise an influence on business policy. It has been suggested, for example, that government might as a permanent policy use a veto on price changes as a method of seeing that the decisions of separate firms conformed to public policy on checking fluctuations in the business cycle. Could Congress frame a standard to guide in the determination of price policy?

The questions arise also in regard to proposals for control of the economy through adjustment of taxes, public expenditures, and credit policies according to the ebb and flow of the economic tide. During the past several years credit policy has been largely a result of pure executive management, for it has been geared—subject to modification effected in the spring of 1951—to Treasury policy of maintaining a low interest rate on government obligations. During the war, decisions on use or non-use of fiscal methods of preventing inflation were matters of executive discretion. Congress did in 1951 prescribe the maximum credit limitations on consumer purchases,

[50] For a limited number of industries operating locally the States might use the test of wages, or other terms of employment, set by collective bargaining in comparable industries; but it is doubtful whether such a test would be acceptable or practicable for large, national industries. At any rate, if compulsory settlement were expanded to a considerable number of key, national industries, government would have to forge its own labor policy.

For a good summary of the problems involved, see Jerre S. Williams, "The Compulsory Settlement of Contract Negotiation Labor Disputes," *Texas Law Review*, XXVII, 587-658, particularly pages 653-657 (May, 1949).

[51] See page 83.

but would a practice of specific determinations by Congress seriously reduce the possibilities for effective use of credit controls? And could Congress frame directives which would enable administrators to adjust taxes and public expenditures within legislative formulae? [52] Would such formulae either bind too tight or have a deceptive simplicity?

Government action may not expand materially in any of the directions referred to above. On the other hand, the questions may indicate the challenges to legislative science. The framing of directives in economic regulation may be the most difficult of future legislative tasks.

In spite, however, of the noblest efforts of man to subordinate government business to legislative directive, experience—outside the tax field, at least—indicates that directives will only set broad and general guides which leave the development of program to those who carry the continuous responsibility for special tasks. The Congress may seek to avoid vagueness in its directives but experience gives force to the judgment that "effective regulation does not permit a rigid and detailed statute." [53]

[52] Discussing compensatory tax policy, Alvin H. Hansen says:
"To make this machinery effective, it is evident that the standard or basic income-tax rate would have to be subject to administrative control. Within limits established by Congress, the President should be empowered to raise and lower the standard income-tax rate."
"The proposal, then, is that the President should be required to review quarterly the revenue receipts from the income tax applicable to individuals for the purpose of ascertaining the extent to which the current and anticipated revenues from this source contribute to stability and employment. Subject to such principles and standards as the Congress may set forth in applicable revenue acts and other statutes, the basic income-tax rates levied on individuals and the relevant withholding schedules should be varied within limits imposed by legislative enactment to such extent as the President may determine to be necessary or desirable for the purpose of maintaining full employment and economic stability, due consideration being given to the combined effect of this action and other measures taken." Alvin H. Hansen, *Economic Policy and Full Employment*, 41 and 142. Copyright 1947 by McGraw-Hill Book Company, Inc.
[53] Task Force of the Hoover Commission, *Regulatory Commissions* (Washington, 1949), 19.

ADMINISTRATIVE APPROACHES IN PROGRAM DEVELOPMENT

Although a cross-section of administrative control would show many areas in which administrative decision could have little or no effect on program content and coverage, there is an extensive area in which the economic policy of the nation gets its substance from administrative decision. The way this occurs differs in the various settings in which control is exercised. Both the extent and the general methods can, however, be illustrated by three examples chosen to illustrate each of three aspects of administrative shaping of the substance of control.

Elaboration of Directives

Program is developed by the elaboration of the standards prescribed in delegations. This may be done by a case-to-case method, as when an agency like the Federal Trade Commission tries to establish precedents in particular cases which will give definite meaning to statutory language. Or it may be done by the framing of rules or policy statements to supplement those in the basic regulation.[54] The example of wartime price control shows possible aspects of the latter procedure.

First, in this instance policy standards came from a "hierarchy of sources."[55] Largely as the result of the Stabilization Act of 1942 the President possessed authority to issue directives on pricing of commodities.[56] An example of the exercise of this authority was the "hold-the-line order" of April, 1943, which, among other things, directed the Price Administrator to allow no further increases in prices affecting the cost-of-living "except to the minimum extent required by law."[57] Next in the line of sources were directives to the Price Administrator issued by the Economic Stabilization Director or his superior, the Director of War Mobilization and Re-

---

[54] For discussion of rule making see pages 95-101, 112-120.
[55] James B. Eckert, ed., *Problems in Price Control: Pricing Standards* (Washington, 1947), 1.
[56] 56 *U. S. Stat. at Large,* 765.
[57] Executive Order No. 9328, April 8, 1943, 8 Fed. Reg. 4681.

conversion, both of whom had been delegated authority by the President. Then came the further elaboration of standards within O.P.A. Here so extensive a set of standards was developed that it has been said that "the use of the administrative standard was probably carried further than had ever previously been the case."[58] The standards were contained in various forms of policy statements by the Administrator, in provisions of price regulations which prescribed standards for the agency to follow in fixing prices upon sellers' applications, and in "price operating instructions" containing further guides to the staff for administering the price standards set in the regulations.[59]

The standards developed within O.P.A. served a triple purpose. They met, first, the agency's need to clarify specifically the policy it would follow in particular circumstances; second, the agency lawyers' need for standards so that they could assure the Administrator that even-handed treatment was given to all persons subject to regulation; and third, the Administrator's need for objective standards so that the work could be passed down the line and to the field, safely.

Although there was a high degree of centralization in the issuance of the standards developed within O.P.A., the actual process of elaboration involved the work of a hierarchy of officials. The general statements were developed largely in the Office of the Deputy Administrator for Price. Their translation into more precise standards or their elaboration in specific action was done at lower levels—in the divisions, the branches, or in some cases even in regional offices. Thus, O.P.A. experience illustrates the possibilities of the policy-elaborating function being carried deep into the administrative hierarchy.[60]

How can lines be drawn between the functions of Congress, the

---

[58] *Problems in Price Control: Pricing Standards,* 6.

[59] Important also were the understandings reached informally in conference. The minutes of some early conferences have been published in the Historical Reports on War Administration: Office of Price Administration: *Minutes of the Price Administration Committee* (Washington, 1946).

[60] This is a frequent feature of the institutional process in administration. For further aspects of this process, see pages 200-209.

chief executive, coordinating officials, the agency head, and the latter's subordinates? Except for Congress each works within some framework of guiding policy, but each also moves further in elaboration of policy. Policy making and administration get mixed in the vast middle area of the government hierarchy.

A second noteworthy fact was the tremendous significance of the standards evolved outside the Congress, including those at the agency level. The words "generally fair and equitable" were only a starting point. The content and effect of program depended upon the elaborating standards and the tightness or looseness of their application. Thus, the program's meaning was found in such O.P.A. standards as these: the "industry earnings" standard under which prices would be adjusted upward for an industry only if it were shown that the industry's earnings before taxes were not equivalent to its annual average earnings before taxes from 1936 to 1939 (adjusted for changes in investment);[61] the "minimum product" standard, which "as finally formulated" "required that the ceiling prices for a particular product or product line of a multiple-product industry be high enough to permit the producers of the bulk of the output (by dollar volume) to receive their out-of-pocket costs";[62] or the various standards under which individual seller's prices could sometimes be adjusted—to "relieve hardship," to prevent "local shortage," to bring his prices "in line" with those of other sellers.[63]

The complex of standards had to be adjusted to circumstances within industries and to surrounding factors, such as the shift to reconversion and decontrol. Standards were continuously measured against conditions. Policy framers had to consider how the standards could be "tailored" to the conditions in particular industries, what

[61] *Problems in Price Control: Pricing Standards*, 15, 27-89.
[62] *Ibid.*, 91, and see generally pages 91-121. Ultimately, out-of-pocket costs included only factory costs.
[63] *Ibid.*, 20, and see generally, 389-420. For judicial decisions on some of O.P.A.'s pricing standards see Nathaniel L. Nathanson, "The Emergency Court of Appeals," in *Problems in Price Control: Legal Phases* (Washington, 1947), Part I, 5-15. Readers not having access to this source may refer directly to leading cases discussed by Nathanson, including particularly Philadelphia Coke Co. *v.* Bowles, 139 F. (2d) 349 (1943); Interwoven Stocking Co. *v.* Bowles, 141 F. (2d) 696 (1944); Gillespie-Rogers-Pyatt Co., Inc. *et al. v.* Bowles, 144 F. (2d) 361 (1944); and Armour & Co. *v.* Bowles, 148 F. (2d) 529 (1945).

prices could be "lived with," and other practical factors which place limits on government.

Decisions on broad policy matters inevitably had political effects. Those in industry who were dissatisfied with pricing standards complained through political channels, and more and more the Congress became a forum for discussion of O.P.A.'s pricing standards. One result was amendments of the governing statute as it was renewed at successive dates. The most significant of these contained new directives which liberalized pricing standards[64] or, in the final period, limited O.P.A.'s discretion as to speed and choice of areas for price "decontrol." [65] Disagreement over such matters led in 1946 to a presidential veto of the extension act and a 25-day period without control while an extension act was being passed. It is not too much to say that the policies of O.P.A. became engulfed in political controversy to an extent which made it impossible for an administrative agency to operate effectively.

What is the lesson of this experience? Does it show only the need for a stable legislative foundation for administration? The most vulnerable aspect of O.P.A. was the necessity for periodical renewal of its directive. This was accentuated by the decline of executive leadership in the Congress and the dissatisfaction of the people with controls. But one could not say that this was the whole lesson of the experience. Does it not indicate that there are areas in which administration cannot be insulated from politics? Under the conditions, was it not necessary to have administrative elaboration of standards? But did this not inevitably bring politics into the amplification of standard? Does it show that administration, to be successful, must have a measure of political acumen? Or that even that sometimes is not enough, administration itself sometimes being expendable?

These questions do not affect the fact that elaboration of directive is an administrative function. They do indicate the unreality of a concept of government which assumes that policy making can

---

[64] See *Problems in Price Control: Pricing Standards,* Chapters VI and VII.
[65] *Ibid.,* 500-503 and Price Control Extension Act of 1946, 60 *U. S. Stat. at Large,* 664.

move down into administration without involving the latter in politics. They show also that the significance of the facts presented here lies in the large issue of the relation of the political organs of government to the process of regulation, which must therefore be discussed in later chapters.

Reconciliation of Economic Factors

The dependence of policy upon administrative action is revealed in other situations where administration seems to be, in the main, only a mechanism for continuing adjustment of opposed economic interests and considerations. Railroad rate making offers a clear example.

In the Transportation Act of 1920 Congress tried to give a definite directive on rate making. It directed that the Commission's powers over rates should be used so that

carriers as a whole (or as a whole in each of such rate groups or territories as the Commission may from time to time designate) will, under honest, efficient, and economical management and reasonable expenditures for maintenance of way, structures and equipment, earn an aggregate annual net railway operating income equal, as nearly as may be, to a fair return upon the aggregate value of the railway property of such carriers held for and used in the service of transportation.[66]

Making allowance for the qualification "as nearly as may be" and the exercise of Commission discretion on rate groups, economical management, and reasonable railroad expenditures, the basic guide of "annual . . . fair return upon the aggregate value" looks like a rule for rate making.

But when is a rule not a rule? It is clear, first, that this one had some gaps. It gave no guide on composition of rates but only referred to the level of rates as a whole. And neither it nor the Valuation Act of 1913 told the Commission how to put its manifold pieces of evidence on value into a single-sum statement of total value of a railroad.[67] Without a rule for determining aggregate value

---

[66] Sec. 15a(2), 41 *U. S. Stat. at Large,* 456, 488.
[67] On this problem see Sharfman, *The Interstate Commerce Commission,* III-A (New York, 1935), 246-267.

the rule for rate making was no rule. Second, the authority of the rule vanished because its motive did not square with practicalities. The purpose of the rule was stated by the I.C.C.: "Both the present rate-making rule and the recapture provisions were founded upon the theory that the rates charged by the railroads could be so adjusted—moved up and down from time to time—as to maintain a comparatively stable level of aggregate earnings." [68] The Commission stated that this would require the lowering of rates in prosperity and raising them in depression. The latter, of course, would have an adverse effect on the amount of traffic moving by rail and thus defeat its purpose. The I.C.C. soon "found it necessary to take into consideration existing industrial conditions and the effect of freight rates upon the movement of traffic," [69] and criticized the rule as cherishing "elusive hopes that by mere changes in rates railroad earnings can be made stable regardless of business conditions." [70]

The I.C.C. recommended a change in the directive on rate making,[71] and a change was made in the Emergency Railroad Transportation Act of 1933. The new rule reads:

In the exercise of its power to prescribe just and reasonable rates the Commission shall give due consideration, among other factors, to the effect of rates on the movement of traffic; to the need, in the public interest, of adequate and efficient railway transportation service at the lowest cost consistent with the furnishing of such service; and to the need of revenues sufficient to enable the carriers, under honest, economical, and efficient management, to provide such service.[72]

This directive really says no more than that the I.C.C. shall make a judgment based on all the relevant factors. It fits a different pattern of thought than the rule in the Act of 1920. The earlier act tried to extend the principle of the rule of law through

[68] *Annual Report,* 1932, 16.

[69] Letter from Joseph B. Eastman, Chairman, Legislative Committee, I. C. C., to Hon. James Cousens, Chairman, Committee on Interstate Commerce, Jan. 21, 1931, printed as Appendix G in *Annual Report, 1931,* 347-357. Quoted words are at page 350.

[70] *Annual Report, 1931,* 109, quoted from its own decision in *Fifteen Per Cent Case, 1931. 178 Interstate Commerce Commission Reports,* 539, 581.

[71] See *Annual Reports for 1930,* 96; *1931,* 107-110, 347-367; *1932,* 16-18.

[72] 48 *U. S. Stat. at Large,* 211, 220. Compare the multiple standards for rate making in the Civil Aeronautics Act of 1938, 52 *U. S. Stat. at Large,* 973, 998.

a definite directive, the latter accepts the judgment of men. For the traditional idea of the "rule of rules," the 1933 statute substitutes discretionary measuring of economic effects—a method similar to that of an informed board of directors of a railroad. Borrowing phrases from Landis we may say the pattern follows the "industrial" rather than the "political analogue."

This approach in rate making accords with the general character of the I.C.C.'s processes. Professor Sharfman has characterized these as pragmatic in nature. He has referrrd to the "relatively minor rôle played by precedent," the absence of "any controlling degree of finality" in decisions, the use of "trial-and-error methods," the frequent recourse to modification and supplementary action, the fact that "the Commission's rulings" are "predominantly a matter of informed judgment, flexibly adjusted to changing circumstances and conditions, with the pressure of legal necessity emerging only on relatively rare occasions." [73]

Factors affecting the composition of rates are too complex for brief discussion. It is possible, however, to say that here too administrative discretion is exercised in terms of a multiplicity of factors. Distance and cost of transportation, desire of the carriers to attract traffic, the desire to avoid too great a disturbance to existing commercial relationships are among the many factors which influence decision on rate structures. To a large extent the revision of rates has been based on carrier initiative, and Commission action has only partially modified the historical pattern. The rate structure remains unrationalized in accord with clear and consistent principle. The I.C.C.'s "task is not primarily to achieve a goal, but to maintain a moving balance between ideal ends and immediate practical considerations." [74]

The "moving balance" has not always been satisfactory to group and geographical interests. This is illustrated in two of the significant protests. That of the farmers led to the Hoch-Smith Resolution

[73] I. L. Sharfman, *The Interstate Commerce Commission*, II, 367-384. Copyright 1931 by The Commonwealth Fund.
[74] I. L. Sharfman, *The Interstate Commerce Commission*, III-B, 766. Copyright 1936 by The Commonwealth Fund. For Sharfman's full discussion of the composition of rates, see pages 309-768 of the volume cited.

which directed the Commission "to effect with the least practicable delay such lawful changes in the rate structure of the country as will promote the freedom of movement by common carriers of the products of agriculture affected by that depression, including livestock, at the lowest possible lawful rates compatible with the maintenance of adequate transportation service." [75] The balance among the interests was not altered by the Resolution, first because of uncertainties as to the legal effect of the Resolution, and second, because by the time the I.C.C. bowed to the Resolution in the grain rate case the Supreme Court thought the railroads were too much in need of help from the depression to allow help to the agricultural interests.[76] More successful was the protest of the South against what it regarded as sectional discrimination in freight rates. The protest led to amendment of statutory directives and to initiation of rate investigations in the I.C.C. which ultimately resulted in changes favorable to the southern plea.[77] Congress in 1940 amended the antidiscrimination provisions of the Act to Regulate Commerce so as to include the words "region, district, territory" [78] and directed the I.C.C. to investigate rates between and within classification territories for the purpose of determining whether such rates were unjust and unreasonable or unlawful in any other respect in and of themselves or in their relation to each other.[79] The I.C.C. had not waited for the passage of this legislation to initiate an investigation of some of the freight rates involved (known as class rates). After lengthy investigation it decreed an increase in such rates in so-called Official Territory (east of the Mississippi and north of the Ohio and Potomac Rivers plus most of Virginia) of 10 per cent and an equal percentage decrease in all other parts of the country, except the "Mountain-Pacific Territory," and between

[75] 43 *U. S. Stat. at Large*, 802.

[76] See Harvey C. Mansfield, *The Lake Cargo Rate Controversy* (New York, 1932), 248-256, and Sharfman, *The Interstate Commerce Commission*, II, 469-472, III-B, 740-744.

[77] For a readable and careful summary of the southern movement see Robert A. Lively, *The South in Action: A Sectional Crusade against Freight Rate Discrimination* (Chapel Hill, N. C., 1949).

[78] 54 *U. S. Stat. at Large*, 898, 902, Section 5 (a) (1).

[79] Section 5 (b).

these points of the country and Official Territory.[80] Thus, a new point of balance was fixed in the rate structure of the nation.

In these instances Congress showed its dissatisfaction with I.C.C.'s resistance to shipper pressures for change in the status quo. More often, Congress has let the Commission "take the heat." And in some instances the Commission has succeeded in devising compromises that have so commended themselves as to be written into the statute later. A classic example is the principles of interpretation of the long-and-short haul rule of the Mann-Elkins Act of 1920 which were later substantially incorporated in the Transportation Act of 1920.

The position of the I.C.C. in reconciliation of conflicting economic interests has thrown appointments to the body into the very vortex of politics. Thus, the controversy over lake cargo coal rates prevented confirmation of Commissioner Esch's reappointment and was a dominating factor in appointments to the Commission for a number of years.[81] Out of the controversy came a southern demand also for representation, and over the years the northeasternly balance in composition shifted to one in which the southerners and the westerners were in the majority. It has been the habit of commentators to condemn sectional and other political influences on nominations, but a realistic view will recognize that the entry of politics often will be the inevitable result of delegation of power to mediate economic conflicts.

It is significant, nevertheless, that the conflicting transportation interests of groups and sections have been resolved in large measure within an administrative structure. Whatever weaknesses it may have had in other respects, the I.C.C. has been quite successful in moderating and absorbing the strains between interests within its own process. But what is the nature of this function? With its heavy facade of judicial procedure, the I.C.C. has been called "the Supreme Court of the transportation world." But the word "court" has its own connotations and does not capture the larger meaning of

---

[80] *Class Rate Investigation*, 1939, 262 I.C.C. 447 (1945), upheld in New York v. U. S., 331 U. S. 284 (1947).
[81] See Harvey C. Mansfield, *op. cit.*, 161-194.

this administrative operation. In railroad regulation the administrative process is not one of law application merely; on the contrary, the policy of the nation takes form in discretionary and "pragmatic" administrative resolution of complex economic factors and conflicting group interests.

Political Adjustment

Economic control may involve a process of adjustment which is clearly political. This, it appears, is the case in present-day tariff making.

In tariff changes the ideal of decision in accord with definite guide and mathematical data has been lost since 1934 in the new realities of trade agreements. The statutory guides in the Reciprocal Trade Agreement Act have been too general to confine the discretion of our negotiators.[82] The program derives its content from the bargaining with other nations and the compromise of forces at home.

The latter results inevitably from two factors. First, the parties in interest at home must be heard. Experience has shown that tariff making cannot be insulated from group pressure;[83] but in the trade agreements program, procedure has safeguarded the right of group protest. The Reciprocal Trade Agreement Act of 1934 provided that "reasonable public notice of the intention to negotiate an agreement . . . shall be given in order that any interested person may have an opportunity to present his views to the President, or to such agency as the President may designate." [84] Executive order has provided that, prior to negotiation, a Trade Agreements Committee shall recommend to the President a list of items for consideration; the items approved by the President are then published in the Federal Register and issued to the press. Interested parties may then present their views to an interdepartmental Committee for Reciprocity Information. Thereafter, the Trade Agreements Committee, with representations so obtained and information from the Tariff

[82] 48 *U. S. Stat. at Large,* 943, 19 U. S. C., Sec. 1351.
[83] See Herring, *Public Administration and the Public Interest* (New York and London, 1936), Chapter VI.
[84] 48 *U. S. Stat. at Large,* 943, Sec. 4; 19 U. S. C., Sec. 1354.

Commission, the Department of Commerce, and perhaps other agencies, makes recommendations to the President relative to the trade agreement under consideration.[85] Initially, the fact that the composition of the two committees was different enabled the "hearing" committee to form a kind of buffer between those who determined American policy and the group pressures. In 1937, however, the membership of the two committees was made identical. Initially, also, the notices of intention to negotiate contained no statement of the items for negotiations, but this too was soon changed.[86] Thus, procedure provides the maximum encouragement for group intervention in the tariff-making process.

The second conditioning factor is found in the position of the various organs of the government. Trade policy is an aspect of foreign policy; but the departments concerned with home affairs consider that it is also important to American industry, agriculture, and labor. The position of these departments with respect to the promotion and protection of group interests may lead them to take a different view on tariff concessions from that of the Department of State. The military now also claims an interest in these matters. The result of this multi-agency interest has been recognized in the creation of the two committees mentioned above, both of which today contain representatives of the U. S. Tariff Commission, the Secretaries of State, Treasury, Defense, Interior, Agriculture, Commerce, and Labor, and of the Administrator for Economic Cooperation. The purpose, according to the executive order, is to coordinate the interests of American agriculture, industry, commerce, labor, and security, and of American financial and foreign policy.

The final result is that tariff changes are not a matter of application of standard, but of compromise of forces. The Department of State may be able to exert a certain directional force, particularly if manned by personnel who have a fervent belief in the economic and foreign policy values of free trade; but such force is qualified by

[85] The most recent executive order is No. 10170, October 13, 1950, 15 F. R. 6901.
[86] For a discussion of these changes and the early history of the procedural requirements see Carl Kreider, "Democratic Processes in the Trade Agreements Program," *The American Political Science Review,* XXXIV, 317-332 (1940).

the factors of group interest and opposed conceptions of public policy. The process of government here follows neither the industrial nor the legal analogue; it is essentially political wherever it is located in the governmental structure.[87]

Beyond Examples

There may be danger of overstatement in use of examples. Many agencies can translate general statutory directive into specific rules without the framework of hierarchical policy determinations which characterized wartime price control. Agencies which must reconcile a complex of economic factors may find more immediate relevancy in the statutory directives than has been the case in directives on railroad rate making. The example on the tariff is not typical, though it may become so if foreign policy becomes more intertwined with domestic economic control or if government action in different areas of economic control and service has to be reconciled at the executive level into a coordinated economic program.

The examples do show the three main elements which affect the content of program. Regulation takes form *by movement from directive, resolution of economic factors, and compromise of group pressures.* Different programs exhibit varying combinations or degrees of effect of each of the three factors.

The examples not only show the scope of administrative participation which often exists now but indicate that which may exist in future programs. Broad functional regulation, e. g., of wages, prices, rate of production, would, as in wartime, call for administrative elaboration of statutes in order that program could be consistent in the various industries. Industry management, at least where regulation is initiated in an industry whose organization and practices are already developed, is likely to reveal aspects comparable to a con-

[85] It might be argued that this process has been lifted above the level of administration. But it is a delegated task. Also, the task of government is being carried forward by continuing, specialized committees. The Trade Agreements Committee even has responsibility for keeping "informed of the operation and effect of all trade agreements which are in force" and the Committee for Reciprocity Information for allowing interested persons opportunity to present their views "with respect to the operation and effect" of such agreements. Executive Order 10004.

siderable degree to those which characterize control by the I.C.C. Control of currency and credit also calls for continuous discretion on the proper balance among economic factors. Any effort to coordinate the activity of administration toward a defined major economic objective—either of expansion of economic activity or of temporary restraint—would inevitably lift the everpresent adjustment of group interests to that higher level of political reconciliation which has characterized reciprocal tariff agreements.

SOME OTHER ASPECTS OF ADMINISTRATIVE DEVELOPMENT OF PROGRAM

Creation, Expansion, and Contraction of Program

Engrossed as it has been in the problem of standards, the literature of public administration has taken insufficient note of the actual creation, expansion, and contraction of the program of government outside the Congress.

Creation and expansion of government program by administrative and executive action was apparent in the emergency created by World War II. Price controls were imposed over a large number of industries under the President's broad emergency powers before the Congress enacted a price-control statute; wage controls emerged prior to their authorization by Congress in the Stabilization Act of October, 1942.[88] Moreover, the scope of controls over production, price, wages, and manpower was, on the whole, matter for administrative and/or executive discretion.

The same had been true in the early days of the New Deal when a flurry of activities developed under the most tenuous Congressional directives. Sometimes the process of government

---

[88] The National War Labor Board had been created by Executive Order No. 9017, *Federal Register*, VII, 237, and it succeeded the National Defense Mediation Board, created by Executive Order No. 8617, *Federal Register*, VI, 1532. By the summer of 1942 limitation on wage increases by the 15 per cent or "Little Steel" Formula had become the policy of government. On the necessity of voluntary methods in production controls, due to lag in Congressional authorizations, see John Lord O'Brian and Manly Fleischmann, "The War Production Board Administrative Policies and Procedures," *George Washington Law Review*, XIII, 1-60, particulary pages 8-9 (December, 1944).

seemed to be inverted. With a minimum of legislative authorization or collaboration administrative agencies evolved specific programs; subsequent legislative history, in appropriations and organic acts, selected and confirmed some of the specific programs for survival. For example, as late as 1946, Congress passed the National School Lunch Act,[89] which confirmed a program which had evolved years before—partly as part of the process of disposing of agricultural surpluses and partly for relief of the needy—and had been continued on the basis of year-to-year appropriation acts.

Leaps in program occasionally occur even in "normal" periods. For example, after more than forty years of national bank supervision a new Comptroller of the Currency initiated the practice of considering community need for more banking facilities before chartering new national banks;[90] this marked a turn from official sanction of free enterprise in banking to an official policy of protecting existing establishments against the competition of new enterprises. In the twenties the Federal Reserve Board gave new meaning to open-market negotiations. Whereas prior to 1922 these negotiations had been conducted separately by the Federal Reserve Banks[91] with objectives related to banking operations only, the Federal Reserve Board in 1923 initiated, through an open-market investment committee, a policy of coordinating the operations of the reserve banks "with primary regard to the accommodation of commerce and industry, and to the effect of such purchases or sales on the general credit situation." This policy was confirmed in the Banking Act of 1933.[92]

Program may be contracted, diverted, or vetoed in the administrative process. In the twenties the Federal Trade Commission

---

[89] 60 *U. S. Stat. at Large,* 230.

[90] Thomas P. Kane, *The Romance and Tragedy of Banking* (New York, 1923), 393-394. Note also the discussions in *Annual Report of Comptroller of the Currency,* 1910, p. 19, and *Annual Report of the Secretary of the Treasury on the State of the Finances* (1909), 406.

[91] Steps were taken in 1922 by the reserve banks to coordinate the placing of their orders.

[92] See E. W. Kemmerer, *The ABC of the Federal Reserve System* (Princeton, 1938), 51-52, 200-204. The quoted words in the text are those of the Federal Reserve Board.

moved to a considerable degree away from the cease-and-desist technique prescribed by law to a policy of "helping business help itself." [93] The I.C.C. stalled for several years on the directive of Congress to develop a consolidation program for the railroads. [94] The whole grand design of the Transportation Act of 1920, which looked toward deliberate and constructive promotion of public ends, [95] was substantially stalemated in the I.C.C.'s existing pattern of "pragmatic" regulation. [96] The Commission's almost complete inactivity in the regulation of pipe-line rates for twenty-eight years followed by inadequate and dilatory proceedings during the next fourteen years has quite aptly been called "nullification of the Congressional intent to regulate pipe-line rates." [97]

Normally administration cannot under the restraints of legal order jump to new program. [98] New departures must be linked to power delegation. The latitude for elaboration, contraction, or diversion, is, however, very wide. In this respect, administration moves almost, if not quite, to the top level of policy determination.

Development of Technique

Policy development is often contingent upon administrative invention of special technique.

The big task in allocation of scarce materials during the war-

[93] See Herring's general summary on "Personalities, Politics, and the Federal Trade Commission" in *Public Administration and the Public Interest*, 125-138.

[94] Sharfman concludes that in its failure for 6 years to adopt a final consolidation plan "the Commission chose to disregard . . . the statutory mandate. . . ." I. L. Sharfman, *The Interstate Commerce Commission*, III-A, 482. Copyright 1935 by The Commonwealth Fund. For fuller discussion see his elaboration at pages 474-501, and W. N. Leonard, *Railroad Consolidation under the Transportation Act of 1920* (New York, 1946), particularly pages 271-281.

[95] See Sharfman, *op. cit.*, I, 176 ff.

[96] Administrative discretion with respect to carrying out law is not confined to regulatory agencies. See, on discretion exercised by local law enforcement officers, Schuyler C. Wallace, "Nullification: A Process of Government," *Political Science Quarterly*, XLV, 347-358 (1930).

[97] By Kenneth Davis, after a graphic account of the amazing story. "Administrative Powers of Supervising, Prosecuting, Advising, Declaring, and Informally Adjudicating," *Harvard Law Review*, LXIII, 193, 225 (1949).

[98] The C.A.A. may establish classifications or groups of carriers and exempt any air carrier or class of carrier from economic regulation. Civil Aeronautics Act of 1938, Section 416. This has enabled it to limit and subsequently extend the coverage of its controls.

time emergency was the discovery of appropriate techniques of allocation. The search for technique led to priority orders, limitation orders, conservation orders, controlled materials plan, set-aside orders, consumer rationing, and other methods.[99] The use of these sometimes called for a further search for auxiliary technique, as in rationing, where local board issuance of ration coupons, ration banking, dealer accountability, and plans for determining "who would get how much" grew out of the administrative process.[100] Likewise, in price control the elaboration of standard described above was accompanied by a search for techniques of pricing. Price controllers discovered a group of techniques such as the freeze of prices at the level existing on a certain date, the use of margin above costs or other formulae, the fixing of the price in dollars and cents, and preticketing, in which the manufacturer put the retailers' price on the merchandise.[101] Through all the war agencies inventiveness in technique was the major test of administrators. Technique was comparable to strategy and tactics in military operations.

These are illustrations of regulatory technique. Probably more important in the long run was the application of new mechanical techniques in the 'thirties and thereafter in large-scale government operations. Beginning with the first AAA benefit payments and the veterans' bonus distribution, multiple check writers and presently IBM card checks enabled the government to issue checks at many times the rates known in the 'twenties. This made manageable, for example, the WPA program of the 'thirties. In nonspending operations, also, mass production techniques have made program operations physically possible. For example, the system of enforcement in gasoline rationing, where all coupons turned in by consumers were checked to detect counterfeiting, could not have been undertaken except for advances in mechanical technique.

[99] On the search for technique in the War Production Board see John Lord O'Brian and Manly Fleischmann, op. cit., pp. 24-37.

[100] See Joseph Kershaw, A History of Ration Banking (Washington, 1947); Judith Russell and Renee Fantin, Studies in Food Rationing (Washington, 1947); and my Field Administration of Wartime Rationing (Washington, 1947).

[101] See Peter G. Franck and Milton Quint, eds., Problems in Price Control: Pricing Techniques (Washington, 1947).

The New Deal period indicates that administrative development of technique is characteristic of emergencies. A wide variety of techniques were embodied in codes of fair competition and in the measures developed within administration for relief and aid to agriculture.

The history of any agency with large, discretionary powers will probably reveal occasions of creation of new technique. The F.C.C. created the six months term for broadcast licenses, and retained it for many years, thus providing a technique for continuous control. The S.E.C. used the cooperation of the New York Stock Exchange. The F.T.C. developed the trade conference and the stipulation.[102]

Often, however, new techniques must be authorized by amendatory legislation. Thus, the technique of administrative setting of future maximum rates for railroads was authorized by the Hepburn Act[103] and that of suspending new rate schedules during a period of study was authorized by the Mann-Elkins Act.[104] The contest over the technique of unit development of oil fields is being fought in state legislative halls. In civil aeronautics, former Commissioner Landis has suggested that instead of its present open-end system of subsidization without stated limits, Congress might require imposition of air mail budgets; the budget would then become a new managerial technique of the Civil Aeronautics Board.[105]

In the next four chapters we shall analyze the *standard* methods which are used in administrative control and further emphasize the responsibility of administration for choice of techniques of application. At this point, the conclusion may be stated that search for appropriate technique is unavoidably an administrative responsibility. Moreover, where there is lack of statutory authority to use effective technique, the responsibility for recommending legislation is inescapable.

[102] See page 123.
[103] 34 *U. S. Stat. at Large*, 589.
[104] 36 *U. S. Stat. at Large*, 552.
[105] James M. Landis, "Air Routes under the Civil Aeronautics Act," *The Journal of Air Law and Commerce*, XV, 295-302 (1948).

Detail and System

As national economic program is refined in the administrative process a web of detail is created. This is the result of the number and variety of situations to which general policy must be adapted in a nation-wide economy.

Wartime wage control offers a relatively simple illustration of this tendency. The key standard was the Little Steel Formula under which the basic wage rate could be adjusted upward by 15 per cent, which accorded with the percentage increase in the cost of living under the defense program up to the end of April, 1942. But other standards developed. Wages could be raised to correct inequities and inequalities, to correct substandard wages, and to aid in the prosecution of the war. The inequity and substandard tests had to be elaborated by definition. As time passed special increases which did not fit any of the standards were allowed and ultimately the nation became familiar with so-called "fringe" adjustments, which allowed some form of additional compensation without raising the basic wage rate.[106]

Could compulsory arbitration be substituted for collective bargaining without a progressive refinement of standards of decision? Wartime labor control certainly offers no hope that this could be done.

Much more extensive detail developed in price and production control. Industry cried for simplification and the author knows that in one agency at least (O.P.A.) a drive was made toward the objective; but inevitably regulation had to be adjusted to differences within industries, and this produced long and detailed regulations.

This has been the development also in long-range regulation of particular industries. The statutory components are broadened as experience shows loopholes and new problems. The Interstate Commerce Act has expanded from a few simple prohibitions to an extensive set of directives to the I.C.C. The experience

[106] For a brief summary of wartime wage controls see Harold W. Metz, *Labor Policy of the Federal Government* (Washington, 1945), 183-194.

in railroad regulation has been copied in the acts providing for regulation of communications, power and gas holding companies, power operating companies,[107] civil aeronautics, and to an extent of other fields. Other experience supplements that of the I.C.C. in leading to a statutory pattern of regulation which is broader and deeper.[108] From the various statutory directives administration proceeds with elaboration and adjustment to particulars. The result *in each area* is a new system of law and management.

Can escape from detail be found in general measures which play along the whole economic front, that is, by regulation of the general framework of the economy and by fiscal measures? This, it would seem, is a desirable objective; but the hopes are sometimes dimmed. The chief element in the maintenance of framework— the policy of maintaining competition in industry—now seems to lead to prolonged struggle in anti-trust suits and an effort to find a solution adapted to the problems in a particular industry? Does antitrust even lead to adjustment to particulars? Fiscal measures offer hope in theory as alternatives to detailed control, but the nation shrank in wartime from adequate use of these and relied instead too much on price-wage controls.

Whatever approaches are used, ultimately there evolves in each area a system of control. It may take a long time for it to evolve, as in railroad regulation, or it may require a period of strenuous reform action, as under the holding company act, but ultimately an agency will move within the confines of its evolved system of standards and techniques. It will find its point of balance within the conflict of forces, though it may be a "moving balance" in an unstable situation.

Will it then restrict itself to minor adjustments within its larger system? Can more be expected of institutions if these are insulated against politics? Is it the function of politics to supply any needed

---

[107] The Natural Gas Act of 1938, 52 *U. S. Stat. at Large*, 821, did not establish the comprehensive controls which have characterized national regulation in other fields.

[108] In connection with the point made above, the massive income tax code of today may be compared with the slim statute first passed after the adoption of the Sixteenth Amendment.

corrections of major import in an evolved administrative system—either through new directives or new appointments? And does the commission system insulate against the latter and allow for major change only through new directives or through creation of new agencies?

AID TO CONGRESS BY ADMINISTRATIVE AGENCIES

The aid of administrative agencies in the work of Congress is one of the necessities of modern government. This is true, first, because of the volume of legislative enactments which deal with administration. It was found that "Out of the total of 429 public acts exclusive of appropriation acts in the first session of the Seventy-fourth Congress (1935), 270 referred to the organization or functioning" of administrative organs.[109] The aid of administrative agencies is necessary, also, because of the technicality of modern legislation and the accumulation of information and experience on technical matters in the administrative agencies.

Included in this aid is administrative recommendation of legislation. Those who administer turn to the legislature for correction of defects in directives, for legislation which will improve administrative performance, and even for extensions in program coverage.

Administrative initiative of legislation is no new development, having been practiced in early administrations, including President Washington's; but the volume of administrative proposals has increased with the growth of administrative activity and the increased participation of chief executives in legislative leadership.[110] A competent authority stated in 1926 that "Probably more than half

[109] Edwin E. Witte, "The Preparation of Proposed Legislative Measures by Administrative Departments," in President's Committee on Administrative Management, *Report with Special Studies* (Washington, 1937), 361.

[110] See O. Douglas Weeks, "Initiation of Legislation by Administrative Agencies," *Brooklyn Law Review*, IX, 117-131 (1940). So little attention has been given to administrative aid in statute making that Edwin E. Witte found this was the only article on the subject prior to his own in 1942. Edwin E. Witte, "Administrative Agencies and Statute Lawmaking," *Public Administration Review*, II, 116-125 (1942).

the business [of Congress], measured by importance, comes directly or indirectly from the Departments or Bureaus of the Government." [111] Since 1926, the expansion of administration has led to an expectancy that much new legislation will either be recommended by administrative agencies or developed with their aid.

Congress has often imposed upon administrative agencies a definite duty of assisting in its work.[112] Statutes sometimes impose a general duty of recommendation of measures of legislation, at other times they contain directions that recommendations be made on particular subjects, and at other times they provide that either house of Congress may call upon an agency for an investigation and report. Statutes creating the most significant regulatory agencies have customarily required annual reports to Congress, and these may serve as media for recommendations of legislation.

The significance of administrative initiative of legislation in development of program is shown in the experience of some of our older regulatory agencies. The Interstate Commerce Commission has from the beginning urged the adoption of new legislation which it thought was needed for support of the regulatory program. From its earliest annual reports to its support of the basic features of the Reed-Bulwinkle Bill, passed by Congress in 1948,[113] the advice of the I.C.C. has been, to say the least, one of the most influential factors in the evolution of the legislative pattern of railway regulation. Sharfman has concluded that "While the Congressional response has often been tardy, it has seldom swerved, in

[111] Congressman Robert Luce, *Congress* (1926), 3, quoted by Weeks, *ibid.*, 123.

[112] One of the outstanding examples was in the Securities Exchange Act, 48 *U. S. Stat. at Large*, 881, Sections 11 (e), 12 (f), 19 (c) and 211, providing for studies by the S.E.C. The advisory function with respect to legislation was emphasized at an early date. See Cushman, *The Independent Regulatory Commissions*, 55, for emphasis on this function in Congressional deliberations from the report of the Windom Committee to the enactment of the Interstate Commerce Act in 1887.

[113] 62 *U. S. Stat. at Large*, 472. See Commissioner Clyde B. Aitchison's statement for the Commission in *Hearings before a Subcommittee of the Committee on Interstate and Foreign Commerce*, House of Representatives, 79th Cong., 1st Sess., pursuant to H. R. 2536, p. 9.

essence, from the direction of the Commission's recommendations." [114]

Carl McFarland drew a sharp contrast between the records of the F.T.C. and the I.C.C. prior to 1933 in the recommendation of legislation. He showed that whereas "the Interstate Commerce Commission kept up an insistent demand for legislation," the F.T.C. had failed to make its annual report an instrument for obtaining more effective regulatory powers and had reported noncommittally "For the most part, lack of authority and reverses at the hands of the courts." He believed that the weak position of the F.T.C. before the courts and the strong position of the I.C.C. were due, in the main, to the difference in aggressiveness in asking for strengthening legislation. After saying that I.C.C. experience shows that "the judiciary . . . does respond to a determined legislative policy," he concluded significantly: "Effective regulation under such a system [joint action of judicial and administrative agencies] is secured by the active cooperation of the legislature with the administrative arm of government." [115]

In the period immediately following the date of McFarland's publication the F.T.C. pushed recommendations for legislation which would strengthen its position. It is significant that the strengthening legislation of 1938 (the Wheeler-Lea Act) included provisions which had been recommended by the Commission in several successive annual reports.[116]

There are possible dangers in administrative influence on legis-

[114] I. L. Sharfman, *The Interstate Commerce Commission*, I, 290. Copyright 1931 by The Commonwealth Fund. And see the following page for Sharfman's list of examples of the conspicuous part played by the Commission in legislation. See also the long list of recommendations of the I.C.C. from 1920 to 1930 in Carl McFarland, *Judicial Control of the Federal Trade Commission and the Interstate Commerce Commission: 1920-1930*. (Cambridge, 1933), 168, footnote 206.

[115] From pages 181-183 and 188 of Carl McFarland, *Judicial Control of the Federal Trade Commission and the Interstate Commerce Commission: 1920-1930*. Copyright 1933 by The President and Fellows of Harvard College. Final quotations in text are from page 188.

[116] Public Law No. 447, 75th Cong.; *Annual Reports* for 1935, 1936, 1937, at pages 14-15, 16-17, and 15, respectively.

lation. Oftentimes the pressures of the administrators and the interest groups coincide, and it has been said by one observer that "Congress cannot cope with the combined interests of these private associations and the bureaucracy." [117] It has been said, also, that there is an "inevitable tendency toward narrowness and provincialism in administrative circles." [118] The bureaucrat is indeed "likely to have a disproportionate view of values," [119] due to engrossment in his specialty, continuing contact with a limited set of interest groups, lack of contact with the general public, and the inevitable tendency to think of new problems in relation to the evolved pattern of control within which he is imbedded.[120]

In spite of the dangers, the fact of administrative influence on legislation must be accepted. Moreover, it is suggested that administrative aid and initiative on legislation should be emphasized as a major administrative responsibility. The bureaucrat has facts and experience; these create responsibilities. Also, the fact of delegation creates the responsibility of searching for, proposing, and urging better methods of attaining the objectives underlying the delegation. Finally, administrative initiative of policy recommendations is one of the means by which change in program by administrative effort solely can be avoided. It is a means by which an agency may avoid overextension of its own policy-determining functions and too deep involvement in decisions which will have political results. It is a way of pointing responsibility back to the representatives of the people.

The dangers—in whatever degree they may exist—parallel those of program development by administrative agencies alone. In both cases the problem of achieving a larger view and of bringing new purpose and freshness in approach are present. The remedy may lie in use of supplementary sources of legislative information. One

---

[117] James M. Beck, *Our Wonderland of Bureaucracy* (New York, 1932), 92.
[118] Edwin E. Witte, "Administrative Agencies and Statute Lawmaking," *Public Administration Review*, II, 116-125 (1942), at pages 124-125.
[119] *Ibid.*, 123.
[120] See H. J. Laski, "The Limitations of the Expert," *Harper's*, CLXII, 101-110 (1930).

such is the commission of inquiry, another is continuing organs of planning with broadly inclusive jurisdiction. The first—sometimes appointed by the executive, sometimes representative of legislative bodies, occasionally representative of both—is a well-known and often-used method of getting a fresh and comprehensive view of an economic or social problem.[121] The second has had much discussion in recent years and offers hope for a view of policy needs from a different angle than that of the separate agencies immersed in their particulars.[122] Administrative aid in legislation is a natural result of agency expertness but it need not be trusted as the exclusive source of ideas about the "moving balances" in society.

CONCLUSION

The relation of politics to administration presents a set of anomalies. The program of government is made to a considerable extent in administration, and yet the claim that administration should be independent from politics is strong. The belief of two generations ago that legislative power could not be delegated has disappeared, but the doctrine of the same period that administration was separate from politics has had a stouter life. The idea of administration as an organ of social adjustment has paralleled the dream of administrative stability and permanence of tenure. Some would say that if the agencies are run like the courts all will be safe, but the politicians and the pressure groups seem to know that regulatory administration is a different kind of process from that of the courts.

Perhaps an answer will be found on middle ground. Perhaps it will be recognized that the business of making policy does run deep in the stream of government and yet the place of the expert in the process be accepted. But perhaps also more attention

---

[121] For recent discussions see Carl M. Marcy, *Presidential Commissions* (London, 1945), and Phillips Bradley, "Blazing New Legislative Trails," *Survey Graphic*, XXXIII, 234-238 (May, 1944), the latter being a discussion of the New York State Joint Legislative Committee on Industrial and Labor Conditions (Ives Committee).

[122] For further discussions see pages 254-255.

will have to be given to the problem of political direction and oversight.

We shall return to this subject in Chapters 10 and 11. In the meantime we take a closer look at the tools of administrative control.

Chapter V

Administrative Tools
and Techniques:
Traditional Instruments

INTRODUCTION

It is clear from the foregoing discussion that responsibility for attainment of the various public objectives in economic control lies heavily in administrative centers. It is appropriate, then, to discuss the tools and techniques which are available for use in these centers. This is the purpose primarily of Chapters V to VIII, inclusive.

The principal purpose is to show the choices which are available to Congress and administrative agencies in their search for effective methods, and wherever possible to indicate what decisions on regulatory technique are necessary if program objectives are to be achieved. The task is difficult because no complete summary of the technology of administrative control appears to have been compiled, nor even a complete classification of the contents of the administrator's tool kit.[1]

[1] Harold D. Smith presented a "'Tool Chest' of Government Activities," but his summary was not of administrative methods but of government policies which could be used to assure full employment. *Hearings before a Subcom-*

Because of the maze of regulatory techniques used or which may be used, discussion is possible only within a framework of classification. The methods of administrative control are classified herein as instruments of control, facilitative arrangements, and operating methods. The instruments of control are the primary means—such as licensing and benefit payments—through which the program of government is carried to the people. They are types of action to be used for attaining the objectives of regulation. Facilitative arrangements are additional means employed to secure effective execution of programs. They are mainly of four types: those of a legal nature which strengthen the administrative authority to pursue a course of action; those which enable the administrative agency to obtain the information needed for intelligent action; sanctions, i.e., the ultimate compulsive techniques for overcoming resistance to public authority; and communications, i.e., the enlistment of compliance by trade and public relations. Operating methods include arrangements of procedure and internal organization used to get the job of an agency done efficiently and fairly. The instruments of control will be discussed in this and the succeeding chapter, facilitative arrangements and operating methods in the two chapters immediately following.

The word "instruments" has been chosen to emphasize the purposive nature of public administration. A statutory enactment sets the governing objectives of public policy; public administration supplies a number of means or instruments for carrying these objectives into practice. Moreover, the word "instruments" is used in a broad sense to encompass the full content and effect of the administrative action. Instruments are more than forms of action. True, a form of action, such as the license, may be regarded as an instrument of control. But licensing as a means of control has a broader significance than is indicated on the face of licenses, for it often includes an enveloping system of initial discretion and continuous supervision. It is more meaningful, therefore, to regard licensing, rather than the license, as the instrument of control.

---

mittee of the Committee on Banking and Currency, U. S. Senate, 79th Cong., 1st Sess., on "Full Employment Act of 1945," 681, 691-696.

Instruments should be distinguished from powers.[2] Powers are legal grants of authority to use instruments and facilitative arrangements. Rule making is an instrument for translating a general declaration of policy into specific guides for future conduct; the rule-making power is the authority to use the instrument. An instrument may involve use of an aggregation of specific powers, e.g., licensing may involve powers of initial grant or refusal, supervision, amendment or cancellation. An instrument may also involve non-legal factors, such as use of influence or pressure or even of concession in order to achieve selected goals.[3]

One set of instruments available to administrators may be called traditional instruments because they have formed the basis of a system of overhead legal controls commonly used in this country in administrative control of private action. The set of instruments includes executory instruments, rule making, directory action, enabl-

[2] Much of the discussion of administrative acts has been conducted in terms of powers exercised. A trail-blazing discussion of administrative powers was given by Ernst Freund in his *Administrative Powers over Persons and Property* (Chicago, 1928). He distinguished between non-determinative and determinative powers. The former included two types of powers which he insisted should be distinguished from each other, namely, enforcing and prosecutory powers. Determinative or ruling powers were powers exercised in case-to-case administration to produce "an immediate effect on legal rights or status" of the individual. (Freund never defined the word determinative; the definition given here is part of that given by John Dickinson in his review of Freund's book in *American Political Science Review*, XXII, 981 [1928].) Determinative powers included enabling (licensing) powers, directory powers (powers to issue orders), and dispensing, examining, and summary powers. They did not include rule making, for Freund did not think of the rule-making power as "necessarily" an administrative power. See particularly Freund's discussion at pages 10-18.

For two very comprehensive classifications of administrative acts see James Hart, *An Introduction to Administrative Law* (New York, 1940), Chapters VI and VII. Hart's classifications were made for the purpose of throwing "some light on the distinctions that the courts make in setting the bounds of official powers and in deciding what forms of action are available against their misuse."—P. 131. His first classification is based on the "types of functional characteristics involved," his second on "types of administrative action involved."—P. 132.

For another classification of "The Forms of Administrative Action," see F. F. Blachly and Miriam E. Oatman, *Federal Regulatory Action and Control* (Washington, 1940), Chapter IV.

[3] For the importance of non-legal factors see particularly the sections on Sanctions and Communications in Chapter VII.

ing action, the veto, and the exemption. These will be described, compared, and evaluated in this chapter.

These instruments are commonly referred to in the literature of public administration and administrative law. A review and comparison here is of practical value for several reasons. First, the names and terms are words in common use as well as terms of professional art, and are used by different people and in different contexts in so many different senses that clarification of the substantive aim and place of each in the system of control is needed. Second, the names of forms of action cannot be relied on to tell the purposes of their employment, since form and substance are not always the same—e.g., the form of an order may be used merely to require compliance of one party or it may be used to make a determination which becomes in effect a rule for the future. Third, and most significant, the several forms of action (particular and general, prospective and retroactive, enabling, suspensory, prohibitory, etc.) emphasize the several—often conflicting—considerations which administrative agencies need to take into account in various situations: speed, workload, flexibility, uniformity, justice to individuals, overriding social necessities. Administrators must balance these competing values in or before acting, and the weight they give to one consideration as against another determines their choices among the available instruments. Congress must balance these values too in deciding which instruments will be placed at the disposal of an agency; that is, what range of discretion it will have in the choice and combination of instruments.

EXECUTORY INSTRUMENTS

The term "executory instruments" is used to include the conventional methods of enforcement and prosecution. There is the enforcement activity of the police, which includes not merely apprehension of law violators but preventive duties, as exemplified by the traffic officer. There is, next, an amplification of the system of enforcement in the act of inspection. This instrument is inherently an extension of the function of policing, having as its purpose the detection of cases of noncompliance with standards. Though a weapon long exercised in England and the United States, its use has been extended in the last hundred years or so to numerous fields. Public use of the instrument may be frequent, comprehensive, penetrating, and detailed.[4] There is involved sometimes an examination of books and records, as in the case of bank and insurance examinations. Closely related to policing activity, though usually put in separate hands, is the prosecuting function. Prosecution involves a review and check on police activities, and serves as a link between the policing and the ultimate decisional authorities, when the process of enforcement is carried forward to its completion.

These instruments are an essential preliminary to judicial action. They are used also in support of other administrative instruments, being normal accompaniments of the power to govern by administrative license, order, or rule. Finally, they may have a substantial governing effect of their own. Thus, the mere threat of prosecution, or of more frequent and intrusive inspections, may bring change in a business concern's practices.

An administrative agency may have little or no choice on the use of these instruments, but much choice on the way they are used. It can develop plans on the frequency and rigor of inspections. It can determine the places where its resources for enforcement will be used, the degree of noncompliance which will be tolerated, and the conditions under which violations will be compromised. It can take a "get tough" or "go easy" attitude toward major or minor violations. Its discretion may, however, be limited by many factors. The chief of these will be the availability of personnel and appropriations, the necessity of obtaining cooperation from other agencies having law enforcement functions, and the general climate of opinion concerning the degree of rigor which should exist in the enforcement of regulatory legislation. Success in the use of these instruments depends therefore on political

[4] For a discussion of inspection see Leonard D. White, *Introduction to the Study of Public Administration* (3rd ed., New York, 1948), Chapter XXXIII.

support and on the coordination of law enforcement activities, as well as on the wisdom and efficiency of particular agencies.

RULE MAKING AND DIRECTORY ACTION

Two main instruments of control are the prescription of rules of *general* applicability and the issuance of directives applicable to particular parties or situations. Historically, these two have been distinguished in the literature of public administration and public law as rule making and direction through particular decision (normally through a so-called order). Thus, Professor Fuchs could write in 1938: "The most obvious definition of rule making and the one most often employed in the literature of administrative law asserts simply that it is the function of laying down general regulations as distinguished from orders that apply to named persons or to specific situations." [5]

The line between general regulations and specific directives is, however, blurred. First, a so-called order might operate over a comprehensive situation and govern a variety of related particulars. We may note, for an example, the order of the Securities and Ex-

---

[5] "Procedure in Administrative Rule Making," *Harvard Law Review,* LII, 259 (1938), quoted in *Federal Administrative Procedure Act and the Administrative Agencies,* New York University School of Law Institute Proceedings, VII, 494, footnote 3. Fuchs' statement accords with the definition of rule making given by James Hart in his report to the President's Committee on Administrative Management: "The rule-making power may be defined as the legal authority of administrative officers or agencies of government to prescribe discretionary or interpretative rules and regulations of general applicability and legal effect, or to determine the existence of conditions under which contingent statutes are to become operative." "The Exercise of Rule-Making Power" in President's Committee on Administrative Management, *Report with Special Studies* (Washington, 1937), 319. It accords also with the view of the Attorney General's Committee on Administrative Procedure, which initiated a discussion of "The Development of Administrative Rule Making" with the following sentence: "The promulgation of general regulations by the executive, acting under statutory authority, has been a normal feature of Federal administration ever since the Government was established." *Final Report of the Attorney General's Committee on Administrative Procedure* (Washington, 1941), 97. Subsequent discussion in the report does not indicate any different conception of the meaning of rule making. Fuchs' statement also accords with much judicial authority. Note, for example, the following from Mr. Justice Cardozo's dissenting opinion in Panama Refining Co. *v.* Ryan, 293 U. S. 338, 448: "Investigation resulting in an order directed against a particular person . . . is not to be confused with investigation preliminary and incidental to the formulation of a rule."

change Commission directing the simplification of a holding company system. The action is particular only in a very restricted sense; it covers a particular case, but the case itself might be very inclusive. Second, the line between a particular situation and a category of situations cannot always be drawn clearly. Freund gave the following example of the varying degrees of particularity of an administrative act:

Rate-making illustrates the gradations: (1) a rate for a particular person for a particular shipment; (2) a rate for a particular person for many shipments, or for a particular shipment for many persons; (3) a rate for a particular class of merchandise between two specified places; (4) a mileage rate for a particular class of merchandise; (5) a tariff of charges for a particular road; (6) a tariff of charges for many roads.[6]

All of the things listed by Freund might be done in the form (i.e., under the name) of order, in which case the substantive distinction between rule making and directory orders would be obscured by language usage. A change in the relation of freight rates between geopgrahical areas (discussed at pages 72-73) was done by order but this obviously was a use of the word "order" to cover categories of shipments. Conversely, so-called rules, like special legislation, may apply "to named persons or to specific situations."

The draftsmen of the legislation which became the Administrative Procedure Act were faced with the necessity of drawing a workable distinction between rules and orders. The bills were framed upon the assumption that there should be two types of administrative procedure, one adapted to rule making and the other to adjudication, which was to be defined in the Act as "agency process for the formulation of an order." The early drafts began with the traditional definitions of rule making and rules, and called anything which was not a rule an order. The original bill read:[7] " 'Rule' means the whole or any part of any agency state-

[6] Ernst Freund, *Administrative Powers over Persons and Property*, 15. Copyright 1928 by the University of Chicago.
[7] *Administrative Procedure Act, Legislative History*, 79th Cong., 2nd sess., Senate Doc. No. 248, 156, quoting from H. R. 1203 which was the same as the original McCarran Bill.

ment of general applicability designed to implement, interpret, or prescribe law or policy or to describe the organization, procedure, or practice requirements of any agency. 'Rule making' means agency process for the formulation, amendment, or repeal of a rule."

In later drafts there was departure from the simple test of "general applicability." There was doubt as to whether these words would encompass certain types of administrative decisions which agencies thought should be exempted from the strict procedures prescribed in the drafts for "orders." Hence, words were added to remove doubt as to classification of several types of decisions. In the Committee on the Judiciary of the Senate the following words were added at the end of the provision quoted above: "and includes the approval or prescription for the future of rates, wages, corporate or financial structures or reorganizations thereof, prices, facilities, appliances, services, or allowances, therefor, or of valuations, costs, or accounting, or practices bearing upon any of the foregoing." [8] In this form the bill passed the Senate.[9] Subsequently, in the Committee on the Judiciary of the House of Representatives the added language was placed at the end of the first sentence in the initial draft and the definition of "rule" was expanded to include "any agency statement of general or particular applicability and future effect." [10] These changes brought the definition to the final form in the Administrative Procedure Act, reading as follows:

[8] *Legislative History,* 218. S. 7 as reported by the Senate Committee on the Judiciary on November 19, 1945—Sen. Rep. No. 572, 79th Cong., 1st sess. Attorney General Clark commented as follows on the added language: "Proceedings are classed as rule making under this act not merely because, like the legislative process, they result in regulations of general applicability but also because they involve subject matter demanding judgments based on technical knowledge and experience. As defined in subsection (c), for example, rule making includes not only the formulation of rules of general applicability but also the formulation of agency action whether of general or particular applicability, relating to the types of subject matter enumerated in subsection (c)." *Legislative History,* 225.

[9] On March 12, 1946. *Legislative History,* 339.

[10] *Legislative History,* 236, quoting from House Report No. 1980, 79th Cong., 2nd sess., May 3, 1946.

"Rule" means the whole or any part of any agency statement of general or particular applicability and future effect designed to implement, interpret, or prescribe law or policy or to describe the organization, procedure, or practice requirements of any agency and includes the approval or prescription for the future of rates, wages, corporate or financial structures or reorganizations thereof, prices, facilities, appliances, services or allowances therefor, or of valuations, costs, or accounting, or practices bearing upon any of the foregoing. "Rule making" means agency process for the formulation, amendment, or repeal of a rule.[11]

The addition of the words "of particular applicability and future effect" seems to be an abandonment of the old distinction between general and particular applicability for another test, often used to distinguish legislative and judicial action. The House Committee Report rationalized as follows: " 'Rules' formally prescribe a course of conduct for the future rather than pronounce past or existing rights and obligations." [12] The test of rule making, in this form of rationalization, is futurity rather than generality.[13] Thus rules, like statutes, might be special or general.

[11] Section 2 (c).

[12] *Legislative History*, 254, quoting from House Report No. 1980.

[13] Commenting on the final definition of rule making Congressman Walter said:

"In this bill the accepted analytical terminology has been adopted. Accordingly we speak of rule or rule making whenever agencies are exercising legislative powers. We speak of orders and adjudications when they are doing things which courts otherwise do." *Legislative History*, 355.

But vain have been the efforts to find single absolute tests for distinguishing legislation and adjudication. Justice Holmes once made the following statement: "The establishment of a rate is the making of a rule for the future, and therefore is an act legislative, not judicial, in kind. . . ." Prentis *v.* Atlantic Coast Line Co., 211 U. S. 210, 226 (1908). The simple test of future applicability of a rule of conduct has been criticized. See, for example, Chief Justice Cullen's answer to Justice Holmes in People *ex rel.* Central Park, N. and E. River R. Co. *v.* Willcox, 194 N. Y. 383, 87 N. E. 517 (1909). But Justice Holmes must not have meant to argue a simple test of future applicability. The quoted sentence must be considered in its context. It followed these sentences: "A judicial inquiry investigates, declares, and enforces liabilities as they stand on *present or past facts and under laws supposed already to exist.* That is its purpose and end. Legislation, on the other hand, looks to the future and *changes existing conditions by making a new rule,* to be applied thereafter to all or some part of those subject to its power." (Author's italics.) And note his opinion in In re Janvrin, 174 Mass. 514, 55 N. E. 381 (1899), in which it was held that the Supreme Judicial Court of Massachusetts might be given the power on petition to fix rates for the future, the ground of the decision being that the court was

Actually, however, the Act strengthened the old distinction in an important way. Most of the things done historically under the formal name of "order," but which are general in their effects, are included in the special list of things which are called rules. Thus, an "order" prescribing a change in a territorial schedule of rates is under the Act a "rule." In fact, what the framers of the Act did was to conclude that USUALLY certain categories of decision had effects which were general rather than particular and hence to list these as rule making. But since sometimes these things might be done by particular action, the basic definition of rule making was changed.

The distinction between general regulations (whether called rules or orders) and orders (or special rules) applying to particular persons is still the most important distinction to be made among administrative instruments. Procedure will inevitably tend to be different in general and particular action. The tightness of judicial review may appropriately differ as between general rule making and orders limited to particular persons or situations. More important, the choices made by Congress and administrators between general rule making and particular orders as alternative means of applying and developing policy may affect materially the success of government and the position of parties subjected to its control. For this reason, the values in general rule making (whether in the

---

called upon only "to fix the extent of actually existing rights." In other words, Holmes recognized that judicial power might extend to the determination of a future rule of conduct in a case where the decision was made on existing rights or duties of particular parties. Viewed in its entirety his view seems to be closely similar to that expressed by Professor Green in the definitions quoted herein, page 25, footnote 10.

In contrast to the prospective or non-prospective nature of the action, its particularity or generality has sometimes been considered as the basis of distinction between a legislative and a judicial act. That this test is difficult of application is likewise revealed by rate determinations.

Note also the following: "What distinguishes legislation from adjudication is that the former affects the rights of individuals in the abstract and must be applied in a further proceeding before the legal position of any particular individual will be definitely touched by it; while adjudication operates concretely upon individuals in their individual capacity." John Dickinson, *Administrative Justice and the Supremacy of Law*, 21. Copyright 1927 by the President and Fellows of Harvard College.

form of a rule or a general order) and in the various forms of case-to-case administration, including orders and rules applying to particular persons or situations, are discussed fully at the end of this chapter.

In the meantime, a few additional comments about the varieties of rule making and of directory orders, and about their use in the past will further clarify the elements in the traditional system of legal control.

It has been said that there are two chief forms of rule making: "The one may be called supplementary or detailed legislation, the other, contingent legislation." [14] In the case of the latter, the operation of statutory provisions is contingent upon an administrative decision that certain conditions exist or a certain event has occurred. Early examples of this type of delegation of power are found in the legislation of Congress from 1790 to 1824 governing commercial intercourse with foreign countries.[15] Later examples are the authorities granted the President in the Tariff Act of 1890 to impose retaliatory duties in the event he deemed the duties of a foreign country "to be reciprocally unequal and unreasonable," [16] and in the Tariff Act of 1922 to raise or lower duties as much as 50 per cent whenever he found that duties fixed in the act did not equalize costs of production between the United States and a principal competing country.[17]

"Supplementary or detailed legislation" is of two types. First, there are interpretative rules, which are administrative declarations of the meaning of statutory provisions.[18] Second, there are rules which "fill up the details of the law." The making of the latter has sometimes been called supplementary legislative power, or at other times discretionary rule making to emphasize the agency's freedom in the development of the content of the rules.

[14] John P. Comer, *Legislative Functions of National Administrative Authorities* (New York, 1927), 26.

[15] The series of acts is summarized in Field *v.* Clark, 143 U. S. 649 (1892), and by Comer, *op. cit.*, 64-72.

[16] 26 *U. S. Stat. at Large*, 567, 612. Upheld in Field *v.* Clark.

[17] 42 *U. S. Stat. at Large*, 858. Discussed above, page 59.

[18] See Comer, *op. cit.*, 29, 137-169.

Discretionary rule making may itself take two forms, namely, internal policy standards to guide officials in making further decisions,[19] and rules which prescribe standards to govern private action.

Comer has said that "It is an erroneous supposition that the great mass of administrative legislation now playing such an important part in the government of this nation sprang full-grown out of the complex conditions of modern life."[20] He shows that Congress has from the beginning granted rule-making power to officials in the executive branch of the government. Nevertheless, the conditions of modern life have led to an increasing tendency toward legislation in general terms,[21] and toward the use of rule making as one means of implementing general law. A calculation in 1936 showed that there were no fewer than 115 federal agencies that, under 964 statutory provisions and 71 executive orders and proclamations, issued rules and regulations that affected the public.[22] The preponderant portion of such delegations are grants of supplementary legislative power, contingent legislative power being somewhat exceptional. It is this grant of supplementary legislative power, exercised through policy standards or general rules, which has most significance as an instrument of economic control.[23]

It should be noted, also, that there are several types of directory orders.[24] First, there is the order of convenience or benefit. The traf-

---

[19] For examples see pages 67 and 118-119.

[20] *Op. cit.*, 50.

[21] See pages 55-61.

[22] "Report of the Special Committee on Administrative Law" in *Annual Report of the American Bar Association*, LXI, 720, 783.

[23] For further discussion of administrative rule making see, in addition to the works cited, James Hart, *Ordinance Making Powers of the President* (Baltimore, 1925); F. F. Blachly and Miriam E. Oatman, *Administrative Legislation and Adjudication* (Washington, 1934); Committee on Ministers' Powers, *Report* (London, 1932, Cmd. 4060); John Willis, *Parliamentary Powers of English Government Departments* (Cambridge, 1933); F. J. Port, *Administrative Law* (London and New York, 1929), Chapter IV.

[24] For classifications of types of orders, directory or otherwise, see White, *op. cit.*, 3rd ed., 532-534, and F. F. Blachly and Miriam E. Oatman, *Federal Regulatory Action and Control* (Washington, 1940), 68-70. White lists four types: orders of convenience, ancillary orders, corrective orders, orders of exemption. Blachly and Oatman give two classifications. In the first, orders are classified according to their legal nature as procedural, legislative, legislative in form but procedural in effect, judicial. The second may be given in the words

fic officer, alternately giving go and stop signals, is an example.[25] Within this class are all orders issued for the purpose of clarifying rights which are protected or obligations which should be met. [26] Second, there is the corrective order. An example is the cease and desist order of various government agencies. The majority of administrative orders having economic significance will fall within this group; Freund has, in fact, called directory action "a system of corrective intervention." [27] Third, there is the redressive order. This designation is given to the type called by Blachly and Oatman "Reparation and Analogous Orders" and includes reparation orders, damage orders, and awards for payment of money.[28] An example is the reparation order of the Interstate Commerce Commission. It commands a carrier to make reparation to a shipper for an unfair charge already made.

Freund concluded that directory action had been adopted in England and the United States tardily and with apparent reluctance,[29] but shows nevertheless the trend toward its use in modern programs of control.[30] It may be added that directory action has been authorized in every comprehensive regulatory statute passed by Congress since the Interstate Commerce Act.[31] Economic legislation which is corrective in objective, that is, designed mainly to correct abuses, has relied chiefly or solely on this instrument of control. It is the instrument used by the Federal Trade Commis-

---

of the authors. "It is more generally useful to use a mixed scheme of classification, based on subject matter, legal nature and legal effect. According to this scheme, orders may be classified as follows: legislative regulatory; procedural; administrative controlling; injunctive and command; reparation and analogous orders; penalty orders; orders in respect to licenses, registrations, etc.; orders *in re* declarations and designations; and negative orders." A fuller elaboration is contained in very complete outlines and accompanying discussion at pages 276 to 304.

[25] Compare White, *op. cit.*, 3rd ed., 532.
[26] Compare Freund, *op. cit.*, 146-147.
[27] Ernst Freund, *Administrative Powers over Persons and Property*, 581. Copyright 1928 by the University of Chicago.
[28] *Federal Regulatory Action and Control*, 293-294.
[29] *Op. cit.*, 173.
[30] *Ibid.*, 141-146.
[31] "But above all it was the Interstate Commerce Act which brought this phase of administrative power into prominence." *Ibid.*, 145.

sion against unfair methods of competition, by the National Labor Relations Board against unfair labor practices, and by a number of other agencies enforcing a standard of conduct. Freund, writing before the new phase of quasi-partnership of the public in regulated industries had become so apparent, concluded that the order had become "the chief instrumentality of federal economic legislation." [32] In the more developed phases of public control heretofore referred to as industry management,[33] directory action has been retained but only as a part of a more complex battery of administrative instruments.

ENABLING ACTION

By enabling action (commonly called licensing) is meant the grant of consent in particular cases. Governmental authorization is granted for a particular thing otherwise forbidden.[34] It has been described by Freund as "a system of advance checks," [35] for public power is exerted prior to private action and constitutes an authorization or denial of such action.

The extent of enabling action may be obscured by the various names employed to describe its particular uses. The word "license" is most frequently used. "Licenses" are required to engage in many learned professions, occupations(e.g., merchant marine officer), and service trades; to sell insurance, as insurer, agent, or broker; to operate radio stations; and for many other purposes. The term "certificate of convenience and necessity" is employed in other fields, notably the household utilities and transportation. The word "certificate" is used for merchant seamen, airmen, and aircraft. The word "permit" is sometimes used, as the "permit" to drill an oil well or the "permit" of a foreign corporation to do business within a state. The corporate charter is a device for giving consent for

---

[32] *Ibid.*, 145-146.

[33] See Chapter II.

[34] "In simplest terms, a license is an official permit to carry on a particular business or profession, or to do a particular thing otherwise forbidden." White, *op. cit.*, 3rd ed., 518.

[35] Ernst Freund, *Administrative Powers over Persons and Property*, 581. Copyright 1928 by the University of Chicago Press.

the use of a particular form of business enterprise. The franchise grants consent to a utility to use city streets. Registration, certification, consent, approval, are other words which may be used in statutes to describe the act of giving consent.

The Administrative Procedure Act recognized the many forms of enabling action but used the word "license" to include all of these. In defining terms it says: "'License' includes the whole or part of any agency permit, certificate, approval, registration, charter, membership, statutory exemption or other form of permission." [36]

The use of this instrument normally extends further than an original grant or denial of authorization. It may extend, also, to the following: (1) imposition of conditions as a part of authorization; (2) modification of the terms or conditions at the discretion of the granting authority; (3) renewal or denial of the authorization at periodic intervals; (4) revocation of the authorization.[37]

With these additions, enabling action becomes more than a power of initial check; it becomes also a means of continuing control. The continuing control may be exercised in two ways. Private parties may be required to make further petitions for public consent, as in the renewal of radio broadcast licenses and the approval of utility rate changes. Or it may be exercised through public intervention for correction or withdrawal of previous consent.[38]

The manifestations of the enabling (licensing) function were summarized in the following definition in the Administrative Procedure Act: "'Licensing' includes agency process respecting the grant, renewal, denial, revocation, suspension, annulment, withdrawal, limitation, amendment, modification, or conditioning of a license." [39]

The formal exercise of the licensing function will normally be done through the form, or name, of an order. Thus orders will be

---

[36] Sec. 2(e). We have classified the exemption separately. See pages 111-112.
[37] See Freund's discussion of enabling powers, *op. cit.*, Chapter VII.
[38] Perhaps strictly speaking this would be directory action rather than enabling action, but to call it such would add complexity to any discussion of the forms of action and it is just as reasonable to say that in this instance the two instruments of control overlap.
[39] Section 2(e).

issued denying or granting, amending, or revoking licenses. Licensing is also, like the directory order, a means of applying policy in particular instances. It is not surprising, therefore, that the Administrative Procedure Act (which provided one general pattern of procedure for many particular acts) defined "order" as "including licensing," and "adjudication" as likewise including "licensing."

The use of terms should not obscure the fact that licensing provides another instrument of public action. In addition to rule making and roving intervention through directory orders, the public has the option of preventing action by private parties except with prior and continuing consent.

The option has been chosen in much of our economic legislation. It has been a familiar element in regulation by the states under what the courts have been accustomed to call the "police power." It was the instrument of control adopted in the first national system of control over an industry, namely, banking in 1863. It was not used in national railroad regulation at first, but large use of licensing was contemplated under the Transportation Act of 1920. It has been extensively used in utility regulation and in late patterns of regulation, as in radio, air transport, and security regulation. The Atomic Energy Act contemplates the use of the instrument in the development of industrial use of atomic energy. These examples indicate the important place of licensing in the system of economic controls.[40]

The option on use of licensing is sometimes a choice between this instrument and no control, for it may be the only feasible approach. The option may also be a choice between the ends which can be obtained, or the dangers which can be avoided, in alternative instruments. Licensing may be chosen because it pro-

---

[40] White has summarized the growth of the licensing function. *Op. cit.*, 3rd ed., 521-525. See also Charles V. Koons, "Growth of Federal Licensing," *Georgetown Law Journal*, XXIV, 293 (1935-36). National banking supervision, accomplished largely through enabling and inspection (examining) powers, has been too much overlooked in the literature of public administration. A good study on the subject is Guy Fox, *Control of Banking by the Comptroller of the Currency* (Ph.D. dissertation, The University of Texas, 1948). If patents and copyrights are a form of enabling action, then the use of licensing in our national legislation goes back to the eighteenth century.

vides the means of establishing a very tight system of control. This can be achieved through conditions attached to an original author-ization, requirements for periodical renewal, or imposition of li-censing control over particular decisions of private management. On the other hand, licensing may be avoided because it may virtually terminate public control in that rights may be created or rigidities developed in the economy which will impair the ability of the government to protect the public interest in the various con-tingencies of the future.

Decisions on use of the instrument of licensing will be affected by the views of economic groups as to its proper use. They fre-quently desire the limitation of entry into a profession, occupation, or business, the grant of a privilege, or the advance approval of a desired business policy. For these purposes they are willing—per-haps anxious—to accept a licensing power. On the other hand, they will object to certain forms of continuous supervision of their activities through licensing requirements. They will dislike petitions for renewal of licenses, preferring the certainty of permanent or long-run authorizations. As to requirements for submission of day-to-day policy decisions for public approval, they may object to the burden and delay involved in this and may regard such re-quirements as a particularly obnoxious interference with the liberty of enterprise. Licensing may be welcomed if it creates rights or special advantages but resisted if it seems to make trade a privi-lege. If there is necessity for continuous control private parties will usually prefer a standard of personal responsibility enforced through retroactive action against those who violate the standard rather than a system of advance public check. The struggle against censorship of the press illustrates the deep-seated antagonism to continuous exercise of licensing functions.

Decisions on use of licensing may also be affected by adminis-trative considerations. Freund saw administrative advantages in li-censing in that the individual had to assume the burden of moving and that any incidental delays would operate against him; also, the techniques of public action were simpler in licensing than in di-rectory orders. On the other hand, he saw that the administrative burden in licensing could be so great as to prevent its use; he thought this difficulty accounted for Congress' requiring, in 1910, merely notification, not preliminary approval, of railroad rates.[41]

In spite of the variety of considerations which may affect decision on use of licensing, it is possible to summarize types of situations in which the instrument does or does not have utility. It appears that enabling action may be used advantageously in the following situations:

First, where the degree and normal expectancy of danger from departure from a minimum standard of conduct is sufficient to require advance check. It is this factor of danger that accounts for the frequent use of this instrument under health and safety legislation, and in banking and other legislation designed to insure financial solvency. Even with a continuing exercise of the implementory power of inspection, the same results could be obtained by the order only if summary power of enforcement existed.[42]

Second, where a license is necessary to indicate a standard of competence. The license is recognized to be the appropriate approach in regulating professions and service activities in which the chief interest of the public is in personal competence.

Third, where knowledge of those subject to regulation and a minimum amount of knowledge as to their activities is essential. In this case enabling action may be a preliminary but not the substance of public control. Such is the effect of the provisions for registration of holding companies under the Public Utility Holding Company Act and of the requirements for registration of dealers and dispensers of narcotics. Such, also, seems to have been the purpose of some proposals for federal incorporation or licensing of corporations engaged in interstate commerce.

[41] *Op. cit.*, 59-64.

[42] A careful balance between a licensing power and a summary power of enforcement is maintained in Sec. 404 (a) of the Federal Food, Drug, and Cosmetic Act of 1938, 52 *U. S. Stat. at Large*, 1040, 1048. For the protection of health, power is granted to the Secretary of Agriculture to issue emergency permits governing the manufacture, processing, and packing of any class of food. Summary suspension of permits subject to reinstatement after hearing is authorized. A private right of hearing is preserved but the public is protected during the pendency of the hearing.

Fourth, where restriction on number of units, on capital invest-ment or new undertakings, or on use of public privileges or prop-erty is a point of policy. The franchise and the certificate of public convenience and necessity, two forms of enabling action, have been fundamental elements in utility regulation because of, first, the obvious disadvantages of competition and overexpansion, and second, the necessity of restricting the grants of use of city streets and of the power of eminent domain. Licensing of developments on federal property and navigable streams were the first forms of federal control of power utilities. Prevention of physical or eco-nomic waste in oil production may require restriction of the num-ber of wells.

Fifth, where action on private initiative will have a continuing and perhaps irrevocable effect upon the organization and conduct of industry. This factor probably accounts for the requirement of the consent of the Interstate Commerce Commission for the acquisi-tion of control of one railroad by another, and for similar restric-tions on acquisition of control in many other regulated industries.

In certain other types of situations the directory order appears to be a more appropriate form of control. These situations are:

First, where the activities subject to control are numerous and varied. It would not be practicable to solve the problem of unfair methods of competition by prior approval of all selling practices and advertising copy or to control motor carrier rates by advance consent. If the action in such cases must be particular rather than general (through legislation or general rule making), then it must be under a roving power of occasional intervention rather than a blanket power of advance check.

Second, where the exercise of public power cannot conveniently be made to depend upon a conditional benefit. Enabling action can be used only where public purposes can be attained by the pe-tition of private parties who will derive benefit from the removal of a restriction; but it may be advantageous to depend upon the initiative of rival parties in interest, or of a public agency repre-senting weaker parties or general interests.

Third, where the requirements of public policy cannot be expressed in advance action. Just as the limits of prevision circumscribe rule making,[43] so likewise they partially determine the appropriateness of enabling action. It may be undesirable to give a conditioned consent if the conditions may need frequent or radical revisions; and where foresight is lacking, unconditional authorization may result in the sacrifice of interests that should be protected or in the premature crystallization of a situation. Even conditional approval tends to solidify business organization, practices, or channels of trade. It is for these reasons that many have looked with suspicion on prior consent, or even advisory action, as an alternative to the traditional pattern of action in anti-trust cases.

Finally, the scope of licensing may be limited by use of rule making. Rules of general applicability may take the place of conditions attached to licenses or of advance approvals of particular acts of private management. To the extent that this is possible, the arguments in the final section of this chapter on the superiority of rule making will apply.

THE VETO AND THE EXEMPTION

Two approaches in control are related closely to the instruments heretofore discussed but have distinctive functions in the system of control. These are the veto and exemption.

Freund defined the "veto system" as a "system intermediate between license requirement and occasional intervention." He described the system as follows:

The method is to require the individual to give notice of his proposed action to the administrative authority, which is then given an appropriate time to forbid the action; but after the lapse of the designated time without administrative prohibition, the individual is free to proceed. The system may or may not include subsequent corrective action by new orders.[44]

The veto system is illustrated in the Securities Act of 1933. The act made it unlawful to sell securities in interstate commerce or

[43] See page 120.
[44] Page 62 of Ernst Freund, *Administrative Powers over Persons and Property.* Copyright 1928 by the University of Chicago Press.

by use of the mails unless a registration statement was filed. If the regulatory organ found that the statement was "on its face incomplete or inaccurate in any material respect," it could refuse to permit the statement to become effective, and if it appeared "at any time" that the statement included "any untrue statement of a material fact" or omitted "to state any material fact," a stop order suspending the effectiveness of the statement could be issued.[45]

The veto system is a customary feature in administrative regulation of utility rates. The pattern set in our railroad legislation, under which rates must be filed but may be disapproved, has been widely copied. The system has also been recommended for supervision of industrial combinations and agreements. President Theodore Roosevelt, desiring some form of advance action in such cases, once made the following recommendation to Congress:[46]

Probably the best method of providing for this would be to enact that any contract subject to the prohibition contained in the Anti-Trust Law, in which it was desired to enter, might be filed with the Bureau of Corporation or other appropriate executive body. This would provide publicity. Within, say, sixty days of the filing—which period could be extended by order of the Department whenever for any reason it did not give the Department sufficient time for a thorough examination—the executive department having power might forbid the contract, which would then become subject to the provisions of the Anti-Trust Law, if at all in restraint of trade. If no such prohibition was issued, the contract would then only be liable to attack on the ground it constituted an unreasonable restraint of trade.

Proposals for administrative veto over industrial contracts have been made by others, a notable example being that of a committee of the United States Chamber of Commerce in 1931. It was proposed that

business concerns desiring to enter contracts for the purpose of equalizing production to consumption and so carrying on business on a sound basis, may file such contracts with some governmental authority, the contracts to take effect and to remain effective unless the governmental authority

[45] Sections 8 (b) and 8 (d), 48 *U. S. Stat. at Large,* 74, at p. 79.
[46] *Congressional Record,* XLII (March 25, 1908), 3853.

having supervision finds on its own initiative or on complaint that such agreements are not in the public interest, in which event such agreements would be abrogated.[47]

The intermediary veto system may have certain advantages where the actions under control are numerous. A filing requirement gives the administration notice of contemplated action, and may also give it a basic body of factual data. An administrative bottleneck may, however, be avoided by substitution of roving intervention for definite decision on each private action. On the other hand, where each action must be carefully analyzed, as under the Securities Act or under the proposals in regard to industrial agreements, the administrative burden is similar to that in licensing—and, in fact, the substantive action itself is closely similar.

Exemption, in form, is not a method of control but a relaxation of control; nevertheless, grant or refusal of exemptions can be made a positive means of control. Administrative use of the instrument may be by rule or order. The first method is illustrated by a number of provisions in the Federal Food, Drug, and Cosmetic Act granting power to make exemptions by "regulation." [48] A notable example of the second is found in the practice of the Railroad Commission of Texas. Rule 37 of the Commission provides a rule for spacing of oil wells, but a very considerable administrative burden exists in the handling of numerous petitions for exceptions. In some cases, as in some of the provisions of the Public Utility Holding Company Act of 1935, the administrative agency is given the choice of exemption by rule or order.[49]

Exemption by order upon the petition of parties bears a close resemblance to enabling action. And yet it is different, for licensing sets a standard, exemption allows departure from a standard.[50] Moreover, it has its own peculiar function in the system of

[47] See Charles A. Beard, *America Faces the Future* (Boston and New York, 1932), Chapter V, for a copy of the report of the Committee. Quoted words are at page 204.
[48] Sections 403 (e), 403 (k), 405, 502 (e), 502 (l), 503, 505 (i), 602 (b), 603. 52 *U. S. Stat. at Large*, 1040 ff.
[49] Sections 3 (b), 9 (c)(3), 13 (a), 13 (b). 49 *U. S. Stat. at Large*, 803 ff.
[50] Freund, *op. cit.*, 129.

control for it facilitates government by general rule by providing a means of relaxing rules to meet particular conditions.

THE CHOICE BETWEEN GENERAL RULE MAKING AND CASE-TO-CASE ADMINISTRATION

The most significant problem with respect to the traditional instruments of control is that of choice between general rule making and case-to-case administration. Though the problem is of particular significance with respect to choice between general rule making and directory action, it has significance in relation to all the instruments of case-to-case administration, namely, licensing, special rule making, directory action, the veto, and the exemption.

The nature of the problem may be partially revealed by reference to the functions of case-to-case administration. First, case-to-case administration may be executory in nature, its purpose being the application of a fairly definite statute to a particular fact situation. As such, it is similar to judicial application of definite statutory provisions. Second, case-to-case administration may be used to apply an indefinite or general statutory guide without the purpose of evolving a policy being a primary consideration. In each case an attempt would be made to make a decision which was proper with reference to the particular facts presented. Third, case-to-case administration might be used under a general statutory provision as a means of developing a policy or administrative program. In this instance, decisions in particular cases might be regarded as having precedent value. Agencies might even choose cases for consideration which offered opportunities for the establishment of precedents. The positive efforts of administration would thus be combined with judicial methods of creating law.

With respect to the first of these types no question of use of general rule making arises. But as to the last two types the question is presented as to whether general rule making would not be a more satisfactory approach. Where case-to-case administration and general rule making may both be used as means of applying and/or elaborating general law a number of advantages may be claimed for the general rule making power.

Some of these were ably summarized by James Hart in a special report to the President's Committee on Administrative Management. Hart argued that there was danger of arbitrary and discriminatory exercise of authority in case-to-case administration. "The rule-making power thus has inherent checks that do not operate in the exercise of power in individual cases. It is there that arbitrariness creeps in, personal spite finds expression, and favoritism and discrimination are readily possible." [51] For this reason, Hart concludes: "On the whole, then, discretion as to uniform rules is less dangerous than discretion as to individual cases and discretion as to individual cases is less dangerous if guided by preexisting rules than if untrammeled." [52]

Hart argued also that administrative rule making was a useful means of "increasing the certainty of law." He saw a double disadvantage in uncertainty as to the precise legal obligations of parties, and this whether general law was administered by administrative or judicial decision. There was a disadvantage in the effects on business initiative and trade. When the business man is unable "to discount the future," there is "a depressing or deflationary effect on trade." [53] The complementary result is the ineffectiveness of regulatory effort. "Indeed, there is some reason to believe that such statutes tend to simmer down, especially when conservatives are at the helm, to rather ineffective forms of control, for the simple reason that it seems impracticable to hold business to standards which it can learn only retroactively, after there has been litigation." [54] Hart concluded that administrative rule making would supply "a satisfactory middle term between legislation and final adjudication," particularly if parties were given immunity from liability for any act done or omitted to be done in good faith in conformity with an administrative rule.[55]

[51] President's Committee on Administrative Management, *Report with Special Studies* (Washington, 1937), 324.

[52] *Ibid.*

[53] *Ibid.*, 326-327.

[54] *Ibid.*, 327.

[55] *Ibid.* Hart refers to the "new technique" in the amendment to the Securities Act in 1934 which gave immunity to parties for "any act done or omitted in good faith in conformity with any rule or regulation . . . notwithstanding

Hart connected these two arguments in favor of administrative rule making with the traditional concept of the rule of law. He believed that this concept had value and defined its meaning as follows:

That idea can no longer mean the rule of detailed statutes. It means rather, first, that Congress should guide the administrator by as careful a definition of general policy as is possible, and, second, that the gap between congressional mandate and administrative orders in particular cases be bridged, though by no means narrowed to mere red tape, by the rule-making power.[56]

A few qualifying remarks may be made concerning these arguments. First, the very real and ever-present danger of discriminatory action in case-to-case administration may be overemphasized. A certain objectivity results from the continuous handling of similar cases and from the responsibility before the public and affected groups for defensible solutions, and this objectivity may be increased by improvements in the process of administration. The opportunities for objective action appear to be greater in public administration than in legislative halls or the jury system of judicial action.[57] Moreover, the argument on uncertainty is subject to several comments. First, informal administrative procedure may exist for advising individuals concerning their rights or for actual settlement of disputes concerning rights. Second, declaratory orders may now be issued in appropriate cases by administrative agencies. The Administrative Procedure Act authorizes an agency

that such rule or regulation may, after such act or omission, be amended or rescinded or be determined by judicial or other authority to be invalid for any reason." 48 *U. S. Stat. at Large,* 908.

[56] *Ibid.,* 326. Note also the following from page 324: "By the rule of law is here meant the system whereby governmental action in the individual case is guided by uniform rules to which the administrator may be required to conform by appeal to a tribunal which is impartial in the sense of being independent of the administrator."

[57] After commenting on the tendencies in use of discretion by juries and particularly on "the play of sympathy," Freund concluded that "the new administrative power" "substitutes for the more or less arbitrary judicial action—arbitrary because delegated to a jury—a fixed and responsible rule." "The Substitution of Rule for Discretion in Public Law," *American Political Science Review,* IX, 666, 667 (1915).

"in its sound discretion . . . to issue a declaratory order to terminate a controversy or remove uncertainty."[58] Such a process is feasible only where the "critical facts can be explicitly stated, without possibility that subsequent facts will alter them."[59] Nevertheless, where it can be used, it provides a kind of complement or alternative to the "middle term" suggested by Professor Hart, for declaratory orders have "like effect" with "other orders."[60] Finally, the problem of certainty is connected with sanctions. The history of the Sherman Anti-Trust Act shows the hesitancy to impose penalties in cases of violation of statutes of uncertain meaning; but the case is different where the cease and desist technique is employed, that is, where the administrative order applies prospectively only.

As for the relation of the positive arguments in favor of rule making to the concept of the rule of law, the author believes there is need for revision of that concept in a more fundamental way than that suggested by Professor Hart. The essence of the concept is the absence of caprice. And caprice may be eliminated, not merely by a rule of rules, but by objective attitudes reenforced by regularity in the processes of administration.

The various comments only partially reduce the force of Professor Hart's very cogent arguments. Improvements in the process of administration may not be expected to remove fully the deficiencies in case-to-case administration. Moreover, they would perhaps fall short of counteracting public suspicion of unequalness in application and impact of case-to-case decisions.

Another argument which has been advanced in favor of rule-making authority is that it has an advantage over directory action with respect to judicial review.[61] Whereas the courts will hold rules

---

[58] Sec. 5 (d).

[59] From an argument for use of declaratory orders in *Final Report of the Attorney General's Committee on Administrative Procedure,* 30-33.

[60] Administrative Procedure Act, Sec. 5 (d).

[61] Some students of public administration see advantage in choice of the power which will be least subject to judicial control. See, for example, Hart, *Report with Special Studies,* 326. Blachly and Oatman have emphasized the confusion on judicial functions which results from judicial review of administrative action under general statutes. *Administrative Legislation and Adjudication,* 41, 242.

to be invalid only if ultra vires under the statute or in violation of constitutional provisions, they may pass on the substance of an administrative order applying a generic statute. The effect is to give to the judiciary rather than the administration the function of statutory elaboration, with a loss in expertness of consideration and in the positive effort that appertains to administrative action.[62]

Another argument emphasizes the deficiencies of case-to-case administration as a means of developing administrative policy. These deficiencies have been summarized ably by Professor Milton Handler in certain comments on the work of the Federal Trade Commission:

The definition of unfair competition by administrative legislation is incomparably superior to definition by administrative decision. The method of judicial exclusion and inclusion does not permit of a sustained, consistent, comprehensive and speedy attack upon the trade practice problem. The case to case determination takes years to cover even a narrow field; it leaves wide lacunae; false starts are difficult to correct and the erroneous decision is just as prolific as a sound ruling in begetting a progeny of subordinate rules. In a controversy between two litigants or between a Commission and a private party, the law making function is distracted by factors which are important to the contestants but irrelevant to the formulation of future policy. The fusion of law and economics, the detailed investigations and hearings, and the precise formulation of rules, all of which are so essential to a proper regulation of competition, are not feasible when law making is but a by-product of the adjustment of controversies.[63]

Though, as Dean Landis has pointed out, Professor Handler may place too great faith in the power of men to make advance de-

---

For the view that greater judicial control may constitute an advantage for the directory power over the enabling power, see Freund, *Administrative Powers over Persons and Property*, 174.

[62] See the chart showing the fate of orders of the Federal Trade Commission in Carroll H. Wooddy, *The Growth of the Federal Government, 1915-1932* (New York, 1934), 186. In later years the record of the Commission in the courts was much improved. See Milton Handler, "Unfair Competition and the Federal Trade Commission," *George Washington Law Review*, VIII, 399, 402-404 (1940).

[63] Milton Handler, "Unfair Competition," *Iowa Law Review*, XXI, 175, 259 (1936). Compare Blachly and Oatman, *Administrative Legislation and Adjudication*, 51.

cisions covering "the full range of our industrial problems, from aluminum to zinc," [64] he has directed attention to a major deficiency of case-to-case administration. It is a slow, piecemeal, and indirect method of evolving policy. It may lead to a "very narrow view of the public interest," [65] to what Dean Landis calls "administration myopia that fails to see the woods because of the abundance of the trees." [66] It is a method of government which encourages the administrator to take the easy road of deciding only the issues presented rather than the hard road of finding fundamental solutions for economic maladjustments.

To the convincing reasons for preference for general rule making given in the preceding discussion there may be added another, namely, administrative necessity. Rule making is an expedient for reducing the volume of administrative actions to manageable dimensions. This may be illustrated by reference to the experience of a few wartime agencies.

Two officials of the War Production Board summarized trends in its methodology as follows:

The history of the regulatory activities of the Office of Production Management–War Production Board may be described as a progression from the particular to the general. The original priorities statute was administered solely by the assignment of priority to individual transactions through the issuance of preference rating certificates. . . . Applications for preference ratings frequently exceeded 10,000 per day. It soon became apparent that the on-rushing torrent of paper would engulf the agencies administering the system and industry as well, unless simplified means of regulating production and distribution could be achieved.[67]

The various succeeding types of issuances, though usually referred to as "orders," came more and more to have the character of general rules and had the effect of reducing the number of particular decisions.

[64] James M. Landis, *The Administrative Process*, 87. Copyright 1938 by Yale University Press.
[65] Wilson K. Doyle, *Independent Commissions in the Federal Government* (Chapel Hill, 1939), 75.
[66] *Op. cit.*, 68.
[67] John Lord O'Brian and Manly Fleischmann, "The War Production Board Administrative Policies and Procedures," *The George Washington Law Review*, XIII, 1-60, at pages 28-29 (December, 1944).

In O.P.A., where the basic method of control was from the beginning general rule making (price schedules; price, rationing, and rent regulations), the issue between particular action and general action arose frequently with respect to adjustment policy. In price regulation adjustment of prices for particular concerns might be allowed in order to make a regulation which was "generally fair and equitable" more "fair" as to particular parties, or adjustments might be allowed to maintain concerns which were essential for the war effort or domestic welfare. Moreover, a generally tight pricing policy might sometimes be maintained only if there was an adjustment provision for the marginal concerns. Nevertheless, the administrative burden in adjusting particular prices for particular concerns was so great that the agency tried to escape from it, first, by moving toward the essentiality test, under which adjustments were to be given only to keep essential concerns in operation, and second, by seeking for substantive rules on pricing which avoided the charge of individual inequity.[68]

Another example in O.P.A. experience will illustrate the administrative necessity of general rule making. Administrative approval of prices on new products, products built to special specifications, and in other cases where special pricing seemed essential, would have constituted an impossible burden. The answer was to devise pricing rules under which business management could determine its prices. Sometimes a series of pricing rules designed to cover most of the situations which would arise would be incorporated in the regulation. Though administrative approval remained in some cases, the administrative task was reduced to manageable or near manageable dimensions.[69]

There is one aspect of rule making which requires special mention. Hart said that "On the whole . . . discretion as to individual cases is less dangerous if guided by preexisting rules."[70] The rule-

[68] On price adjustments in O.P.A. see James B. Eckert, ed., *Problems in Price Control: Pricing Standards* (Washington, 1947), Chapters IX, X, and XI.

[69] Many with experience in the agency would argue that the burden of pricing new products under Maximum Price Regulation 188 was one which O.P.A. was never able to handle satisfactorily.

[70] *Report with Special Studies*, 324. Compare Ernst Freund, "The Substitution of Rule for Discretion," *American Political Science Review*, IX, 666 (1915).

making power can be used as an instrument of internal administration, that is, internal regulations may provide instructions to the staff which will insure uniform administration in case-to-case action. Publication of these guides for administrative decisions acquaints interested parties with the "common law of the agency," and may serve either to ward off pressures for special concessions or to canalize these into an attack on general policy, which generally is preferable to a multiplication of particular pressures. Where case-to-case decisions are made by a scattered staff, as in field administration, general rule making as a guide for particular decision is imperative.[71] Even where licenses, exemptions, and directory orders are issued in the national office, the advantages of internal regulations in insuring uniform application and preventing public suspicion of discriminatory action are so great that it may be said that an administrator should usually try to maximize the reduction of discretion in case-to-case administration by advance rules.[72]

It may be concluded that the various arguments on the superiority of general rule making are so convincing as to indicate the need for continuing consideration of the possibilities for making greater use of this instrument. The challenge of the future is to economize administrative effort, to search for general solutions, and to minimize the suspicion of favoritism. These ends may perhaps be best attained if administrators and their staffs are trained to look above particulars for the inclusive rule.

It would appear to be undesirable to prescribe a blanket requirement that all general statutory provisions must be supplemented by general regulations;[73] but it likewise may be wise to require in some cases, and to authorize in most cases, the use of the instrument. To a considerable extent, however, the responsibility for maximizing

[71] See the author's discussion on "The Problem of Discretion versus Rule" in *Field Administration of Wartime Rationing* (Washington, 1947), 104-108.

[72] General standards may also be laid down to guide in the framing of future rules. For an example see the discussion of standards in O.P.A. at pages 65-68.

[73] Proposal of a mandatory requirement that agencies implement their statutes with rules and regulations was made in "Report of the Special Committee on Administrative Law," *A B A Advance Program,* 169, 186-193, and 224 (1937). Such a provision was incorporated in the Logan-Walter Bill, vetoed by the President on December 18, 1940.

the use of the instrument will rest with administrative authorities themselves.

Nevertheless, it must be recognized that case-to-case administration is one indispensable means of administering general law. For first, the administrator may not be able to foresee in advance the multiple and varied circumstances arising under a statute. To extend specification beyond the limits of prevision may result in artificiality of requirement, in multiplication of loopholes for escape from control, in misdirection of restraints.[74] And second, adjustment to particulars may be essential for justice to individuals and for administrative efficiency. Hart says, "new or even unique situations" may arise and there must be room "for flexibility and individualization." [75] And finally, there may be some areas of public action in which the best attainable is a pragmatic decision based upon all the relevant factors in the particular case.

CONCLUSION

This leads to the final conclusion of this chapter. The attainment of the objectives of public control requires the use and combination of a number of instruments of control. These supplement each other in the battery of administrative instruments. Licensing must be supplemented by policing and prosecution, perhaps also by rule making and exemption. Rule making and directory orders may be complementary means of achieving purpose. Choice between the instruments is important, nevertheless, and particularly choice in favor of maximum use of rule making. Beyond this it may be said that even this kit of instruments has been inadequate, and that others have been selected; these constitute the subject of the next chapter.

[74] Landis says that after the Securities and Exchange Commission had attempted to define "public offerings," it found that advantage was being taken of the definitions. It then abandoned the attempt. *The Administrative Process*, 83.

[75] *Report with Special Studies*, 324.

Chapter VI

Administrative Tools and
Techniques: Other Instruments

Policing and prosecution, licensing, direction by order, rule making, the veto, and the exemption, have been the main elements in the traditional system of regulatory administration. Three features of this system are apparent. It is a system of overhead controls, in which the authority of the state appears to be exercised vertically rather than laterally. It is, as it has now developed, a system of authoritative controls, in which command rather than suasion appears to be the attribute of action. It is, finally, a system which has been more or less assimilated in legal doctrine concerning sovereignty, government of law rather than men, and in the literature of administrative law. If these features appear in our discussions to be sometimes more fictitious than real, they are, nevertheless, clearly established as formal attributes of the traditional system.

There are two other types of instruments used in control of economic activities which may be contrasted with the traditional ones. The first is a group of instruments characterized by reliance on consent and collaboration of parties. The second includes those arising out of financial, commercial, and proprietary operations of government.

121

INSTRUMENTS REQUIRING CONSENT
AND COLLABORATION OF PARTIES

Consent or active collaboration of parties may be an important factor in exercise of the instruments discussed in the preceding chapter. In licensing, consent of parties is implicit in the petiton for government action. Moreover, parties subject to regulation may be given a role of active collaboration in making and enforcing public policy through the instruments discussed. For example, codification of industries under N.R.A. was an exercise of rule-making power with the active participation of industrial groups. Industry advisory committees have been extensively used in rule making and other traditional forms of control.[1] Consent or participation of parties may, therefore, be a technique employed in the use of instruments which have normally been exercised by government alone. On the other hand, there are also instruments in which participation of parties in the final action taken is a necessary element.

The Agreement

One such instrument is the contract or agreement, a form of action which is illustrated in the agricultural marketing agreements. The Agricultural Adjustment Act of 1933 authorized the Secretary of Agriculture to enter into marketing agreements with handlers and producers of agricultural commodities, an authorization which was extended in subsequent acts and is now given by the Agricultural Marketing Agreement Act of 1937.[2] The agreement is in the nature of a contract between the Secretary and those who sign. Agreements have most frequently been used to govern the marketing of milk and fruits and vegetables. They are usually administered by committees of growers or handlers, or both, selected by the Secretary, ordinarily after nominations have been received from the industry.

That voluntary agreement may be an inadequate means of carry-

[1] For discussion of advisory committees see pages 258-264.
[2] 50 *U. S. Stat. at Large*, 246.

ing a program into effect has been recognized in the statutes authorizing these agreements. Prior to 1935 the Secretary possessed a reserve power of licensing the marketing of agricultural products; since 1935 he (or the President) has had the authority to govern marketing by order. Under the act of 1937, an order may supplement an agreement if specified percentages of handlers and producers approve, or an order may be issued without an agreement if a specified proportion of the producers approve. In April, 1950 there was no agreement which was not accompanied by an order, and milk marketing areas were in every case governed by order only.[3]

Consent Prior to Completion of Legal Action

Another instrument is control through consent without resort to or prior to completion of legal action. Many agencies have devised means for settlement of issues by consultation followed by adjustment or agreement to desist.

One notable example of consent prior to completion of legal action is the stipulation of the Federal Trade Commission. The stipulation is an agreement to discontinue alleged illegal practices. Such an agreement may be made prior to the service of complaint by the Commission. It "always consists of three elements: an admission of certain facts; an agreement to cease and desist from designated unfair methods of competition or unfair or deceptive acts or practices; and a consent that the admissions of fact may be used against respondent if subsequently the Commission has reason to believe that the stipulation is being violated and accordingly issues its complaint against him." [4] Whereas during the fiscal year ended June 30, 1948, 70 complaints were issued by the Commission, 99 cases were settled by stipulation.[5]

[3] See Production and Marketing Administration, *Price Programs of the United States Department of Agriculture* (April, 1950).

[4] Attorney General's Committee on Administrative Procedure, *The Federal Trade Commission* (Sen. Doc., 76th Cong., 3d. Sess., 1940), 25. For a statement of the Commission's policy on stipulations see *Federal Register*, August 29, 1947, printed also in *Annual Report* (Fiscal year, 1948), 113-116.

[5] *Annual Report of the Federal Trade Commission for the Fiscal Year Ended June 30, 1948,* 6.

Another example is the consent decree in antitrust cases. The consent decree is really an injunction entered by consent rather than as a result of contested proceedings. It differs from the stipulation in that violation of the decree is a basis for the imposition of sanctions. The initiative in arranging for a consent decree must come from the parties against whom charges have been made. If the Department of Justice considers the proposed agreement to be satisfactory, it will recommend a *nolle prosse* to the court. Thus, although the final decision is made by the court, administrative approval is the major element in the solution.

The consent decree, like the injunction in contested cases, may be a means of obtaining more substantial change in the organization and practice of an industry than could be achieved through the criminal case alone. It may contain provisions which in isolation appear to extend beyond the requirements of the antitrust laws but which, when considered in connection with all the acts of the defendants, are regarded by the Department of Justice as being essential for achieving the purpose of the laws. The Department may begin with a proceeding in equity, or with concurrent criminal and civil proceedings, and gain a consent decree which is more comprehensive in its content than the specific charge of violation. The consent decree is, therefore, a constructive, not merely a negative, instrument. It has been said that there are dangers in use of the instrument, in that it could, along with the threat of prosecution, be employed as a kind of bludgeon to obtain more than the law required, or conversely, that public benefits could be sacrificed by a lenient departmental policy; also, the Department of Justice could be led into work which is "regulatory in nature." [6] Against these dangers, there is some protection in the position of the court. As to the potential regulatory character of the instrument, many have believed that the purposes of the antitrust laws are often best achieved when the injunction, either in consent or disputed cases, is used as a regulatory instrument, that is, as a means of setting forth the conditions of organiza-

[6] Blachly and Oatman, *Federal Regulatory Action and Control* (Washington, 1940), 81.

tion and practice within an industry which consist with the letter and the spirit of the statutes.

The Appeal for Voluntary Cooperation

Still another instrument is the appeal for voluntary cooperation. Increasingly it is being recognized that this is an approach which dovetails with the power to govern by authoritative controls, and is in fact a means of economizing the use of sanctions or of supplementing legal sanctions as a means of obtaining compliance with legal directive.[7] At times, however, the appeal for voluntary cooperation is the sole or primary means by which the government strives to attain its objective. An outstanding example was the program of the government to save grain for its European relief program in the fall of 1947. President Truman enlisted the aid of Mr. Luckman, a leading business executive, for a campaign to obtain voluntary adherence to the limitations on grain use requested by the government.

The danger is that the limitations on the effectiveness of this as an independent instrument of control may not be appreciated, particularly in view of the necessities for and the advantages of the appeal for voluntary cooperation as an auxiliary to authoritative controls. Where there are a small number of concerns, the public demand is insistent, and the program of government is not opposed to industry interests, the appeal for voluntary cooperation from industry may be reasonably effective. Where the appeal must be made to many, whether consumers or sellers, and where denial of desire is requested, the program may be expected to wither quickly unless supported or followed by authoritative instruments. Initially, the appeal may be supported, as it was in O.P.A. prior to the enactment of the Emergency Price Control Act of 1942 by what was called "jawbone controls," that is, the use of strong talk or threats, or again, as it was in N.R.A. (where appeal and authoritative controls were mixed) by stigmatizing the non-cooperative before the bar of public opinion. Ultimately, however, there comes need

[7] For discussion of sanctions see pages 164-175.

for a sanction against the few who initiate the noncompliance which threatens to destroy the general purpose.

Mediation and Fact Finding

Government has had to give increasing attention to the settlement of labor-management conflicts in key industries to avoid prolonged interruption of production and service. The tendency in recent years has been toward efforts to accomplish this objective by making the procedure of collective bargaining work effectively. The government's efforts, by and large, have been along two lines. First, it has used traditional instruments of control to protect the rights of parties and bring them to the conference table. This has been done through such agencies as the National Mediation Board and the National Labor Relations Board. Second, it has tried to aid the parties to come to an agreement through mediation and fact finding. These last are other instruments in which reliance for the attainment of public objectives rests on consent of parties.

Mediation and fact finding were combined and fully developed as instruments of public policy in the Railway Labor Act of 1926.[8] In the fall of 1946 the President supplemented the government's conciliation machinery in industrial disputes with the use of special fact-finding boards. Thereafter, the Taft-Hartley Act adopted, with variations, the system of mediation and fact finding which had been used in railway labor.[9]

These instruments are probably the final alternatives to a system of compulsory settlement through the traditional techniques of order and rule. Already compulsory settlement has appeared in state legislation relative to disputes in utilities and in exceptional national action.[10] Only the future will disclose the extent to which

[8] 44 *U. S. Stat. at Large*, 577.

[9] Title II of the Act, 61 *U. S. Stat. at Large*, 136, 152-156 (1947).

[10] The outstanding examples in national action are the Adamson Act, upheld in Wilson *v.* New, 243, U. S. 332 (1917), and the work of the National War Labor Board in World War II. Ten states had legislation in effect in 1949 for compulsory settlement of disputes in certain utilities. For a comprehensive discussion see Jerre S. Williams, "The Compulsory Settlement of Contract Negotiation Labor Disputes," *Texas Law Review*, XXVII, 587-658 (May, 1949).

mediation and fact finding will be successful instruments of public policy.

Government Counsel

At times government control is exerted through advice, either solicited or imposed. For example, persons desiring to make investments abroad have often approached the Department of State for its advice and at times the Department of State has let it be known that it desired to express its views. Again, bank examiners' counselling with bank officers on loans which should be granted is a normal feature of bank control. The examination and the counsel at the end of the examination are the true instruments of control, and the authoritative weapons possessed by the Comptroller of the Currency are in reality only sanctions to buttress the control exerted on the spot by the examiner.

Nevertheless, the value of counsel as an instrument is dependent upon the existence of authoritative power in the background or upon the possibility of government withholding some favor or benefit which is at its command. As in the case of the agreement, consent prior to completion of legal action, and voluntary cooperation, the weight of the instrument in the economy of control is dependent upon the possibilities for use of other instruments.

The Collaboration of Private Organization

In a later chapter the relation of interest groups to administration is discussed. It will be seen that interest groups participate in various ways in the regulatory process. In most cases this participation is distinctly internal. It is either procedural as when an advisory committee is used, or is organizational as when interests are represented on boards or when exercise of public powers is delegated to supervised groups. There are times, however, when private organizations are taken into the regulatory process in such a way that their participation is a distinct and primary means of conveying a program from government to people. The line of division in classification may not be clear or really important; what is important is the fact that use of private organization can be a significant alternative to direct authoritative control by rule, order, or license.

An outstanding example is the incorporation into the control program of government of commodity and security exchanges. The function of regulation is really shared or divided between the exchanges and the government. This sharing and the collaboration of the exchanges is not merely a concession of government—it is also a technique of government regulation. This is particularly emphasized in the fact that government suggestion and pressure has sometimes been used to get exchanges to adapt their own self-regulatory activities to conform to public purposes. It is reflected in a broader way in the very choice of government to use the collaboration of existing organizations rather than try to extend direct, authoritative controls to the whole area in which it was desired that public policy should prevail.[11]

The value of this approach depends, in the main, on the ability to achieve a consensus of purpose. Where conflicts between the public interests represented in the administration and industry interests represented in private organizations are likely to be continuing, the extension of the area of direct, authoritative controls is the unavoidable result in government technique.

FINANCIAL, COMMERCIAL, AND PROPRIETARY OPERATIONS OF GOVERNMENT

In recent years there has been so large an expansion in government's loans, benefits, taxing and borrowing, and general expenditures, and in the market and proprietary operations of government, as to emphasize the importance of these as instruments of economic control.

Loan and Benefit Operations

Loan and benefit operations have a significance beyond the service rendered to individual economic units; they form an important part of the larger economy of controls through which the trends in private economic action are influenced. Government credit

[11] For discussion of the relation of government to the exchanges see Avery Leiserson, *Administrative Regulation: A Study in Representation of Interests* (Chicago, 1942), Chapter 8.

in the agricultural field, for example, has had a strong regulatory effect on interest rates on agricultural loans. Government loans may be used for such broader control purposes as the fostering of small business, the conservation of business assets, the maintenance of an exiting system of ownership (individual proprietorship on farms or occupant ownership of homes), for influencing a larger flow of capital investment into selected fields, or to encourage production of scarce commodities. Likewise, benefit payments may be used for regulatory purposes, such as the restriction of production of particular commodities or the promotion of production of others, or for even broader control objectives, such as the increase in purchasing power of particular groups.

The control aspects of loan and benefit operations are particularly apparent in the conditions attached to or running with the grants.[12] In making loans to banks in the 1930's the Reconstruction Finance Corporation sometimes exercised control over features of internal management, such as the selection of officers. Loans of the Farmers Home Administration for purchase of farms are made under conditions designed to ensure good farm management. Federal Ship Mortgage Insurance (similar to insurance of F.H.A. loans) is granted only if the Maritime Commission approves the mortgage and the terms of construction, operation, etc. Under the Agricultural Adjustment Act of 1938, loans were to be made by the Commodity Credit Corporation only to cooperators in the marketing control program. It is, of course, general knowledge that benefit payments have been made to farmers on conditions which were regulatory in effect.

In a sense loan and benefit operations are like the instrument of licensing. In both there is an advantage to the recipient, and in both there may or may not be a strong control element. As for the immediate effect on private parties, the service or control aspects may predominate depending on the existence and severity of conditions running with the consent or grant.

[12] Where a benefit payment is automatic upon compliance with requirement the rule prescribing the requirements is the instrument of control; only where the acceptance of the benefit is optional is the benefit operation the channel of control.

Nevertheless, loans and benefits may reveal distinct and contrary administrative characteristics. The loan is granted only on petition and a separate consideration of each petition is required. The administrative burden is comparable to that in other particularistic controls. Moreover, the discretionary element in the exercise of the administrative authority is usually large. Even though narrowed by rules on types of borrowers, types of security, and other factors, decision may still involve discretion on business integrity and financial risk. On the other hand, benefit payments may be made to large groups in accordance with standards which practically eliminate discretion and which reduce the administrative burden to clerical operations.

The utility of loan and benefit operations as means of control will depend mainly on two factors. First, it will vary with the need for the service offered. Second, it is dependent upon the ability of the government to render the service under conditions sufficiently inviting to counterbalance objections to any accompanying restraints or inconveniences. In any form of conditional service, acceptance of service will follow measurement of conditions.

Tax and Debt Management Policies

The regulatory uses of taxation have long been recognized. The tariff is the most familiar example of the use of taxation for economic as well as for revenue purposes. Proscription of undesired economic activity through prohibitory taxes, rather than by direct legislation, is a familiar, though not a frequent, means of control. Thus, it was used effectively in national banking legislation to kill state bank note issuance, was tried as a means of obtaining national regulation of child labor, and was long used to restrict the sale of colored oleomargarine. Taxation is also used to stimulate or restrict economic activity. A current example is the use of tax amortization certificates as a means of encouraging expansion of defense plant facilities. Beyond the many particular uses of taxation, it is now widely contended that government should use the instrument as a means of economy management, raising taxes to check inflationary trends and lowering them when recession is threatened.

Debt management policies may incidentally or purposely have large regulatory effects. The potentialities of debt management policy were first recognized in this country by Alexander Hamilton. The potentialities have been revealed in many ways in recent years. Debt management may have a material effect upon the interest rate and thus be used to stimulate or restrain investment. It may or may not be used to absorb excess purchasing power, i.e., through sales of bonds to the general public rather than to the banks. It may be combined with taxation and control of volume of public expenditures, and with these and direct controls over wages and prices, in a comprehensive system of economic controls.

Taxation has in the past been almost exclusively a legislative rather than an administrative weapon. Debt management, on the other hand, has been an administrative instrument. Adventures in economy management through taxation might call for extensive shifts of discretion of administrative agents.

General Expenditures

Public expenditures for defense, social welfare, public works, and foreign rehabilitation and relief have become so large a part of the total income of society that they may at times be the largest single influence on economic operations. Their rate, timing, and direction, and their effect on government's fiscal operations are significant. Their rate and timing may coincide with other forces in a business cycle and thus accentuate inflationary or deflationary trends; or their rate and timing may have a compensatory effect, raising the level of economic activity in depressed periods. Their direction may have a selective influence on industries, as when purchases for foreign aid create domestic shortages and inflation of prices in particular industries, or when public works expenditures stimulate the building trades and their supply sources. Their volume affects the tax and borrowing policies of government, which in turn may be used for regulatory purposes.

In a sense, the expenditures of government, including benefit payments, are a service to the economy. The effects listed above may be purely incidental. Expenditures can be manipulated, however, in such a way as to be an element in economy management.[13] To the extent that this is done, public expenditures are a further instrument in the kit of economic controls.

The proper uses and the potential effectiveness of public expenditures as an instrument of economy management are problems for the economists to study. But the instrument has significant administrative aspects. The use of this and other approaches in fiscal policy may offer hope for a significant measure of control over the general trends in the economy without an excessive increase in direct, overhead, authoritative controls such as were outlined in the preceding chapter. They thus offer a hope for economy in administrative effort and in the burden of administrative control on private interests. A further administrative aspect of fiscal controls is their strictly public nature. The directions and volume of public expenditures are matters of public interest, and need not be affected by claims of legal right in the way that exercise of the traditional instruments has been. Regularization of the use of the instrument might create rights against discrimination in detailed application, but the basic decisions on policy might escape entirely from legal limits in favor of private rights. Finally, the discretion exercised through administrative channels, or through political and administrative channels combined, is likely to be large. Flexibility is an inescapable requirement for effectiveness in use of expenditures as a means of economy management, and flexibility accrues only where there is continuing discretion.

Expenditures may have a control aspect in a narrower sense. As in loan and benefit payments, particularized objectives may be sought through the attachment of conditions. An outstanding example is the Walsh-Healey Act, which requires that contractors on government projects must conform to prescribed labor standards.

Market and Proprietary Operations

In miscellaneous ways the government's purchases and sales may have a regulatory effect. Credit controls are exercised through open-market purchases and sales of government securities by the Federal

[13] See pages 17-18 for an explanation of the term "economy management."

Reserve System; and by the timing of sales, and the form and conditions of issue, of government securities by the Treasury Department. Purchase of agricultural surpluses by the government has been a part of the larger regulatory and promotional program in agriculture. Purchase of scarce commodities for stockpiling has been a means of conserving needed materials for future production. In war and defense emergencies, contracts for purchase of commodities and facilities for military use have been a means through which price and production schedules were fixed, and thus have supplemented the efforts toward allocation and stabilization by order and rule. Though avoided in World War II, government's predominant position as a purchaser could be used as a means of compelling compliance with the various regulations issued by its agencies.

One method of control which has been proposed and sometimes used is the competitive sale of commodities or service by the government. Competitive service as a means of forcing reduction in prices is thus presented as an alternative to use of the system of overhead regulation through rule, license, and order.

Competitive rendition of service has been a recurring option for determiners of policy in this country. It was the proposal of the Windom Committee of the Senate in 1874 for solution of the problem of railroad rates, then thought to be excessive.[14] Some municipalities have used the threat of competitive service as the chief weapon in the "armory of control."

Expansion of government enterprise may often have regulatory effects. Postal savings and parcel post had regulatory effects on interest rates and express charges. Government entry into direct financing of farm mortgages in the second decade of this century had a material effect upon interest rates in all agricultural financing. In recent years, multipurpose river development programs, as in the Tennessee Valley and on the Colorado River in Texas, have led to reductions in rates in areas adjacent to the river projects.

Analysis of the utility of the instrument of competitive service would fill a volume. It may be remarked here that competition has not actually been used extensively as a regulatory instrument in the

[14] Senate Report 307, 43rd Cong., 1st Sess., Part I, 242-243.

past. Normally, either private enterprise or government enterprise has supplied a particular commodity or service in a particular geographical area. The threat, as a gun behind the door, has been more significant. It may be, however, that in low-cost housing two forms of government action, subsidized private supply and government supply (also with subsidy to user) will be used; a measure of competition between public and private supply would thus be the result.

Government might exercise control through investment of money in enterprises which have previously been wholly under private management. We have noted that the R.F.C. bought preferred stock in banks and used this as a method for control of management. Some years ago Professor W. Y. Elliott suggested that the government acquire control through stock ownership in existing power holding companies.[15] He thought that this method of control was preferable to competition. He also saw that it would offer a means of reorganizing holding company structure; and this would therefore have been an alternative to the method of overhead control chosen in the Public Utility Holding Company Act. During the depression some believed that what industry needed was not more credit but equity financing; and the suggestion was made, therefore, that government establish a corporation to take stock in small industries. Such a corporation could—though this did not appear to be the purpose of the suggestion—have used its voting powers for control of management.

Government investment might be made in a supercorporation and thus become the means of a new form of overhead control; or government could become partial owner of stocks in existing corporations, giving rise to a dual system of management.[16] If control

[15] *The Need for Constitutional Reform* (New York and London, 1935), 107.

[16] After summarizing the use of mixed corporations in foreign countries and in the First and Second Banks of the United States, Fainsod and Gordon conclude: "Ordinarily, however, mixed enterprise with the government predominating is transitory; it tends to become transformed into purely public enterprise.

"Mixed corporations in which private stockholders predominate have more fruitful possibilities. The presence of government directors on the board may provide a more effective means of continuing regulation than outside agencies coming into operation after complaints of malfeasance. To be effective, however, such participation must be supplemented by special authority for the government directors, which sets the framework within which the impact of

were to be an objective, investment in voting securities might be a more acceptable approach than loans. It is more direct and it accords with traditional notions of rights of management.

CONCLUSION

On the whole, the first set of instruments discussed in this chapter reveals a tendency to economize in the use of government authority. Government seeks to attain its objectives without use of the legal imperative. It seeks to win its objectives by suggestion, suasion, and pressure. It holds its authority in reserve and in the meantime softens its impact as sovereign and yields to the desire of men to act without compulsion.

The same tendency will be revealed in the subsequent discussion on sanctions, procedure, and relationships with regulated interests. These discussions will reveal the immense value of cooperation and consent. On the other hand, the discussions in the subsequent chapters will reenforce the conclusion stated above that it is normally necessary for government to hold its reserve power in readiness in order to achieve a sufficient measure of cooperation and to overcome the resistance of opponents in interest. The next chapter will seek to show the formal elements of authority which are essential for effective public control.

The second group of instruments discussed in this chapter also reveal a tendency to use other approaches besides those which have been part of the traditional legal pattern. As government uses its money for loans, benefit payments, expenditure for various public purposes, purchases and sales, and acquisition of ownership, it becomes a business agent in economic society. Controls over private action may be incidentals in this development, or they may be a part of the purpose in the use of the money. Formally, action may be taken by rule or order; frequently, however, the form of action

---

public policy will operate. . . . As yet only in its infancy in this country, the mixed corporation may well find considerable employment in sectors of the economy where neither wholly private enterprise nor its complete displacement by government meet the needs of policy." Merle Fainsod and Lincoln Gordon, *Government and the American Economy* (Rev. ed.), 733. Copyright 1948 by W. W. Norton and Company, Inc.

will be simply an operating decision not formalized in rule or order. Irrespective, however, of these differences, the expansion of the state as business agent, or as user of money, results in relationships between government and citizen which are sometimes more comparable to those between units in the business world than to those characteristic of the traditional legal pattern.

Chapter VII

Administrative Tools and Techniques:

Facilitative Arrangements

Attainment of policy objectives through administrative action will involve more than selection and combination of instruments of control and service. Further techniques will be required to facilitate the execution of programs. Some of these are primarily procedural, such as are to be discussed in a chapter on operating methods; but others are more than procedure. The term "facilitative arrangements" best captures their breadth and import.

Four types of such arrangements may be distinguished. Discussion of these will carry us deep into the details of administrative control, but anyone familiar with past regulatory experience will realize that failure or success in regulation is materially dependent upon arrangements of the several types discussed in this chapter.

ARRANGEMENTS TO SECURE AN ADMINISTRATIVE COURSE OF ACTION

Experience has shown that when powers of decision (determinative powers) are given to administration, arrangements are usually required to insure that the benefits of an administrative course of action may be obtained. These arrangements are particularly important where directory action is involved, but some are significant also where other types of action are used.

Administrative Initiation of Action

Authority to administrators to act on their own initiative is normally needed. Without this authority, advantages inherent in the position of the administrative agency may be lost. The agency is constantly obtaining information which indicates the points at which the public policy embodied in its directives is most seriously threatened. It can, moreover, make investigations which provide information for selection of areas of activity. Only if it possesses the power to act on its own initiative can it deploy its resources where they will be most productive.

Public initiative has been generally accepted in the exercise of executory powers (policing and prosecution). It would appear to be equally desirable, with possible exceptions, where the function of deciding has been vested in administrative agencies.[1]

The Act of 1887 gave the Interstate Commerce Commission the same power to proceed on its own initiative as it had on the receipt of a complaint.[2] When, however, the Hepburn Act delegated determinative powers on rates to the Commission, complaint was made a condition of administrative action.[3] By the Mann-Elkins Act the provision was changed to allow the Commission again to act on its own initiative.[4]

Today, the power to initiate action without complaint or petition normally rests in administrative agencies which govern by rule or order. Thus, the F.T.C. may as a result of study of advertising copy in its Radio and Periodical Division or of other investigations issue a complaint and set it down for hearing. This is not always true, however. For example, the National Labor Relations Act apparently required a complaint from an outside party in unfair labor practice proceedings; as a result, the Board has sometimes been forced to

---

[1] This leaves open the question as to whether deciding and initiating should be in the same agency. See pages 209-213, 292-303.

[2] Sections 13 and 15, 24 *U. S. Stat. at Large,* 379, 383-384.

[3] 34 *U. S. Stat. at Large,* 584, 589, amending Section 15.

[4] 36 *U. S. Stat. at Large,* 539, 551, amending Sections 13 and 15.

resort to the clumsy, if not embarrassing, expedient of seeking for a party to make a complaint when administrative investigation indicated a violation of law.[5]

The significance of administrative initiative has been emphasized by state utility regulation. Some commissions do not have authority to institute proceedings except upon complaint. Moreover, there has been a strong tendency among state commissions to emphasize their judicial functions and assume the attitude of waiting judges, a tendency defended by some who have argued that the judicial impartiality of the agencies should be protected in that way. Others, including a number of special commissions of inquiry, have noted the deleterious effects: the dissipation of administrative resources in the handling of minor complaints while more serious situations went unchallenged, the failure to attack abuses comprehensively, and the loss of positive effort for protection of the public interest.[6] A competent source has said that one test of the quality of administration is the extent to which such a commission "uses its own initiative in making investigations to bring about adjustments," [7] not waiting for the action of municipal councils and quasi-public groups.

The energy sources for a public program may be diverse. The complaint of private parties is a necessary source of information and push. The petition of local governments and agencies carrying collateral responsibilities may be equally, or even more, important. But the initiative of those carrying primary responsibilities for government programs is also important, particularly where broad regulatory functions over particular industries or economic functions have been delegated to an agency. This is true, among other reasons, because of the intricacy of the problems, the need for comprehensive planning, the importance of the general investigation, and the reservoir of expert knowledge in the agencies. Under these conditions,

[5] See Attorney General's Committee on Administrative Procedure, *National Labor Relations Board* (Sen. Doc. 10, 77th Cong., 1st Sess., 1941), 7. The Labor Management Relations Act did not change the governing provision.

[6] See James W. Fesler, *The Independence of State Regulatory Agencies* (Chicago, 1942), 13-15; C. O. Ruggles, *Aspects of the Organization, Functions, and Financing of State Public Utility Commissions* (Boston, 1937).

[7] W. E. Mosher and F. G. Crawford, *Public Utility Regulation* (New York and London, 1933), 34.

reliance must inevitably be placed heavily upon an administrative course of action, arising out of administrative investigation and selection of areas of action.[8]

Initial Decision and Completion of Process

An administrative course of action depends upon the safeguard of the twin principles of exclusive original jurisdiction and exhaustion of administrative remedies.[9]

These are principles of administrative-judicial relationship. The first preserves the administrative power to make the initial decision by barring prior proceedings in any other forum. The second, under which the courts refuse to take jurisdiction until a petitioner has exhausted all remedies available in the administrative process (e.g., appeal for reconsideration or appeal to a higher administrative authority), preserves the authority of the administration to complete its process.[10] Initial decision and completion of process might be

---

[8] On the purely enforcement plane, the example of O.P.A. is significant. In the early days of the price and rationing programs the enforcement staff dissipated much of its energy in following up complaints received from individuals. Later, its energies were directed largely to locating through investigation, in rationing the large leaks of commodity, and in price the violations which had the most significant effect on the program. In other words, there was an effort to use the investigation staff in such a way as would contribute to the maximum safeguarding of the programs.

[9] Exclusive original jurisdiction is sometimes referred to as the "doctrine of prior resort" or as "preliminary resort" or as the "doctrine of exclusive administrative jurisdiction," or, still more often, as "primary jurisdiction" of the administrative agency. On the other hand, the author of the note on "Primary Jurisdiction—Effect of Administrative Remedies on the Jurisdiction of Courts," *Harvard Law Review*, LI, 1251-1267 (1938), uses the term "primary jurisdiction" to include exclusive jurisdiction and exhaustion of remedy. P. 1252.

[10] This is not, of course, the way the courts have rationalized the doctrines. It is a way of placing emphasis on the administrative need behind the doctrines, as is also the inversion of the term "exhaustion of administrative remedy" in the author's term "completion of process." There is often need for stating the substance of a principle in more than one way. In this case, "exhaustion of administrative remedies" serves well in the context of judicial action for safeguarding private rights, but a term like "completion of process" serves a complementary purpose in expressing the same principle in the context of the administrative process.

There is a third problem closely related to exhaustion of remedies and primary jurisdiction, namely, that of "ripeness for review," as Kenneth Davis describes it. See his analysis of the cases and practical considerations relating to all three doctrines in "Administrative Law Doctrines of Exhaustion of Remedies,

regarded as two aspects of a broader notion that the administration should be allowed to exercise its delegated functions before the courts intervene.

Exclusive original jurisdiction will normally be granted to an agency by statute. Expressly or by definite implication it will be clear that the courts have no jurisdiction until after the administrative decision is made. On the other hand, a judicial doctrine of exclusive original jurisdiction arose in cases under the Interstate Commerce Act in which the Supreme Court interpreted away express provisions of the Act which gave concurrent original jurisdiction to the judiciary.[11] The Court apparently thought that these provisions were inconsistent with the purpose of the statute to provide an administrative course of action, and itself crystallized the notion that exclusive original jurisdiction is an inevitable concomitant of administrative control.

The doctrine of exclusive original jurisdiction of the regulatory agency was first stated by the Supreme Court in 1907 in the famous Abilene Case,[12] in which it was held that a shipper could not resort to a court for reparations for an alleged unreasonable charge, when the charge had been filed with the Interstate Commerce Commission and no decision had been made by it on the issue of reasonableness. Subsequently, after the courts had refused in many types of cases to take jurisdiction prior to a determination by the Commission,[13] Justice Brandeis summarized succinctly the reasons in public policy

---

Ripeness for Review, and Primary Jurisdiction," *Texas Law Review*, XXVIII, 168-193, 376-408 (1949-50). Davis discusses questions of ripeness in two parts: (1) may one challenge a general regulation prior to its specific application to him? (2) may one challenge "administrative interpretations not embodied in orders or regulations, including findings, valuations, announcements, statements of policy, determinations of status, 'directive orders,' conditions attached to approvals or permits, advisory opinions, threats of enforcement, and advice or rulings provided for the benefit of other agencies"? P. 376. Discussion of these leads into topics, such as the declaratory judgment, which extend beyond the scope of the discussion in our text.

[11] Sections 9 and 22 of the Act as amended in 1906.

[12] 204 U. S. 426.

[13] I. L. Sharfman, *The Interstate Commerce Commission*, II (New York, 1931), 401-403. Sharfman's discussion of "The Doctrine of Primary Jurisdiction" at pages 393-406 presents a full analysis of the development and effects of the doctrine.

for maintaining the primary jurisdiction of the administrative agency:[14]

It is required because the enquiry is essentially one of fact and of discretion in technical matters; and uniformity can be secured only if determination is left to the Commission. Moreover, that determination is reached ordinarily upon voluminous and conflicting evidence, for the adequate appreciation of which acquaintanceship with many intricate facts of transportation is indispensable; and such acquaintanceship is commonly to be found only in a body of experts.

Initial decision by the I. C. C. has not, however, been required in all cases, the application of the rule of the Abilene Case being dependent apparently on the Court's judgment as to whether the needs stated in the above quotation really existed. Where the questions presented are regarded as issues solely of interpretation of law and do not call for the exercise of administrative discretion on facts, then the rule is not applied.[15]

Exhaustion of administrative remedy has had a more complex background than that of exclusive jurisdiction. At least three factors have been of significance in its development.[16] First, it has arisen because of the belief of courts of equity that equity jurisdiction could not exist if there were adequate remedies without appeal to equity. Second, the factor of comity toward state agencies has been of some significance, as in the leading case of Prentis v. Atlantic Coast Line Co., where the Supreme Court refused to enjoin the enforcement of railway rates prior to the final determination of the rates by the state commission and the highest state court.[17] Third, the courts have seen the values of "orderly procedure" in which they gain "the assistance of specialized tribunals for a preliminary

[14] Great Northern Ry. Co. v. Merchants Elevator Co., 259 U. S. 285, 291 (1922).

[15] Compare the case last cited with Texas and Pacific Railway Co. v. American Tie and Lumber Co., 234 U. S. 138 (1914). See also Sharfman, op. cit., II, 403-406.

[16] For a fuller discussion of these see Raoul Berger, "Exhaustion of Administrative Remedies," Yale Law Journal, XLVIII, 981-1006 (1939).

[17] 211 U. S. 210 (1908). Berger points out that, although the exhaustion doctrine is commonly identified with this case, it had already been enunciated in tax cases and an immigration case. Op. cit., 981-982. It is the leading case in the area of economic regulation.

sifting of the complicated technical problems that are a concomitant of an industrialized society." [18] Accordingly, the doctrine is applied today in cases at law as well as of equity.

Although the exhaustion doctrine is firmly fixed by a half-century of case law, there is much confusion and uncertainty concerning its application.[19] This is the result of the inevitable conflict of purposes. On the one hand, the courts see the procedural advantages of allowing the completion of the administrative consideration through all of its stages, and see also the desirability of withholding their intervention as long as the parties affected by administrative action appear to have a remedy within the administrative process; also, statutory intent for delay of judicial intervention is often obvious. On the other hand, the courts are likely to be sensitive to threats of real injury to be suffered during the pendency of administrative consideration and may feel also that it is their peculiar responsibility to pass without delay on certain types of questions, such as constitutionality, jurisdiction of the agency, and clear errors of law.[20]

Although the exhaustion doctrine arose as a rule of judicial self-limitation, statutes may now play a significant rôle in defining the scope for application of the doctrine. The growth in the size of the tasks of agencies has resulted in arrangements for delegation within administrative agencies, and for internal appeal or reconsideration, which give added importance to the exhaustion rule. It is desirable that legislative provision for such arrangements be accompanied by a positive concept on the place of completion of process in the total framework of administrative decision. Moreover, the threat of delay to new programs by premature judicial intervention suggests the wisdom of statutory clarity on the intended scope for application of the rule and of appropriate statutory support for it.

Statutes can, for example, make it clear that courts shall not review while the process of appeal within the agency is underway,

---

[18] Berger, *op. cit.*, 1006.

[19] See, in addition to Berger, *op. cit.*, E. Blythe Stason, "Timing of Judicial Redress from Erroneous Administrative Action," *Minnesota Law Review*, XXV, 560-587 (1941), particularly pages 568-576 where Stason discusses the uncertainties with respect to seven different types of cases.

[20] See Davis, *op. cit.*, for a fuller statement of the considerations leading to application or relaxation of the exhaustion rule.

or, as was provided in the Federal Power Act,[21] unless a party shall have made application for reconsideration, thus providing the agency with an opportunity to correct its errors. The Administrative Procedure Act, however, seems to place a brake on expansion of the doctrine of exhaustion. On the one hand, it provides: "Every agency action made reviewable by statute and every final agency action for which there is no other adequate remedy in any court shall be subject to judicial review." [22] Thus, all "final agency action" is subjected to review. On the other hand, the same subsection provides:

Except as otherwise expressly required by statute, agency action otherwise final shall be final for the purposes of this subsection whether or not there has been presented or determined any application for a declaratory order, for any form of reconsideration, or (unless the agency otherwise requires by rule and provides that the action meanwhile shall be inoperative) for an appeal to superior agency authority.

This seems to allow resort to the courts while there is pending an administrative ruling on a rule or general order, a request for administrative reconsideration, or an administrative appeal on a rule or order which is in the meantime effective,[23] or, more significant, it seems to allow evasion of such processes by direct resort to the courts. The reservation "Except as otherwise expressly required by statute" saves past legislative support for the exhaustion doctrine and points to the need for legislative consideration of the doctrine in future regulatory statutes.[24]

---

[21] Section 313 (a), 49 *U. S. Stat. at Large,* 803, 860. And the Natural Gas Act, Sec. 19 (b), 52 *U. S. Stat. at Large,* 821, 831.

[22] Section 10 (c).

[23] "The provision . . . apparently applies when a party asks for agency review of an examiner's initial decision." Davis, *op. cit.,* 198-199.

[24] Davis points out that the only substantial problem in applying the last sentence of Section 10 (c) is discovering when agency action is "inoperative." "If a veteran's claim for a benefit is turned down but the veteran has a right of appeal, how can the agency make its action in denying the claim 'inoperative'? If the C.A.B. suspends the license of a pilot pending a hearing on the question of revocation of the license, and the examiner files an initial decision calling for revocation, must the pilot be permitted to fly and endanger others pending appeal to the Board? If an applicant for a broadcasting license loses before the examiner, how may the F.C.C. make that action inoperative?" *Op. cit.,* 193.

The significance of positive legislative support for one or both of the principles discussed in this section may be illustrated by two cases. The first, Myers *v.* Bethlehem Shipbuilding Corporation,[25] arose out of a petition to enjoin the National Labor Relations Board from holding hearings on charges of unfair labor practice, it being alleged by the plaintiff corporation that its business did not concern interstate commerce, and hence that the Board lacked jurisdiction. The federal district court granted a preliminary injunction and its action was affirmed by the court of appeals. The decision was overturned by the Supreme Court, which ruled that the Board had exclusive original jurisdiction, and this even though the issue was one of jurisdiction reaching to the constitutional power of the United States.[26] The Court rested its decision in part upon Section 10a of the National Labor Relations Act which, in addition to empowering the Board "to prevent any person from engaging in any unfair practice affecting commerce," provided: "This power shall be exclusive, and shall not be affected by other means of adjustment or prevention that has been or may be established by agreement, code, law, or otherwise." But the Court also based its decision on "the long-settled rule of judicial administration that no one is entitled to judicial relief for a supposed or threatened injury until the prescribed administrative remedy has been exhausted." [27]

Two comments may be made about the case. First, the statement above seems to absorb the prior resort (exclusive original jurisdic-

[25] 303 U. S. 41 (1938).

[26] The Court of Appeals stated the issue: "In applying the test laid down in the Jones and Laughlin opinion to individual business organizations, some uncertainty as to which are under federal control in their relations with their employees and which under state control will at first be unavoidable. When the question is raised, as in this case, we think it devolves on the National Labor Relations Board to show that the business involved is probably within its jurisdiction." 89 F (2d) 1000, 1000-1001.

[27] More recently the Supreme Court has upheld the right of agencies to determine "coverage," i.e., whether a particular concern was included under federal legislation, and to have the benefit of compulsory process to obtain information prior to the decision on coverage. Endicott Johnson Corp. *v.* Perkins, 317 U. S. 501 (1943) and Oklahoma Press Publishing Co. *v.* Walling, 327 U. S. 186, 214 (1946). In the former case, the question of coverage arose under a contract under the Public Contracts Act. In the latter, it was a question as to whether the Fair Labor Standards Act was applicable to the publishing company, and one of the claims was that it was not for constitutional reasons.

tion) rule into the doctrine of exhaustion of remedy, or at least, to indicate the parallelism in the logic lying beneath the doctrines.[28] Second, it indicates that no type of substantive issue, not even one of constitutional jurisdiction, which depends upon analysis of technical fact relating to application of law to particular parties is immune from the application of the twin doctrines of initial decision and exhaustion of remedy.

Some reservations must, however, be listed. First, cases where questions of law can be determined from the face of a statute or administrative rule or order are obviously different from the Myers Case where decision depended upon analysis of technical facts. Thus, the Supreme Court has refused to apply the exhaustion rule where the orders of a Commission were "on their face plainly invalid."[29] Second, the Myers Case involved the determination of applicability of a statute to particular parties, but different questions are raised where parties wish to contest the validity of a statute.[30] Stason's argument that no agency is likely to hold invalid its own enabling legislation seems compelling reason for undelayed judicial decision on constitutionality of statutory provisions.[31] In Lichter v. U. S. [32] the Supreme Court passed upon the constitutionality of the Renegotiation Act on its face, without a prior administrative consideration of the issue, and at the same time that it held that petitioners had lost their right to present issues of coverage

---

[28] See also the further statement of the Court at p. 51. And note the following: "The fact that the exhaustion cases were thus cited to buttress the primary jurisdiction doctrine underscores the essential identity, for practical purposes, of both rules. . . . With the extension of the exhaustion doctrine to courts of law, and the establishment of the non-discretionary nature of the rule, the sole real point of difference disappears." Berger, op. cit., 995. But contrast Davis's statement: "The differences between the two concepts are clear, and the names 'exhaustion of administrative remedies' and 'primary jurisdiction' are well supported by usage. Mr. Justice Frankfurter's characterization of the Myers case as involving primary jurisdiction therefore seems unfortunate." Op. cit., 400-401. We suggest that Justice Frankfurter was correct in calling the issue one of primary jurisdiction and also in seeing that it fuses with the issue of exhaustion of administrative remedy.

[29] Public Utilities Commission of Ohio v. United Fuel Gas Co., 317 U. S. 456 (1943).

[30] See Pike-Fisher, Administrative Law, Section 45a.22.

[31] Op. cit., 576. And note Davis's supporting view, op. cit., 185.

[32] 334 U. S. 742 (1948).

and amounts of profits because of failure to exhaust special statutory remedies. Finally, there are questions concerning the extent to which the Myers Case will be followed, the answer to which may be dependent upon such factors as the immediate effects upon the rights of parties, the procedural aspects of cases, and most assuredly, the extent to which legislation fixes a clear rule of administrative jurisdiction.

The other case is Yakus v. U. S.[33] Here the Supreme Court upheld the legislative prescription of an exclusive method of testing the validity of wartime price regulations. The system prescribed had for its purpose the prevention of the crippling effects of court action, such as had been experienced in utility regulation.[34] It included the following features:

1. Protest to the Administrator within 60 days after issuance or change of a regulation.
2. Hearing and decision by the Administrator.
3. Appeal to the Emergency Court of Appeals, created for the purpose of acting as the exclusive court of review on price and rent regulations.
4. Prohibition of any temporary restraining order or interlocutory decree by the Emergency Court of Appeals and prescription of a thirty-day period before a permanent injunction could become effective.
5. Review by the Supreme Court by writ of certiorari.

Upholding the provision for consideration of the validity of his own regulations by the Administrator, the Court referred to the Abilene Case (on initial jurisdiction) and said:

As with the present statute, it was thought desirable to preface all judicial action by resort to expert administrative knowledge and experience, and thus minimize the confusion that would result from inconsistent decisions of district and circuit courts rendered without the aid of an administrative determination.

---

[33] 321 U. S. 414 (1944).
[34] "Congress, in enacting the Emergency Price Control Act, was familiar with the consistent history of delay in utility rate cases." Chief Justice Stone for the majority in the Yakus Case. 321 U. S. 414, 432.

Moreover, the Court held that the defendant had lost his right to contest the validity of the regulation affecting him because of his "failure to make timely assertion" of his right "before the tribunal having jurisdiction to determine it." This decision was reached even though the defendant argued that the time allowed for decision by the process prescribed would have left him no alternatives except operation at a loss, closing his business, or operation in violation of the regulation.

The case shows how definite legislative support for the twin principles of initial decision and completion of process can safeguard an administrative course of action. In Yakus v. U. S. the issue was formally one of initial decision; but it was presented on a statutory scheme which encompassed all that initial decision plus exhaustion of remedy normally accomplishes, for the protest procedure was in reality a request for reconsideration rather than an initial decision of the Administrator.

Decision on the Final and Complete Record

Where decision must be made on the basis of evidence in the record, it is necessary to establish administrative authority to build the complete record on which the final decision is to be based. There is no value in initial decision if parties may withhold evidence at the administrative stage and wait until a court hearing to present the meat of their case. This would make the administrative hearing a sham and place the regulatory power in the courts rather than the administrative agency.

Although this seems self-evident, it was necessary to travel the hard road of experience before the lesson was learned. The Supreme Court affirmed the position of lower courts that new evidence could be admitted on judicial review of decisions of the I.C.C. under the acts of 1887 and 1889.[35] The results were stated by the Commission:[36]

[35] See particularly Interstate Commerce Commission v. Alabama Midland Ry. Co., 168 U. S. 144, 175 (1897).
[36] *Annual Report*, 1897, 31-32.

The same case is not tried before the court which is tried before the Commission. The trial before the Commission, therefore, with all its attendant expense and consumption of time, goes practically for nothing. The decisions of the Commission are made upon one statement of facts, while the decisions of the courts may be, and usually are, made upon an entirely different statement of facts. . . . A practice like the present one tends to bring that body into disrepute and is grossly unfair to it and to the complainants who appear before it.

Over the years the practice has changed. Appeal is through the statutory bill in equity to a three-judge district court, from which appeals go directly to the Supreme Court. The Commission's position is safeguarded by the judicial practice of considering only the evidence submitted to the Commission. Recently, when a district court took new evidence in the territorial class rate case, the Supreme Court reaffirmed the traditional practice by stating that if "additional evidence was necessary to pass on the issue of confiscation, the cause should have been remanded to the Commission for a further preliminary appraisal of the facts which bear on that question." [37]

Decision on the administrative record is the general rule in judicial review today. This is true whether the form of appeal be the statutory bill in equity, to a court of appeals, regular district court, or to a special three-judge court, or the statutory appeal, appearing in the Federal Trade Commission Act, under which appeal goes to a court of appeals.[38] For the bill in equity, decision on the

---

[37] N. Y. v. U. S., 331 U. S. 284, 336 (1947). See also the comments of the Court in St. Joseph Stock Yards Co. v. U. S., 298 U. S. 38, 53-54 (1936), where the procedure for judicial review was the same as in I.C.C. cases.

[38] For a summary of methods of access to the courts from administrative agencies see Joseph P. Chamberlain, Noel T. Dowling, and Paul R. Hays, *The Judicial Function in Federal Administrative Agencies* (New York, 1942), 164-193.

Some variations may be noted. In some cases, the appeal to a designated reviewing court may be made by either party. E.g., for decisions of the I.C.C. or of the F.C.C. except for those affecting radio licensing. In other cases, any interested party may use the statutory appeal and the agency alone may bring the equity case in a district court. E.g., the Civil Aeronautics Act and the Federal Power Act, in which cases it is a regularly constituted district court. In other cases, the statutory appeal is the only procedure for review.

administrative record has been a rule of practice established within the courts; in the case of the statutory appeal, which is now the more common procedure for review of regulatory decisions, statutes normally provide for remanding the case to the administrative agency for taking of any additional evidence, but only with safeguards designed to insure that parties will make reasonable effort to produce the testimony in the initial hearing. The statutory language usually follows closely that of the Federal Trade Commission Act:[39]

If either party shall apply to the court for leave to adduce additional evidence, and shall show to the satisfaction of the court that such additional evidence is material and that there were reasonable grounds for the failure to adduce such evidence in the proceeding before the commission, the court may order such additional evidence to be taken before the commission and to be adduced upon the hearing in such manner and upon such terms and conditions as to the court may seem proper. The commission may modify its findings as to the facts, or make new findings, by reason of the additional evidence so taken, and it shall file such modified or new findings . . . and its recommendation, if any, for the modification or setting aside of its original order, with the return of such additional evidence.

Since 1933 several regulatory statutes have also tried to insure that parties present all contentions before the administrative agency. Such statutes provide simply that "No objection to the order of the Commission shall be considered by the court unless such objection shall have been urged before the Commission," or add to this a provision for court consideration of new objections if there were grounds for failure to present these at the administrative stage.[40]

---

[39] Section 5 of the original act, approved September 26, 1914. 38 *U. S. Stat. at Large*, 717, 720. Among other statutes providing similarly are Securities Act of 1933, the Securities Exchange Act of 1934, the Public Utility Holding Co. Act of 1935, the regulatory section of the Federal Power Act amendments of 1935, and the Natural Gas Act of 1938. Similar also in effect is the provision in the Communications Act concerning decision on the administrative record in cases affecting radio licensing.

[40] The Securities Act of 1933 (Section 9a) and the Securities Exchange Act of 1934 (Section 25) contained the language quoted in the text. The Public Utility Holding Company Act (Section 24), the Civil Aeronautics Act of 1938 (Sec. 1006e), the Federal Power Act (Section 313b), and the Natural Gas Act (Sec. 19b) add the qualifying words "unless there were reasonable grounds for

A breach in the administrative authority to build the complete record was made in the decision of the Supreme Court in Crowell *v.* Benson in 1932.[41] Crowell, a deputy commissioner of the U. S. Employees' Compensation Commission, had made an award against Benson, based upon a finding that an employee was injured while (1) in the employ of Benson and (2) performing service upon the navigable waters of the United States. The Court distinguished these from other determinations of fact, these being "fundamental" or "jurisdictional" in the sense that the constitutional authority of the United States depended upon their determination. It was said that Congress' power depended on the occurrence of the injury on the navigable waters of the United States and that liability without fault depended also on the master-servant relationship. As to these "basic facts" the Court saw "a question of the appropriate maintenance of the Federal judicial power in requiring the observance of constitutional restrictions." After emphasizing that the judiciary must be able to make its own judgment on questions of fact when constitutional rights are involved, the Court came to the question: "Upon what record is the determination to be made?" The answer was: "We think that the essential independence of the exercise of the judicial power of the United States in the enforcement of constitutional rights requires that the Federal court should determine such an issue upon its own record and the facts elicited before it." [42]

Although once regarded as a major obstacle in the development of administrative powers, the case may now have lost its significance. First, it is clear that a *de novo* hearing on jurisdictional facts is not required where only a question of statutory power is raised. The Supreme Court has held *de novo* trial was not necessary on the question of whether a railway fell within the group exempted from

---

failure to do so," and the National Labor Relations Act of 1935 said "unless the failure or neglect to urge such objection shall be excused because of extraordinary circumstances." (Section 10e). The Federal Trade Commission Act still does not carry language preventing consideration of objections not raised in proceedings before the Commission.

[41] 285 U. S. 22.

[42] There was a strong dissenting opinion by Justice Brandeis for himself and Justices Stone and Roberts.

the Railway Labor Act.[43] Second, the doctrine of Crowell v. Benson has been strictly limited in workmen's compensation cases, not being applicable to a determination as to whether an injury arises out of and in the course of employment,[44] or whether death results from suicide or accident,[45] or whether the employee is the type covered in the Act but admittedly within Congressional jurisdiction.[46] Finally, the case is inconsistent with some later decisions. The requirement of *de novo* hearing in Crowell v. Benson seems to have resulted from the Court's conviction that the initial decision on a constitutional issue should be made by the courts; but the Myers Case sanctioned initial decision by an administrative agency on an issue of federal jurisdiction. In State of New York v. United States, the Supreme Court said: "Thus, we think that if the additional evidence was necessary to pass on the issue of confiscation, the cause should have been remanded to the Commission for a further preliminary appraisal of the facts which bear on that question." [47]

This comparison of two later cases with Crowell v. Benson shows the place of the power to build the record in the arrangement of administrative powers. Although it might be argued that there are administrative advantages in gathering all evidence in one hearing, even though some issues were reserved for decision at a later stage, safeguarding authority to build the complete record is most significant, from the viewpoint of administrative regulation, because initial decision and completion of process are meaningless without it. Moreover, it is even more essential where the initial decision has legal effect, for a binding decision on a partial record is indefensible.[48]

---

[43] Shields v. Utah Idaho R. Co., 305 U. S. 177 (1938).
[44] Voehl v. Indemnity Insurance Co., 288 U. S. 162 (1933).
[45] Del Vecchio v. Bowers, 296 U. S. 280 (1935).
[46] South Chicago Coal and Dock Co. v. Bassett, 309 U. S. 251 (1940).
[47] 331 U. S. 284, 336 (1947).
[48] This is true whether the decision has (1) binding effect on parties unless set aside upon a review, or (2) has a measure of binding effect on reviewing courts as a result of doctrines limiting the scope of review, or (3) has both of these attributes.

Authoritative Administrative Decisions

It has long been settled that an administrative rule may be given the force and effect of law, with violators being subject to penalty for violation of a valid rule.[49] Moreover, it has been the general practice to give administrative rules automatic legal effect. On the other hand, recognition that the benefits of an administrative course of action could not be secured without providing for the authoritativeness of directive orders has come slowly.

Orders of the I.C.C. under the Act of 1887 could be violated with impunity until approved by a federal court. This placed upon the Commission the burden of going to the courts to get its orders approved. This increased the administrative burden, slowed the administrative process to a snail's pace,[50] and with other factors destroyed any hopes for effective regulation under the existing statute.

The Hepburn Act added arrangements for facilitating the attainment of substantive objectives which have formed the backbone of the system of administrative regulation in this country. The Act provided:[51]

All orders of the Commission, except orders for the payment of money, shall take effect within such reasonable time, not less than thirty days, and shall continue in force for such period of time, not exceeding two years, as shall be prescribed in the order of the Commission, unless the same shall be suspended or set aside by the Commission or be suspended or set aside by a court of competent jurisdiction.

Penalties provided in the regulatory act applied from the date of effectiveness of an order. Except for orders for the payment of money (reparation orders), the appropriate court, upon petition of

---

[49] U. S. v. Grimaud, 220 U. S. 506 (1911). In licensing cases the decision of the agency usually has the support which comes from statutory provision for penalties for operation without a license.

[50] "The average duration of the cases which have been actually prosecuted for the enforcement of the orders of this Commission has been about four years." Interstate Commerce Commission, *Annual Report*, 1897, 32.

[51] Section 15 as amended, 34 *U. S. Stat. at Large*, 584, 589.

the Commission or the Attorney General, was to enforce such orders if "regularly made and duly served." [52] Moreover, injunctions could not be issued suspending or restraining the effect of an order except upon notice to the Commission and decision, after hearing, of a three-judge court.[53]

The backbone was left out of the Clayton and Federal Trade Commission Acts. No sanction was provided for an administrative order to "cease and desist" and once again administrative agencies carried the burden of going to court for affirmation of their orders, during which time parties could ignore the administrative order with complete impunity. This was changed in amendments in 1938 to the Federal Trade Commission Act, which provided that cease and desist orders of the Commission issued under the Act, would become "final" sixty days after "service of such order" by the Commission unless petition for court review had been filed by a party subject to the order.[54] Penalties were provided for violation of an order which had "become final." [55] Thus, the burden of going to court was placed upon the contesting party.

It is still true, however, that cease and desist orders under the Federal Trade Commission Act are ineffective during appeal, subject to the authority of the reviewing court to issue such writs as "are necessary in its judgment to prevent injury to the public or to competitors pendente lite." [56] The tendency in regulatory measures is, nevertheless, to maintain the effectiveness of orders during appeal. Statutes now often provide that appeal proceedings "shall not, unless specifically ordered by the court, operate as a stay of" an ad-

[52] Section 16, as amended.
[53] *Ibid.*
[54] "As a consequence the Commission rarely finds it necessary to resort to the courts, and that method of enforcement has in the main become obsolete." Joseph P. Chamberlain, Noel T. Dowling, and Paul R. Hays, *The Judicial Function in Federal Administrative Agencies,* 184. Copyright 1942 by The Commonwealth Fund.
[55] Sections 5 (g) and 5 (1) of amended act, 52 *U. S. Stat. at Large,* 111, 113-114. The same system of final effect of cease and desist orders if not appealed within specified time and with penalties provided had been included in the provisions relating to packers in the Packers and Stockyards Act of 1921, 42 *U. S. Stat. at Large,* 159.
[56] Section 5 (c) of the amended act.

ministrative order. This language appears in all three of the major regulatory statutes administered by the Securities and Exchange Commission,[57] and in other recent regulatory statutes.

Sanction for administrative orders has sometimes been withheld in regulatory statutes where the cease and desist technique was employed. The Clayton Act has never been amended so as to give weight to cease and desist orders issued by enforcing agencies.[58] The National Labor Relations Act still does not provide any penalty for violation of Board orders. On the other hand, the authoritativeness of orders has been safeguarded in other types of regulatory statutes, and particularly in those statutes which have provided for comprehensive regulation of particular industries.[59]

Summation

An agency which can act on its own initiative in appropriate cases, which has authority to make the initial decision and to complete its process without interference, which can build the complete and final record, and whose rules and orders are effective without further process has several of the basic essentials for an administrative course of action. Support must, however, be found in other expedients. Orders must have some authority with the reviewing court;

[57] Securities Act of 1933, Sec. 9 (b), Securities Exchange Act of 1934, Sec. 25 (b), Public Utility Holding Company Act of 1935, Sec. 24 (b).

[58] Even weaker are cease and desist orders against monopoly and restraint of trade issued by the Secretary of Commerce in the fishing industry and the Secretary of Agriculture for producers' associations, for here the orders not only have no effect on the individual but also are by statute given little effect on the courts, where the order is to be only prima facie evidence of the facts. See Chamberlain, Dowling, and Hays, *op. cit.*, 138. Cease and desist orders normally are conclusive on the courts if based on substantial evidence. See pages 331-332.

[59] There are exceptions. Thus, penalties for violation of an administrative order do not apply to action taken under Section 11, Subsection (b), (d), (c), and (f) of the Public Utility Holding Act, presumably because of the extensive industry reorganization which might be required by such an order. Illustrative also is the exemption of administrative orders for the payment of money (reparation orders) from the penalty provisions of the Hepburn Act.

Authoritativeness of orders is an example of the change in locus of control, discussed at pages 31 ff. The early statutes "put the courts between the administrative agency and the parties against whom the agency's orders ran." Chamberlain, Dowling, and Hays, *The Judicial Function in Federal Administrative Agencies,* 187. Copyright 1942 by The Commonwealth Fund.

otherwise, their authoritativeness as to persons pending and during appeal will be unrewarding ultimately. This subject must await discussion in a separate chapter, but the other arrangements which facilitate use of major instruments may be discussed immediately.

ARRANGEMENTS FOR OBTAINING INFORMATION

Facts—lots of facts, facts about the details of industry operation— are the *sine qua non* of intelligent public control. It is not surprising, therefore, that regulatory statutes try to provide ample administrative power to obtain information.

A number of elements of authority comprise the modern battery of such powers. First, administrative agencies having control of particular industries are granted power, patterned after the grant in the Interstate Commerce Act, to require regular and special reports. Second, power is usually granted to require the submission, sometimes under oath, of specific information relating to matters subject to regulation.[60] This may include power to require the attendance and testimony of witnesses and the production of documentary materials. Third, authority to prescribe forms of accounting and to examine accounts may be granted. This power customarily accompanies rate-making powers or powers of control over financial institutions and practices.[61] Fourth, power to inspect premises and products, test equipment or analyze samples may be granted.[62] Fifth,

---

[60] Such grants of authority vary. They may have a general effect. The Interstate Commerce Commission may require from "carriers" and "lessors" "specific answers to all questions upon which the Commission may need information." 49 U. S. C. 20 (1). Or they may be limited to a particular purpose. The S.E.C. has authority to require that a security registration statement be accompanied by such documents as are "necessary or appropriate in the public interest or for the protection of investors." Securities Act of 1933, Sec. 7. One such type of provision, recurring in many statutes, is that requiring the filing of tariffs or rates of charge.

[61] Powers over forms of accounting were first granted to the Interstate Commerce Commission in 1887 but were expanded in 1906. For an example of extensive authority over accounts, see Section 15 of the Public Utility Holding Company Act of 1935.

[62] An interesting variant of the testing power was stated in Section 204b of the Civil Aeronautics Act of 1938. The C.A.A. was authorized to "purchase and exchange modern aircraft, completely equipped in such manner that such aircraft can be used in testing and checking every phase of light operation."

special or general investigations may be authorized.[63] Sixth, hearings may be held at which interested parties will present testimony. Seventh, with or without statutory authorization, agencies may confer with and obtain the advice of selected persons or groups. Eighth, information may be obtained from other government agencies or from the research reports of private organizations.

How can these powers be enforced? First, violation of administrative rules and orders relative to the filing of reports and the keeping of accounts may be subjected to penalty in the same way that other rules and orders now usually are. Second, failure to comply with a lawful administrative subpoena may likewise be subjected to penalty. Third, an administrative agency may be authorized, in case of failure to comply with a subpoena, to invoke the aid of a court which, upon determination of the validity of the subpoena, may order production of information.[64] Since this procedure, coupled with the power of the court to punish by summary contempt proceedings, is more expeditious than a criminal trial, and since it effects the end desired, namely, the production of the data, it is the method which is customarily employed to enforce obedience to a subpoena.

No national administrative agency has ever been granted authority to compel production of testimony by its own process. An old bit of dictum in a Supreme Court decision[65] and a strong antipathy toward the administrative power of subpoena have prevented this. Nevertheless, the procedure for enforcement brings delay and expense, and it has been suggested that the authority granted to ad-

---

[63] Note the various purposes of such investigations in the following grant in Sec. 18 (a) of the Public Utility Holding Company Act of 1935: "The Commission, in its discretion, may investigate any facts, conditions, practices, or matters which it may deem necessary or appropriate to determine whether any person has violated or is about to violate any provision of this title or any rule or regulation thereunder, or to aid in the enforcement of this title, in the prescribing of rules and regulations thereunder, or in obtaining information to serve as a basis for recommending further legislation concerning the matters to which this title relates."

[64] I.C.C. v. Brimson, 154 U. S. 447 (1894).

[65] Referring to the I.C.C., the Supreme Court said, "Such a body could not, under our system of government, and consistently with due process of law, be invested with authority to compel obedience to its orders by a judgment of fine and imprisonment." I.C.C. v. Brimson, 157 U. S. 447, 485 (1894).

ministrative agencies in some of the states to punish for failure to comply with a subpoena be granted in some circumstances to national agencies.[66]

In addition to the procedural problem of preventing delay, there have been questions concerning the scope of the authority to obtain information. The power to obtain information has been limited by several constitutional restrictions, but the effect of these has now largely withered away. The compulsory production of records was held to be within the protection of the Fifth Amendment against compelling any person "in any criminal case to be a witness against himself";[67] but the effects of this were almost completely destroyed, first, by statutory provisions for immunity against prosecution on matters on which testimony was exacted by compulsory process,[68] and second by judicial decision that the self-incrimination provision did not protect corporations or their officers acting in official capacity,[69] or unincorporated labor unions and their officers.[70] In many cases, particularly in Federal Trade Commission investigations, information has been refused on the ground that it did not

[66] See E. F. Albertsworth, "Administrative Contempt Powers: A Problem in Technique," *American Bar Association Journal*, XXV, 954-958 (1939), and Foster H. Sherwood, "The Enforcement of Administrative Subpoenas," *Columbia Law Review*, XLIV, 531-547 (1944). Kenneth Davis has argued: "The proposition that the present system rests on constitutional interpretations which are no longer valid seems unanswerable. Furthermore, the procedure requiring agencies to apply to courts for enforcement orders is needlessly inconvenient and expensive." "The Administrative Power of Investigation," *Yale Law Journal*, LVI, 1111-1154, at p. 1140 (August, 1947).

But Mr. Justice Murphy protested against the existing power, though long recognized as constitutional, of agencies to issue subpoenas. Even though enforcement required judicial action, he thought many persons yield because "of the air of authority" with which administrative agencies issued the demand. Dissenting alone in Oklahoma Press Publishing Co. *v.* Walling, 327 U. S. 186, 218-219 (1946).

[67] Boyd *v.* U. S., 116 U. S. 616 (1886).

[68] Brown *v.* Walker, 161 U. S. 591 (1896).

[69] Hale *v.* Henkel, 201 U. S. 43 (1906); Wilson *v.* U. S., 221 U. S. 361 (1911); Interstate Commerce Commission *v.* Baird, 194 U. S. 25 (1904).

More recently the effects of the self-incrimination provision have been limited by holdings that records required to be kept by law, as under O.P.A., were quasi-public records and that the constitutional privilege against self-incrimination did not extend to such records. See Shapiro *v.* U. S., 335 U. S. 1 (1948).

[70] U. S. *v.* White, 322 U. S. 694 (1944).

relate to interstate commerce or other matters subject to federal jurisdiction;[71] today, the administrative demand for information will be enforced pending determination of jurisdiction,[72] probably even on issues of constitutional jurisdiction, when exclusive original jurisdiction lies in the administrative agency.[73] The courts have taken note of the protection of the due process clause against excessive public demands for information, but the decline of due process as a limit on regulatory power must inevitably be accompanied by a similar decline in its effects on the power to obtain information. However, the question of due process has been swallowed up, in the past, in the issues arising under the Fourth Amendment.

Until recently, the Fourth Amendment, whose purpose was to prevent the general warrant for search and seizure, was a major limit on public power to require the submission of business records for inspection. This resulted from a holding in 1886 that compulsory production of papers (subpoena duces tecum) "is within the scope of the Fourth Amendment in all cases in which a search and seizure would be." [74] Moreover, courts have acted on the assumption that the protection of the Fourth Amendment extended to corporations.[75]

For a period there was a judicial tendency to avoid constitutional questions by construing narrowly the intent of statutes granting the authority to issue the subpoena duces tecum. Courts thought in terms of criminal law enforcement, and were loath to allow the use of the subpoena for supervisory purposes or for getting information on which to base rules or recommended legislation. Thus, the Interstate Commerce Act was interpreted so as to allow the subpoena only where there was a complaint or might be a complaint of viola-

---

[71] See particularly F.T.C. *v.* Claire Furnace Co., 285 Fed. 936 (App. D. C. 1923), and the discussion in Thomas C. Blaisdell, Jr., *The Federal Trade Commission* (New York, 1932), Chapter VIII.

[72] See footnote 27 at page 145.

[73] See the discussion of Myers *v.* Bethlehem Shipbuilding Corporation, *supra,* 145-146.

[74] Boyd *v.* U. S., 116 U. S. 616, 622. A request for production of papers is obviously not an "actual" search and there is no seizure; it is referred to as "constructive" search and seizure. See the comments of Justice Rutledge in Oklahoma Press Publishing Co. *v.* Walling, 327 U. S. 186, 202 ff. (1946).

[75] Hale *v.* Henkel, 201 U. S. 43 (1906); Silverthorne Lumber Co. *v.* U. S., 251 U. S. 385 (1920).

tion.[76] Moreover, judges found it difficult to believe that Congress, even in delegating general investigatorial functions, would authorize broad or sweeping requests, not describing with particularity the information requested. Hence, the Federal Trade Commission Act was interpreted with the same spirit as though the courts had been determining the proper scope of a grand jury request for information. The court decisions left doubts as to the extent of right of use, or as to whether sufficiently broad subpoenas might be used, in the general investigatorial functions given to the Federal Trade Commission. The results of this and other legal obstacles were that the Commission was "shorn of power" as an investigatory agent.[77] Beyond this, doubts were left as to whether administration would be hampered in its broader purposes by vestigial notions which would assimilate a request to an interstate corporation for information needed for supervisory or legislative action to a search of an individual's home for something which might turn up upon which he could be sent to jail.

The tide has now changed in favor of administrative power. First, strict judicial interpretation of statutes has been met by broader statutory language. Thus, the Public Utility Holding Company Act, after broadly defining investigative authority so as to include the S. E. C.'s supervisory and legislative powers,[78] grants the power of subpoena in aid "of any investigation or any other proceeding." [79] Second, Congress's power to use the subpoena for obtaining information as a basis for legislation has been upheld,[80] and the doctrine of the nondelegatability of legislative power has been so clipped that it should not stand in the way of delegation of the subpoena power from Congress to administrative agencies which are given power to make rules or to recommend legislation.[81] Third, the Supreme Court's

[76] Harriman v. I.C.C., 211 U. S. 407 (1908).
[77] Blaisdell, *op. cit.*, Chapter VIII.
[78] See footnote 63.
[79] Section 18 (c). Kenneth Davis says, "Not a single important regulatory statute fails to provide broad powers of investigation supported by powers to compel production of evidence." "The Administrative Power of Investigation," *Yale Law Journal*, LVI, 1111-1154, at p. 1119 (August, 1947).
[80] McGrain v. Daugherty, 273 U. S. 135 (1927).
[81] See pages 55-61.

language contains much broad doctrine on a number of aspects of this problem. In 1917, Justice McKenna, speaking for the Supreme Court, said, "it is not far from true—it may be it is entirely true, as said by the Commission—that 'there can be nothing private or confidential in the activities and expenditures of a carrier engaged in interstate commerce.'" [82] But what is the difference between such a carrier and any other corporation engaged in interstate commerce and subjected to public regulation in this day when the concept of two types of industries, those which are and those which are not "affected with a public interest," has lost its legal significance? Recently, the courts have developed the idea that records required to be kept by public authority are "quasi-public" records.[83] And in a recent full analysis by Justice Rutledge for the Supreme Court it was said:[84]

It is not necessary, as in the case of a warrant, that a specific charge or complaint of violation of law be pending or that the order be made pursuant to one. It is enough that the investigation be for a lawfully authorized purpose, within the power of Congress to command.

Also, it was said that the only protection from the Fourth Amendment (if it gave any protection) was against a subpoena which was too broad or indefinite;[85] and it is unthinkable that, in view of the repetition of statutory authorities for broad investigations, the courts should not be influenced by purpose of investigation in determining whether a subpoena is too broad. Inevitably, this question of breadth or particularity must become one of interpretation of statutory purpose; issues of particularity of subpoenas must be swallowed up in those of delegation. If information is relevant to a statutory purpose, how can the request for it be too broad? Finally, the language and

[82] Smith v. I.C.C., 245 U. S. 33, 43 (1917).
[83] See the discussion and cases cited in Davis, "The Administrative Power of Investigation," *Yale Law Journal*, LVI, at pages 1136-1138 (August, 1947).
[84] Oklahoma Press Publishing Co. v. Walling, 327 U. S. 186, 208-209 (1946).
[85] " . . . and the Fourth, if applicable, at the most guards against abuse only by way of too much indefiniteness or breadth in the things required to be 'particularly described,' if also the inquiry is one the demanding agency is authorized by law to make and the materials specified are relevant. The gist of the protection is in the requirement, expressed in terms, that the disclosure sought shall not be unreasonable." P. 208.

holdings of the courts have long indicated that the limitations of the Fourth Amendment ended with orders for production of papers, and would not extend to requirements for reports or answers to questionnaires.[86]

This leads us to the final comment about the trend toward administrative power to obtain information. Except in the exercise of enforcement powers, production of papers is usually only an essential reserve weapon, not the primary one, in the battery of information-getting powers. Reports, financial statements, and questionnaires supply basic data for supervisory purposes and for legislation. This is why business men in general became more interested in checks against excessive requirements for reports and filling in questionnaires than against demands for documentary evidence. And this is why the Federal Reports Act was passed.

This act[87] was designed to reduce to the minimum the burden on business enterprises and the cost to government in the gathering of facts. It authorized the Director of the Bureau of the Budget to designate a single agency to obtain information needed by more than one agency and to determine on request of any party having a substantial interest or on his own motion whether the collection of any information by a Federal agency was necessary for the performance of its functions; and prohibited agencies from collecting information upon identical items from ten or more private persons without approval of its plans or forms, and related regulations, by the Director.

[86] In I.C.C. *v*. Goodrich Transit Co., 224 U. S. 612 (1910), the Supreme Court upheld the authority of the Commission, as granted by statute, to prescribe methods of accounting and require a financial report. It was pointed out that a reservation had been made in the Harriman Case that the decision did not apply to requirements as to "systems of accounting and reports" and there was reference in the opinion to the necessity of information in order that the Commission might carry out the act and make the reports to Congress which were required by law. More recently, in Isbrandtsen-Moller Co. *v*. U. S., 300 U. S. 139, 145 (1937), the Supreme Court, in upholding an order of the Secretary of Commerce which required the company to file copies or summaries of its books and records on stated subjects, said: "The argument that the order amounts to an unreasonable search and seizure forbidden by the Fourth Amendment, is answered by the fact that it does not call for the production or inspection of any of appellant's books or papers."

[87] 56 *U. S. Stat. at Large*, 1078 (1942).

Years ago a federal justice pointed to the need for balance between public need and private burden:[88]

Very possibly, to sustain any right of inspection and searching, it must also appear that there is some reasonable proportion between the public value of the information likely to be obtained and the private annoyance and irritation it will occasion.

The justice was speaking about a test for the courts; but on requests for information to be directed to a number of parties the proper place for the test is in an organ like the Bureau of the Budget which can examine the request in advance, eliminate the unnecessary, secure coordination and lack of duplication among agencies, improve the form of the request, and thus reduce the burden on government and citizen alike.

The requirement for clearance in the Bureau of the Budget is not without its dangers. Yards of tape, and delay in needed clearances, may sometimes result. The arrangement for clearance recognizes, nevertheless, the essentials of government power and the legitimate fears of private annoyance. Implicit also is the recognition that the respective government agencies can frequently turn to each other for information and that research techniques may often be used which avoid or reduce the necessity for further private burden.

On this matter the future should be free of the difficulties and uncertainties of the past. The agencies of economic control now have access to a vast outpouring of economic data from governmental and private sources, they have their own research techniques, and they have statutory powers to call for information from private sources. And it may safely be predicted that the Congressional will that agencies must have adequate information will have its way, that the Fourth Amendment will not prevent reasonable requests made under authority of law, and that the ever-present danger that agencies will ask for too much will be met, by and large, and except for enforcement proceedings against particular parties, by internal administrative checks rather than by corrective judicial process.

[88] Justice Rose in Federal Trade Commission *v.* Baltimore Grain Co., 284 Fed. 886, 889-890 (1922).

SANCTIONS

Definition and Need of Sanctions

There is little literature on sanctions and the word itself has been variously defined. Landis used the word broadly to include all "the methods that exist for the realization of policies." [89] Leonard D. White has defined a sanction more narrowly as "a means of enforcement; in formal terms 'a conditional evil annexed to a law to produce obedience to that law.' " [90]

Landis' definition would adequately describe all the arrangements we have discussed in this and the preceding two chapters. This is more than is customarily included in use of the word "sanction." White's definition, though closer to common usage, requires amendment and elaboration. It should be amended, in this day of diverse government approaches, to include a conditional advantage annexed to obedience to law, e.g., the advantage of favorable publicity. If so amended and if construed so as to include not only the evil or advantage itself, but all those official actions which threaten evil or promise advantage, the definition provides bounds for a category of actions which implement public programs.

Sanctions then are the means of enforcement available to government because of the individual desire to obtain advantage or to avoid disadvantage. The word "sanction" may be used generally, also, to refer to the coercive authority which government possesses as a result of the existence of particular sanctions.

For administration, the significance of sanction lies not in its punitive aspect, but in its effect in maintaining the solvency of programs. Sanction, therefore, has meaning in administration of law because it is *the compelling force which may be exerted by government to effect compliance.*

[89] "These implements or remedies to effectuate policies can appropriately be called sanctions. . . . Sanctions, or the methods that exist for the realization of policies, may be thought of as constituting the armory of government." *The Administrative Process,* 89-90 (New Haven, 1938).

[90] *Introduction to the Study of Public Administration* (3rd ed., 1948) 548, quoting 56 *Corpus Juris* 125.

Some men will conform to the requirements of law because of their respect for law, based perhaps upon their conviction concerning its place in society. Others will conform because of their conviction of the justice of the particular rule or set of rules to which they are subject.[91] Still others will conform, consciously or unconsciously, only because of the measurement of advantages and disadvantages. Some, perhaps many, in the first two groups, will remain there only if they do not see an advantage accrue to those in the third group, which gives rise to the danger of the snowballing of violations. Because many do act upon the basis of comparison of advantages, and because others follow the tide, sanctions are necessary in the battery of public weapons. Their rôle may be minimized by the enlistment of understanding and conviction, by making regulation less burdensome, or by choice of service rather than control; but where men's actions are controlled in ways which they do not like then sanction is the reenforced concrete in the foundations lying beneath public purpose.

Types of Sanctions

Sanctions may be classified as inherent or external, and there are many forms of each.

Sometimes the sanction inheres in the instrument of control. Where government grants a conditional benefit, as in conditional benefit payments in agriculture, the sanction for the conditions lies in the power to withhold or withdraw the benefits. Where government competition with private enterprise is used as an instrument of control, the primary instrument and the sanction are identical. In such cases control is facilitated by avoidance of the necessity for external sanction.

Similar is the voluntary acceptance which results from the value in economic markets of services rendered. Grain standards fixed by the Secretary of Agriculture could be evaded easily by individuals facing only the authority of government; but these standards "have been voluntarily adopted throughout the country as the basis of trading not only on boards of trade and grain exchanges but at

[91] See pages 175-176.

country elevators, terminal markets, for warehousing and financing purposes, for future trading and in foreign markets." [92] In this case the sanction rests in the service that results from control, uniform and reliable standards being a facility of commerce.

In other cases the sanction inheres, in part at least, in the position of the administrative agency. Those who must continue to deal with an agency will often desire to maintain its good will. Much, of course, will depend upon the strength of the agency, perhaps also on the breadth of its functions. Thus, various actions taken to strengthen and extend the authority of agencies have the automatic effect of economizing the use of external sanction.

A sanction inheres in the action of the agency in those cases where penalty for violation of administrative decision is virtually automatic. There is a sanctionary element in the authoritative order where the penalty for violation is sufficiently certain that coercion is carried in the order itself. The fact that operation without a license normally subjects one automatically to penalty gives to refusal or withdrawal of license a similar sanctionary force. The sanctionary element in these cases will be strong only if the result appears certain on judicial review. Thus, authority of administrative decisions plus occasionality of judicial correction provides a system of coercion within administrative action which is complementary to ultimate or pure sanctions.

External sanctions may be called judicial or administrative, depending on the type of agency (judicial or administrative) through which they are applied. Judicial sanctions are of two types—criminal and civil. The forms of civil sanction are many, but of two types. There are civil penalties (punitive or remedial), to be recovered either by government or injured parties. And there are writs of mandamus and injunction, having as their final sanction the power of a court to impose penalties for violation. Some of the many types of administrative sanctions are:

1. Threat of prosecution.
2. Fines or pecuniary penalties which have the effect of fines.

[92] Attorney General's Committee on Administrative Procedure, *The Administration of the Grain Standards Act* (Sen. Doc. 186, 76th Cong., 1st Sess., 1940), 2.

3. Power to remit or mitigate statutory penalties.
4. Award or benefit for approved conduct, which may have
   a) A contractual aspect merely, as when the position of government as contractor is used to impose "a penalty for disapproved conduct . . . directly connected with the activity sanctioned by its award," or
   b) A punitive aspect, as where extraneous standards are enforced.
5. Publicity, either favorable or unfavorable.
6. Revocation, annulment, modification, suspension, failure to renew licenses.
7. Summary seizure or destruction of goods.
8. Award of damages.[93]

Tendencies in Sanctions for Administrative Action

Although most statutes prescribing standards of conduct or providing comprehensive regulation in particular areas of economic life carry the threat of fine or imprisonment, there has been a marked tendency in regulatory statutes to authorize the administrative agency to secure injunctions as an alternative to criminal prosecutions. In this way the delays of criminal proceedings, the pitfalls of jury trial, and the reluctance to punish business men, particularly when statutes and regulations may leave an area of uncertainty as to precise requirements, can be by-passed.

There has also been a tendency toward greater reliance on administrative sanctions. A variety of reasons may account for this. There may be need for prompt action, as in the action of S.E.C. on security issues; or an opportunity for automatic application of sanctions, as in deduction of penalties from interest on bonds held by the Treas-

[93] See Chamberlain, Dowling, and Hays, *op, cit.*, 79-163, for discussion of these. Included also in their discussion are (1) deportation and additional taxes (by revenue agencies), neither of which are significant in our analysis of economic controls; and (2) many types of action which are sanctions in the broad meaning of the authors but not in the narrower meaning in which the term is used here. Among these are exhortation, education, and propaganda (note our next section on communications as a parallel to sanctions in the armory of government); preparatory sanctions, such as inspection and investigation; administrative report of violation to the Attorney General.

urer of the U.S. when national banks fail to transmit required reports. Any agency will prefer to use its own sanctions if by this means the costs, delays, and uncertainties of the court room can be avoided. Also, sanctions may be linked with the system of administrative control. Thus, in licensing the sanction of withdrawal by revocation, suspension, or failure to renew is part and parcel of the system of control. Correctly or incorrectly, it may be thought that the power to award reparations for excess rate charges in the past is so close to other determinative powers of administrative agencies that it should not be separately allocated. More significant than other causes, however, is the greater availability of sanctions of appropriate weight and effect in the kit of administrative tools. Chamberlain, Dowling, and Hays state the point concisely:[94]

The immense power of administrative agencies to enforce their policies is largely due to the character and variety and the effectiveness of the sanctions available to the agencies. A single agency may have a wide choice of means of enforcement from which it can select those most appropriate in furthering the policy adopted for the regulation of an industry subject to its control, or in molding the relationships between conflicting interests in the field in which the agency operates. This wide choice of sanction is a valuable aid to the purposes of regulation.

Third, there is a tendency toward inclusion of non-judicial types of sanctions in the battery of sanctions applied by administrative agencies. The threat of prosecution, the use of publicity, and the economic penalties of government as licensor, benefit bestower, and contractor are today among the most potent of the coercive weapons of government. The reasons for use of these sanctions is clear. The economic penalties often arise automatically with the use of certain instruments of control. But, also, use of these various sanctions is the result of that search of administrative agencies for effective sanction which Chamberlain, Dowling, and Hays stated.

[94] Joseph P. Chamberlain, Noel T. Dowling, and Paul R. Hays, *The Judicial Function in Federal Administrative Agencies,* 223. Copyright 1942 by The Commonwealth Fund.

The Quest for Effective Sanction

This search for effective sanction is one of the major challenges in administrative control.[95] How can sanctions be found which meet the three tests of promptness, certainty, and appropriate degree of severity?

A few examples will show that the toughest problem is that of severity. For enforcement of the Walsh-Healey Act, for example, there are two sanctions: civil action for damages to the employee (payment of amount of wages lost to the employee for violation of the act) and withholding of government contracts for three years. The inappropriateness of these sanctions has been noted: "Indeed, it may well be asked whether the statute is adequately implemented, for on the one hand the only penalty for violation is that restitution be made, an extremely light club with which to compel obedience to the Congressional command; while on the other hand the penalty of blacklisting is so severe that its imposition may destroy a going business and, with it, the employment opportunities of those whom the statute was intended to benefit." [96] The latter penalty does not adequately implement the statute, for administrative officers will seldom apply a sanction which is so disruptive of established business. In a recent year only eleven firms were placed on the black list, but for about 850 other firms found to be in violation only the lighter penalty was applied.[97] One may wonder how heavy a deterrent is placed upon the employer by so light a penalty, particularly when only a limited percentage of those subject to the Act can be inspected by the Public Contracts Division.

[95] There is the converse problem of "fair play and individual justice." The increase in administratively applied sanctions and particularly in those of a non-judicial type makes it imperative that proper internal safeguards exist in administration. See Chapter XI. The problem of safeguards is emphasized in Dalmas H. Nelson, "Administrative Blackmail: The Remission of Penalties," *Western Political Quarterly*, IV, 610-622 (December, 1951).

[96] Attorney General's Committee on Administrative Procedure, *Division of Public Contracts* (Sen. Doc. 186, 76th Cong., 3d Sess., 1940), 4.

[97] *Annual Report of the Wage and Hour and Public Contracts Divisions*, 1947, 8-9.

Similarly, the Fair Labor Standards Act of 1938 until recently could be enforced by the laborer's bringing his own suit in the courts, or by public action for injunction or to apply the criminal penalties provided in the Act. Laborers were not in a position to enforce their rights by private suit. The public procedure was too cumbersome for the nearly 20,000 violations found in a year's inspection, and hence the Wages and Hours Division tried to get voluntary restitution of back wages due. But in one year employers agreed to restore only $13,400,000 of $21,600,000 found to be due. The administrative agency said, "The direct and simple way to handle this problem is to give the Administrator specific authority in the act to bring suit for the payment of wages due under the act upon request by employees to whom such wages are due."[98] This was done in amendments in the Fair Labor Standards Act in 1949,[99] and thus a sanction of more appropriate weight was provided.

The lack of sanction of appropriate severity may be seen in national banking laws. Until recently the only sanctions available to the Comptroller of the Currency were appointment of a receiver or proceedings in a Federal District Court to dissolve a banking association. These sanctions were too drastic for the thousands of minor violations of law,[100] and administrators over a long period of years recommended "intermediary penalties."[101] Finally, in 1933, two additional sanctions were added. The power to publish an examiner's report was granted, but had not been exercised up to February, 1940, because it was felt "that the results in terms of public reaction might be disastrous."[102] A new power to remove officers has like-

[98] *Ibid.*, 1946, 64.

[99] 63 *U. S. Stat. at Large*, 919.

[100] One author has stated that fully one-third of the banks "violate the law in some respect in the conduct of their business" and that "probably seventy-five per cent of the examiners' reports disclosed violations of one kind or another." Thomas P. Kane, *Romance and Tragedy of Banking* (New York, 1923), 320, 366.

[101] See, for example, statement of George B. Cortelyou to the National Monetary Commission, *Suggested Changes in the Administrative Features of the National Banking Laws* (Washington, 1910), 196.

[102] Attorney General's Committee on Administrative Procedure, *Federal Control of Banking* (Sen. Doc. 186, 76th Cong., 3d Sess., 1940), 42.

wise been deemed too severe for frequent use. The result is summarized in the following statement:[103]

The paradox in the situation is that the sanctions are so compelling that the authorities almost never use them. Because the banks are so important in an industrial-commercial economy, compulsive steps which might shake confidence are withheld. Although there is in fact an iron hand within the velvet glove of the banking authorities, the glove is seldom removed.

On the other hand, Louis Caldwell has commented on the failure of an administrative* agency to use intermediary sanctions. He pointed out that the F. C. C. has made extensive use of the procedure for renewing licenses periodically as a method of discipline, and that use of this method means "no alternative between the death penalty and acquittal." He argued that the penal provisions of the Act gave a more appropriate remedy, for "The courts have a wide latitude in assessing anything from a normal fine to a heavy one." [104] The Commission's view is that criminal penalties and license refusal and revocation are both cumbersome, and it has recommended that it be given the power to issue cease and desist orders.[105]

The usual need is for a scale of sanctions, and where these are not provided by law the agency will search for extralegal sanctions. This has been true, for example, of the Comptroller of the Currency. "Constructive guidance" by way of suggestion and "moral suasion" are used by bank examiners to obtain adherence to regulations. Letters setting forth corrective requirements are sent from the Comptroller of the Currency. Some Comptrollers have required directors of banks to reply over their signatures to letters from the Comptroller, thus establishing a record for the future. Banks may be put on a "special list" for closer surveillance, involving more frequent examinations or more frequent or comprehensive reporting—a strong sanction because banks will desire to avoid excessive burden or the

---

[103] *Ibid.*, 43.

[104] George Warren, ed., *The Federal Administrative Procedure Act and the Administrative Agencies* (New York, 1947), 82-84, 90. Actually, the statement about death penalty or acquittal is overput for it overlooks correction as a result of administrative threat.

[105] Hearings before a Subcommittee of the Committee on Interstate and Foreign Commerce on S. 1333, 80th Cong., 1st Sess. 14, 51.

danger of public knowledge of special treatment. Tactful suggestion, pressure, and special surveillance provide a scale of lighter
sanctions, which derive their potency from the existence in the background of the heavier sanctions provided by law and inherent in the
threat of public suspicion.[106]

The development of a scale of sanctions is illustrated in the experience of O.P.A., where this was necessary because of the multitude of affected parties and the variations in importance of violations.

The sanction of publicity was extensively used. Those who failed
to cooperate in rationing, price and rent control had the stigma of
"chisellers" attached to them. Although the agency policy in the later
days called for abstaining from appeals to patriotism, the appeal was
used in the beginning, with the converse implication on the violator.
Also, the Enforcement Department put much emphasis on publicity
of names and penalties in cases in which successful court action was
obtained. Publicity was depended upon as an important deterrent
to potential violators and for prevention of snowballing of violations.

Special means were devised to handle the great number of small
violations. In rationing, revocation of gasoline rations by district
office or local board was used to penalize violation in use of rations
by the individual user of gasoline.[107] In price control, a range of
sanctions for minor retail violations was created by administrative
action, particularly for retail food stores. Representatives of the local
price panels checked stores periodically and called the operators'
attention to violations; this might be followed, if violations were repeated, by written warnings from the price panel, and, if further
repeated, by admonitory conferences in the hearing room of the
price panel. Later, the price panels were given the authority, in the
case of small violations, to negotiate a settlement of the Administrator's claim under law for penalties. Final failure of a panel to

---

[106] A chapter on "Sanctions" in the unpublished dissertation by Guy Fox, *Regulation of Banking by the Comptroller of the Currency* (The University of
Texas, 1948).

[107] See the author's *Field Administration of Wartime Rationing* (Washington,
1947), 116-117.

obtain compliance could be followed by report to the enforcement officials in district offices, who could then seek a voluntary settlement or move to the courthouse.

This experience is significant in the general story of sanctions for national law. First, it calls attention to the lack of localization of national enforcement machinery. There are no local courts and local police. Federal district courts cannot handle a mass of small business. In the absence of provision for further use of state machinery, an administrative agency whose regulations touch the general public or little business must build its own grassroots tribunals. Second, it shows that sanctions must be complementary and cumulative.[108] Fairness to individuals and effectiveness of program both depend upon the balanced use of sanctions of differing weights. Third, it emphasizes the significance of non-judicial approaches. Education, then warning and conference, pressure applied lightly and then strongly, may be the typical method of administration. Compliance, not punitive action, is the basic administrative objective. Moreover, conservation of energy is an important aim in good administration, and methods which are time-consuming must be reserved for those who yield only to drastic measures.

In rationing also, O.P.A. used a sanction which was administratively created and administratively applied. This was the famous suspension order procedure under which a seller of a rationed commodity could be suspended from the handling of such commodity.[109] The sanction had many advantages. The procedure be-

[108] For a summary of "complementary" and "cumulative" sanctions in another agency, see Attorney General's Committee on Administrative Procedure, *Securities and Exchange Commission* (Sen. Doc. 10, 77th Cong., 1st Sess., 1941), 11-18.

[109] The sanction was created by O.P.A. General Order No. 46, 8 Federal Register, 1771 (1943). It was held valid in L. P. Steuart and Bro., Inc., *v.* Bowles, *et al.*, 322 U. S. 398 (1944), as a proper exercise of the power to allocate scarce commodities under the Second War Powers Act. The Court thought that the suspension order was not designed to punish offenders but to prevent the distribution of a "scarce and vital commodity" in "an inefficient, inequitable, and wasteful way." For an explanation and defense of the suspension order see Arthur L. Brown, "The Office of Administrative Hearings," *Cornell Law Quarterly*, XXIX, 461-488 (1943-1944), and for opposite views see Second Intermediate Report of the Select Committee to Investigate Executive Agencies, H. Rep. No. 862, 78th Cong., 1st Sess. (1943); Roscoe Pound, "The Chal-

fore the O.P.A. officials who heard and decided, called hearing commissioners, was simple and expeditious. Prompt application of the sanction was possible. Moreover, the period of suspension could be adjusted to accord with the gravity of the offense. Thus a single sanction provided a scale of penalty.[110]

The suspension order is perhaps the outstanding example of administrative search for and creation of formal, legal sanction. Along with the more informal methods used in the rationing and price panels, it shows the importance of administrative inventiveness in the development of appropriate sanctions. As a result of these techniques, the threat of sanction was widened to include more parties and the burden on courts and attorneys was reduced. The injunction could be reserved in price control for the larger offenders, or for those whose violations threatened the program most seriously, and in rationing for those to whom the suspension order could not be applied.[111] The criminal proceeding could be reserved for the flagrant violator whose punishment by this means was necessary to preserve the idea that the programs had teeth. The purpose of the scale, or the bundle, of sanctions was compliance, or to put it differently, the solvency of the programs.

lenge of the Administrative Process," *American Bar Association Journal*, XXX, 121-126 (1944); and San Francisco Bar Association, *Committee Report on the Office of Administrative Hearings of the Office of Price Administration* (December, 1943). For an answer to the latter see National Lawyers Guild, San Francisco Chapter, *Report on Office of Administrative Hearings of the Office of Price Administration* (January, 1944). For use of the suspension order by the War Production Board, see O'Brian and Fleischmann, "The War Production Board Administrative Policies and Procedures," *George Washington Law Review*, XIII, 1-60, at pages 46-54 (December, 1944).

[110] The chief weakness of the suspension order lay in the fact that it applied *in personam* and not *in rem*. Investigations within O.P.A. showed that filling stations frequently continued to operate under essentially the same management, but with a paper change in ownership. This led to a proposal from the Enforcement Department in 1945 that the suspension order operate *in rem*, but this was successfully opposed by those responsible for trade relations in the Rationing Department and for public relations in the Information Department.

[111] The suspension order could not be applied against those whose continued operation was essential in order to maintain channels of distribution.

Conclusion

The problem in sanctions is to find those which carry appropriate force in particular situations. This may call for administrative discretion and creativeness. This may result in a range of sanctions. It may result in a variety of sanctions—some inhering in the instrument of control, some judicially or administratively applied by formal processes, and some being informal and even extralegal. The over-all purpose is compliance and solvency of program.

COMMUNICATIONS

In recent years the significance of communication of purpose and the limitations of authoritarian methods, as means of attaining internal cohesion and unity within organizations, has been emphasized.[112] Workers within an organization follow orders and other directives with zeal and enthusiasm only when they understand and believe in the purpose of the directives.

Communications, or to put it differently, the use of the fine art of trade and public relations, is at least equally important in obtaining the compliance of private citizens subject to administrative action. Sanctions must exist, but administrators will know that solvency of program depends upon minimizing the necessity for sanction by use of techniques for gaining understanding and consent.

One essential is to gain understanding in the affected industries of the precise requirements of the law. This may be easy where the concerns subject to regulation are large and few, or where strong trade associations channel information to all members of affected industries. It will be easier where regulation has become customary in an industry. The task will be more difficult where regulation af-

[112] The leading book on the subject is Chester I. Barnard, *The Function of the Executive* (Harvard University Press, 1942). Note the following from page 89: "The possibility of accomplishing a common purpose and the existence of persons whose desires might constitute motives for contributing toward such a common purpose are the opposite poles of the system of cooperative effort. The process by which these potentialities become dynamic is that of communication. Obviously, a common purpose must be commonly known, and to be known must be in some way communicated."

fects a large number of concerns, particularly if these are small operators and they have not become accustomed to public control.

Wartime agencies, with new controls affecting vast numbers, gave much attention to trade education. They found it necessary to establish field offices whose primary function was trade education.[113] They found it necessary to plan educational programs to reach the trade. They sometimes had to put on drives within administration to simplify regulations or the trade releases explaining these, so that they would be understood in the trade. They often found that maintenance of solvency of program involved a continuous battle against trade ignorance of requirement. The task was complicated immensely by the multitude of regulations and the inevitability of detail in requirement. This conclusion may be made: as regulation is extended to more concerns and becomes more intricate, the necessity for a trade relations arm of administration increases.

It is essential not only to inform but to win consent from the regulated. An experienced public administrator and newspaper editor once remarked to the author, "The American people regard it as part of their liberty not to obey a law they do not believe in." This may be the Achilles heel of regulation, for consent can be won if requirement is easy but public need may sometimes call for hard measures. The subject must be discussed more fully later.[114] At this point, it is sufficient to say that a major task of administration is to gain consent for the purpose of regulation from a sufficiently large percentage of those affected to reduce, to manageable proportion, the dependence upon sanction.

Still another essential is some measure of understanding of purpose and requirements from the public generally. An agency can count on attack. It will become a failure unless it readies itself for this attack by winning support from the public. But this is hard because Mr. Citizen faces limits on his span of attention. There is only so much he can keep up with. The answer must lie partly in

[113] See the author's *Field Administration of Wartime Rationing,* and Carroll K. Shaw, *Field Organization and Administration of the War Production Board and Predecessor Agencies: May 1940 to November 1945* (Civilian Production Administration, 1947).

[114] See Chapter IX.

cultivating those particular groups which may be counted on for support for the policy of the law. But these may be weak, and this problem may indicate that there are two vulnerable heels in regulation.

The problem of communications between government and the people has not been sufficiently studied.[115] Some fear the weight of government publicity on public opinion; others fear the weakening of administration through ignorance and adverse publicity. The problem seems to be one of balance in the general system of communications. In that balance one need is for channels through which the administrative agency can reach the public. In what cases will field offices help meet the problem? Must the publicity sections of control agencies be strengthened? Should government sometimes use paid advertisements as means of reaching the people? These and many other questions have not yet had the attention they deserve.[116]

CONCLUSION

The reader of this chapter will have seen that facilitative arrangements are the stuff out of which administration is bulwarked. Purpose will be thwarted, action will miss its goal, if these several types of arrangements are lightly regarded.

Experience from 1887 through World War II has revealed some main essentials. Some of these are now regularly incorporated in legislation, others have become part of judicial practice. The growing points of the future are in many cases indicated. In the main, the areas in which difficulties are faced have changed. Formerly, it was the lack of arrangements to secure an administrative course of action and the restrictions upon power to obtain information which created difficulties. In the future, more attention must be

[115] See, however, James L. McCamy, *Government Publicity: Its Practice in Federal Administration* (Chicago, 1939).

[116] The Commission on Freedom of the Press recommended that the government inform the public with respect to its policies and the purposes underlying these, and that the government employ its own media of communication to the people where private agencies of mass communication were unable or unwilling to supply media. *A Free and Responsible Press* (1947), 81, 88-89.

given to the problems of sanction and communication. These run into questions of acceptance and support which challenge the efficacy of economic control, and which will be discussed further in subsequent chapters dealing with the troublesome external factors affecting the success of administrative agencies; it can be said, nevertheless, that ingenuity in choice and combination of sanctions, and ingenuity and art in trade and public relations, will widen the area of administrative effectiveness.

This chapter further reveals the extent of administrative responsibility. A previous chapter (Chapter IV) showed how administrative responsibility includes elaboration of policy; this chapter shows that such responsibility may extend even to administration of sanctions and to winning support for public policy. From where, to where, does the administrative course run? From directive to compliance.

Chapter VIII

Administrative Tools and Techniques:

Operating Methods

INTRODUCTION

No other aspect of administrative action has received as much attention during the past fifteen years as the operating methods of administrative agencies. The discussion centered on the procedure in administrative "rule making" and administrative "adjudication" and the related problem of allocation of responsibilities among agency participants in administrative proceedings.[1]

On the whole, this has been a lawyers' discussion. On the whole,

[1] The discussion was stimulated by the activities of the Committee on Administrative Law of the American Bar Association, created in 1933. The committee soon centered its attention on problems of procedure. The Attorney General of the United States appointed a Committee on Administrative Procedure in 1939 which made its final report in 1941. Already, the discussion on procedure had started in the Congress. Its first enactment, the Logan-Walter Bill, was vetoed by the President in 1940. Subsequent consideration led to the passage of the Administrative Procedure Act in 1946. The best source of information on the background of this act is *Administrative Procedure Act, Legislative History* (Sen. Doc. No. 248, 79th Cong., 2d Sess., 1947).

179

also, the approach has been from the judicial analogy. There has been much comparison between administrative and judicial proceedings and search for ways of insuring that administration would operate in line with standards followed in judicial proceedings.

There has been danger that this approach would lead to too narrow a view of administrative processes. The danger has been avoided to some extent by the empirical approach of the Attorney General's Committee on Administrative Procedure. Its careful studies of the procedure of about thirty agencies and its final report contributed materially to an understanding of the nature of administrative processes and revealed the immense diversity of administrative activities for which procedure must be devised.

It has been shown in the preceding pages that much of the task of administrative control is distinctly different from the judicial function. Routine performance, managerial discretion, and general determinations of future policy bulk large in the total task. Even where administrative work has an adjudicatory aspect, certain distinctive features of administration are significant. The Attorney General's Committee on Administrative Procedure noted that four characteristics of administrative agencies are of fundamental importance in relation to problems of procedure.[2] There is, first, the factor of size. Most agencies are large and must handle a large volume of work, giving rise to the necessity for delegation of authority and informal settlement. Second, the agencies "specialize in particular tasks and they include specialists on their staffs," and hence "they can accomplish much" of their work "without the necessity of informing themselves by the testimonial process." Third, they are responsible for results, and therefore "cannot take a wholly passive attitude toward the issues which come before them." Finally, the variety of duties makes generalization in description and prescription difficult. "A procedure which would be for the protection of the individual in one situation may be clearly to his injury in another. A set of standards evolved to meet one problem may fail wholly to meet another." To these four factors should be added a

[2] *Final Report of the Attorney General's Committee on Administrative Procedure* (Washington, 1941), 18-20.

fifth which the Committee emphasized throughout its report—the need for expedition.[3]

A more general and all-pervading characteristic of administration was tacitly recognized by the Committee and might have been clearly set up as the dominant feature. Each administrative agency is *in itself an institution* carrying an *institutional responsibility* for getting a job done. The institutional resources must be used in the most effective manner for the performance of the whole task of the agency. In handling particular tasks use may be made of its reservoir of specialists. And, as with any institution with a large volume of work, of varied nature, and requiring varied specializations, a regulatory institution must combine coordination and supervision with delegation.

It is in this institutional quality of administration that the clue to the administrative process as a whole is to be found. Administrative processes are a problem of institutional management, as well as of legal technique; and the science of management may have more to contribute to their development than the science of law.[4] Judicial techniques for reaching an informed judgment should be used in many types of administrative decision. On the other hand, these techniques should be reserved for situations where they serve a useful function; and even when used they must be adapted to the institutional process of which they are a part.

This does not mean that individual right and interest and "fair play" with respect to each person or concern are not fully as important as administrative effectiveness. In some cases efficiency will have to yield to procedures which are generally believed to be essential for fair play. By and large, however, there need be no conflict. Efficiency requires that the administrative judgment shall be an informed judgment; this accords with the legitimate interest of particular parties.[5] And fair play does not require that there be no

---

[3] See particularly page 61 of the *Final Report*.

[4] Factors of management as well as of legal technique were, it should be noted, considered by the Attorney General's Committee.

[5] Parties may, of course, have other legitimate interests in procedure, as those protected in the rules of exclusion in evidence, e.g., protection for trade secrets or against self-incrimination.

arrangements for facility in the affairs of government. On the contrary, arrangements for doing the whole job in the most expeditious manner may be the chief expedient for protection of individual interest.

To carry forward the task of government with efficiency and fair play, administrative processes must take account of many needs. Among the most important problems are those of saving time and expense, of providing the administrator with adequate and proper factual material, and of organizing administrative operations in such a way as to insure efficiency and fair play in the process of decision. These three, and the main outlines of the Administrative Procedure Act and certain recommendations of the Hoover Commission, will be discussed in this chapter.

ECONOMIZING ADMINISTRATIVE EFFORT

An administrative agency will need to plan for the effective use of its time and resources. In order to get its whole job done, and to dispose of its several tasks expeditiously, it will need to save time and expense.

It should also strive to save the time and expense of those affected by administration. If to the burden of keeping informed about governmental policy and of keeping accounts and submitting reports is added the necessity of attending or being represented at excessively prolonged and complicated proceedings, the exaction of the administrative process will often be exasperating. Now and then a party may be interested in stalling administration or relatively unconcerned with the expense of proceedings, but most persons will appreciate an expeditious and inexpensive handling of their affairs.

A variety of expedients may be employed to save administrative time and expense, most of which will also result in savings for those affected by administration.

Expert Performance

Expert performance of preliminary and basic tasks eliminates or reduces the burden of formal contest. If tests to licensees are given with sufficient care, proceedings for revocation may be rare.[6] If grain or cotton is graded carefully by persons who have been qualified under high standards, appeals from their decisions will be infrequent. If inspection is competent, or if basic data are expertly analyzed, prior to the issuance of complaints, time will not be lost in the hearing of baseless cases. If rules are framed carefully, petitions for exemption may be relatively infrequent. If the work of preliminary study by expert divisions is competently done, the task of hearing officials is simplified.

Routinizing Tasks

The most familiar administrative technique for economizing time is the routinizing of tasks. Every administrative agency conserves its time by reducing to routine the simple, less disputable, minor—even some major—repetitive tasks.

Routine is merely a set process of handling recurring situations. It is a form of institutional habit. It may result from overhead prescription of standard practices. Or it may be attained by specialization of function, for where the same persons repeatedly perform the same task the processes of performance tend to become automatic. Although it creates the danger of inattention to new and special circumstances, it yields regularity and dispatch.

An example from OPA's experience may be cited. Each two months every institutional user of food (restaurants, hotels, etc.) was issued rations. Although the decision on each grant was supposed to be an "adjudicatory" decision by a local board, the burden was so heavy that clerical issuance of rations without close examination of applications was a frequent practice. The opportunity for abuse was great, for overstatement by an applicant of the number of persons served or of revenue received during the past period would lead to an excessive grant. In 1945, when the job of issuance was

---

[6] In regard to revocation of grain inspectors' licenses, it has been said: "The care exercised in licensing inspectors has practically eliminated incompetency as a cause for suspension or revocation." Attorney General's Committee, *The Administration of the Grain Standards Act* (Sen. Doc. 186, 76th Cong., 3d Sess., 1940), 19.

moved to district offices, it was necessary to solve the problems of load and fraud. This was done by arranging for a historical record card for each user, from which an experienced technical employee at relatively low salary could detect, by comparison of a current application with the record for past periods, whether there was evidence of overstatement. If not, issuance was an automatic clerical process; only the questionable applications were "flagged" for more careful consideration by superiors.

Informal Settlement

The most successful technique for avoiding the burden of adjudication is informal settlement. This term applies to any method of settling *particular issues* without a formal hearing.[7] A decision is made on the basis of an inspection of premises, an examination of books, a testing of samples, a physical examination. An inquiry concerning a right or interest, an objection to administrative action, a complaint against another party—these are settled by correspondence or in conference. A complaint having been issued or being imminent, parties enter into an agreement to abstain from the practice alleged, or (as in National Labor Board proceedings) to take affirmative action to remove the cause of complaint.

The Attorney General's Committee reported that "The great bulk of administrative decisions are made informally and by mutual consent."[8] In addition to pointing out the myriad decisions resting on inspection or test, the Committee stated some figures which proclaim forcefully the significance of informal settlement:

In labor relations one might expect a high percentage of contested cases, yet in the first four years of its existence the National Labor Relations Board closed 12,227 unfair labor practice cases, in only eight per cent of which were formal complaints issued and in only four per cent of which were formal decisions made. The Interstate Commerce Commission over a period of ten years has arranged settlements in all but five of the 3,500 demurrage complaints filed with it. In the entire Department of Agricul-

---

[7] This is the sense in which the term "informal" is used in the *Final Report* of the Attorney General's Committee. See pages 35-42. See also Walter Gellhorn, *Federal Administrative Proceedings* (Baltimore, 1941), Chapter II.

[8] *Final Report*, 35.

ture, which administers over a score of regulatory statutes, the total proceedings under all statutes which have gone to formal hearing have in the
three years ended in June, 1940, averaged 253 a year, and of these only 37
in the last year progressed to the stage of exceptions to the examiner's
report.[9]

The Federal Alcohol Administration in one year passed on more than
93,000 applications for label approval or exemption; the Department of
Agriculture has registered some 1,700 live poultry dealers; the Securities
and Exchange Commission examines annually hundreds of registrations
of securities and registers as many more dealers and brokers. Virtually all
of these applications are disposed of without formal proceedings.[10]

The Federal Trade Commission during the year ended June 30, 1938,
settled 564 cases by stipulations to cease and desist without the issuance
of complaints. During the same period it issued 310 formal complaints.[11]

When the experience in World War II is more fully recorded
many techniques for handling a large volume of cases by informal
processes may be revealed. One of the expedients was the use of
local boards in rationing and selective service. In one year local
rationing boards of unpaid citizens made adjudicatory decisions on
68,000,000 applications for supplementary gasoline and on 18,-
000,000 applications for tires. Necessarily, the procedure was informal. In such cases, the important safeguards for private interests
and public efficiency are the proper selection, instruction, and
supervision of personnel.[12]

Gellhorn has written as follows:[13]

Just as only a comparative handful of administrative decisions can ever
be examined by the courts, so a similarly minor number of these determinations can—or should—be preceded by formal hearings of a judicial-

---

[9] *Ibid.* For a discussion of informal settlement by the Interstate Commerce
Commission see Sharfman, *The Interstate Commerce Commission,* IV (New
York, 1937), 72-73, 170-177, 280-282. An illuminating discussion of the meth-
ods of disposing of complaints by the National Labor Relations Board is given
by R. R. R. Brooks, *Unions of Their Own Choosing* (New Haven, 1940),
Chapter I.

[10] *Final Report,* 39.

[11] *Ibid.,* 41.

[12] See my *Field Administration of Wartime Rationing,* 97-118, for an appraisal of adjudication by local boards.

[13] Walter Gellhorn, *Federal Administrative Proceedings,* 45. Copyright 1941
by The Johns Hopkins Press.

ized character. If really effective protections of private interests are to be devised, they must be founded upon recognition that the "life blood of the administrative process" is its informal procedures.

Judicialized procedures are a luxury. In the administrative process, as in the courts, the delays resulting from their use are often intolerable.[14] The amount of staff time required is great. Except where precedents are needed or other special reasons exist for judicial procedure, avoidance of formal contest by use of informal methods will be one measure of administrative success.[15]

Techniques in Formal Hearings

Where a formal hearing is employed, techniques may be used to save time and expense and insure maximum dispatch.

Two devices "to narrow the field of testimony to those issues in which there is actual disagreement between the parties" were recommended by the Attorney General's Committee.[16] These are the prehearing conference and stipulations of fact. It found that a number of agencies, particularly the Civil Aeronautics Board, had used the former. It recommended the use of the latter to cover a portion of the issues, as was the practice of the National Labor Relations Board on issues of interstate commerce, as well as to cover the entire case, as in the Federal Trade Commission and other agencies.

Notable success has been achieved by the Interstate Commerce Commission in the use of the so-called shortened procedure under which sworn memoranda of fact and argument are substituted for the usual oral hearings. A memorandum by the complainant, an answer by respondent, and a reply by complainant supply the basis for an examiner's report, after which the procedure is the same as in formal cases heard orally. The shortened procedure is used only if designated by the Commission and accepted by the parties; upon the request of the Commission or any party at any stage prior to the service of the examiner's report, the case will be set for oral

---

[14] See *Final Report*, Appendix G, "Time Consumed in Reaching Administrative Decisions," 327-374.

[15] Rule making may be another means of conserving time. See pages 117-118.

[16] See *Final Report*, 64-68.

hearing. It has been said that this procedure, "through which, from its inauguration in 1923 to November 1, 1936, about a third of all formal complaints filed during that period have been handled, has proved to be a very acceptable method of conducting the more simple regulatory proceedings, with substantial savings of both time and expense." [17] Present rules also provide for "modified procedure" under which, if the case is set for hearing, the matters on which oral evidence will be taken are limited.[18]

Use of Staff Work

Another method is the use of staff work to gather data. Thus, in adjudicating a large number of small cases in the Veterans Administration, the Railroad Retirement Board, and the Federal Security Administration, the facts are accumulated by agency correspondence and investigation and used without cross-examination as part of the basis of decision.[19] In larger proceedings where economic data must form a large part of the basic factual record, the staff may gather much of the data prior to the hearing. Even though the facts so gathered are put on the record, time and expense are saved in use of staff research rather than the testimonial technique for pulling the facts together.

INFORMING ADMINISTRATIVE JUDGMENT

Whether formal or informal methods are employed, the objective must be an informed judgment. This is a basic purpose of procedure. It aids decision by providing for gathering and testing of facts and insuring that the decision will be made upon the basis of the facts and the applicable rules of law or policy.

It is not possible in brief span to analyze all aspects of the procedure for informing judgment. To insure informed judgments in administration it is necessary to use many techniques and safeguards both for gathering facts and for reaching decisions. Primarily, at-

---

[17] Sharfman, *The Interstate Commerce Commission,* IV, 226. Copyright 1937 by The Commonwealth Fund.

[18] Interstate Commerce Commission, *General Rules of Practice,* as adopted July 31, 1942, Rules 5 (j), 5 (k), 44 to 54.

[19] See Gellhorn's discussion, *op. cit.,* 102-105.

tention is focused in this section on the factual basis of decision.[20]

The judicial process has provided society with one technique for assembling and analyzing facts. It has been refined and tested more completely than any other technique, except perhaps the more recent laboratory technique of the natural sciences.

Nevertheless, it is only one of the techniques available to administration. Questionnaires, surveys, general inquiries, search in the files of the agency, expert knowledge of the staff, and other techniques may be used.[21] As a result, thorny questions concerning the place of the judicial hearing and the combination of techniques for informing judgment have arisen.

The Judicial Hearing

In the judicial hearing reliance is placed upon the testimonial process and the contest of adversaries. Sworn testimony, subjected traditionally to test by cross-examination, forms the factual basis for decision. The hearing is restricted to issues between opponents in interest, and these carry the burden of presenting testimony and showing its significance under applicable rules of law and policy.[22]

Since this type of procedure is especially adapted to decision on disputed facts and issues in application of law or policy to particular parties, it is frequently, though by no means always, required by law or allowed in practice if desired by parties, before a final adverse decision is entered. In regulatory administration a highly publicized example is the procedure used before cease and desist orders are issued. Here the charge of government against citizen produces an adversary relationship in which a judicial type of procedure is obviously required. A judicial hearing is also customary prior to final adverse decision in such varied proceedings as reparation cases, revocation of licenses and many other forms of disciplinary action, requirement of expenditure of money or

---

[20] The succeeding section focuses attention on the institutional process, which is the key factor in the process of reaching decisions.

[21] See pages 156-157 for a list of information-getting powers of administrative agencies.

[22] Where the facts are not in dispute the hearing will be more limited, but the adversary character of the proceedings is retained.

alteration of business organization or practice by individual concerns, and final denial of a license, permit, or benefit.

The basic essentials of the judicial hearing as they have been defined for administrative practice are

1. Notice to affected parties of action being considered;

2. Opportunity to know the claims of those in opposition and to
meet these with evidence and argument; and

3. Decision on the basis of the record made in the hearing.

Beyond this there are many points of detail and controversy.
Many of these center around the question as to the extent to which
administrative agencies should follow the rules of evidence in
courts. In general, it may be said that either by statute or judicial
acceptance most agencies are allowed considerable freedom from
rules of competency, relevancy, and materiality of evidence, reliance
being placed upon the skill and fairness of the agencies in determining what should be accepted and considered.[23] On the other
hand, the courts have guarded closely the requirement that all
facts which form the basis of decision must go on the record and
be subject to attack and reply, whether these facts come out of the
records of the agency or are a part of the expert knowledge of the
staff.

Other issues in controversy have related to the organization of
administration for the judicial hearing. These issues will be discussed
in the final section of this chapter.

Non-judicial Proceedings in Particular Cases

Objective Data. The greater proportion of particular decisions
of many administrative agencies will be based on tests, inspections,
or facts state on a form. In some situations there may be an occasional judicial hearing on appeal, but normally even appellate

[23] But while the original National Labor Relations Act provided that in proceedings before the N.L.R.B. relative to unfair labor practices "the rules of
evidence prevailing in courts of law or equity shall not be controlling," (Sec.
10 b), the amendments of 1947 provide that such proceedings shall "so far as
practicable" be conducted under the rules of evidence applicable in the district
courts of the United States.

administrative procedure would not involve a judicial type of hearing.

Test of a sample is the method used in determining appeals from grain inspectors' gradings. Grain is regularly graded by state or private inspectors, licensed by the national government. A dissatisfied buyer or seller may appeal to the Department of Agriculture. A supervising inspector in the department makes a decision on the basis of a new test made by him. A further appeal may be taken to a board of grain supervisors which makes a decision on the basis of its own test or that of the supervising inspector. No hearing with testimony and attorney's arguments is held, but a decision is made quickly on the basis of expert analysis of objective data. A right to a hearing before the Secretary of Agriculture is preserved by statute, but records showed only one such appeal in twenty-three years.[24]

There are many other cases where decision is based upon physical examination of person or inspection or test of property.[25] The conclusions of the Attorney General's Committee seem inescapable:[26]

The soundest procedure in cases of this type is that which recognizes the reality that the inspection is and must be the decisive element. . . .

Protection, in cases such as these, can be afforded by a right to reexamination or reinspection by another and more experienced inspector, far more than by any right to a formal hearing before an official who must merely listen to testimony.

[24] For a fuller analysis of the procedure see Attorney General's Committee, *The Administration of the Grain Standards Act*, 29-33. Procedure outlined in 7 CFR 26.46-26.65.

[25] For other examples see *Final Report*, 36-37. And for a particularly good summary of the necessity of basing administrative decisions on engineering data, without any hearing, see Kenneth Culp Davis and York Y. Willbern, "Administrative Control of Oil Production in Texas," *Texas Law Review*, XXII, 149, 157-159 (1944), and for fuller discussion Willbern's *Administrative Control of Petroleum Production in Texas* (Ph. D. Dissertation, The University of Texas, 1943), *passim*.

[26] *Final Report*, 37-38. Questions of a more difficult type are raised where, as in North American Cold Storage Co. *v.* Chicago, 221 U. S. 306 (1908), it seems necessary to destroy property before an administrative reexamination can be made. In such cases, a hearing can be held, if requested, to test the justification for the action which was taken.

Somewhat similar are many of the cases where decision is made on the basis of simple accounting data. Illustrative were applications for adjustment of individual prices in OPA days. Most of these could be determined by the balancing of figures. The main safeguard to individual and agency was perfection of the instructions to applicants and of the forms on which applications were made. Beyond this the individual was protected by agency practices of informing the applicant of additional information which was needed, of having agency accountants help prepare the data, and of allowing a right of appeal. Also, the doors of the agency were open for consultation; but this was of more value for good will and for belief in fairness than for information obtained.

Decision on the basis of data on a form is the most common of administrative methods. For the multitudes of men who do not appeal the first decision (or whose appeal must still be decided primarily on data from a form), the safeguard for correct decision lies in part in the efficiency and integrity of the person who examines the completed form, but also in the proficiency of those who devise the forms, for theirs is the task of seeing that the form brings the objective data needed for accurate decision. The form expert is, therefore, one of society's most valuable procedural technicians.

Administrative Investigation and Check. One example will show that there are other cases in which the judicial technique may not be considered useful or appropriate. Information for the decision of the Comptroller of the Currency on an application to establish a national bank is obtained largely through field investigation by an examiner. This investigation includes a study, among other things, of the community, the adequacy of existing banking facilities, and the business history of those who would serve as directors and officers of the bank. The basic information is acquired by officials who have a responsibility to go searching for the facts.

Although a monograph of the Attorney General's Committee was critical of the failure of the Comptroller to provide a precise statement of the grounds for disapproval of applications, it recognized that it would be undesirable, in view of the need "of securing frank and complete information from those who would be reluctant to speak if their identity were disclosed," to reveal "to the applicants all of the material adverse to them, including the names of informants." The following significant conclusion followed:[27]

In this instance, the protections customarily available in the form of cross-examination or of direct rebuttal must be replaced by the safeguards of careful checking by experienced investigators and of corroborative investigations by the Federal Reserve Banks and the F.D.I.C. . . . Particularly in this field of banking, where the matters to be decided rest not only on objective data, but also (and more importantly, perhaps) upon the experienced judgment of the Comptroller's ranking subordinates, a record made at a public hearing would have little practical value as a basis for subsequent review. And the investigative technique now in use is probably superior to the device of formal hearings as a method of obtaining necessary information, preliminary to decision.

Methods of Informing Judgment in Rule Making

Four methods of informing judgment in rule making may be distinguished, namely, institutional research and staff analysis, consultation, the legislative hearing, and the adversary hearing.

An example of the first is found in the practice of the Federal Reserve Board in general credit controls. The procedure is

almost wholly internal, based upon the special knowledge and research of the board and staff. Credit conditions are under constant scrutiny and study. Banks are required frequently to report such conditions, and a staff of economists in Washington, generally regarded as highly expert and able, analyzes credit and business conditions from day to day. By means of graphs and indices and general reports prepared by its staff, the Board is constantly informed of current situations and considers whether and what steps ought to be taken.[28]

Consultation with outside parties is illustrated in the practice of the Board in exercising another power—that of issuing regulations. After a tentative draft of a regulation is prepared it is customary to submit it to such organs as the Federal Reserve Banks (which may

---

[27] *Federal Control of Banking* (Sen. Doc. 186, 76th Cong., 3d Sess., 1940), 29-30. The full account of the procedure of the Comptroller will be found at pages 13-31.
[28] Attorney General's Committee, *The Federal Reserve System*, 20.

in turn submit it to banks and persons in their districts), the American Bankers' Association or its appropriate committee, the Federal Advisory Council (which is selected by the Boards of Directors of the Federal Reserve Banks), and interested governmental agencies. Two methods have been used by these organs to present their views, namely correspondence, and conferences or round table discussions, with members of the Federal Reserve Board's staff.[29]

Considerable variation exists among agencies in the form of consultation. A draft regulation may be sent to a selected list of persons. It may be discussed with advisory committees composed of interested parties. Or it may be circularized widely, through the trade press or otherwise, giving to a larger group an opportunity to make its views known.

Somewhat different is the legislative hearing, in that it is "publicly announced in advance and any interested party is permitted to attend and testify." [30]

The special nature of the legislative hearing should be noted. It is a general inquiry conducted preliminary to the promulgation of a general rule. The basic analogue is congressional procedure rather than judicial procedure. It may be very informal or it may be held under statutory requirements which give it a close resemblance to a judicial proceeding. But even then courts recognize the difference between the legislative and the judicial hearing. Thus, in Norwegian Nitrogen Products Co. v. U. S., the procedure of the Tariff Commission was attacked on the ground that evidence was kept secret and not subjected to cross-examination. The Supreme Court took note, among other things, of the legislative nature of the proceeding and held the procedure did not violate the statutory requirement that the Commission should give notice and "reasonable opportunity to parties interested to be present, to present evidence, and to be heard." [31] And in the Assigned Car Cases, where the claim was made

[29] *Ibid.*, 32-38. For a discussion which shows the extensive use of staff analysis, consultation with other government agencies, and consultation with private groups, see George L. Back, *Staff Report on the Federal Reserve System* (unpublished monograph prepared for the Hoover Commission), Part II. The discussion is illustrated by three examples in Appendix III.

[30] *Final Report*, 105.

[31] 288 U. S. 294 (1933).

that the evidence taken by the I.C.C. related to only a few carriers and was not shown to be typical, the Supreme Court upheld the procedure, saying[32]

In the case at bar, the function exercised by the Commission is wholly legislative. Its authority to legislate is limited to establishing a reasonable rule. But in establishing a rule of general application, it is not a condition of its validity that there be adduced evidence of its appropriateness in respect to every railroad to which it will be applicable. In this connection, the Commission, like other legislators, may reason from the particular to the general.

The legislative hearing may have quite different functions than the judicial hearing. The primary purpose may not be to gather and test facts, for these may be gathered largely by other processes and may not be available for challenge to all who are affected by the hearing. The purpose of the hearing may be to gain new viewpoints, to uncover resentments, to give persons a feeling that they have had a chance to be heard, or to aid in obtaining understanding and compliance with the rule to be adopted.

Different, however, is the adversary or judicialized legislative hearing. This has been judicially developed in rate-making cases. The courts developed the ideas, first, that decisions could not be upheld upon review unless based upon evidence in the record, and second, that evidence from the agency's files or elsewhere could not be used as a basis for decision if notice of use and opportunity to rebut had not been given to those rendering the service to the public. The requirements were further elaborated in the second appeal in Morgan *v.* U. S.[33] The Secretary of Agriculture had issued an order fixing maximum rates chargeable by market agencies at the Kansas City stock yards. Testimony was taken before an examiner, and findings were prepared for the Secretary by subordinate officials. But no tentative report on evidence was prepared by the examiner for submission to the parties, so that they would have an opportunity to make exceptions and address arguments to the points which governed decision. It was held in this case, *where the*

[32] 274 U. S. 564, 583 (1926).
[33] 304 U. S. 1 (1937).

Secretary himself did not hear the evidence and where no other means of focusing an issue was used, that the statutory mandate for a "full hearing" required that an intermediary report be prepared and an opportunity be given to answer claims made therein. "The right to a hearing," the Court declared, "embraces not only the right to present evidence but also a reasonable opportunity to know the claims of the opposing party and to meet them."

This requirement arose out of the Court's interpretation of the nature of the proceeding. It was said that the proceeding was not a general inquiry but was "of an adversary character," with the "Department prosecuting the proceeding against the owners of the market agencies." "The proceeding had all the essentials of contested litigation, with the Government and its counsel on the one side and the appellants and their counsel on the other. It is idle to say that this was not a proceeding in reality against the appellants when the very existence of their agencies was put in jeopardy."

The Procedural Problem in General Rule Making

It has been argued that one advantage of rule making was the opportunity for "objective responsibility" among administrators, arising from their adherence "to precedent, to expert opinion, and to professional ethics." [34] On the other hand, some have emphasized certain weaknesses of the administrative bodies in comparison with the Congress, such as the lack of breadth in knowledge and opinion which are possessed by a body representing a cross-section of the nation, the lack of responsiveness to public opinion, and the lack of awareness of political expediency.[35] And some have feared that sufficient protection might not be given to acquired property interests. The question arises, therefore, as to whether appropriate procedures can reduce the alleged dangers in rule making.

[34] James Hart in President's Committee on Administrative Management, *Report with Special Studies* (Washington, 1937), 324, with reference to Carl J. Friedrich, "Responsible Government Service under the American Constitution," in *Problems of the American Public Service* (New York, 1935), 37-38.

[35] See Ernst Freund, *Administrative Powers over Persons and Property* (Chicago, 1928), 220-223; J. Roland Pennock, *Administration and the Rule of Law* (New York, 1951), 47; Hart, *Report with Special Studies,* 337.

In the author's opinion, the answer can rarely, if ever, be found in a complete adoption of the judicialized hearing. First, such a procedure is ill-adapted to general rule making. The difficulty has been stated as follows:[36]

The issues are normally complex and numerous; the parties may be diverse and not alignable into classes; the outcomes will involve a judgment concerning the consequences of rules to be prescribed for the future and a discretion in devising measures to effectuate the policies of the statute. These factors differentiate these proceedings from the normal judicial trial in which adversary hearings are traditionally employed and accordingly limit the possibility of defining issues in advance, of addressing evidence to them, of permitting systematic cross-examination, and of stating the findings and conclusions fully.

Second, the procedure is too burdensome. Commenting on its use under three statutes, the Attorney General's Committee said:[37]

The record and exhibits lying back of the recent bituminous coal price order totaled over 50,000 pages; the trial examiner's report embraced approximately 2,800 pages in addition to exhibits, and the Director's report consisted of 545 single-spaced legal-size pages, exclusive of indices, annexes, and price appendices. Wage-order records under the Fair Labor Standards Act run from 600 to 10,000 pages each. The hearing process under the Food, Drug, and Cosmetic Act has required from 5 to 11 months for completion. The bituminous coal price order was issued more than two years after the present phase of the procedure leading to it was begun.

Unavoidably, and irrespective of what methods of gathering and testing data are used, the record of facts or file of data upon which decisions affecting the nation are based will often be large. The burden of the judicialized proceeding may be reduced by written submission of facts and arguments.[38] But still, the judicial

[36] *Final Report,* 109.

[37] *Final Report,* 110.

[38] See the suggestions of Ray A. Brown for written submission of data in public utility cases. "Public Service Commission Procedure—a Problem and a Suggestion," *University of Pennsylvania Law Review,* LXXXVII, 139, 160-164 (1938). Also Kenneth C. Davis, "An Approach to Problems of Evidence in the Administrative Process," *Harvard Law Review,* LV, 364, 402-410 (1942), in which it is argued that a distinction should be made between "legislative facts" and "adjudicative facts" and with recognition that "Briefs and oral arguments are often (though not always) better vehicles for presentation of legislative facts than testimony and documents."

hearing tends toward a record which is bulky and full of minutiae and encourages the extension of contest over numerous details of evidence. Third, in spite of the argument of the Attorney General's Committee that there are cases where persons with adversary interests can be depended on to bring in needed facts,[39] there is danger that overdependence on that method will lead to an impression that rule making is primarily a matter of private rather than public interest. The logic of the second Morgan decision, in which the making of a rate for the future is compared to a prosecution against individuals, may be wrong in theory and dangerous in result. Finally, adversary hearings in rule making may "strain a gnat" to protect a party on a particular and still leave the problem of responsive and expert solution of conflicts of interest.

What about the method of consultation with interested parties? Part of the answer is that it is often an essential means of informing the agency of the limits of regulation or of the technical or political effects of proposed policy. The rest of the answer is that it may be too narrow. It may fail to reach many of the private interests immediately affected by the rule, leading to an identification of the regulatory agency with the large and the near. Or it may fail to reach peripheral interests or persons representing the general public, leading to an identification of the agency with the regulated interests and a lack of responsiveness to public opinion.

It must be recognized that in many cases it is impossible to enlist interest in regulation outside of a small group. The rules relate to technical matters and lie outside the reach of public discussion. Breadth in agency research and viewpoint may, therefore, be more important than minute procedural safeguards.

Nevertheless, there is advantage in trying to reach a wider group. This may be done by broader notice. Publicity may be used to bring a proposed rule to the attention of diverse groups. The broader notice may be supplemented in cases by a legislative hearing. The effect of the hearing is to publicize the proposed action and to give a forum for discussion to all who are interested. It may be one means of reconciling specialization with democracy, of making

[39] *Final Report,* 108-109.

experts more sensitive to public opinion, and of checking the adequacy of institutional research in a broader forum.

It may be noted that such safeguards will usually be of value only if the agency has crystallized its thinking to the point that it can submit a proposal or alternative proposals for consideration. To make the legislative hearing meaningful the research must be substantially completed, the data organized, and the alternatives of decision defined.

The Administrative Procedure Act contains three main sets of provisions regarding proposed rule making. First, Section 4 (a) requires notice in the Federal Register of proposed general rule making with this set of exceptions:

Except where notice or hearing is required by statute, this subsection shall not apply to interpretative rules, general statements of policy, rules of agency organization, procedure, or practice, or in any situation in which the agency for good cause finds (and incorporates the finding and a brief statement of the reasons therefor in the rules issued) that notice and public procedure thereon are impracticable, unnecessary, or contrary to the public interest.

The exception in the words "impracticable, unnecessary, or contrary to the public interest" was essential. The need for speed or secrecy may make notice "impracticable" or "contrary to the public interest." [40] The minor or technical nature of an amendment may make notice "unnecessary" and "contrary to the public interest."

A question is left, however, by the requirement. If the agency can within its own discretion determine when notice shall not be given, then the necessary flexibility in administrative methods may be retained. If, on the other hand, the issue is one for judicial determination (and the use of the words "for good cause finds" may provide a basis for court jurisdiction), then the agencies may use the notice procedure when they believe it is unwise or unnecessary

---

[40] Normally, secrecy in public business is undesirable. But there are occasions on which notice of the possible amendment of a rule would disturb the markets in a manner that would be contrary to the public interest. In price and rationing control during World War II it was often necessary to keep prospective action secret in order to avoid private advantage and market disturbance.

in order to avoid the possibilities of court contest and of the setting aside of the rule.[41]

Second, Section 4 (b) provides:

After notice required by this section, the agency shall afford interested persons an opportunity to participate in the rule making through submission of written data, views, or arguments with or without opportunity to present the same orally in any manner; and, after consideration of all relevant matter presented, the agency shall incorporate in any rules adopted a concise general statement of their basis and purpose.

This provision leaves the agency the discretion as to whether to use the oral legislative hearing or limit the opportunity of participation to submission of written material. The requirement of a "general statement" of "basis and purpose" encourages careful consideration and gives the lawyers in an agency a legal basis for questioning the sufficiency of the showing of "basis and purpose." Will it, in addition, lead to court contest over the legality of stated "purpose" and the sufficiency of the showing of "basis"?

Third, Section 4 (b) provides that, instead of the above, the requirements in the act relative to adjudicatory hearings[42] shall apply "Where rules are required by statute to be made on the record after opportunity for an agency hearing."

The act indicates the impossibility of uniform prescription. It leaves much scope for adjustment of the rule-making process to practical need; the "$64 question" is, of course, whether the determination of these questions of practicality will be shifted into the arena of judicial contest.

ORGANIZING ADMINISTRATIVE OPERATIONS

In large agencies with extensive responsibilities attainment of the two objectives discussed in the preceding sections will require spe-

[41] See Nathaniel L. Nathanson, "Some Comments on the Administrative Procedure Act," *Illinois Law Review*, XLI, 368, 381-386 (1946). See also the statements in Senate and House Committee Reports, *Administrative Procedure Act, Legislative History*, 200 and 258.

[42] The Act says that the requirements of Sections 7 and 8 shall apply. There are some exceptions or qualifications applicable to rule making in these sections but, on the whole, the requirements are the same as for "adjudication."

cial arrangements in organization. For dispatch and economy delegation of duties is required, and to insure an informed judgment varied institutional resources must often be used and coordinated. The proper organization of administrative operations is, therefore, a requisite for administrative efficiency. What, we may now ask, have been some of the problems of efficiency and "fair play" to individuals which have arisen in organizing the work of administrative agencies?

Institutional Operations

A decision of the Supreme Court in 1936 in the first of the series of decisions in Morgan *v.* U. S. concentrated attention on two opposed modes of decision.[43] Where the statute had placed upon the Secretary of Agriculture the duty of setting rates for stockyards, the Court held that it was his duty personally to consider and appraise the evidence. This decision was based upon the Court's conclusion that the rate-making proceeding had "a quality resembling that of a judicial proceeding" and that the requirement of a "full hearing" in the statute had "obvious reference to the tradition of judicial proceedings in which evidence is received and weighed by the trier of facts." In such cases the Secretary has a duty "akin to that of a judge."

The judicial process has made us familiar with one mode of decision. It places authority to decide on persons and makes decision a personal responsibility.

Chief Justice Hughes, for the Court, took note of another type of process. He said there was "no basis for the contention that the authority conferred . . . is given to the Department of Agriculture, as a department in the administrative sense, so that one official may examine evidence, and another official who has not considered the evidence may make the finding and the order." The alternative process referred to is the institutional process, in which responsibility is not personal but institutional, and the name of an official on a rule

[43] 298 U. S. 468.

or order merely shows that the organization has considered and decided.[44]

We have seen that the distinguishing feature of administration is the use of organization to get jobs done. This is, of course, obvious where action must be taken on a mass of particulars. In such cases, tasks are spread downward, performed at various levels in the organization, and only the unusual case sifts to the top.

Nevertheless, certain aspects of organization for performance of volume jobs are often overlooked. First, legal distinctions as to type of function are not significant. Decisions are made throughout the hierarchy of organization and by quick, often by routine, process, without reference to whether they are "adjudicatory" or "administrative" in nature. Second, the decisions may require teamwork among a group of officials or may be made by a single official; but in either case decision is not significant as an exercise of personal responsibility, but signifies a sharing of the organization's responsibility. The decision is that of an organization. The individual responsibility is exclusively to the organization for doing the job assigned according to the rules and habits governing the organization or the proper standards of organizational behavior.

Institutional operations also are characteristic of policy making. This may be illustrated by a relatively simple example. In OPA a number of amendments to rationing regulations were issued each week. These went to the Federal Register over the name of the Administrator. But he never read the amendments, had personal knowledge of the general contents of only a few, and his name was affixed by the Secretary. The Secretary affixed his name automatically if the initials of the head or assistant head of the Rationing Department were on the clearance sheet. Back of this stood the

[44] For a careful analysis of this type of decision, see Kenneth Culp Davis, "Institutional Administrative Decisions," *Columbia Law Review*, XLVIII, 173-201 (1948). See also Walter Gellhorn, *op. cit.*, 25 ff. Speaking of certain propositions to be kept in mind, Gellhorn said: "The first is that an administrative agency ought not to be personalized. It is not comparable to an individual, but is a highly complicated and organized structure of many men and many parts." *Federal Administrative Proceedings*, 25. Copyright 1941 by The Johns Hopkins Press.

contribution of many persons. Lawyers, business specialists, special analysts, and operations officers had participated at the branch level. Consultation had occurred with officials at division, department, or agency levels, and usually also with officials in other agencies. An advisory committee or selected contacts in industry might have been consulted. In the end, a clearance sheet carried the approval of branch, division, and department executives, of attorneys, of persons responsible for banking and currency operations in rationing, and of those responsible for local board and field office administration.

There is danger that the implications of what is obvious and recurrent in administrative policy making will be overlooked. What affects the welfare of 150,000,000 people is usually too big to entrust to a person. Organization is an expansive technique—it makes it possible to match bigness of problem with sufficiency of analysis. Moreover, the clearance sheet is evidence of the sometimes friendly effects of administrative tape. It records that nothing has been overlooked, that all the experts have been consulted, that there is unity within the organization on the final solution.[45]

Institutional operations have also developed in formalized case-to-case administration. The pattern as it had developed by 1940 in cease and desist proceedings in the F.T.C. and N.L.R.B. may be generally summarized.[46] First, there was a preliminary investigation

[45] An indication of the lack of recognition of the institutional nature of administrative processes is apparent in the following extreme statement of Justice Roberts in his dissent in Bowles *v.* Willingham, 321 U. S. 503, 537 (1944), in which the Supreme Court upheld rent control provisions of the Emergency Price Control Act against the charge that too much authority was delegated to the Administrator. "Without further elaboration it is plain that this Act creates *personal* government by a petty tyrant instead of government by law. Whether there shall be a law prescribing maximum rents anywhere in the United States depends solely on the administrator's *personal* judgment. When that law shall take effect, how long it shall remain in force, whether it shall be modified, what territory it shall cover, whether the different areas shall be subject to different regulations, what is the nature of the activity that shall motivate the institution of the law,—all these matters are buried in the *bosom of the Administrator* and nowhere else." (my italics) A very large bosom indeed! And a great vacuum in the Rent Department of OPA!

[46] The summaries are based largely on Attorney General's Committee on Administrative Procedure, *The Federal Trade Commission* (Sen. Doc. 186,

to determine whether there was sufficient evidence of violation of law to justify a complaint.[47] In the F.T.C. the basic work was done in the Chief Examiner's Division;[48] its recommendation was studied by a commissioner who reported to the Commission, which made the decision on issuance of a complaint. In the N.L.R.B. the basic work was done by the regional office, which transmitted a recommendation to Washington, where it was considered in the Secretary's Office, which might authorize issuance of a complaint or refer the issue to the Board. In any event, whether in the Chief Examiner's Division of the F.T.C. or the regional office or national office of the N.L.R.B., a number of persons with different duties participated in the process. And in either agency there might have been settlement along the road by informal methods. Second, there was a hearing on the complaint before a trial examiner. In both the F.T.C. and the N.L.R.B. he was assigned from a trial examiners' division composed of persons having this function exclusively. In the F.T.C. the case against the defendant was presented by public counsel assigned from the Chief Counsel's office, while in the N.L.R.B. the case was prosecuted by someone from the office of the Regional Attorney.[49] The hearing before the trial examiner followed the judicial pattern, except that it was "somewhat more flexible than procedure at law."[50] In the N.L.R.B. briefs and oral arguments followed the taking of testimony, after which the trial examiner prepared an intermediate report containing findings of fact and recommendations for decision. In the F.T.C. there was no presentation of briefs and no oral argument at this stage, and the examiner

---

76th Cong., 3d Sess., 1940) and *National Labor Relations Board* (Sen. Doc. 10, 71st Cong., 1st Sess., 1941).

[47] In proceedings under the Federal Trade Commission Act it was necessary also to determine whether a proceeding was in the "interest of the public" for this is a statutory prerequisite to a complaint. See F.T.C. *v.* Klesner, 280 U. S. 19 (1929).

[48] Except that a great volume of false and misleading advertising cases were handled in the Radio and Periodical Division.

[49] It was the practice in the N.L.R.B. to make the parties who filed charges parties to the complaint also. Attorney General's Committee, *National Labor Relations Board*, 30.

[50] Attorney General's Committee, *The Federal Trade Commission*, 42, and *National Labor Relations Board*, 36-47.

prepared a report on the facts but no recommendations. In both cases the examiner's report was served on the parties and submitted to the Commission or Board. Third, there were further proceedings to inform the Commission or Board. In both agencies written exceptions to the trial examiner's report would be filed, briefs submitted, and oral argument presented. The Commission was aided by a full analysis by a single commissioner, and might also ask for aid from the Chief Counsel.[51] The Board was aided, both before and after the oral hearing, by a review attorney and his superiors in the Review Division. The review attorney prepared an analysis of the case[52] and reviewed it with the Board prior to the oral hearing, made a report to the Board after the hearing, and prepared a draft of the decision when this was made.

Features of this process have been typical of formal case-to-case administration, whether there was a charge of law violation or a regulatory decision as in rate making. Preliminary examination has provided opportunity to dismiss or settle informally. When cases are set for hearing, the examiner is the central figure in many agencies. The final decision has been made with the aid of review attorneys and other staff experts.

The decision in the first Morgan Case did not undo all of this. It had, of course, no meaning except for case-to-case administration where the process had "a quality resembling that of a judicial proceeding"—an exceedingly vague area. Even there it did not prevent staff conduct of preliminary investigations nor the use of examiners and other technical aid. The Court said that its rule did not "preclude practicable administrative procedure in obtaining the aid of assistants in the department. Assistants may prosecute inquiries. Evidence may be taken by an examiner. Evidence thus taken may be sifted and analyzed by competent subordinates."[53] Thus, the

---

[51] "The Chief Counsel . . . does not confer with members of his staff who have previously been connected with the case." Attorney General's Committee, *The Federal Trade Commission*, 56.

[52] The review attorney sometimes sought the advice of the Division of Economic Research on technical questions of labor relations and also sometimes consulted at this stage with his supervisor. Attorney General's Committee, *National Labor Relations Board*, 59-60.

[53] 298 U. S. 468, 481.

Supreme Court accepted, to a large extent, the necessities of institutional process. All it required was a final personal examination by the department head. Even this became only a rule of administrative guidance and not a judicially enforceable practice, where the record itself did not reveal the extent of personal examination. This was the result of the decision in the Fourth Morgan Case. After the district court had put the Secretary on the stand to determine whether he had made the examination required by the Supreme Court's rule, the Supreme Court said "the Secretary should never have been subjected to this examination." [54]

Elsewhere a more sweeping attack has been made on the institutional process in adjudicatory proceedings. The Bar Association Committee favored both the elimination of staff aid in the final process of decision and of the exercise of judgment by the decider as to the extent to which he personally should examine the record. It proposed: "All hearing, deciding, or reviewing officers shall personally consider the whole or such parts of the record as are cited by the parties, with no other aid than that of clerks, or assistants who perform no other duties; and no such officer, clerk, or assistant shall consult with or receive oral or written comment, advice, data, or recommendations respecting any such case from other officers or employees of the agency or from third parties." [55]

It has been said that "This proposal seems wholly irresponsible." [56] Nevertheless, the limitations on staff aid were incorporated in the Labor Management Relations Act. Referring to the N.L.R.B., it provided:[57]

The Board may not employ any attorneys for the purpose of reviewing transcripts of hearings or preparing drafts of opinions except that any attorney employed for assignment as a legal assistant to any Board member may for such Board member review such transcripts and prepare such drafts. No trial examiner's report shall be reviewed, either before or after its publication, by any person other than a member of the Board or his

[54] U. S. v. Morgan, 313 U. S. 409, 422 (1941).
[55] Proposed Federal Administrative Act, Section 7d, 30 A. B. A. J. 226, 228 (1944).
[56] Kenneth Culp Davis, "Institutional Administrative Decisions," *Columbia Law Review*, XLVIII, 173-201, at p. 197 (1948).
[57] Title I, Section 4 (a).

legal assistant, and no trial examiner shall advise or consult with the Board with respect to exceptions taken to his findings, rulings, or recommendations.

Thus, the system which had been developed in the Board for review attorneys, with the help of other staff members, to aid in the process of decision was destroyed; aid could come only from persons isolated from the rest of the organization.

Moreover, the Attorney General's Committee recommended a system which it believed would allow the elimination of review staffs, except for legal assistants, and insure the mastery of the record by agency heads. In regard to the function of the legal assistants and the duty of the agency heads, it said: "But these assistants should be aides and not substitutes. The heads of the agency should do personally what the heads purport to do." Their review of the case "should include a personal mastery of at least the portions of the records embraced within the exceptions." [58]

The system which the Committee thought could accomplish these results was one of delegated responsibility.

Institutional Decisions and Institutional Delegation

The decision in the first Morgan Case placed the government in an absurd position. The effect of the Court's rule has been summarized as follows:[59]

The Secretary of Agriculture administers forty-two regulatory statutes. In addition, he administers a host of non-regulatory statutes, some of them, like the Soil Conservation and Domestic Allotment Act, of high national importance. Finally, he is a major political officer and takes part in the formulation of national policy as a member of the Cabinet. If he were to give to every order which he signs the consideration which the Morgan case requires, he would probably have to devote all his time to the conduct of matters which must be considered petty from a national viewpoint.

How escape from this situation? First, it would appear to be unwise to try to solve it by transferring functions from departments

---

[58] *Final Report,* 52. And see pages 243-244.
[59] A. H. Feller, "Prospectus for the Further Study of Federal Administrative Law," *Yale Law Journal,* XLVII, 647, 662 (1938).

to commissions. The same problem exists in commissions with large responsibilities. They are, in fact, overwhelmed with decisions on particular cases. To solve this problem by placing government "in commission" would entail the multiplication of commissions and would increase the difficulties of over-all coordination.[60]

Can it be solved by delegation within the departments or commissions? In part, this would seem to be the answer. Its value, however, might not rest in the elimination of the institutional decision, but rather in the greater freedom it would give to top administrators to plan broadly. One evil in big administration is the failure to shake particulars away from top officials.

Delegation of authority within the agency is now a familiar technique in case-to-case proceedings. In the I.C.C. authority to make decisions has been delegated, subject to reconsideration by the whole Commission, to divisions of the Commission under statutory authority reaching back to 1917; and similar delegations have been made to single commissioners since statutory authorization was given in 1933. The F.C.C. tried but abandoned the use of divisions. The N.L.R.B. has delegated authority to divisions of three members under authorization given in the Labor Management Relations Act of 1947.[61] The Schwellenbach Act gave the Secretary of Agriculture the authority to delegate regulatory power, and such delegation has been made, to a judicial officer.[62]

The Attorney General's Committee recommended delegation of the authority to make initial decisions in adjudicatory proceedings to examiners (called hearing commissioners in the *Final Report*).[63] This was to be the solution provided in the Administrative Procedure Act for rule making and adjudication where statute required that decision be made on the record after opportunity for hearing.[64]

But delegation to examiners may not always be an appropriate

[60] On this problem, see Chapter X.
[61] For discussion of panelization on commissions see Commission on Organization of the Executive Branch (Hoover Commission), *Task Force Report on Regulatory Commissions*, 50.
[62] See page 303.
[63] *Final Report*, 50-51, 244.
[64] See page 212.

solution. For one thing, there is the question of the actual weight and finality of the decision of a subordinate authority. Will parties accept its decision as final? Or will more acceptance be obtained if the order is issued in the name of the agency head? Would the examiner's decision have even less force if he were attached to a bureau? And would there be a relaxation of responsibility if there was no consideration or review from higher officials.[65]

But bigger questions arise. Those above do not seem too significant where law and policy are so definite that the examiner's decision on particular applications may be expected to follow lines which will almost always be approved upon appeal. But where there is a lack of clarity in the law and policy which guides in particular decisions or where the case method is used to make decisions of large and broad import, other questions combine with those above.

First, there is the problem of agency unity. Can unity be maintained without central review before decision? Will the agencies get into difficulties because of internal divisions which are revealed? Will the issues on which there is appeal become issues for battle in the wider arena in which agencies are fought? Will these difficulties be accentuated if the examiners have a large measure of independence, as recommended by the Attorney General's Committee? Any agency will desire to avoid the weakening effects of a public exhibition of disunity, and the public will not often benefit from the airing of differences which can be resolved by institutional study and internal collaboration.

Second, in matters of large import where decision is based upon complex fact situations and policy considerations, no single right answer may appear from the record. The judgment of men may differ on the choice among alternatives. In such cases, should not procedure aim at a single authoritative decision, rather than a decision correctable from above?

Third, is the examiner the proper recipient for delegated authority where issues of policy are mixed with those of law application? The examiner's responsibility ends with decision of the particular

[65] Questions of this kind were raised by Feller, *op. cit.*, 662-663.

case; he does not have to assume continuous responsibility for the results of a course of decision. If gaps in policy are really present and the economic effects of decisions are extensive, then delegation within a department or commission should probably go to bureau or division chiefs who carry over-all responsibility for a segment of the control program.

Irrespective, however, of the extent and locus of delegation, one fact remains. Decision on significant issues of economic policy such as are now often handled by case-to-case methods require team-work. Examiners or bureau chiefs will need the aid of other persons. It is not merely the overloading of agency heads which creates the need for institutional collaboration; it is, in addition, the extent of the effects and the dangers of inadequacy in the projection of a single mind forward into the area of economic effects that produce the need at any level of authoritative decision on significant issues for the collaboration of men of complementary competencies. Delegation may allow some single person to assume final mastery of the whole case, as was desired by the Attorney General's Committee; but it cannot always avoid the need for aid to that person from other persons in the agency, as was assumed in the Bar Association's recommendation.

But even the ideal of the Attorney General's Committee may not be universally applicable in administration. Delegation is not a universal remedy for the problems of big administration. The heads of agencies may for good reasons hold the decisional power at the top, even in some cases where case-to-case administration is used. If so, the head may have to use trusted assistants to make decisions which go over his name. The safeguard in such cases would not lie in what the head could do himself but in his ability to insure the competency of staff work in the final, as well as the preliminary, stages of institutional decision.

Separation of Functions

In spite of the facts noted above, much progress has been made in the separation of judicial and quasi-judicial from other functions through the use of examiners. Moreover, it has been generally recognized that one type of official should not participate in the making of an agency decision. Where the procedure is really of an adversary nature and officials in the agency act as advocates on one side of the case, then it has been regarded as a requirement of good practice and "fair play" not to allow those who act as advocates to assist or advise those who decide.

In the generation of development which preceded the passage of the Administrative Procedure Act, administrative practice had moved toward a full separation of the judicial functions in the subordinate staffs of the agencies. The pattern included features noted above in the discussion of the F.T.C. and the N.L.R.B.[66] First, the full record of testimony was made before an examiner, who served in a division which—whatever its name—was really a hearing division. Except in small agencies where it was impracticable, the examiner performed no other duties except those of hearing officer. Second, members of the prosecuting staff were not consulted by the examiners concerning the disposition of the case. Third, attempts were made to immunize the examiners from the prosecuting staff. In addition to staff training on this matter, special arrangements were made. In the N.L.R.B. the examiners went out from the national office; the prosecutors were from a regional office. Attempts were made in some agencies to assign examiners and prosecutors so that the same men performing the two functions did not work together regularly, or even to prevent the two men from travelling together. Although there were variations, and some departures from these standards, tendency had crystallized in the direction of separation.

The position of the examiner varied. In some agencies he merely presided; in others he exercised a strong control in the development of the record.[67] In some, he could recommend a decision; in others, he only made findings of fact.[68]

[66] Pages 202-204.

[67] Note the contrast between the F.T.C. and the N.L.R.B. Attorney General's Committee, *The Federal Trade Commission*, 37-38, and *National Labor Relations Board*, 36-39.

[68] These differences are shown in our discussion above at pages 202-204 on the F.T.C. and the N.L.R.B.

At the agency level, practice had moved in the direction of using for assistance in analysis of fact and preparation of opinions only persons who had not participated as advocates in the earlier proceedings. Though a general counsel's office might aid in the process of decision, persons in the office who had served as prosecutors would not be allowed to participate.[69]

Many thought that further safeguards should be provided. Some desired a separation of judicial functions from the agencies.[70] Others desired only to confirm the tendency for separation of functions in the subordinate staff. Although a minority of the Attorney General's Committee desired "adjudication by wholly independent agencies" in issues between the government and private parties, the majority sought only to strengthen the examiner's position. It proposed that an independent office participate in their selection and removal, that they have full control of the hearing, and that their decisions "should be final and binding" unless the case were called up for review by the head or heads of the agency.

The Administrative Procedure Act

The Administrative Procedure Act contained provisions relating to the separation of functions, the delegation of power and use of examiners, and the institutional process.

First, the provisions in regard to separation of functions and the institutional process (contained in Section 5[c]) extend only to adjudication "required by statute to be determined on the record after opportunity for an agency hearing" and those in regard to delegation and use of examiners (contained in Sections 7 and 8) only to adjudication or to rule making "required by statute . . . on the record after opportunity for an agency hearing."[71] They do

---

[69] G. C. Henderson's findings concerning the participation of trial counsel in preparation of findings of the F.T.C. must have had an influence toward the later practices on separation in the F.T.C. and other agencies. *The Federal Trade Commission* (1924), 85-86.

[70] See Chapter X.

[71] Section 4 (b). Further exclusions from particular provisions will be noted in the discussion which follows. See also the exclusion of certain matters in Section 5 and to the Act itself in the definition of "Agency" in Section 2 (a).

not apply to rule making generally, to most grants of licences, nor to many other types of informal or semi-formal "adjudication." [72]

Second, the position of the examiners (today called "Hearing Examiners" in civil service nomenclature) is strengthened. They are "to perform no duties inconsistent with their duties and responsibilities as examiners," can be removed only "for good cause" determined by the Civil Service Commission "after opportunity for hearing upon the record thereof," shall receive "compensation prescribed by the Commission independent of agency recommendations or ratings," shall have broad powers in the conduct of hearings, and as noted below may exercise a substantial delegated authority. It may be, however, that the independence from agency control provided to examiners will be a practical limitation on agency willingness to delegate.[73]

Third, as to delegation the Act avoids prescription of a single system. On the one hand, it authorizes initial decision by examiners who preside at hearings. On the other hand, this system is not required of an agency. The board or executive who heads the agency may preside at the hearing. If an examiner presides, the agency may "in specific cases or by general rule" require that the record be certified to it for initial decision. A member of the agency (i. e., member of a commission or board) may preside instead of an examiner. Moreover, the statutory authority of agencies, such as the I. C. C., to use boards or other officers for hearings and initial decisions is preserved. Also, in the broad category of cases, including rule making, exempted from the requirement of separation of functions, any officer qualified to preside at hearings, whether or not he was the presiding officer in the case, may make the intial decision.[74]

It is contemplated that the hearing officer who does not make the initial decision shall recommend a decision, as was the practice in some agencies. But the applicability of the provision is limited in

[72] See the definition of "adjudication" as "including licensing" in Section 2 (d).
[73] On the issue of independence see Chapter X.
[74] See Sections 7 (a) and 8 (a).

the case of rule making or determining applications for initial licenses.[75]

Thus the Act leaves much discretion to an agency in solving the problems of delegation discussed in a section above and after a period of years a study of experience should be helpful.

Fourth, in addition to giving an independent position to the examiner, the Act in famed Section 5 (c) seeks to embody into law the past tendencies on separation of functions among subordinate personnel. In general,[76] it provides (1) that the initial or recommended decision shall be made by the officer who presided at the hearing, (2) that such officers shall not consult with "any person or party" except upon notice and opportunity for all parties to participate, (3) that hearing officers shall not be subject to supervision or direction from officers engaged in investigative or prosecuting functions, and (4) that investigative and prosecuting officers shall not participate or advise on decisions except as counsel or witnesses.

The application of the provision is limited, however, in that it does not apply to (1) rule making, (2) "determining applications for initial licenses," (3) "proceedings involving the validity or application of rates, facilities, or practices of public utilities or carriers," nor (4) to participation by the agency or its members.

It may be said that the provisions will in instances require more than has been crystallized in agency practice and in other cases will require less than agencies themselves have required.

Fifth, what does the Act do in regard to institutional decisions in cases of "adjudication required by statute to be determined on the record after opportunity for an agency hearing"? On the one hand,

---

[75] Section 8 (a) provides: "Whenever the agency makes the initial decision without having presided at the reception of the evidence, such officers shall first recommend a decision except that in rule making or determining applications for initial licenses (1) in lieu thereof the agency may issue a tentative decision or any of its responsible officers may recommend a decision or (2) any such procedure may be omitted in any case in which the agency finds upon the record that due and timely execution of its function imperatively and unavoidably so requires."

[76] For qualifications see Section 5 (c).

it does not prevent the use of review attorneys or other aides where the decision is made by the agency nor does it require any degree of mastery of evidence by the agency. The institutional decision remains unencumbered at the agency level.[77] On the other hand, the language of the Act apparently isolates the examiner from staff aid in all cases where Section 5(c) applies, for this provision says that no hearing officer "shall consult any person or party on any fact in issue unless upon notice and opportunity for all parties to participate." It has been argued, however, that "the general objective and the legislative history" of the Act show a strong case for interpretation of the words "person or party" as not being intended to exclude staff members; and that "from the standpoint of practical desirability, the reasons in favor of permitting the examiner to consult other members of the staff are overwhelming." [78]

Litigation will solve the issue of interpretation. But it will be recalled that we have urged that matters of large import involving decision which will have extensive economic effects will not ordinarily be delegated to officers who cannot receive staff aid. All matters of this type are probably not exempted from Section 5 (c). Perhaps the independent position of the examiner and his lack of responsibility for total results will prevent the delegation of such matters; but in addition to these limitations on delegation it would seem that extensive delegation to examiners, which seems to be a purpose of the Act, will be limited if teamwork is not possible.

The Hoover Commission

We have been led in this discussion, unavoidably we think, down the narrow bypaths of procedure and through the crisscrossing paths of adjudicatory proceedings and rule making "on the record after opportunity for an agency hearing." We think, however, that through all this discussion the fact stands out that the network of procedure is understandable only in terms of its total character,

---

[77] Kenneth Davis has noted that a remark of the House Committee is inconsistent with such a conclusion, but he sufficiently answers the point made by the Committee. "Institutional Administrative Decisions," *Columbia Law Review*, XLVIII, 173, 186-188 (1948).

[78] *Ibid.*, 199.

which is the unfolding of institutional process, the allotment of institutional functions, and the adaptation of the work of pieces of structure to the institutional system of which they are a part.

The Hoover Commission and its task force on regulatory commissions lifted their vision above the intricacies of the network of procedure and charted some trunk highways into which the by-paths must lead. They struck at the problem of organizing institutional resources in a more effective manner.

The task force advanced four major suggestions for better internal operation of the regulatory commissions.[79] First, it emphasized that it was the basic responsibility of the heads of an agency to define standards and plan the regulatory program. Since the case-by-case method was "extremely costly in time and effort," the commissions "should make a more strenuous effort to clarify and establish governing criteria." This would have the advantage of

1. Assuring more equal treatment,
2. Materially relieving the commissions in the handling of their work load, and
3. Facilitating delegation.

But "standards for specific situations . . . should be part of a general program of regulation." And the time of commissioners was "so occupied in disposing of the daily case load that they had little chance to consider the program of the agency as a whole or to decide where its time and resources can be expended to the best advantage." For this there were many possible causes, including reliance on judicial types of procedure; the remedies suggested were delegation and provision for the aid of a small staff unit for planning and research.

Second, the task force proposed that housekeeping duties and administrative supervision of the bureaus and divisions of the commissions should be made the responsibility of the chairmen but that this work should be done for them by an executive officer. This proposal for a way of delegating internal managerial responsibility in commissions is merely a reflection of the larger administrative

[79] *Task Force Report on Regulatory Commissions*, 39-55.

principle that the time of administrators responsible for program should be conserved by delegation of auxiliary and preliminary tasks. This leaves open the question of the extent and method of delegating authority for program decisions.

Third, it was proposed that the staff experts be grouped in bureaus *according to the major functions of the agency* rather than according to professional skills. Although the task force did not comment on this aspect of the problem, this suggestion provides an alternative or complement to delegation to examiners. The opinion of lawyers and the trend in legislation on procedure have been toward delegation of decisional authority to semi-independent persons with specialized professional skill; the suggestion of the task force would lead to the creation of strong bureaus or divisions which could serve as centers for decision based upon the complementary contribution of the experts within the bureau. Examiners, when used under this system, could report to the division chief, and the larger responsibilities outlined for examiners in the Administrative Procedure Act might be assumed in part by the division chiefs.

Fourth, the task force noted that "the formal quasi-judicial hearing is an expensive or clumsy device for obtaining necessary information and the fruitful exchange of views" and recommended greater use of conference techniques. The Hoover Commission expressed its concern over procedure in general terms:[80]

> The Commission makes no comment as to the fairness of existing administrative procedures, but the Commission is concerned with the growth of cumbersome and costly administrative procedures. All of this detail is not required for "due process," or essential for fair and full solution of the various problems.

Thus, while the lawyers have been concerned over the internal arrangements for contribution of specialized groups to institutional decisions in particular cases, and have desired to regularize or restrict this in formal case-to-case administration, the Hoover Commission and its task force on regulatory commissions have looked at the over-all use of agency resources and have suggested straight-line delegation to officials in the chain of administrative responsi-

---

[80] *Regulatory Commissions*, 10.

bility and the use of methods of operation which would delimit the use of the case-to-case approach. The two approaches are complementary, but improvement along the lines suggested by the task force would reduce the area in which the lawyers' questions would have significance.

CONCLUSION

This chapter shows the complexity of operating methods in administrative action and the necessity for adjusting these methods to varying factors. This is especially true in economic control where the variety of situations is so great, where the decisions vary from the minutest detail to broad managerial judgment, where factual records must be supplemented by discretionary judgment, and where organization is the expedient for disposing of volume and informing judgment on big problems.

Although statutory directive and judicial corrective have played a part, the agencies themselves had, in the main, prior to 1946 developed the modern system of administrative operations. The process had been experimental. Yet the trends were unmistakable. Agencies sought methods of informal disposal. Formal processes were, to a large extent, held in reserve, to be used on appeal or request, or as a supplementary method of gathering and testing data. Institutional teamwork was the chief feature of the administrative process, but was accompanied by a trend toward separation of judicial tasks in the subordinate organization and toward use of "orthodox trial techniques" in cases with adversary characteristics.[81]

About a decade ago a movement for statutory directive on procedure gained force. The American Bar Association and the Attorney General's Committee proposed legislation. Some wanted to require that adjudicatory proceedings be "cast in the judicial mold," and the Logan-Walter Bill, which was vetoed by President Roosevelt, "rested solidly on this proposition." [82] In the preparation of a new bill account was taken of the diversities and peculiarities of the

[81] *Final Report*, 61.
[82] Gellhorn, *Federal Administrative Proceedings*, 44. Copyright 1941 by the Johns Hopkins Press.

administrative process, which had been revealed in the study of the Attorney General's Committee. Attorney General Clark sought to reconcile the differences between the administrative agencies and the Congressional committees, which initially had shared the views of the severe critics of the administrative process. The result was the Administrative Procedure Act of 1946.

Although the effects of the Act cannot be foretold yet, a few comments can be made. It accepts diversity in administrative procedure. Adjudicatory proceedings are required in rule making only where statute requires decision on the record; otherwise, only notice and some form of opportunity to present views is required, and this may be avoided by findings that it is "impracticable, unnecessary, or contrary to the public interest." In adjudicatory proceedings, agencies are left much discretion about delegation to examiners and exceptions are made to the requirements for separation of functions. On the other hand, there is basis for concern about the effects of the Act. Some provisions will mean increased work for agencies.[83] The independence of examiners from agency control may limit their utility in large or novel proceedings. There are many uncertainties concerning the requirements of the Act.[84] Where qualifications or exceptions to stated procedure are allowed in the Act agencies may feel constrained to follow the stricter procedure (even though regarded as unrealistic) to avoid judicial test over whether the action fell within the qualification or exception.[85] The most serious uncertainty is the extent to which litigation will be encouraged over procedural questions.

There is room for doubt as to whether it would "have been better

[83] See comments of Bradford Ross in George Warren, ed., *Federal Administrative Procedure Act and the Administrative Agencies* (New York, 1947), 191-195.

[84] The uncertainties are revealed on page after page of the comments of representatives of the agencies in George Warren, ed., *The Federal Administrative Procedure Act and the Administrative Agencies.*

[85] E.g., notice may be given in rule making even though the agency thinks it is "contrary to the public interest" or an agency may give a party another chance rather than revoke a license even though it thinks the revocation would be in the public interest. See Section 9(b), second sentence, and the comments on the sentence in Warren, *op. cit.*, 540-542.

to move forward with the development of a 'common law' of administrative procedure through the sharing of experience and the adaptation of procedure to substantive approach rather than to try to partially 'codify' at a midway point." [86] But whatever the answer to this question, it may still be that the adaptation of operating method will be largely an administrative responsibility. Moreover, it appears that the problem should be studied continuously by some agency of government. Such an agency might take a new start on the problem of procedure. It might search for ways of expediting public business—from routine performance to rate making. It might, agency by agency, ask: do present institutional processes result in more delay than is necessary to get an informed judgment? What expedients of delegation can be employed without loss of unity?

Proposals for continuous study of administrative methods have been made by recent investigating groups. The Attorney General's Committee proposed an Office of Federal Administrative Procedure, headed by a board composed of two ex-officio members of the judiciary and a Director of Federal Administrative Procedure; a major function of the latter would be to study administrative practice and procedure.[87] The task force on regulatory commissions also proposed such an office, to be located in the Executive Office of the President, and to "analyze organization, procedure, and methods." The Hoover Commission itself recommended that the Bureau of the Budget "should, with the aid of carefully selected legal consultants, suggest ways and means to improve and thereby reduce the cost of disposing of business before administrative agencies." [88]

The Hoover Commission has placed the problem of regulatory operations in the proper perspective. It is a division of the problem of administrative management. But legal experts need to be brought into company with management experts. The "science of management" and the "science of law" should meet in the larger study of all aspects of getting public jobs done.

[86] My review of Warren, *op. cit., The Southwestern Social Science Quarterly,* XXIX, 167-168 (September, 1948).

[87] *Final Report,* 123.

[88] *Regulatory Commissions,* 10-11.

Chapter IX

The Problem of the Interest Groups

GENERAL ASPECTS OF THE PROBLEM

Administrative agencies are created to put into effect public purposes, that is, purposes set by the organs of government representing the whole public and presumed to accord in some way with the interests of the public generally. Society, on the other hand, is split into economic groups, each having its own interests and each seeking to protect or advance such interests. The relations between administrative agencies—operating under the concept of the public interest, and the economic groups—with their preoccupation with their own ends, give rise to the most difficult problems in public administration.

The administrative mechanism is intertwined with the contest of interests in myriad ways. Interests demand and oppose its creation, expansion, and invigoration. They contest in legislative halls over its purposes, powers, and methods. Once established, it becomes a potential center of influence on the gains and losses and the power and freedom of the interests. They seek, therefore, to control or evade its operations, to obtain its favor, or to mitigate their subjection to it. Inevitably, the administrative mechanism occupies some kind of position in the push and tug of interests.

220

In this interplay between administration and interests it is the group interest which has weight. Single individuals or concerns will have interests in administrative action; but such interests may have a temporary impact, be absorbed entirely in administrative procedure, or be too weak to affect the trend of administrative action. On the other hand, those who perform specific economic functions, or perform them in specific ways, tend to have identities of interest which are continuing; as a result, they may seek and achieve a long-run influence on administration. The term "group interest" has come into common use for description of these functional identities. The term "group" has two connotations: one is that of persons associated in organizations or associations; "the other is that of a category of persons presumed or observed by the investigator to possess attributes in common." [1] Both types of "group" may have weight in the contest of interests, though organization may be expected to enhance the impact of a group having a common interest.

The existence of group interests has long been recognized. Madison distinguished various economic interests of men and found in these "the most common and durable source of factions" in society.[2] The dominance of interest motivation in the historic struggles of American parties has also been recognized.[3] Recently, however, and particularly within the last half century, interests have been structurally integrated in associations and unions, and these have become centers of power and influence in society. Today, group interests are brought to bear on government both in the appeal of party and Congressmen for the support of the interests in the franchise of the people and in the pressure of inter-

[1] The quotation and the distinction are from page 6 of Avery Leiserson, *Administrative Regulation: A Study in Representation of Interests.* Copyright 1942 by the University of Chicago.

[2] James Madison, Federalist Paper No. 10, *The Federalist* (Lodge, ed., 1888), 54.

[3] A. N. Holcombe, *The Political Parties of Today* (New York and London, 1924), and C. A. Beard, *Economic Origins of Jeffersonian Democracy* (New York, 1915), *The Economic Basis of Politics* (New York, 1922), and *The Economic Interpretation of the Constitution of the United States* (New York, 1913).

est organizations on the political and administrative structure of the government.[4]

There have been some efforts toward generalization concerning the relation of the interest groups to administration. Several of these, in one way or another, place a heavy emphasis on the position of the interests.

One form of generalization is the group process theory. According to this theory government is only a process through which group pressures are exerted. "All phenomena of government," says Bentley, "are phenomena of groups pressing one another, forming one another, and pushing out new groups and group representatives (the organs or agencies of government) to mediate the adjustments."[5] Law, also, "is a group process. . . . It is a forming, a systematization, a struggle, an adaptation, of group interests, just as government is."[6] Stated in its most extreme form by a critic of the view, the group process theory means that[7]

At any given moment, public policy is the resultant of a parallelogram of operative forces; the substance of public policy is redefined as the balance of power shifts. Government institutions thus tend to be transformed into mere pawns in a struggle for supremacy. Deprived of independent creative force, the purposes which they serve simply mirror the changing fortunes of battle. . . . The idea of public interest becomes a fiction used to describe an amalgam which is shaped and reshaped in the furnace of their conflicts.

Another view shifts emphasis to the function of government in relation to group interests. This is the reconciliation theory. The outstanding presentation of the idea advances it with balance and a hope for some "independent creative force" in government. Herring has said "that the purpose of the democratic state is the

---

[4] E. Pendleton Herring, *Group Representation before Congress* (Baltimore, 1929), and *Public Administration and the Public Interest* (New York and London, 1936).

[5] Arthur F. Bentley, *The Process of Government* (Chicago, 1908), 269.

[6] *Ibid.*, 272.

[7] Merle Fainsod, "Some Reflections on the Nature of the Regulatory Process," in C. J. Friedrich and Edward S. Mason, *Public Policy*, 298. Copyright 1940 by the President and Fellows of Harvard College.

free reconciliation of group interests." [8] This, in Herring's view, cannot be done without "a great administrative machine" which will synthesize the group interests into a unified conception of the public interest. [9] In achieving this synthesis, government may find a standard of public interest which gives it some independent weight among the contenders for power. [10] Nevertheless, government must find an accord with at least some of the interests. "Inescapably in practice the concept of the public interest is given substance by its identification with the interests of certain groups." [11] "The public interest can be realized only through promoting certain special interests." [12] Moreover, there must be compromise between the bureaucracy and the groups [13] establishing "a harmonious relationship" between the two: "The solution of the liberal democratic state must lie in establishing a working relationship between the bureaucrats and special interests—a relationship that will enable the former to carry out the purpose of the state and the latter to realize their own ends." [14] "Administrative efficiency demands the elimination of all possible friction between the ruler and the ruled." [15] All in all, Herring looks for concord in a setting of conflicts.

Another approach is the evaluation of government action in terms of its acceptance by the interest groups. This might be called the acceptance theory of the public interest. Leiserson has ex-

[8] E. Pendleton Herring, *Public Administration and the Public Interest*, 9. Copyright 1936 by McGraw-Hill Book Company, Inc. Also, at page 209: "Hence the public interest cannot be given concrete expression except through the compromise of special claims and demands finally effected. Special interests cannot be banished from the picture, for they are the parts that make the whole. . . . The experience of the Interstate Commerce Commission in its relations to carrier and shipper associations suggests that the 'pressures' of such groups can be directed to useful ends and that the influence of partisanship and sectionalism can be subdued by a salutary functionalism."

[9] *Ibid.*, 6-9 particularly.

[10] *Ibid.*, especially pages 348 and 377. Vaguely and without elaboration Herring thinks some class interests may have an "intrinsic social import" which the state "can mobilize." P. 348.

[11] *Ibid.*, 24.

[12] *Ibid.*, 259.

[13] *Ibid.*, 16.

[14] *Ibid.*, 24-25.

[15] *Ibid.*, 26.

pressed the idea in an unqualified way: "It is suggested that a satisfactory criterion of the public interest is the preponderant acceptance of administrative action by politically influential groups. Such acceptance is expressed through compliance on the part of such groups affected by administrative procedural requirements, regulations, and decisions, *without seeking legislative revision, amendment, or repeal.*" [16] Implicit in this statement is the idea that the administration should act in such a way as to prevent influential groups from being sufficiently dissatisfied that they will resort to politics. This, of course, would mean that the administrator would test his action by the reaction in front rather than solely by the directive behind. This Leiserson recognizes:

The administrator who conceives his task solely in terms of executing a legislative mandate has but a limited view of his public and social functions. Such a view does not consider the opportunities for differential and discriminatory treatment of group interests. . . .[17]

In another mode of generalization, actual participation of groups in the process of government is defined as an element of democratic government. The guild socialists and the pluralists have, of course, thought that representation of the vocational interests of man was a democratic necessity. Of more practical influence in this country has been the underlying idea among many that bureaucratic government was undemocratic or brought dangers of regimentation, and hence should be checked by citizen participation.[18]

[16] Avery Leiserson, *Administrative Regulation: A Study in Representation of Interests*, 16. Copyright 1942 by the University of Chicago. The italics are mine.

[17] *Ibid.*, 13. Other factors to be considered are also listed by Leiserson.

[18] After commenting on N.R.A. code authorities and the possible values of part-time boards composed of "persons whose intellectual interests or business enterprises were not far removed from the public work entrusted to them," Lindsay Rogers concluded:

"For, in extending controls over economic life, democratic states must seek methods of administration which are more flexible, more informed, and more representative than is possible through a bureaucracy. If they are to escape the evils which are the inevitable concomitants of direct regimentation, governments must more and more content themselves with laying down the rules of the game and permitting their application by persons who enjoy some measure of 'official independence,' who are not constantly held to political responsibility. Many experiments in this direction are now in progress."—Lindsay Rogers, Foreword, xiv, to R. H. Connery, *The Administration of an N.R.A. Code.* (Public Administration Service, Chicago, 1938).

There is a parallel notion that consultation and voluntary aid of affected parties is democratic procedure. Thus, farmer participation in agricultural programs has been called "agricultural democracy" or the "new democracy." [19] Discussing lay participation in administration, Gellhorn concluded: "affected private interests are shaping the course of official action. It is Democracy at work." [20]

Here are four aspects of theory: government is a pawn before the interest groups; government's function is to reconcile the groups by a working relationship with them; acceptance by groups is the test of the public interest; group participation is democracy. Separately or together they put a set of questions. Is government, inevitably, only a pawn or to a considerable extent only a pawn? If a possibility for an independent will is admitted, how can it be discovered and find expression? Can a counterpoise be found to group pressures for their own particular interests? Can a larger view of community purpose be made effective in administration? Can group participation be reconciled with the promotion of the public interest?

The questions are toughest in the context of administrative regulation. The directives to administration may express a policy which is antithetic to the interests of power groups among the regulated. Because of this, the control activities of government present a different type of problem from the service activities. In the latter, there is usually a large measure of identity between the government as server and the people who are served; except for the conflict with the taxpayer over payment of the social cost of services, there is frequently no strong opponent in interest. A harmonious relation between the bureaucrat and the groups may be achieved without great difficulty, and without threat to the purpose of statutory directives. In contrast, control activities are often initiated in a setting of strong conflict between the regulatory

[19] Among others, Dale Clark uses the term "agricultural democracy" in "The Farmer as Co-Administrator," *Public Opinion Quarterly*, III, 482-490 (July, 1939); John D. Lewis says "new democracy" in "Democratic Planning in Agriculture," *American Political Science Review*, XXXV, 232-249, 454-469, at p. 469 (April, June, 1941).

[20] Walter Gellhorn, *Federal Administrative Proceedings*, 130. Copyright 1941 by The Johns Hopkins Press.

purpose and the most powerful of the affected groups. "The elimination of all possible friction between ruler and ruled" might have to be purchased by a material watering down of the objectives of law. Moreover, the acceptance theory of the public interest would run counter to the purposes embodied in law.

New regulatory statutes are usually enacted in a period of agitation when the sentiments of the community at large are aroused behind some ideal or concept of the general welfare. Thereafter, the public at large gives its attention to other matters and the interests which are prepared for continuous pressure or resistance are provided a more favorable setting for the achievement or protection of their specific purposes. Is the community will ephemeral and transient? Does the political will expire with the framing of the directive? Or may force be assembled within the administrative mechanism behind the concept of public interest embodied in the directive?

The problem of implementing a policy antithetic in some measure to the interests of power groups among the regulated is complicated by certain necessities of administration. First, the administrative agency may have to maintain close contact with the regulated in order to know what is feasible. Its own resources of information may not provide a sufficiently intimate view of technicalities, variations, and resistances. The technicalities lie so deep and the variations are so numerous in modern industry that the bureaucracy may find it impossible to be informed without the aid of experts in industries.[21] Resistance to the agency's efforts, often existing in the minds of the regulated, must be known in order that judgment of the degree of requirement may be realistic. On purely technical matters, such as rules of safety in railroad transportation, consultation with the interests may provide the technical information which is needed and reveal the level of requirement which is technically possible. On larger matters also, the administrative agency may need to consult with the interests in order to know what standard of requirement the agency "can live with," i.e., to know the maximum level which will be accepted.

[21] Compare Herring, *Public Administration and the Public Interest*, 191.

Second, close contact with the regulatory interests may be necessary as a technique of gaining consent and support. This is partly a matter of compliance. The regulators must reach the minds of the regulated if compliance is to be obtained. This may require consultation and the winning of adherence, perhaps even cooperative efforts between administration and friendly elements among the interests. It is more, however, than a matter of compliance. An agency must have friends and it must not have too many or too powerful enemies.[22] Whether the agency is interested in moving forward with new program activities or in the survival of the evolved system of control, it will have to build a dependable liaison with some groups which will give it support in Congress and the presidential office.

Third, there are times when special arrangements with the regulated seem to be necessary in order to give them a sense of participation, or to reach widely scattered parties, or to incorporate existing mechanisms of social control. These arrangements are illustrated in our later discussion of control of agriculture and of commodity and security exchanges.

These several factors and the demands of the interest groups have led to arrangements for participation of interests—through advisory channels or otherwise—in the process of administration. In this way the "conflicts of economic groups" are integrated with the exercise of public authority and such groups are given a chance "to bring public policy into conformity with their own particular demands."[23]

It may be expected that such integration would over a long run lead toward (1) moderation in administration, (2) adjustments to particular groups or influences, and (3) more identity of view between the regulators and the regulated. Thus, the realities of administration give force to the questions presented by the conclusions of theory. Can administration which is closely associated

[22] See Norton E. Long, "Power and Administration," *Public Administration Review*, IX, 257-264 (1949).

[23] Avery Leiserson, *Administrative Regulation: A Study in Representation of Interests*, 1, 4. Copyright 1942 by The University of Chicago.

with controlled interest groups maintain any substantial independence of view and vigor in policy? [24]

Leiserson has noted that there are two "dilemmas of theory." The first, as he says,

goes to the very foundations of the state and its political processes. . . . Carried to its extreme as a constitutional principle, interest representation would be almost the negation of positive government. . . . Functional interest does not seem to be a force tending toward social unity.[25]

The second dilemma was summarized as follows:

The objection to "democratizing the organization of authority" on the basis of a shared responsibility between administrators and group representatives is that it may in practice become a means of reflecting the views solely of the organized sector of a single private interest.[26]

The fundamental problem posed by all of this discussion is whether government in its continuing operations can give expression to an inclusive and over-all, a large rather than a narrow, view of the public interest. Unavoidably, the influence of the interest groups is exerted for their own particular ends. Can administration be a channel through which a broader perspective can be implemented?

This problem is posed repeatedly and continuously through Herring's exploratory volume. He and others have indicated the practical methods of partial remedy. In our opinion, however, these would be given more meaning if fitted against a restatement of the concept of the public interest. It seems to us that the reconciliation and acceptance concepts of the purpose of the administrative process, though they must form part of the tools of thought of the administrator and though they may in the hands of

---

[24] "The Interstate Commerce Commission was devised as a means for ensuring public control that at the time would be unbiased and competent. To act competently it must have the coöperation of the carriers and shippers. Can the commission remain objective in the execution of its duties?" E. Pendleton Herring, *Public Administration and the Public Interest,* 193. Copyright 1936 by McGraw-Hill Book Company, Inc.

[25] Pages 264 and 266 of Avery Leiserson, *Administrative Regulation: A Study in Representation of Interests.* Copyright 1942 by The University of Chicago.

[26] *Ibid.,* 268.

a broad-gauged interpreter allow an inclusive view of public policy, do not, nevertheless, provide a sufficiently positive concept for the administrator.

First, the extreme implications of the group process theory need not be accepted. Fainsod's conclusions carry conviction. The "wielders of these [regulatory] instruments" may have "independent creative force and manipulative power" by "virtue of their special competence or their strategic position in the regulatory hierarchy." [27] This "manipulative power of regulatory agencies may be utilized to maintain an existing equilibrium of interests; it can be used to tilt the scale and create a new equilibrium." [28]

How should this manipulative power be organized and used? Partly in synthesis and partly by way of new rationalization, we suggest one basic and three subsidiary approaches. The first constitutes a restatement of the positive element in the administrative function.

The basic approach has two aspects. The first is expert search for solutions of public problems and methods of carrying these solutions into effect. The second relates to the purpose of the search. The solutions should be oriented toward the larger concepts of public or community purpose. Thus, putting the two needs together, we may say that the central need is a publicly-oriented or publicly-conditioned expertness. The words require explanation and the concept of public purpose is admittedly vague; neverthe-

[27] In Friedrich and Mason, *Public Policy*, 299. Copyright 1940 by the President and Fellows of Harvard College.

[28] *Ibid.*, 320. Since this chapter was written David Truman's *The Governmental Process* (New York, 1951) has provided many new insights on the relations between government and groups. In his discussion of the administrative process (Chapter 14) he says that although some "dramatic instances tend to support" the conclusion that administrators are "pawns of the dominant organized groups" that "No responsible account of the governmental process . . . would generalize from such examples." (Pp. 446-7). He discusses as factors refuting such an interpretation the influence of the administrator's view of his role ("the influence of office"), his group memberships, and his identification with the administrative unit. (Pp. 446-457). Our discussion in the following pages states a concept of the role of the administrator and of the ways in which the role can be protected. The quotations here and at other places from *The Governmental Process* are made under publisher's (Alfred A. Knopf, Inc.) general authorization of use.

less, the idea here presented has a sufficient core of clarity and captures the heart of administrative purpose in policy development.

By publicly-conditioned expertness we mean a capacity for finding solutions in government action which accord with the thread of unity in the community ideal and the possibilities for effect on the economic organism. There are at a given period certain unities in community purpose. Thus, the community at large may be interested in fair dealing among men, in the efficient conduct of publicly-regulated industries, in minimizing the cyclical changes in economic activity. For the administrator these purposes may be expressed in preambles of statutes, in statutory standards like the "public interest" and "public convenience and necessity," or may be derived by implication from statutes as a whole and the legislative and historical background of these. All the administrator's efforts should be oriented toward such public purposes. Their translation from vague expression into substantive action is the motive which conditions his search for solutions.

This translation requires expert consideration of the possibilities for change in the operation of the economic organism. This organism is a complex of technologies, institutional framework, and behavior patterns. Within this complex the administrator finds points of resistance and of pliability. *Expert analysis consists in the discovery of the areas of pliability and the means of manipulating these.*[29] *The maximization of this ability and its conscious utilization for the community ideal provide the best attainable measure of the public interest.*

On a narrow plane, publicly-conditioned expertness is the ability to resist the pressure for a decision in favor of a particular party or interest which is contrary to the statement of the public interest which delimits and prescribes the area of expert decision. But the concept we are urging has a broader significance. In the broad sense in which we have described it above, *publicly-conditioned expertness consists in finding ways to make the eco-*

---

[29] I am indebted to Merle Fainsod's chapter in Friedrich and Mason, *Public Policy, 1940,* for the idea of measuring the contribution of the regulatory agency in terms of its "manipulative power."

nomic organism yield to community purpose.[30] Discovery of the ways and means is the function of the expert in the administrative structure. He should have competence in measuring possibilities and in discovering techniques for manipulating organism in terms of directive. It is the function of the political superstructure to see that he does not forget that his manipulative powers are subordinate powers, to be exercised in terms of the community purpose embodied in directives. It must also be the function of the political superstructure to provide some guiding concept of public purpose.

To carry weight in the contest of forces, the expert must be creative and positive. "The offering of positive proposals by a responsible administration is then the first goal to seek," says Herring.[31] The "independence of administrative initiative," which Leiserson sees as one of the final public safeguards, is significant only as the initiative charts a line of decision and action.[32] The effect of such initiative may be to force the interests to conform to an external standard of action.

What place does this point of view concerning a publicly-conditioned expertness leave for the interest groups? It allows consultation with the interest groups, but this consultation has two purposes. The first is to grasp the possibilities for making directive effective—to obtain more information on what is wise and effective. The second is to enlist understanding and support for the solution or course of action which objective analysis (within the limits of public purpose) has indicated is the "right" one.[33] The purpose of consultation—or of any other method of interest participation—is positive; it aims toward effectiveness rather than limitation.

The view also allows recognition of the *fact* that interests will

[30] The word "purpose" rather than "welfare" is chosen deliberately. The administrator may have an influence on community purpose and he may have much scope under a general directive to put his own concepts of public welfare into his interpretation of public purpose; but he must still be, in theory, a subordinate to the political agents which define purpose.

[31] Herring, *op. cit.*, 383.

[32] Leiserson, *op. cit.*, 284.

[33] See pages 175-177 on the importance of communication of purpose.

exert pressure on bureaucrats, but it accepts this as *only one of the many factors which limit pliability*. The bureaucrat "is restricted in many directions." [34] In the regulation of the oil industry, for example, he cannot change the geology of formation and lift of oil, nor change the technology of drilling and transportation, nor ignore the law of capture and the correlative rights of men, nor move without recognition of the ways men will react to what he does. Each of these will condition the bureaucrat's efforts and leave him with a restricted area in which his talents can be used. Interest group opinion is only one of the conditioning factors. Good administration will include the fine art of seeing what the interests will take and maximizing this area, where desirable for attainment of directive, by communication of purpose and enforcement techniques. Where group interest obstructs and cannot be changed, even with the maximum obtainable support of political organs, it becomes like the hard facts of geology part of the area of resistance and nonpliability. The end of the rope is reached for the administrator in his search for ways of achieving directive. Administrative responsibility must inevitably expire at the point where pliability ends.

The real differences between the resistances in interests and the resistances in geological facts are two. The first is that the obstruction of the interests may be modified or overcome by the enlistment of understanding and support in the interest groups and the general public and by the potentialities for compulsive sanctions. These are the basic links between expert analysis and interest acceptance. The second is that the area of interest resistance is one in which administration is dependent upon politics. Where resistances are technical in nature, the problem is one for the expert exclusively; where they rise to the level of human relations, as most problems do, then administrative force is heavily dependent upon political force. Possibly the administrative agency may start with a strong and conclusive directive, with adequate powers, and sufficient appropriations; but even then, if the resistances in interest are powerful and continuing, the administrative agency

[34] Herring's words at page 237.

must find some political sustenance. Beyond a certain area, the administrator is only trying to lift himself by his bootstraps if he does not tie on to the transmission lines of political power.

This is conclusion drawn from the realm of reality. But the ideals of democratic government also demand that the administrator shall not try to take the full responsibility for the manipulation of interests. His directives set the vague line of division between his responsibility and that of his political superiors. If he has integrity and is loyal to the ideal of democratic government, he will recognize that, beyond a certain point of reasonable adjustment to practicalities, the responsibility for restricting a public program through concession to the interests should rest with the top political, not subordinate administrative, organs. Anything more than this is "administrative absolutism" in a negative form and destroys the integrity of administration by asking too much of it.[35] Also, if the administrator understands the meaning of democratic government he will reach to the political superstructure for a guide on community purpose. Anything less than this is "administrative absolutism" in a positive sense in that it ultimately results in men in subordinate position trying to fill a full vacuum on community purpose by their own unguided efforts.[36]

[35] Compare the following statement from Fritz Morstein Marx in "Administrative Ethics and the Rule of Law," *American Political Science Review*, XLIII (December, 1949), 1119-1144:
". . . public administration obviously has no claim to a political veto. However deep-felt their concern with the common good, government officials are constitutionally out of order in undertaking to serve as a continuing corrective in the political process." Pp. 1136-1137.

[36] For further discussion of the transmission of political force to administration, see pages 83-84, 289-290.

Professors Carl J. Friedrich and Herman Finer have argued the relative merits of "objective" responsibility (the self-limitation of the administrator which results from his habit and capacity for making decisions which accord with technical facts) and political responsibilty, as means of safeguarding public administration. Particularly in Friedrich's chapter in C. J. Friedrich and Edward S. Mason, *Public Policy*, and his "Responsible Government Service under the American Constitution," in Commission of Inquiry on Public Service Personnel, *Problems of the American Public Service* (New York, 1935), 3-74, and in Finer's "Better Government Personnel," *Political Science Quarterly* (1936), LI, 580-585, and "Administrative Responsibility in Democratic Government," *Public Administration Review*, I (1941), 335-350. (Continued, next page.)

It is inevitable, nevertheless, that directives from Congress, or from the top structure of the executive branch where politics and administration are so fully combined, will often be general and vague and that the content of government will take form down in the administration. It is because of this gap between directives and specifics of program that the search for techniques of organization and procedure which will maintain the publicly-conditioned point of view among administrators is the crucial task of administrative science.

Once the need for a publicly-conditioned expertness is accepted as paramount, certain subsidiary expedients for partial attainment are indicated. The first is to organize public authority in such a way that the publicly-oriented point of view and the objective analysis of subordinate factors may prevail at the primary levels of administration, that is, in the bureaus, commissions, and departments. The concepts of public responsibility and independence from special point of view are customarily accepted. The problem is to avoid their attenuation in the organization and personnel

---

In one statement Friedrich has said succinctly much of what we have said here:

". . . we have a right to call such a policy irresponsible if it can be shown that it was adopted without proper regard to the existing sum of human knowledge concerning the technical issues involved; we also have a right to call it irresponsible if it can be shown that it was adopted without proper regard for existing preferences in the community, and more particularly its prevailing majority. Consequently, the responsible administrator is one who is responsible to these dominant factors: technical knowledge and popular sentiment."—*Public Policy*, 12. Copyright 1940 by the President and Fellows of Harvard College.

On the other hand, we concur in Finer's view that there is need for strengthening the channel of overhead political direction. Professor Friedrich expects more of administration than it *should have* to supply; Professor Finer may expect more of representative government than it *can* supply. We have argued that the directive should serve as a link between Friedrich's objective responsibility and Finer's political responsibility. Our earlier discussion (Chapter IV) reenforces Friedrich's conclusion that statutory directives will not give adequate guides, but we shall argue at a later point that this creates a need for a political directorate in the executive branch which will carry the responsibility for partially filling in the gaps left in Congressional directives and which can serve as a channel through which meaningful issues of public policy are raised to the level of Congressional decision.

For a recent argument for an "indispensable" political check, see Charles S. Hyneman, *Bureaucracy in a Democracy* (New York, 1950), Chapter III.

practices of government and in the attitude of the official. As the policy of government moves out of the larger forum of legislative consideration into the agencies of administration the principle of public responsibility may be vitiated by the identities of viewpoint between regulatory organs and special groups whose interests are more particularized than those embodied in the policy of the law. To restrict this by expedients of organization and personnel practice is the first method of making administration an effective weapon of public power. This objective is regarded as controlling in the second and third sections of this chapter dealing with personnel and structure.

The second subsidiary approach is really a corollary of the first. It aims to restrict the participation of interest groups in administration in such a way as will prevent them from bending the policy of administration toward particular objectives inconsistent with the political directives. Gellhorn has urged "that the parties immediately involved should in the main be limited to the rôle of advisors," [37] and Herring has emphasized consultation as the proper means of bringing the interest groups into the process of administration. [38] This need for subordinating interest participation dominates our discussion in the fourth section of this chapter on "The Coordination of Interest Participation."

The third subsidiary approach is to enlarge the structure within which the course of administrative action is determined. This is one of the creative ideas left at the end of Herring's volume. Mechanisms for coordination, and for central planning and overhead direction of administrative operations, are means of insuring that government's view will be more inclusive than that of the particular interests. [39] Judgments will differ as to the precise organizational and procedural methods which are conducive to the larger view. Our suggestions for attaining this objective are given in the main in our chapter on organization but some suggestions will appear in the detailed portion of this chapter.

[37] Walter Gellhorn, *Federal Administrative Proceedings,* 133. Copyright 1941 by The Johns Hopkins Press.
[38] *Public Administration and the Public Interest,* Chapter XXI.
[39] *Ibid.,* Chapters XX and XXIII.

The foregoing comments are made with full recognition of limiting factors. Ofttimes the policy of government, as in labor disputes, aims only to hold a balance between parties or mitigate the strains of conflict between the interests; and ofttimes policy aims to promote rather than to restrict an interest. Second, where control is an objective, the resistance in the interests, and therefore in the will, of the regulated does warn of the limits on the effectiveness of regulation as a device for attaining community purpose. There are inherent limitations on the effectiveness of a system in which public authority is superimposed above private management and seeks to limit or direct its behavior. These may suggest careful consideration in relevant cases of the alternatives of free private action, government management of enterprise, or government regulation. But whatever the policy of government, no change in the fundamental concepts of public power are required. The answer, so far as there is an answer to the problem of the interest groups, is to distinguish between the two factors of community purpose and resistances to its attainment, and to strengthen the factors in politics and administration which maximize the opportunities for generalizing community goals.

PERSONNEL OF THE PUBLIC AUTHORITY

Interest Representation in Agency Composition, Particularly on Boards

The public nature of government office is customarily recognized in several ways. The salary is almost always paid from the public treasury, the official is required to take an oath which affirms his public responsibility, and his appointment almost universally comes from a public authority. The general practice, moreover, is to leave the appointing authority unbound by tight restrictions designed to protect functional or sectional interests. This has been particularly true of federal statutes. In the states many statutes either require technical qualifications, as in tax and utility laws, or provide for representation of groups, as in unemployment compensation, industrial commissions, and professional licensing boards. Such requirements are more exceptional in federal legislation. And yet the problem of maintaining the public viewpoint remains a serious one.

Theoretically, occupational qualifications are different from interest group representation. Actually, however, such qualifications may be designed to provide representation of a point of view. The Bituminous Coal Act of 1937 provided for a commission of seven members of which two "shall have been experienced bituminous coal mine workers, two shall have had previous experience as producers." [40] The face of the act may indicate that these were only standards for complementary competences, but the legislative history shows that the purpose was representation of interests. John L. Lewis had in fact stated that labor representation on the commission was a *quid pro quo* for support of the United Mine Workers for a regulatory measure.[41] Similarly, the negative provision in the rider on the 1944 appropriation act for the Office of Price Administration against paying salaries to persons directing the formulation of price policy who were not "qualified by experience in business, industry, or commerce," [42] looks like a mere statement of competence; but it was in fact an expression of resentment over the lack of representation of the business attitude in the policy-making function.

Occupational qualifications are, however, quite rare in federal statutes. The provision in the original Federal Reserve Act which required that at least two members should be "experienced in banking and finance" was exceptional in federal legislation relating to the composition of regulatory boards.[43]

Also theoretically different from partisan group representation is the idea that a board should be a cross section of the community but without duty of the members to represent any particular viewpoint. This ideal has perhaps been most carefully expressed in the standards for selection of O.P.A.'s local board members. One standard was representation of all the important groups in

[40] 50 *U. S. Stat. at Large,* 72.
[41] See Cushman, *The Independent Regulatory Commissions* (New York, London, and Toronto, 1941), 377-378, 385-386.
[42] 57 *U. S. Stat. at Large,* 522, 526 (1943).
[43] Dropped by amendment to the statute in 1922. 42 *U. S. Stat. at Large,* 620.

the community. "This policy was described as representation of 'the community as a whole,' it being assumed that full representation was unlikely to be achieved in practice without participation by members selected from each of the major distinguishable segments of the community." On the other hand, a personal fitness standard set the goal that all members should have "a high regard for board membership as a public trust, rather than as an opportunity to promote a special viewpoint." The two objectives were not inconsistent; and it is probably true that the widening of membership brought to the board persons, such as women and laborers, whose sympathies lay strongly with the policy of the agency.[44]

Similar is the idea of a balanced board, expressed by the following summary of President Wilson's decision concerning appointments to the Federal Reserve Board:[45]

It was then decided by President Wilson that three members should be men of legal training and experience, and that two members should be men of broadest possible business or industrial experience. It was also determined that the personnel should be chosen from different parts of the country and different industries in order that the broadest possible viewpoint might be the result of the combined judgment of the whole commission.

The history of the Federal Reserve Act is interesting with reference to this distinction between a board which reflects the community composition and one designed to give specific representation to particular interests. President Wilson rejected banker nomination of representatives to the board.[46] However, the original act provided that the President should "have due regard to a fair representation of the different commercial, industrial, and geographical divisions of the country";[47] and demand from agricultural

[44] For fuller discussion see my *Field Administration of Wartime Rationing* (Washington, 1937), 99-104.

[45] Statement of Commissioner Joseph E. Davies, quoted by E. Pendleton Herring, *Federal Commissioners* (Cambridge, 1936), 95.

[46] Carter Glass, *An Adventure in Constructive Finance* (Garden City, 1927), 115-116.

[47] Sec. 10.

interests led to a change of the provision in 1922 so as to direct "due regard to a fair representation of the financial, agricultural, industrial, and commercial interests, and geographical divisions of the country." [48] Yet a member of the board with a background of experience in agricultural activities declared that the members of the Board "without exception, regard themselves as representative not of any group or class interest, but of the common interest and the public welfare." [49]

The line between this ideal and the fact of specialized viewpoint may vanish. The problem is one of attitude. An appointing authority can select a balanced board composed of men who will take the large rather than the specialized view. On the other hand, irrespective of legal limitations on the appointing power, an appointee might be so closely connected with a group viewpoint that he could not assume an independent attitude or the pressure of groups for favorable appointees could compromise the position of a new appointee.[50]

In some cases the line of differentiation of the community-representative and interest-nonpartisan board is conclusively crossed in favor of a definitely partisan composition. On the whole, however, this has been avoided in federal legislation except for agencies dealing with labor interests.

A singular case is that of the Railroad Retirement Board. The statute provides that the presidential nominees shall be one member to be recommended by the carriers, one to be recommended by representatives of the employees, and one to be independent of both these groups.[51] An unusual feature of this requirement is that it seems not to have resulted in partisanship in practice. At

---

[48] 42 *U. S. Stat. at Large*, 620.

[49] Address of Chester C. Davis before the American Farm Bureau Federation, December 10, 1936, as quoted by Leiserson, *op. cit.*, 106.

[50] Sectional representation is similar to group representation. The Federal Reserve Act prohibits appointment of more than one member from each reserve district, the Federal Radio Commission was to have a commissioner from each of five zones, and there have been efforts to obtain sectional representation through statutory requirement or pressure on the appointing authority. See Herring, *Federal Commissioners*, 17-20, and Sharfman, *The Interstate Commerce Commission*, II (New York, 1931), 460-462.

[51] 45 U. S. C. A. Sec. 228j.

least the research group for the Attorney General's Committee on Administrative Procedure concluded that "The Board has consistently acted as a unit, and its members have brought to its deliberations special experience, rather than special and irreconcilable points of view." [52] Especially unusual in federal legislation is this provision for interest nomination of members of an agency whose function is to determine strictly individual claims under definite statutory provisions. The need for objectivity in administration of a statute of this kind is so obvious that it may be hoped that the precedent of interest participation will not be followed in future legislation.

In most cases the use of bipartisan or tripartisan boards in labor matters appears to be related to the dual nature of the governmental function in matters of labor interest. The basic desire on both sides of the labor-management conflict is to avoid the extension of an independent overhead power of determination, and government policy leans strongly toward the concord of parties rather than the fiat of government. As a result, the organization of government agencies confuses the functions of reconciliation of parties and independent determination.

A tripartisan Railroad Labor Board was created in the Transportation Act of 1920. [53] A board of nine would represent equally the public, carriers, and employees; and the representatives of the last two were to be chosen by the President from panels recommended by the affected groups. The board ran into many difficulties and the representation of interests was eliminated in the Railway Labor Act of 1926, which provided for a Board of Mediation of five members. [54] The amendatory legislation of 1934 preserved a board without interest representation, a National Mediation Board of three members. [55] Its main function is mediation and the similar legislation relating to employees in other industries provides for

---

[52] *Railroad Retirement Board* (Sen. Doc. 186, 76th Cong., 3d. Sess., 1940), 14.
[53] 41 *U. S. Stat. at Large,* 456, 470.
[54] 44 *U. S. Stat. at Large,* 577, 579.
[55] 48 *U. S. Stat. at Large,* 1185, 1193-1194.

a Federal Mediation and Conciliation Service, headed by a director for whom no qualifications in interest are prescribed.[56]

Meanwhile, one other aspect of railway labor interests has been vested in a bipartisan board. Disputes growing out of the interpretation and application of agreements go to the National Railroad Adjustment Board, composed of 36 members functioning in four panels with equal representation of carriers and employees. The members are definitely partisans of those they represent. They are selected by, paid by, and hold office at the pleasure of their respective constituencies.

The bipartisan spirit is strong, though it varies in intensity among the four divisions. Experience has shown many deadlocks over procedural points, and a very large proportion of the cases must go to referees selected by agreement of members of the panel or designated by the National Mediation Board.[57]

The word "adjustment" is carried in the title. Would it be better to emphasize the adjudicatory nature of the proceeding by having a nonrepresentative agency which acted in a judicial manner? Gellhorn argues that the difficulties which have been encountered by the Board give substance to the view that decisive functions should be placed in nonrepresentative bodies;[58] but the Attorney General's Committee on Administrative Procedure concluded that it

is a reflection of historical developments and that, with all of its imperfections, it may make for a more workable adjudicatory mechanism than could a plan constructed abstractly . . . . the Committee is not prepared to recommend that the Board be replaced by a new, nonpartisan tribunal until such time as the advantages of that type of organization are acknowledged by all parties concerned.[59]

[56] Labor Management Relations Act, 1947, Title II, Sec. 202, 61 *U. S. Stat. at Large*, 136, 153. (
[57] For further difficulties see Attorney General's Committee on Administrative Procedure, *Railway Labor* (Sen. Doc. 10, 77th Cong., 1st Sess., 1941). The monograph stated that in the fiscal year 1939, 607 cases were decided without referees and 641 with referees, but added that probably the relatively easy and clear cases were settled without referees.
[58] *Federal Administrative Proceedings*, 135-138.
[59] *Final Report*, 185-186. See also Leiserson, *Administrative Regulation*, 123.

Thus, the Committee recognized the significance of the will of the parties in this peculiar area where policy hangs between reconciliation and positive government.

A similar duality in policy and administration is revealed in the experience with tripartisan labor boards in the recent wartime emergency. The National Defense Mediation Board, created March 19, 1941, had eleven members, three representative of the public, four of industry, and four of labor.[60] Its successor, the National War Labor Board, had twelve members, appointed by the President, but with equal representation of the three parties.[61] In both cases, the partisan position of the representatives of labor and management was clear.[62] The strain on the public members was therefore great, particularly since the second board had decisive—not merely mediatory—functions. Again, partisan representation resulted in administrative difficulties and delays. Would a strictly public board have been an improvement? The answer will not be easy for some investigator of the future, for the National War Labor Board had a dual nature in that while it decided particular conflicts and administered a national labor policy, it also held labor and management together during the war under a compromise of interests. Representation for the two may have made them more ready to accept the compromise and the details of successive settlements.[63]

More questionable concessions to interest representation were made in the Fair Labor Standards Act of 1938.[64] Tripartisan boards were to recommend minimum wage rates for industries. The result was that under a façade of legal procedure a kind of bargaining between parties was carried on. In this case the concession to interests would appear to have been unnecessary as a means

[60] Executive Order No. 8617, Federal Register, Vol. 6, 1532.

[61] Executive Order No. 9017, Federal Register, Vol. 7, 237. Continued by 57 U. S. Stat. at Large, 163, 166, Sec. 7.

[62] See Harold W. Metz, *Labor Policy of the Federal Government* (Washington, 1945), Chapter X.

[63] See the discussion by Leiserson in Fritz Morstein Marx, *Elements of Public Administration* (New York, 1946), 333-334. The reader can see parallels in the current experience of the Wage Stabilization Board.

[64] 52 U. S. Stat. at Large, 1060.

of maintaining peace on the labor front. Strictly public decision would have been as feasible as in many other cases of public decision.[65]

What conclusions can be drawn about interest representation on public authorities? It may be necessary in some cases where the public interest lies in the maintenance of peace on the labor front and where the parties are unwilling to yield to a strictly public decision. Even here, however, the burden of proof lies heavily on the advocate of specific representation of interests. In other areas of public action, the weaknesses of interest representation are evident. It is difficult, if not impossible, to include representation of all the interests which might legitimately make a claim for some representation. Moreover, it either puts a man in the position of acting as a partisan at all times or compromising himself both before the public and his group by an effort to recognize a dual responsibility. It makes it difficult also to maintain the "continuing mutual deference and concession so necessary to successful administration."[66] It reduces and destroys objectivity. Whether in the form of occupational requirements or of specific representation, it undermines the integrity of public office and weakens the force of public instrumentalities.

Personal Disassociation or the Non-interest Principle

One notion on the composition of public authority has been that an official should have no personal interest or connection with matters subject to his control as a public official. The narrow meaning of the notion is that a man should not gain in a pecuniary way from his own action as an official, but the broader significance of the non-interest principle is that it is a means of immunizing the official against an attitude of preference toward particular interests subject to control.

The Interstate Commerce Act of 1887 contained two provisions for personal disassociation of commissioners:

[65] Gellhorn, op. cit., 140-144, for an argument that interest representation was a mistake and for citation of other discussions on the procedure.
[66] A. J. Altmeyer, The Industrial Commission of Wisconsin, 318-319, quoted by Leiserson, Administrative Regulation, 133.

No persons in the employ of or holding any official relation to any common carrier subject to the provisions of this Act, or owning stock or bonds thereof, or who is in any manner pecuniarily interested therein, shall enter upon the duties of or hold such office. Said commissioners shall not engage in any other business, vocation, or employment.[67]

Similar provisions have been copied in many of the regulatory statutes.[68] Moreover, there has been a tendency in recent statutes to extend further the first of these prohibitions. The Communications Act of 1934 excluded from membership on the Commission persons having an interest in any business closely connected to the activities subjected to regulation. It also extended the prohibitions to subordinate employees.[69] The acts of 1935 and 1937 providing for regulation of the bituminous coal industry extended the prohibition of excluded financial interests to competing industries, namely oil, gas, and hydroelectric power. The provisions applied to members of the Commission and to the Consumers' Counsel.[70] The act of 1936 creating the Maritime Commission applied the prohibitions to any person having certain excluded interests during the three years prior to his appointment as commissioner.[71]

Less comprehensive are the prohibitions in statutes creating agencies whose regulatory duties extend over a variety of industries. Thus, the acts creating the Federal Tariff Commission, the Federal Trade Commission, the National Labor Relations Board, and the Federal Mediation and Conciliation Service only prohibit commissioners from engaging in any other business, vocation, or

[67] Section 11. The non-interest principle extends the judicial principle that a person shall not judge a case in which he is interested to disassociation from an area subject to continuing control. The older aspect of the principle was embodied in Section 17 of the Interstate Commerce Act of 1887: "No Commissioner shall participate in any hearing or proceeding in which he has any pecuniary interest." Note also the criminal statute which prohibits an officer or a person having pecuniary interests in a private firm from acting for the U.S. in transaction of business with such firm. *U. S. C.*, Title 18, Sec. 93.

[68] Compare, in addition to the acts immediately to be cited, the act of 1930 governing composition of the Federal Power Commission, 46 *U. S. Stat. at Large*, 797.

[69] 48 *U. S. Stat. at Large*, 1064, 1066-1067.

[70] 49 *U. S. Stat. at Large*, 991, 992-993; 50 *U. S. Stat. at Large*, 72, 73-74.

[71] 49 *U. S. Stat. at Large*, 1985, 1985-1986.

employment.[72] This is true, also, of the Atomic Energy Act of 1946.[73]

There was wide departure from the principle of personal disassociation in the agencies created in the emergency of World War II. When Donald Nelson became head of W.P.B. it had about three hundred "dollar-a-year" men and 614 W.O.C. (without compensation) consultants. He accepted the system as a necessity. Efforts were made, however, to protect against the dangers of the system. Rules limiting the appointment of "dollar-a-year" men were adopted, non-industry men were appointed to many top positions, delegations to the divisions of W.P.B.—which were staffed heavily with industry men—were restricted, and arrangements for broadening the internal participation in the making of policy were made.[74]

Other agencies used men who were compensated in whole or in part by private employers. Thus O.D.T. carried some executives on a "without compensation" basis with the employer railroad continuing to pay them their salaries, the Petroleum Administration for War used men whose compensation was supplemented by their private employers, and many representatives of labor organizations served government on a part-time basis with salary also being part-time.[75]

In O.P.A., on the other hand, there was more allegiance to the non-interest principle. Dollar-a-year men were avoided and W.O.C.

---

[72] These are pages at which the provisions appear, though the words may vary slightly: 39 *U. S. Stat. at Large,* 795; 38 *U. S. Stat. at Large,* 718; 61 *U. S. Stat. at Large,* 139 and 153.

[73] 60 *U. S. Stat. at Large,* 755, 757. The statute creating the S.E.C. provided that "No commissioner shall engage in any other business, vocation, or employment, other than that of serving as commissioner, nor shall any commissioner participate, directly or indirectly, in any stock-market operations or transactions of a character subject to regulation by the Commission pursuant to this title." 48 *U. S. Stat. at Large,* 881, 885.

An old criminal statute prohibits a government official or employee from receiving compensation from a private concern for his work as official or employee of the U.S. government. U.S.C., Title 5, Sec. 66.

[74] Civilian Production Administration, *Industrial Mobilization for War—History of the War Production Board and Predecessor Agencies, 1940-1945* (Washington, 1947), 231-233, 969-979.

[75] As summarized by Leiserson in Morstein Marx, *op. cit.,* 323-324.

appointments were sparingly used. At times there was effort to see that employees held no financial interests in industries with which they dealt. The technique of special approval of persons with industry connections was also tried. For local board appointments the rules prescribed the non-interest principle.

These efforts were only partially effective. The principle of disassociation was often forgotten or evaded, both for the paid staff and for the volunteers on the local boards. Moreover, the mere fact of temporary disassociation does not change basic attitudes. Men who are on leave from a salaried position in a business concern or labor organization or who are temporarily without a private connection may have fundamentally the same notions as "dollar-a-year" men. The plain fact is that government needed industry men during the war and that compromise of the normal principle of disassociation was effected in some way or other in the various agencies.

Yet the non-interest principle is reasserted in a recent report of a Senate subcommittee on "Ethical Standards in Government." Discussing employment in present defense agencies, it expressed belief that men who could not give up outside salaries should be replaced as rapidly as possible and that care should be exercised to see that public officials should not deal with cases touching their former employers. It further suggested that, "if at all possible," the highest political positions "should not be filled by persons drawn from the industries which they regulate," and that administrators should select balanced staffs containing some men of great competence who did not come from the clientele industry.[76]

Herring, however, has questioned the desirability of statutory restrictions on financial interest of the heads of regulatory agencies.[77] He shows that the requirement of divestment of financial holdings imposes such a sacrifice on the business man that he is unwilling often to accept appointment. But men of experience, Herring argues, are needed on commissions, not as spokesmen for business,

[76] *Ethical Standards in Government*, Report of a Subcommittee of the Committee on Labor and Public Welfare, U. S. Senate, 82nd Cong., 1st Sess., 1951.
[77] *Federal Commissioners*, Chapter II.

but to bring to commissions knowledge of "the methods and values of the business world." [78] "One or two such men on each board would make these commissions more balanced and better armed to face all comers." [79]

The argument raises fundamental questions. Is there no way of combining competence and detachment? Is acceptance by industry obtainable only by appointment of persons with industry connections? Is financial interest a compromise of the public-service ideal?

It may be assumed that there are men who could serve with a thorough orientation to the public interest even though they had financial interests in the industry regulated. Presumably, however, mental detachment from special and antithetic viewpoint would be more difficult because of the financial interest. Also, the position of the individual is compromised and he automatically becomes subject to suspicion and attack. It may be admitted, also, that disassociation during incumbency is no guarantee of independent judgment. Nevertheless, it is one safeguard whose elimination would compromise a larger ideal—the ideal that the public official should come to his office with no special viewpoint which could conflict with the purpose of the directives to the agency.

It is this larger principle which is vital to the public-service ideal. In selection of a bureau chief the ideal of detachment would be accepted, and technical competence and industry confidence would be sought through staff experts and advisory aids. The board system gives an opportunity to enrich the public service with men who have varied backgrounds, but it seems to be generally admitted that from such backgrounds men should be chosen who can take a large view of the public interest. The principle of disassociation may be an essential means of attaining this end.

Certain Problems in Staff Positions

Agencies have sometimes provided for representation of special viewpoints or needs through special units or positions on their staffs.

[78] *Ibid.*, 24.
[79] *Ibid.*, 32.

The persons holding the positions might be actually affiliated with or closely identified with special interest groups, or they might be persons only presumed to have ability to represent particular interests.

The varying motivations behind such special positions may be illustrated by reference to three notable instances of their use. Within N.R.A. there were three boards, representing the interests of industry, labor, and the consumer. They were called advisory boards; but they had the power to disapprove codes of fair competition, subject to the superior power of the Administrator to overrule their objections. The purpose was to set up a machinery under which it could be assured that the interests of each of three presumably separate segments of the non-agricultural portion of the economy would be considered and given appropriate weight in the balance sheet of results.

In contrast, the urge for special positions in the war production agency came from the desire of labor to have an active participation in the program of the agency. W.P.B. inherited a program which had been initiated under the joint directorship of an industry and a labor chief. When the program was placed under the unified direction of a single chief who was an industry man, an effort was made to retain a place for labor participation in the operation of the agency. Various means were used, such as a Labor Policy Committee with equal representation of the two large labor organizations; a Labor Production Division, for which a significant measure of responsibility could never be found; following lack of success of the Labor Production Division, two vice chairmen of the Board, one for Labor Production, the other for Labor Requirements, and each representing one of the two major labor organizations; and still later, the work of labor's representatives in the agency with the divisions of the agency.[80]

In another agency there was a desire to give certain groups a feeling that their interests were represented in the councils of the agency and also a desire to set up a channel of liaison with these

[80] Civilian Production Administration, *op. cit.*, 235-236, 245-248, 265-266, 589, 590, 748-756, 969-979.

same groups. In O.P.A. there were advisors on labor relations, consumer needs, agricultural relations, and, beginning in 1945, on veterans' problems. In an occasional instance there were industry-contact staff members, but on the whole industry was represented by advisory committees.

In part, then, the special staff unit is only a structural device for insuring that attention is given to a particular and potent interest. Viewed in this respect the primary danger would be that the existence of these units would lead to the development of policy as a mere compromise of interests. To escape this, the administrator could either avoid the use of such units or subordinate them to a higher overhead structure designed to represent the fuller interests of society as a whole.

The likelihood is, however, that these units will be staffed with persons either affiliated with or strongly identified in sentiments with the special viewpoint represented by the unit. This may be demanded by the interest group, adopted by the agency as a means of enlisting confidence in the unit, or be implicit in the tendency of the unit. To the extent that such units are staffed with persons identified with the interests, then the problems discussed heretofore in this section are again presented. The dangers of duality in point of view, or even of loyalty, and the concomitant difficulties for the administrators in charge of the agency in trying to develop a program with some inner consistency and public-interest integrity are present, even though the representation of interests is in subordinate positions.

The dangers arising from special viewpoints corresponding with those of particular outside interests are greatest when staff aids reflecting the special viewpoints are given decisional or operating responsibilities. As for operating responsibilities, it would appear that the interests would have no desire for participation unless they could thereby affect the nature of decision within the agency. But the process of decision is more cumbersome and operates less smoothly if the divergent interests are brought too close to the decisional centers. Even if it were admitted that, in the large, the process of government was one of group reconciliation, the functioning of the process would be hampered if the day-to-day process was one of group collaboration. The difficulties of exploring the pathways to general solutions which accord with the longer and broader interests of men are increased because of the necessity for compromise and the tendency toward bargaining among groups in the agency. It is safe, therefore, to conclude that there is rarely, if ever, any proper place for specific representation of group viewpoint inside the ring where policy is made and executed.[81]

Even internal advisors and liaison officers having close affinity with outside interest viewpoints present problems. To the extent that the affinity exists, the position of the staff aid is compromised and the officials in the channels of responsibility find it difficult to determine how much confidence shall be placed in the advice given. Liaison alone is a difficult limit to impose; but ordinarily more than this will be undesirable, because of the alternative courses which are available to the administrator, namely, the use of expert staff research on effects of government action on interest groups and of channels of counsel from persons representing the interests but standing outside the administrative family.

All of the above deals with hazards to be avoided. Above these negative pieces of argument, the positive and dominant personnel needs should be asserted.

The first is the need for positive search for the type of personnel which will carry a publicly-oriented objectivity. The search will probably be most effective if it reaches for broadly-gauged professional persons, including those who have gained professional competence in general administration.[82] Professional people have canons of integrity growing out of their experience in objective search for data and solutions. If this integrity can be combined with perspective, and the two fertilized with experience which broadens the capacities of men, the personnel base for the maximum possible attainment of the public interest is established.

The second need is to preserve this professional quality in the agency. The professional needs, of course, to be properly geared to

[81] Compare Leiserson's conclusions in Morstein Marx, *op. cit.*, 329-330.
[82] See our further discussion at page 369.

and subordinated to proper channels of political direction; over and over, and unavoidably, this relation of politics to administration conditions discussion of administrative personnel.[83] But though the professional quality is conditioned from above, it may yet be a bulwark against the separatistic and destructive influences operating underneath. The effectiveness of the bulwark will be weakened if professional personnel is scattered in organizational units representing special viewpoints, or if the effort of the professional to manipulate areas of pliability is hampered by nonprofessional representation of interests inside the administrative family.

THE STRUCTURE OF PUBLIC AUTHORITY

Organization may lead toward an identity of viewpoint between the public authority and a regulated fragment of the public. This may occur, first, through the use of the clientele service agency as an organ of regulation. The Departments of Agriculture, Commerce, and Labor have been created and expanded as the result of the demands for action in behalf of special groups. They are oriented toward service to their groups, and they find in them the support and protection which they need in Congress and with the public. Are they, as a result, unfitted for control functions in which there are elements of policy which may be opposed to the desires of their groups?

Second, identity of viewpoint may result from allocation of duties to units of organization which deal continuously with a single commodity, a related group of commodities, or a single industry. During the war a number of so-called "commodity czars" were set up—the Rubber Director, and the directors of the War Food Administration, the Office of Defense Transportation, and the Petroleum Administration for War. In W.P.B. and O.P.A. duties were allocated internally to commodity divisions or branches. In the departments duties have often been allocated in the subordinate structure on the basis of commodity. In such cases a certain

[83] See pages 368-369.

identity of viewpoint may result, first, from the tendency to use personnel in industry units with the same background as the personnel in industry, and second, through constant association of personnel with an outside industry or commodity interest.

Many of our regulatory boards have been set up to deal with the problems of a single industry. They have become organs of industry management. The oldest of these has been praised for its realism and criticised for its railroad-mindedness. The critics have seen the I.C.C. performing the function of "protective guardianship" of the railroads.[84] They have called it a "captive agency." Perhaps guardianship is, in a measure, a proper function. But the use of the term "captive" denotes a suspicion of the nature of public authority.

It would be absurd to argue that the clientele, commodity, and industry principles of organization did not have advantages or that it was not necessary to employ these methods of organization in many instances. Function is generally accepted as the most useful test for organization,[85] but students of administration are not naïve enough to believe that function is either a clearly distinguishable test in all cases or that it should not be measured against other alternatives in particular situations.[86] What is relevant here is that clientele, commodity, and industry organization enlarges the difficulty of avoiding the restrictive and gaining the inclusive point of view. Are there expedients of organization by which this difficulty can be partially surmounted?

One expedient is to transfer the separable regulatory functions from clientele agencies. Experience led some to the belief that the Department of Agriculture was too fully identified with promo-

[84] Commissioner Aitchison himself has spoken of the Transportation Act as creating "a new policy, the 'fostering guardianship' of transportation." *Hearings before a Subcommittee of the Committee on Interstate and Foreign Commerce pursuant to H.R. 2536*, House of Representatives, 79th Cong., 1st Sess., p. 13, 1945.

[85] See W. F. Willoughby, *Principles of Public Administration*, (Washington, 1927), 89-92.

[86] See Schuyler C. Wallace, *Federal Departmentalization: A Critique of Theories of Organization* (New York, 1941), Chapter V, and George C. S. Benson, "Internal Administrative Organization," *Public Administration Review*, I, 474-484 (1941).

tion of agricultural interests to allow one of its units, the Food and Drug Administration, to deal aggressively with processors of agricultural products.[87] It has now been moved to the Federal Security Agency, which presumably may provide a more favorable setting for protection of the consumer interest.[88] The function of conciliation of labor disputes seemed to be inappropriately placed in an agency whose general function was the promotion of the interests of labor. The Labor Management Relations Act transferred the function from the Department of Labor to a new and independent unit.

The feasibility of this approach is limited by the nonseparability of some regulatory functions. Modern governmental programs often fuse promotion and control. This is most obvious in agricultural programs, where production controls are mixed with loans, benefit payments, and soil conservation. In such a case, separation of the control function is not a feasible technique.

A more complete answer to the problem of obtaining the inclusive view is at hand. It is the subordination of the spread of clientele or industry-oriented agencies to policy-forming echelons representing more inclusive viewpoints. Four expedients of organization are related to this objective.

The first expedient is to enlarge the units of administration, thus forcing a broader view of public policy than will be found in the interests of a single industry. Motor, rail, pipeline, and non-oceanic water transportation have now been placed under the Interstate Commerce Commission. From time to time, the suggestion is made that regulation of all transportation facilities be put under a single agency.[89] In the non-regulatory field, the recent creation of a Department of National Defense offers an example of an

[87] For the relations of the Department of Agriculture to the interests, see Herring, *Public Administration and the Public Interest,* Chapter XIV.

[88] But in recommending that the functions of the Food and Drug Administration with respect to foods be transferred to the Department of Agriculture, the majority of the Hoover Commission said:

"We believe, as does our task force, that the Department of Agriculture will be vigorous in the protection of consumer interest." *Department of Agriculture,* 24.

[89] See pages 307 and 311.

attempt to implement a comprehensive objective in public policy. Englargement of the areas of administration may expand the scope for reconciliation of interests, and it may also allow a larger scope for objective analysis and planning. It has its dangers—such as the premature assimilation of a new technological development into a structure where solidified and well-developed interests could block its expansion (e.g., air transport in a world of rails) and the enlargement of the problems of management;[90] but the varying methods of combining unity in planning and deconcentration in operations—discussed in the next chapter—offer potentialities for solution of the management problem.[91]

Second, the advantages of the allocation of duties according to major function merit consideration in all choices of regulatory agencies. Among these advantages are the concentration of attention on purpose and the crossing of industry or commodity lines in the administrative structure, both of which may neutralize particularistic influences.

Where commodity or industry units must be established, as indeed they must in many cases, these are advantages in subordinating them to an overhead structure. In O.P.A. and W.P.B. the commodity structure did not reach to the top level. At that level both staff and line officers were forced to think in terms as broad as those of the regulatory program.

The third expedient is to establish units for staff aid on policy matters at the upper levels of the executive structure. Such units may be staffed so as to obtain the aid of men who are trained by education and experience in the art of problem analysis and also of men who are skilled in the political art of judging the capacity for the manipulation of interests. With such personnel, staff units may be one of the most useful structural arrangements for implementing the idea of a publicly-conditioned expertness. They provide centers for discovery and suggestion of means of manipulating the areas of pliability in the economic organism. When located at the higher levels in the executive structure they are, in addition,

[90] See summary of Landis's views at pages 303-304.
[91] See pages 320-323.

centers through which the long and the large view of economic needs may be injected into the administrative process.

The fourth expedient is to integrate the executive branch of the government so that the President may influence the directions of administrative policy. Independence of administrators, whether in the form of irremovable and non-supervised commissions or of independently operating bureaus in a departmental hierarchy, may be a safeguard for objectivity in the handling of particulars. But it brings adjustment of interests within a framework conditioned by the limited circumference of the agency's program and probable identities of viewpoint with closely-affected groups. There is need for some measure of assurance that agency policy is correlated with the over-all objectives of government and conditioned to the dominant demands of the nation. This requires a channel of overhead check and direction from the President—who must, of necessity, seek to reconcile and subordinate the claims of particular groups to the dominant political demands of the national constituency which he represents. This need is discussed further in Chapter X and in the section on Congress in Chapter XI.

THE COORDINATION OF INTEREST PARTICIPATION

Besides representation in the composition of public authority, how may the interests be coordinated with administration? And what problems of protecting the public interest arise in these methods of coordination?

Influence and Pressure

Coordination between interests and government through the influence and pressure of the former upon the latter is generally condemned. Yet the administrator faces these continuously. And he knows that there are far more angles to this problem of influence and pressure than is appreciated in moral condemnation.

Influence and pressure may come from individual persons or from group interests. Adequate safeguards against personal influence could be found in the statement and enforcement of ethical standards for public officials and in the definition of guides for administrative practice. Adoption of the recommendations of the Senate Subcommittee on "Ethical Standards in Government" [92] would go far toward meeting the first of these needs. It recommended, first, a number of statutory enactments, including (1) amendments to the Administrative Procedure Act prohibiting (with penalty of summary dismissal) the public employee from accepting valuable gifts, becoming unduly involved—through frequent luncheons and expensive entertainment—with persons outside the government with which he does official business, improperly divulging valuable commercial or economic information, or discussing future employment with an outside person with which there was pending official business; (2) amendments to the same act limiting the practice of former government officials before government agencies; (3) legislation to require disclosure annually by top officials of their outside income, assets, and dealings in securities and commodities; and (4) revision and extension of existing criminal statutes on illegal practices of public employees. The subcommittee recommended also that a Court of Ethics be set up to consider practices which could not be prosecuted under criminal law and were not corrected by government agencies. It suggested that requirements for annual disclosure of income, assets, and investments apply to members of Congress. It suggested that professional societies draw up ethical codes governing the participation of their members in public affairs and also that special codes be drawn up for functional groups in the public service, including "regulatory officials."

Other means of combatting personal influence can be developed in the working practices of administration. Though these have not been catalogued in a protective code, a few guides can be listed: conduct business in public offices, get the matter on record, require clearances by professional staff members, prepare for particular pressures by developing a general policy, sink decisions on matters affecting persons or concerns individually deep enough into the administrative hierarchy and procedure to insulate against political direction on particulars.

[92] *Ethical Standards in Government*, Report of a Subcommittee of the Committee on Labor and Public Welfare, U. S. Senate, 82nd Cong., 1st Sess., 1951.

Group pressures which are distributed may also be absorbed and neutralized to a large extent in the administrative structure. Clarification of basic policy and the checks and balances within a large organization may provide much safeguard against distributed pressures. But where an interest is strong enough to exert power politically, or where the demands or dissatisfactions of the different interests are cumulated, a line of administrative defense for a policy antithetic to group interests may not hold unless backed by political support.

The administrator may accept group influence and pressure as part of the inevitables of government and try to organize means by which a part of the process of representing group interests will be absorbed into the regular channels of administration. He may accept the notion that all groups should have channels through which they can make their voices heard, and can present their views as forcefully as they desire, but seek to guide their participation in such a way that the group demands will be considered against the rationalization of public policy in legislation and within administration.

Procedure[93]

The most familiar method of coordination of interest representation with legal authority is through the right of parties to appear and be heard in government proceedings. In the judiciary, advocacy of interests is combined with and made a part of the process of decision. In administration, the same right of interested parties to present their cases may be preserved in formal and informal proceedings. In particularized proceedings, such as the grant of a license, the issuance of an order of individual applicability, the grant of exemption or the use of the administrative veto in particular cases, procedure can be easily adapted to afford adequate representation of interests. In these instances the participation is that of individual parties, but group interests may

[93] Leiserson, *Administrative Regulation*, Chapter III, gives a thorough discussion of interest representation in administrative procedure.

in fact be represented by intervenors or by participation of group representatives in preparation and presentation of the case.

Proceedings may also allow adequate representation of interests in rule making, issuance of orders of broad applicability, or the development of a basic policy which is to govern in subsequent decisions. In such proceedings, group or shared interests may be presented. In proceedings of a legislative type, presentation of representative or typical evidence may result in the presentation of the interests of a category of persons.[94] In less formal proceedings, draft regulations may be submitted to group organizations as well as to individuals, there may be consultation with group representatives, and the actual collaboration of groups may be solicited.[95]

Actually, all participation of interests in a regular and planned way before administrative units may be regarded as procedural. In general, it may be said that the administrator's problem is to provide ample opportunities for the interests to present their claims on matters subject to administrative jurisdiction through regular channels of administration, so as to inform the administration of these claims and their substantiation, and to reduce the presentation of these claims through other channels.

Representative Advisory Boards

Advisory boards are being increasingly accepted as a normal feature of public administration. There are, however, many variations in function and composition. Both of these things are revealed in recent national economic legislation. The Economic Cooperation Act of 1948 provided for a National Advisory Council on International Monetary and Financial Problems which was composed entirely of official members and whose function was coordination of activities of public agencies.[96] The Atomic Energy Act of 1946 required a general Advisory Committee composed of persons from civilian life who would advise the Atomic Energy Commission on

---

[94] See pages 193-194.
[95] See pages 192-193.
[96] 62 *U. S. Stat. at Large,* 137, 141.

scientific and technical matters.[97] The Economic Cooperation Act also provided for a Public Advisory Board, composed of the Administrator and twelve citizens "of broad and varied experience in matters affecting the public interest" to advise on "general or basic policy matters."[98] The Labor Management Relations Act of 1947 created a National Labor Management Panel, composed of six persons outstanding in the field of management and six outstanding in the field of labor, to advise the Director of the Federal Mediation and Conciliation Service.[99] The Emergency Price Control Act of 1942 provided that the Administrator should "so far as practicable, advise and consult with representative members of the industry" affected by regulations, or on request of a substantial portion thereof should "constitute a committee truly representative of the industry." [100]

In these several examples, only the last two base composition on segments of the public, and only the last contemplated a committee which was representative of interests. This latter type of committee provides one method of enriching public administration by external consultation and is a further means of coordinating interest participation with administration.

The many problems in use of such committees relate to function, crystallization, appointment, and scope of representation.

As to function, the basic problem is to define an area of activity which is significant but appropriate. Busy men will not want to give their time unless their work is meaningful. In general, the committee may serve as a two-way channel of communication. For the administrator it is a public relations organ through which he can gain a sympathetic attitude in the industry and enlist aid in obtaining public understanding and support. It is part of the technique of gaining consent. It is, however, also a channel through which he learns of the attitudes in the industry. Normally, the representative committee will not be useful in bringing additional eco-

---

[97] 60 U. S. Stat. at Large, 755, 757.
[98] 62 U. S. Stat. at Large, 137, 141.
[99] Title II, Section 205.
[100] Section 2 (a).

nomic data to the administration, though it may provide some safeguard in a large and diversified country against overlooking some set of facts; more important, it gives the administrator a view of the mind of the regulated and gives to the latter an opportunity to make its views on policy known. The administrator is likely to be interested primarily in molding a friendly group for aid in his public relations problems and may want to withhold from consideration by the committee those matters on which there will be chances of irreconcilable differences of opinion. On the other hand, the committee is usually interested in its impact on the functioning of the agency and will dislike reservation of controversial topics. A cooperative and fruitful relationship is easier if legislation and administrative decision do not impose a policy on industry which appears to it to be too onerous; in this respect, the operation of an interest advisory committee is more difficult in control than in service activities, particularly if the latter is a social service function, such as education or health, where the interests consulted may be professionals (educators or doctors) with an identity of viewpoint with the administration. It may be said, finally, that though committees may sometimes be asked to work out proposals, normally the performance of a successful function will depend on the extent to which staff work in the administrative agency supplies concise information and concrete proposals or alternatives to a committee.

Administrators are often wary of crystallizing advisory committees into permanent existence and form. They may see elements of safety in *ad hoc* committees which can be created and dropped with ease. Assuming that there are continuing functions of vitality for a committee, there are advantages in a standing committee, though permanence can be combined with some flexibility in composition. Such a committee gives an interest group the assurance that it will be consulted and may, therefore, be a means of avoiding, first, a demand for interest representation on the public agency, or second, a too-ready appeal by the interests to the political organs. Permanence provides an opportunity to give the members a fuller grasp of the agency's problems and a sense of responsibility for its over-all results. A standing committee may remove distrust, be a "buffer to criticism," and be a help in "breaking proposed administrative measures on the back of the public."[101] Recent statutes show a tendency to require continuing advisory committees of various types but to leave the administration much freedom to manipulate their composition.

Interest advisory boards may be composed of persons selected as delegates by the interests or of persons selected by public authority to represent economic groups. In the latter case, selection from panels nominated by the interests is a possibility. Choice among these systems is likely to depend upon a number of factors, the chief of which may be the extent to which the interests are organized in representative and group-conscious associations. Such associations are likely to demand that they have a part in determining the appointment of representatives.

During World War II most mobilization agencies worked through trade associations in developing their advisory committees. OPA, on the other hand, tried to deemphasize trade associations, doubting their representativeness, the democratic control of their internal organization, and the feasibility of obtaining the cooperation of association executives for policies which might be unpopular with a portion of the members. It constituted its committees independently, though with some suggestions and check from the associations; it excluded association executives from membership and sometimes from meetings. This effort to prevent association influence was not successful, for association members sometimes caucused prior to committee meetings and maintained influence through lines of communication with industry members who counted most. Association executives could not afford to lose the battle for participation, and as time passed OPA yielded some ground. The experience indicates that some cooperation of the associations must be obtained in the composition and work of advisory committees. On the other hand, an agency will need to retain some independence in the composition of committees, to en-

---

[101] The last of the stated advantages is from Leiserson's quotation from J. A. Salter, *Allied Shipping Control* (London and New York, 1921), 259-262.

sure their representativeness and to safeguard the opportunity afforded by advisory committees to establish agency contact with
cooperative groups.

The crucial problem is that of representativeness. The danger
is that the advisory committee will represent only the large, the
near, or the organized portions of an industry. It may thus provide the administration with a distorted view of interest opinion
and provide a focus through which the strong and strategically-
located interests may exert a disproportionate amount of influence.
In OPA, where every important industry came to have a national
industry advisory committee, criticism from the field offices of the
predominantly northeasternly composition of these committees and
of other unrepresentative elements in their composition led to a
practice of submitting the slates to the field offices for advice. It
was also generally the feeling in the field offices that the small
producer and distributor was represented only through the communication of the field office with the national office. It appears
that an agency must use many sources of information and advice in composing its advisory committees, and that it cannot rely
on such committees as the sole channel for expression of interest
opinion.

A wise administrator may find it possible to increase the support
for his agency's program by giving representation to sympathetic
but unorganized groups. He may search for these groups within an
industry. Or he may give representation to outside groups, such as
laborers, consumers, or outside industry groups. These may be
given representation on a single multi-interest advisory committee
or on separate single-interest committees. The most significant possibility is that of representing the wider interests of the community
through the addition of so-called "public" members to advisory
committees.

A multi-interest advisory committee may be used to obtain
the cooperation of conflicting interests. An example is the effective
use of such a committee in the defense program in 1951. Dissatisfied with the decision on a wage-increase formula by the tripartite
Wage Stabilization Board and with what it regarded as inadequate

direct representation in the defense agencies, a United Labor Policy Committee—set up by major labor organizations—instructed labor members of the Wage Stabilization Board to withdraw and later issued the same instructions to labor representatives in other positions in defense agencies. The United Labor Policy Committee issued a public statement explaining the causes of the "boycott" of the defense agencies. A month later President Truman succeeded in bringing labor back into the fold by constituting a Mobilization Policy Advisory Board, composed of the head of the Defense Mobilization Agency as chairman, and of four representatives each of labor, industry, agriculture, and the public. The committee, though under the chairmanship of the President's immediate subordinate, was accepted by labor as virtually a committee of the President.[102]

Several facts about this episode are of interest with respect to topics discussed in this chapter. First, the compromise of interests was sought at or near the top level of government, where it appropriately belongs. Second, the compromise was sought through an advisory committee, which presumably might reduce the pressure for adding staff positions directly representative of labor interests. Third, the executive order was deftly framed to preserve the fiction—and fiction it was—of a community-representative and non-partisan board. The order said that "All of the members of the board shall represent the general public and the public interest." This apparently was an answer to labor's claim for direct representation within the structure of government, but it quite unrealistically overlooked the fact that an advisory committee is a technique for allowing direct representation without incurring the dangers of such representation on decision-making boards or in staff positions.

This example of use of an advisory committee to meet an immediate problem should not obscure the fact that government devices are tested by their operation. The long-run value of an

[102] For further details see *New York Times*, Feb. 16, 1951, p. 1, c. 4; Feb. 17, p. 1, c. 2; March 16, p. 19, c. 2; April 6, p. 1, c. 5; April 7, p. 7, c. 5; May 1, p. 1, c. 2.

advisory committee will depend upon the continuous skill of the administrator in its use. Professor Macmahon has noted that with all its hopes for more democratic operations the use of advisory committees carries its perils: "It daily sharpens the need for administrative authorities who are skilful in consultation, vigilant in arranging representation that is reasonably comprehensive, sympathetic but wary, and above all independent. Only by careful use of advisory boards will the danger of compromising administration at its core be avoided." [103]

Beyond Procedure and Advice: The Sharing of Responsibility[104]

In 1936 the Supreme Court set a limit on delegation of authority to private groups. The Bituminous Coal Conservation Act of 1936 delegated power to fix maximum hours and minimum wages in mining districts to producers of two-thirds of the tonnage and a majority of the miners. The Court held that this was a violation of due process of law in that it delegated power to the majority "to regulate the affairs of an unwilling minority." [105]

The case shows only the outer limits beyond which the government could not go in 1936.[106] If rule-making power may not be completely delegated to private groups, it may still be shared with them. Moreover, operating functions may also be shared. In various ways national administration has been conditioned by the sharing of decisional and operating responsibilities with private organizations or groups, but in ways which avoided an

---

[103] "Boards, Advisory," *Encyclopaedia of the Social Sciences,* I (New York, 1930), 609-611, at p. 611.

[104] The only full discussion of this topic will be found in Leiserson, *Administrative Regulation,* Chapters II, VII, VIII, and IX.

[105] Carter *v.* Carter Coal Co., 298 U. S. 238 (1936).

[106] Compare Currin *v.* Wallace and U. S. *v.* Rock Royal Cooperative, Inc., ante, page 58. Compare also the closed (or union) shop contract made by representatives of a majority of workers; also, the power of the producer-distributor over the retailer and consumer in fair trade laws, sanctioned by the Supreme Court in Old Dearborn Distributing Co. *v.* Seagram-Distillers Corp., 299 U. S. 183 (1936). See Louis L. Jaffe, "Lawmaking by Private Groups," *Harvard Law Review,* LI, 202-253 (1937-38), for a discussion of the Carter Case in comparison with other areas where private groups have been given a controlling position.

overt and complete delegation of rule-making power as in the bituminous coal act.

Thus, a new act for the coal industry in 1937 provided for a sharing of responsibility but with final decision being reserved for the public authority.[107] The act authorized district boards composed of representatives selected by producers, save for one labor representative, to determine the weighted average of total costs of coal produced in the district upon the basis of figures submitted by the Commission's staff, and, at a later stage, to propose minimum prices upon the basis of weighted average costs submitted by the Commission's staff for the price area. Final decision was made by the Commission. This participation of interests fell short of that in the earlier act but was a step beyond that embodied in the Fair Labor Standards Act where advisory functions were intrusted to interest representatives appointed by the public administrator.[108]

The most extensive sharing of rule making and administrative power with interest groups in our history came in 1933–1935 under the N.R.A., where an attempt was made to establish industrial self-government and a cooperative relationship between the state and interest groups. The statute provided that "trade or industrial associations or groups" might propose codes of fair competition for their respective industries to the President who would approve if he found that these groups were "truly representative" and imposed no "inequitable restrictions" on membership and that the proposed codes did not promote monopoly, eliminate or oppress, or discriminate against, small enterprises, and would tend to effectuate the policy of the Act.[109] Though the President could attach conditions to his approval or on his own initiative impose codes, the initiative came in practice from private groups, usually trade associations. The codes were legally binding and contained penalties for violation. Administration was vested in code authorities representing in the main the industrial groups which pro-

[107] Bituminous Coal Act of 1937, 50 *U. S. Stat. at Large*, 72, April 26, 1937.
[108] *Supra*, page 242.
[109] National Industrial Recovery Act, Title I, Sec. 3 (a), 48 *U. S. Stat. at Large*, 195, 196.

posed the codes, though the public had a representative on each authority and minority industrial groups and labor also had representation sometimes.[110]

Never in a major federal program have the protections for the public interest been so inadequately organized. The speed of the code-making process and the lack of objective policy standards and review facilities in the agency of administration gave industry groups a chance to embody their will into law. The check from labor and consumer advisory committees led to a bargaining process in the making of public law. The code authorities were often unrepresentative; and the national, regional, and local units of these authorities operated without the public supervision which would have been necessary to prevent abuse, discrimination, and overreaching in administration. As for compliance, it resulted more from the unregularized pressure of these organizations upon individuals than from the efforts of the administrative agency or from the authority of a system of law. The experience with industrial self-government revealed the dangers in overextension of group collaboration in a splintered economic system.[111]

The program of agricultural control has allowed for extensive farmer participation. For one thing, imposition of some controls has been contingent upon approval by affected groups. Thus, under the Agricultural Marketing Agreement Act of 1937, marketing orders may be issued by the Secretary of Agriculture if approved by stated percentages of the handlers and of the producers of the commodity or, in stated circumstances, of the producers only.[112] Likewise, the referendum of producers was initiated under the early crop control program of the New Deal and this is continued in the Agricultural Adjustment Act of 1938, which re-

[110] "A survey covering 400 approved codes shows that 218 of the 400 place trade associations in a dominant position, with minority representation for nonmember associations in 101 of the 218 instances. There is labor representation on 21 of the 400 code authorities, and consumer representation on 2." Leverett S. Lyon, Paul T. Homan, George Terborgh, Lewis L. Lorwin, Charles Dearing, and Leon C. Marshall, *The National Industrial Recovery Administration* (Brookings Institution, Washington, 1935), 166.

[111] For full discussion of code making and administration see Lyon and others, *op. cit.*

[112] 50 *U. S. Stat. at Large*, 246, 7 U.S.C. 608 (c).

quires approval of an extraordinary majority of producers of a commodity before imposition of national marketing quotas.[113] This type of provision has been distinguished by the Supreme Court from the delegation in the coal case as being only a statement of the conditions under which Congress desired its policy to be applied.[114]

In addition, farmer participation at the local level has been enlisted in action and planning phases of agricultural programs. Allotment phases of the production and marketing control programs have been administered by local committees of farmers.[115] Following the Mount Weather Agreement in 1938 county land use planning committees, composed largely of farmers, were activated in a majority of counties and for a time gave hope for an expanding program of farmer participation.[116] In soil conservation, agricultural credit, and other programs the farmer affected by the programs has become an active agent.[117]

This enlistment of farmer participation has seemed to carry real advantages. Particularly is this true of the system of local participation. It has been viewed hopefully by those who see the needs of local adaptations in service and planning activities and of "integrating" farmer interests and efforts with the government's program. It has offered opportunities to provide the farmer with a sense of participation in matters affecting his livelihood. It has perhaps provided for the public official a way of understanding

[113] 52 *U. S. Stat. at Large*, 31, Title III, 7 U.S.C., Chapter 35, Subchapter II-B.

[114] Currin *v.* Wallace, 306 U. S. 1 (1939), upholding a statute which forbade auctions of tobacco not inspected by the government at markets designated by the Secretary of Agriculture, but subject to approval of the market designation in a referendum of the growers. Also, U. S. *v.* Rock Royal Coöperative, Inc., 307 U. S. 533 (1939), upholding the Agricultural Marketing Agreement Act of 1937.

[115] For development of farmer participation see Leiserson, *op. cit.*, 205.

[116] See U. S. Bureau of Agricultural Economics, *Annual Report* for each of the years 1939-1941; Lewis, "Democratic Planning in Agriculture," *op. cit.*; John D. Black, mimeographed report for the Agriculture Committee on National Policy on *Federal-State-Local Relations in Agriculture* (1949), 11-19.

[117] See the references cited *Supra*, 225, footnote 19; and Herman Walker, Jr. and W. Robert Parks, "Soil Conservation Districts: Local Democracy in a National Program," *Journal of Politics*, VIII, 538-549 (1946).

farmer opinion and for participating farmers a more intimate view of programs, a wider view of relationships and problems, and a richer experience in group activity.

On the other hand, difficult problems arise in use of a system of farmer participation. In part, these arise out of the heavy dependence of farmers in the localities of the nation upon the paid official for leadership and technical aid in originating and sustaining service and land use programs. In part, they arise out of the difficulties of obtaining a truly democratic participation in local committees[118] and of insuring efficient and fair operation of action programs through farmer committees. They arise, also, out of the fact that agriculture is more than a local, farmer problem. On the one hand, the local farmer community is dependent upon outside financial aid for improvement of land, of dollar crop yields, and other ends; on the other, the community as a whole has an interest in the agricultural foundations of the economy.[119]

It is obvious that the context for consideration of issues of group participation is different when programs are applied to multitudes of little producers in scattered communities, and when these programs combine service, planning, and control activities reaching deep into the everyday pursuit of individual livelihoods. Participation of the affected may be a program necessity and also a necessity for maintaining the feeling that government is "of the people." And yet the obvious principles of public power need still to be maintained. National policy cannot with safety be too restricted by practices of group consent, allotments must be made in strict accord with rules, and national funds should be used in accord with firm lines of guiding policy. If power is shared with interest groups, it must yet be coordinated and properly subordinated.

The most extensive sharing of regulatory responsibilities in present control patterns is with the commodity and security exchanges. In the case of the commodity exchanges and the national security exchanges "the private group had preëmpted the field and the

---

[118] See Lewis's discussion in "Democratic Planning in Agriculture," *op. cit.*
[119] A recent careful analysis of the problem is given by Black in the reference cited in footnote 116.

problems of such regulation long before the advent of government on behalf of interests other than those directly represented in the group organization." [120] The regulatory authorities have left a large measure of self-regulation in the exchanges and have confined their intervention to steps necessary to ensure the proper functioning of the exchanges in the public interest. In the case of over-the-counter exchanges the government itself encouraged the formation of self-regulating associations as a means of bringing under control the thousands of scattered brokers and dealers.[121] In all three cases, the exchanges are incorporated into the system of public control and perform functions which are complementary to those of the supervising public agency.

In these special instances private collaboration has provided a means of attaining public objectives with a minimum of continuing exercise of public authority. The apparent success of the method in these instances may be in part attributed to special circumstances. Brokers and dealers on the exchanges, like bankers, constantly hold considerable sums of other people's money which is withdrawable on demand. They are highly vulnerable to the adverse publicity likely to attend any official suggestion that their behavior warrants investigation. The informal sanctions are often more potent than the formal, therefore, and appear to be a substantial check on the actual exercise of regulatory power by the interest groups. This special situation should not cloud consideration of the great dangers to the maintenance of the public interest in overextension of the principle of self-regulation, as were revealed, for instance, in the experience of the National Recovery Administration. The utility of the system is limited to cases where consensus in objective can be achieved, dangers of unfair treatment to minority groups can be avoided, smooth relationships in divided responsibilties are possible, and too heavy a load of supervisory check and force is not required for maintenance of the public interest.

[120] Avery Leiserson, *Administrative Regulation: A Study in Representation of Interests,* 221. Copyright 1942 by The University of Chicago. See, for full discussion, Leiserson at pages 214-239. See also *Supra,* pages 127-128.
[121] In the so-called Maloney Act, 52 *U. S. Stat. at Large,* 1070 (1938).

CONCLUSIONS

At the risk of being categorical we extract from the preceding three sections several practical guides for maintenance of a publicly-oriented point of view in administrative control:

1. Avoid representation of interests in the composition of public authority, or occupational qualifications which are equivalent, except where necessary to obtain consent of parties to a mediatory process.

2. Preserve the non-interest principle in the composition of agencies, except as emergencies require departure from the principle.

3. Subordinate the position of any staff aides who represent specialized viewpoints and strengthen the professional elements in the staff.

4. Avoid, so far as feasible, allocation of control functions to clientele agencies.

5. Consider the desirability of using administrative units which cut across industry or commodity lines.

6. Strengthen the use of staff aides on policy questions.

7. Provide a channel of over-all political direction and check.

8. Establish the standards of official conduct and administrative practice required to prevent personal influence.

9. Regularize the channels of individual or group contact with administration.

10. Provide ample opportunities for interest representation in procedural processes.

11. Consider the advantages and necessity for advisory committees including committees which are truly representative of interests.

12. Where responsibilities are shared with private groups, provide for true representation of groups and for such supervision as is essential for the maintenance of public purpose and fair treatment of persons.

This is, nevertheless, not all that will be said on the subject. Much of the next two chapters relates directly to this central issue of maintaining a publicly-oriented point of view in administration.

Chapter X

The Problem of Organization

TYPES OF ORGANIZATION

Economic controls have been administered in the national government through three types of organization.

First, many controls are administered in the executive departments.[1] The first comprehensive control program, the regulation of banks, was delegated to the Comptroller of the Currency, who was a bureau chief in the Department of the Treasury. Today, functions of economic control are vested in several departments, including Agriculture, Labor, Commerce, Treasury, Interior, Justice, Post Office, and the Federal Security Agency. Concerning one of these, it has been said:[2]

The Department of Agriculture is one of the largest regulatory agencies in the Federal Government. It administers the greatest number of regulatory acts of any Federal agency—acts which vary widely in subject matter and in administrative and enforcement procedures—and has had long experience in the regulatory field.

In addition to the "regulatory" work referred to in the above statement, the Department through its commodity adjustment programs administers economic controls whose breadth and significance are as great as any in the government.

[1] In this chapter the word "department" is used to include the so-called departments and the Federal Housing Agency, Federal Works Agency, and Federal Security Agency. These occupy a position in the governmental structure similar to that of departments.

[2] Commission on Organization of the Executive Branch of the Government (Hoover Commission), *Task Force Report on Agriculture Activities* (1949), 52.

Second, controls have been administered by independent exccutive agencies, that is, by agencies located outside the regular executive departments but subject unquestionably to the control of the President. This has been an organizational feature of economic control in emergencies. In the early days of the New Deal there was a mushroom growth of new agencies. Some of these, like the Agricultural Adjustment Administration, were placed under department heads, while others, like the giant N.R.A., were put under new officials reporting directly to the President. Similarly, wartime controls in World War II were administered, on the whole, by new agencies outside the departments but under presidential control.[3]

In both of these types control is normally exercised through single officials. This has been the usual practice within departments. In the emergencies, both in the New Deal period and World War II, boards were sometimes established, but even then the authority was usually exercised through the chairman.

The third type of organization is the so-called independent regulatory commission. The term has been applied to agencies which have three features: they are engaged in control of private economic activities, they are headed by a board or commission, and they are independent in some measure from executive supervision. Usually, also, they are independent in the sense of being located outside the departments.[4]

[3] On the New Deal period see Roger V. Shumate, "Development of National Administration in the United States, 1932-35," *American Political Science Review*, XXIX, 842-853 (October, 1935); on controls in World War II see Luther Gulick, "War Organization of the Federal Government," *American Political Science Review*, XXXVIII, 1166-1179 (December, 1944).

[4] Sometimes independence of the commissions is defined only as location outside departments. Examples are the Hoover Commission's report on regulatory commissions and certain definitions by Professor Cushman. See Hoover Commission, *Regulatory Commissions* (1949), 1; Robert E. Cushman, "The Problem of the Independent Regulatory Commissions," in President's Committee on Administrative Management, *Report with Special Studies* (Washington, 1937), 207; Robert E. Cushman, *The Independent Regulatory Commissions* (New York, London, and Toronto, 1941), 4. Usually, however, the other meaning of independence is also stressed. Thus, the task force report for the Hoover Commission defined an independent commission as one "not within an executive department or under the direct control of the President." *Task Force Report on Regulatory Commissions* (1949), 3. Also, Cushman said that the commissions were "wholly free from control by the President." *Report with Special Studies,*

Actually, the contrast is between two methods of administration. After emergencies the agencies located outside of departments but subject to presidential control have usually disappeared or have —as in the case of license control of exports—been absorbed in an old-line department. There remains, therefore, for long-run control programs the contrast between the departmental or bureau type of organization and the commission type. In one there are single heads and executive supervision, in the other plural heads and independence.

Nine agencies were included in the Hoover Commission's studies of the independent regulatory commission. These were the Interstate Commerce Commission, Federal Reserve Board, Federal Trade Commission, U. S. Maritime Commission (since 1950 the Federal Maritime Board), Federal Power Commission, Federal Communications Commission, Securities and Exchange Commission, National Labor Relations Board, and Civil Aeronautics Authority.[5] Among other agencies which might be included in the category are the Atomic Energy Commission,[6] the U. S. Tariff Commission,[7] and the National Mediation Board.[8]

207. With more accuracy, however, Cushman has also written, "Congress has never created a completely independent regulatory commission. The independence of these commissions has consisted in immunity from the President's discretionary removal power; the President has always been given power to remove members for causes stated in the statute." *The Independent Regulatory Commissions*, 460. Independence from removal appears to be a third definition of independence.

Occasionally commissions have been located within departments but not subjected fully to departmental control. This was true of the I.C.C. from 1887 to 1889 and is true now of the Federal Maritime Board. Since 1940 the Civil Aeronautics Board has been attached to the Department of Commerce for housekeeping functions.

[5] Cushman included these nine and the National Bituminous Coal Commission, now extinct.

[6] The Task Force for the Hoover Commission recognized that the Atomic Energy Commission was regulatory and an independent commission but excluded it from study "partly because so large a part of its work is operational, and partly because so many of its problems appear to be unique." *Task Force Report on Regulatory Commission*, 3.

[7] Chairman Herbert Hoover believed that the U. S. Tariff Commission and the Tax Court of the United States should be included in the same category with the nine studied by the Task Force. *Regulatory Commissions*, 1.

[8] See the list given by Lindsay Rogers in "The Independent Regulatory Commissions," *Political Science Quarterly*, LII, 1, at p. 2ff (March, 1937).

It should be noted here that the union of different types of functions exists in both the departmental and the independent commission systems. Sub-legislative, quasi-judicial, and executive tasks, policy making and "pure" administration, have been entrusted to departments and to commissions. Nevertheless, except for the field of agriculture, the commissions have been the chief repository of long-run regulatory functions of a quasi-legislative and quasi-judicial nature; and it mainly is for exercise of these types of functions that the commissions have been created.

THE COMMISSION SYSTEM

Independence: Reality or Myth?

Of the two features of the commission system, independence and plurality, the former has been the center of discussion. This would not have been true if independence had meant no more than location outside of a department, for independence in that sense could present no more than a problem of consolidation of agencies or of special arrangements for coordination by the executive. It is the issue of independence from executive control which has given meaning to the discussion of independence. This is the key issue of organization in public regulation. All of the questions about the nature and purpose of regulation, about segregation of functions, and about the responsibility of administrators are cast in plainer mold in the controversy over whether regulation should be independent from control by the chief executive.

What are the facts about independence in this latter sense? To what extent is it true that these agencies are free from control by the President?

Several factors make for independence. First, appointments of commissioners are for definite, staggered terms extending beyond the date of inauguration of a new president. Since the terms range from four to fourteen years a president may have to wait from three to eight years to appoint a majority of the commissioners.[9]

[9] The Federal Maritime Board, created in 1950, has the shortest term. In this discussion this Board is included as one of the commissions, in place of the old U. S. Maritime Commission.

Second, for seven of the nine commissions studied by the Hoover Commission no more than a majority of the members may be from the same party. Although a president may not find it difficult to locate persons in the opposing party who are sympathetic to his point of view, this provision does insure a lack of political responsibility and confirms a tradition of independence from executive control.

Third, for five of the present commissions the statutes provide that the commissioners may be removed only for neglect of duty or malfeasance in office, or for these causes or inefficiency, or for cause. The limitation by Congress of the President's power of removal of members of the Federal Trade Commission to cases of "inefficiency, neglect of duty, or malfeasance in office" was upheld by the Supreme Court in the famous Humphreys Case.[10] Ofttimes the limitation on the power to remove is "thought of as the distinguishing mark of the independent commission." [11]

Fourth, the President lacks the authority to designate the chairman of the Interstate Commerce Commission.[12] Where the commission selects its own chairman the President may lack a friendly channel of contact with the commission.

Fifth, procedural features limit the President. Where decision must be made on the basis of the record an overhead directive power in individual cases is necessarily excluded, except as to choice and prosecution of cases. Moreover, the very tendency of the commissions to operate so largely by case-to-case proceedings has obscured the opportunities for policy development by overhead directives. The tendency toward emphasis on the judicial aspects of regulation has had the same effect.

Sixth, the commissions' close association with their clienteles and their cultivation of their own channels of contact with Congress

---

[10] Humphrey's Executor v. U. S., 295 U. S. 602 (1935).

[11] Task Force Report on Regulatory Commissions, 14.

[12] This was true, also, prior to reorganization orders of 1950, of the Federal Trade Commission, the Federal Power Commission, and the Securities and Exchange Commission.

have tended to insulate them against novel or disturbing influence from the chief executive.[13]

Finally, tradition has contributed to the development of a theory of independence. L. D. White has said that "The gulf between the Interstate Commerce Commission and the President has been worn deep by usage of a half century." [14] The example of the traditional immunity of the Interstate Commission has helped set a pattern in men's thinking about regulatory commissions generally.

The other side of the picture reveals many limitations on commission independence from executive control and influence. First, the commissions are subject to the exercise of the President's managerial powers. Civil Service rules apply to commission personnel, budgets must be channelled through the Bureau of the Budget, legislative proposals must be referred to it also, and the Bureau may make studies of administrative management.

Second, the President still has significant control of personnel. His power of appointment or reappointment is a means of influencing the trend in regulation, though the limitations have been revealed again in the recent rejection in the Senate of the renomination of Leland Olds as Federal Power Commissioner.[15] The President can designate the chairman for some of the commissions, and it may be assumed that he can remove such a chairman from his duties as chairman. For the Federal Power Commission, the Securities Exchange Commission, and the Federal Communications Commission there are no limitations on his power of removal of commissioners.

Even where limits are placed on his removal power the President may still have extensive influence. Cushman argues that where the statute limits the President to removal for "inefficiency, neglect of duty, or malfeasance in office," the President may use the power

---

[13] See James W. Fesler, "Independent Regulatory Commission," in Fritz Morstein Marx, *Elements of Public Administration*, 211-212 (1946).

[14] *Introduction to the Study of Public Administration* (New York, 3rd ed., 1948), 104.

[15] See Joseph P. Harris, "The Senatorial Rejection of Leland Olds: A Case Study," *American Political Science Review*, XLV, 674-692 (September, 1951).

to (1) "exact reasonable efficiency and absolute integrity" and the authority should extend to "collective as well as individual inefficiency," (2) force compliance with executive orders of general application "which affect the general efficiency of the government," (3) require performance of duties in those cases where the statute allows the President to direct the commissions.[16] Moreover, if the President, after hearing, finds that a commissioner is guilty of "inefficiency" or "neglect of duty," it may be assumed that the courts would not look behind his finding to determine the basis upon which the finding was made.[17]

Third, the President may have a power of direction, or action may require his approval. For example, the Federal Trade Commission has the statutory duty of investigating "alleged violations of the anti-trust laws by any corporation" upon direction of the President. The approval of the President is required for actions of the Civil Aeronautics Board regarding certificates or permits for overseas or foreign air transportation by domestic or foreign carriers, an order of the Securities Exchange Commission suspending trading on exchanges, and decisions by the Maritime Commission for construction of vessels.

Fourth, the President may in conference or otherwise communicate his views to the commissions. This may vary from mere interchange of views with a chairman to strong pressure to follow a presidential policy.

Finally, the President may appoint special study commissions or recommend new regulatory legislation to Congress. Notable examples in the thirties were the National Power Survey and the National Rate Survey, both designed to provide a factual basis for national power policy. More recent examples are the Special Board of Inquiry on Air Safety appointed on June 15, 1947 after a series of disastrous accidents and the temporary Air Policy Committee appointed on July 18, 1947 "to make an objective inquiry into national aviation policies and problems, and to assist me

---

[16] *The Independent Regulatory Commissions,* 464-5.
[17] *Ibid.*

[President Truman] in formulating an integrated national aviation policy." [18]

The presidents since the establishment of the second commission in 1913 have taken no narrow view of their functions. Concerning those prior to Roosevelt, Cushman has said:[19]

There is no doubt that Wilson with his "prime minister" theory of the nature of the Presidential office felt that he was entitled to impress his policies on the independent commissions and to expect their conformity to those policies. President Harding and Coolidge made plain on repeated occasions that they believed Presidential domination of certain of the independent commissions to be essential.[20] Harding, as we have seen, engaged in a long and bitter fight to secure control over the Shipping Board and the Fleet Corporation, and it was clear that President Coolidge agreed with his views in the matter. On at least two occasions President Hoover made public statements indicating how he thought the Interstate Commerce Commission ought to exercise certain of its powers, and the commission somewhat reluctantly yielded to that influence.

Herring has described the effective manner in which the difficulties of independence were avoided in the early years of the Roosevelt period:[21]

The judicial calm of the Interstate Commerce Commission was left undisturbed, but the most able and aggressive commissioner was created Federal Coordinator of Transportation. The United States Tariff Commission was reduced to a harmless condition through the passage of the Reciprocal Tariff Act. The Federal Radio Commission was abolished out-

[18] On August 12, 1948 the President called in the chairmen of the R.F.C. and the C.A.B. and the Director of the Bureau of the Budget to confer with him on the financial situation of the airlines and to find "means by which this industry could obtain the type of financing best suited not only to its immediate requirements, but also to its long run development." He asked the R.F.C. to make a study with the help of the other two agencies. Edward G. Sweeney, *Staff Report on the Civil Aeronautics Board* (Mimeographed for Hoover Commission), Chapter III, 5.

[19] From pages 681-682 of Robert E. Cushman, *The Independent Regulatory Commissions.* Copyright 1941 by Oxford University Press, New York, Inc. On Wilson, however, see E. P. Herring, *Federal Commissioners* (1936), 78, but compare Cushman, *op. cit.,* 222-3, 681, 685.

[20] To Cushman's comments, it may be added that Presidents Harding and Coolidge sought to control commissions by requiring undated resignations of certain commissioners at the time of their appointment.

[21] From page 223 of E. Pendleton Herring, *Public Administration and the Public Interest.* Copyright 1936 by McGraw-Hill Book Co., Inc.

right and a New Deal commission took its place. The President secured the resignation of Hoover's chairman of the Federal Power Commission and added two appointees of his own.

Roosevelt's influence on regulation did not cease with the enactment of New Deal measures. His power of appointment was used to ensure that the general attitudes of the Administration would prevail on the commissions. In several cases the chairman was a continuing channel of presidential contact with the commissions.[22] Even in cases where the president lacked the statutory power to designate the chairman, his desires on choice of a chairman were sometimes controlling.[23] Through his power of appoint-

[22] The reports on some of the commissions prepared for the Hoover Commission's task force on regulatory commissions contain many references to these contacts. A few are cited:

President Roosevelt "had fairly frequent talks with Fly and Porter about all types of important policy questions." William W. Golub, *Staff Report on the Federal Communications Commission* (Mimeographed for Hoover Commission), Chapter III, 2.

"The selection of Douglas as chairman was clearly the wish of the President, and during his incumbency as chairman, there was as close liaison with the White House as at any time in the Commission's history." Carl F. Farbach, *Staff Report on the Securities and Exchange Commission* (Mimeographed for Hoover Commission), Chapter III, 2.

"It is said that most CAB chairmen have had the 'key to the back door of the White House.'" Edward G. Sweeney, *Staff Report on the Civil Aeronautics Board* (Mimeographed for Hoover Commission), Chapter III, 1.

"For the first nine years of its existence, the Commission [Maritime] had two chairmen who assumed an outstanding role which made them much more than first among equals.

"Joseph P. Kennedy, the first chairman, had strong Presidential backing. . . . According to a former official of the Commission, Kennedy would telephone the President in the very presence of a recalcitrant commissioner if a major policy question was involved. . . . Admiral Land was another strong chairman. He, too, was assured of backing from the White House, and was consistently able to obtain a working majority." James MacGregor Burns, *Staff Report on United States Maritime Commission* (Mimeographed for Hoover Commission), Chapter II, 2.

[23] Though the statute provides that, except for the initial appointment, the chairman of the Federal Power Commission shall be elected, the President on July 18, 1933 sent a letter to the Commission which said: "In view of the resignation of George Otis Smith as chairman of the Federal Power Commission, I hereby designate Hon. Frank R. McNinch as chairman and request the immediate concurrence of the commission." Herman Pritchitt, *Staff Report on the Federal Power Commission* (Mimeographed for Hoover Commission), Chapter III, 5, quoting from Federal Power Commission Minutes for July 19, 1933. It is

ment and other means the President tried to remove conflicts on commissions and to improve internal operations.[24] Apparently, his views on policy were occasionally communicated to the commissions;[25] and the leadership of the President on some of the com-

---

said also that the President conveyed to the F.P.C. his desire that Mr. Leland Olds be named chairman, and this was done in January, 1940. Pritchitt, *op. cit.,* Chapter III, 5.

[24] Notably for the Federal Communications Commission. See Golub, *op. cit.,* Chapter III, 1-4 and Chapter XIV, 15. But note also, regarding the Civil Aeronautics Authority:

"After the appointments to the original Authority, it is understood that the objections of the Administrator to subordination by the five-man Authority were carried to the President much to his annoyance. Later, the severe disagreements in 1939-1940 between the two members of the Air Safety Board are said to have been appealed to the President. Largely because the President was bothered by this internal dissension, it is reported, he personally took the initiative in directing the Bureau of the Budget to prepare the Reorganization Plans of 1940 so as to abolish the Air Safety Board and to take the Administrator out from under the five-man Authority and place him within the Department of Commerce." Also, upon adoption of the Reorganization Plans of 1940, the Bureau of the Budget attempted by letter to delineate the functions of Administrator and Board, the letter to serve as a guide to these officials and to the Bureau in preparing the annual budget. Sweeney, *op. cit.,* Chapter III, 3 and 10.

[25] The staff reports for the Hoover Commission's task force contain many general statements about the presidential concern with policy but offer few specific illustrations regarding any president. But see the statements in footnote 22 above. It is said that it was at the President's request that Commissioner Fly raised the problem with the other commissioners of ownership of radio stations by newspapers, which led to a commission order for an investigation. Golub, *op. cit.,* Chapter III, 4. After commenting on Douglas' chairmanship of the S.E.C., the staff report (Chapter III, 3) says:

"But the President did indicate from time to time his desire to 'tighten up' here and there when the Commission seemed to be relaxing a bit too much. A similar situation seems to have prevailed during Frank's period as chairman. Specific approval was sought of the Commission's policy on occasion. Thus, in 1940 when the Commission and the industry had tentatively agreed on an amendment to Section 8(a) of the Securities Act to permit acceleration, the Commission in requesting the President's approval of the amendment pointed out the specific policies that the Commission proposed to follow in granting acceleration if the amendments were enacted."

The staff report on the Maritime Commission says (Chapter III, 5):

"The smoothness with which policies were coordinated between the White House and the Maritime Commission is indicated in the following testimony of Mr. Schnell, the former Executive Director of the Maritime Commission:

". . . Admiral Land, when he was Chairman of the Commission, visited President Roosevelt and discussed our postwar shipping. Admiral Land reported to the Commission at that time and there was a public statement made by President Roosevelt that the time was ripe for us to make bold and daring plans for the future, and it was told to us by Admiral Land that President

missions has been attested by their members.[26] During the war his statutory power to issue directives was used to integrate the work of the commissions with the wartime program.[27] On the whole, however, it is probably not too much to say that it was primarily through the appointive power of the president that the commissions were integrated with the general trend of policy in the nation.

Presidential interest in the work of the commissions is also seen in the record of President Truman. Apparently, he has made less effort than his predecessor to influence the commissions by ap-

---

Roosevelt himself would like to see fast passenger liners . . . and that he would also like to have us resume after the war the round-the-world combination passenger and freight service, which prior to the war the American President Line ran.

"In accordance with the idea of the President the Commission proceeded with the design of the most modern-type vessels to run on those various trade routes. . . ."

On the other hand, the staff report on the F.P.C. (Chapter IV, 3) definitely states: "There is little evidence of Presidential initiative in attempts to influence the general policies of the Commission, and none of efforts to influence Commission decision in particular cases." But the same report concludes:

"Considering the President's constitutional responsibility for the faithful execution of the laws, the need for executive leadership in policy formation, and the problem of coördination of related administrative programs, no theory of complete independence of the Power Commission from Presidential supervision and control can be supported. An example of the record of Presidential relationships with the Commission shows that its independence is in fact substantially circumscribed by executive influence in one fashion or another." Chapter IV, 1. At the same place it is said that the most significant influence of the President has been through the appointive power.

The Task Force Report, 31, concluded: "The investigations of our staff have not revealed that the President has sought to interfere in, or influence the determination of, particular controversies or matters handled by such commissions."

[26] See Cushman, *The Independent Regulatory Commissions*, 682; White, *op. cit.*, 3rd ed., 105. Walter Galenson, *Staff Report on the National Labor Relations Board* (Mimeographed for Hoover Commission), Chapter III, 1, after saying that there is little evidence of direct presidential effort to influence substantive policy of the Board, reports that a former member of the Board told of one instance in which he was called to the White House and asked whether the Board could not alter a certain policy, currently being criticized, to help an election campaign but that the President was persuaded of the unwisdom of the request and did not persist. The name of the President is not given.

[27] For examples of such directives for one commission, see Pritchitt, *op. cit.*, Chapter III, 21.

pointment of commissioners or designation of chairmen.[28] On the other hand, his appointive power has been used decisively,* as when James Landis was not reappointed at the expiration of his term on the Civil Aeronautics Board in 1947,[29] and when Eccles was not redesignated as chairman of the Federal Reserve Board in 1948. It has been shown that his participation in civil aeronautical development through arranging for studies has been considerable. And at least in the case of the Maritime Commission, his views on policy have been presented.[30]

Plainly, there is conflict of trends on the independence of the regulatory commission. Presidential power bucks tradition. Facts run counter to the theory that the commissions are "wholly free from control by the President."

The Arguments for and Against the Commission System

In such a situation inquiry must shift to the logic behind each position. What reasons support the commission idea, including independence from executive control? And what arguments are advanced against it?

The first regulatory commission was the result of compromise. The Senate insisted on a commission; the House seemed unalterably opposed. After years of deadlock a conference committee in 1887 found a give-and-take arrangement under which the House accepted a commission and a flexible regulation of long-and-short hauls and the Senate accepted the stricter prohibitions of the House measure including those against pooling.[31]

Cushman has concluded that state experience influenced Congress toward adoption of commission regulation.[32] Senator Cullom,

---

[28] This seems to be the conclusion of a few of the authors of staff reports for the task force on independent regulatory commissions.

[29] Also significant, in view of cleavages in policy on the F.P.C., was President Truman's reappointment (rejected by the Senate) of Leland Olds in 1949.

[30] See the discussion of the President's requests on sale of tankers and the handling of scrap problems. Burns, *op. cit.*, Chapter III, 6-7.

[31] For a summary see Cushman, *The Independent Regulatory Commissions*, 40-44.

[32] *Ibid.*, 34.

leader for the commission idea in the Senate, had had experience with commission regulation of railroads in Illinois.[33] Thus, the beginning of railroad regulation in the states, with their weak governors and disintegrated administrations, influenced the national government toward the first trimming of executive control and the beginnings of the independent or disintegrated system of regulatory administration.

Even though a commission was established, the twentieth century idea of independence was apparently not present. Cushman has said that "the leaders did not discuss the question of the independence of the commission;" that "independence, if it meant anything, appears to have meant bipartisanship, as a guarantee of impartiality," rather than independence from executive domination; that freedom from removal was not thought of in terms of the effects on presidential authority; and that any independence contemplated was not incompatible with its location in the Department of the Interior, which had certain delegated housekeeping functions.[34]

The example of the Interstate Commerce Commission "undoubtedly influenced Congress to set up other commissions modeled upon it." [35] Other reasons which have led Congress from time to time to set up independent regulatory commissions are:[36]

1. Judicial or quasi-judicial nature of some of the tasks.
2. Desire to keep regulatory functions free from political domination.
3. Complicated and technical nature of the regulatory tasks.
4. Desire to give regional representation on the regulatory agency.

[33] John H. Reagan, leader of the movement for railroad regulation in the House of Representatives, was from Texas, which had no commission at that time. Cushman, *op. cit.*, 34.
[34] Robert E. Cushman, *The Independent Regulatory Commissions*, 61-62. Copyright 1941 by Oxford University Press, Inc.
[35] Cushman, *Report with Special Studies*, 217.
[36] Condensed from Cushman, *Report with Special Studies*, 216.

David Truman argues that use of the commission form after the I.C.C.'s establishment "seems to have been a matter of defensive strategy" of the regulated groups, who prefer the commission "as the least objectionable device." *The Governmental Process* (New York, 1951), 417.

5. Inability to find any logical place in the executive departments for some of the activities.
6. Experimental nature of regulation.
7. Belief that rule-making functions should be performed by a group.

Recently, the arguments for the independent regulatory commission were summarized by the task force for the Hoover Commission. Four arguments were presented.[37] First, was the argument for impartiality. After noting the dangers of "favoritism and unfairness in administration" and the fact that "The regulated interests are powerful and often politically influential," it concluded that "there is a vital necessity" that regulatory agencies be "insulated from partisan influence or control to the maximum extent feasible." Second, was the argument for group policy making and decision. It was said that "the combined judgment" of a group "provides both a barrier to arbitrary or capricious action and a source of decisions based on different points of view and experience." Third, was the argument for expertness. It was argued that the commissioners could obtain expertness through "fixed terms of reasonable duration, and the tradition of reappointment," and through the assistance of members who have served longer. Fourth, was the argument for continuity of policy. It was said that managers in industry, "So far as feasible," "should be able to rely on uniformity and continuity of underlying policy" and this could be sought by "long terms expiring at staggered intervals," "restraints on removal," and "group consultive action." It was recognized that group action could be slow and time consuming, that "the main source of expertness in a commission must lie in its staff," that there has been "for many of the commissions" "excessive turn-over of members," and "that, in practice, the commissions have fallen short" of the ideal of continuity and stability in policy. Nevertheless, it was concluded "that the independent commission has an essential place for certain types of governmental regulation," [38] and this conclusion was accepted by the Hoover Commission.

[37] *Task Force Report on Regulatory Commissions,* 19-25.
[38] *Task Force Report on Regulatory Commissions,* 28.

The arguments against the commission system have not, in the author's opinion, been adequately stated in any single place.[39] For this reason, and because so much of the discussion which follows is based upon the conviction that there is imperative necessity for revision of the assumptions underlying regulatory administration, the author gives seven arguments against the commission system.

First, although the traditional arguments reexpressed by the Hoover Commission summarize real needs in the system of administration, it is actually in the concessions of the Hoover Commission and its study group that the clues for efficient and democratic administration will be found. The reports of the staff admit the deficiencies of commissions as means of obtaining impartiality, expertness, continuity, and group decision and substantiate the view that these advantages result primarily from the complementary contribution of the various staff experts in an institutional process. The reports also acknowledge the inevitability, and even the legitimacy, of presidential interest in the course of commission decision. Staff work and presidential interest are two of the starting points for realistic analysis of the problem of regulatory administration. The weakness of the Hoover Commission study was that it did not concentrate attention on the issue of whether irremovable group organs were a superior in-the-middle channel for assimilation of staff work and accommodation of the legitimate concerns of the President. Quite obviously, the irremovable group is not a perfect means for attaining either objective, and alternatives or correctives in organization deserve attention.

Second, the commission system impedes executive coordination of economic policies. Plurality and independence both make it more difficult for the chief executive to integrate the policies of the commissions with those of other agencies and with the general policy of the government. If prompt and decisive action for coordination is needed, then the commission system stands condemned.

The need for some form and measure of coordination is evident,

[39] Seldom, however, has the knife of logic cut so precisely as in Cushman's analysis of certain aspects of the problem. See pages 293-294.

even under the most obvious demands of public policy. Loans to railroads by the Reconstruction Finance Corporation have a relation to the functions exercised by the Interstate Commerce Commission. The actions of the C.A.B. with respect to the extent of aeronautical facilities and the solvency of aeronautical companies are related to defense policies. Even more is this true of the decisions of the Federal Maritime Board. The Anti-trust Division of the Department of Justice and the Federal Trade Commission are working at the same job. The course of events has necessitated the close and continuous coordination of Federal Reserve Board and Treasury policies. Examples could be multiplied. But no one denies the necessity for some coordination. No theory that an "invisible hand" will guide to paradise under conditions of competition, overlapping, or conflicting action among regulatory agencies has yet been advanced.

The extent of the need for coordination is dependent in part upon the extent to which the policies of government in particular areas of economic control must be correlated with objectives in policy which extend to the economy as a whole. Professor Macmahon put his finger on the test question:[40]

How far the connection of the commissions with the departmental system may seem desirable is likely to depend largely upon the degree to which our society will desire to conduct economic regulation as something more than deliberately insulated bits of compulsory arbitration applied to points of especial strain among conflicting groups. Certainly, if a more deliberately interlocked policy should gain support, we shall have to devise forms of departmental structure which will encompass the hitherto autonomous organs of economic adjustment.

The answer appears to have been, in part, given. Even if society tries to insulate bits of economic control, as in water transportation and banking, the broader purposes of government draw the insulated areas into a larger sphere. More than this, conscious recognition of larger purpose has grown. After 1929 both Hoover and Roosevelt thought in terms of recovery; during the war the

[40] Arthur W. Macmahon, "The Future Organizational Pattern of the Executive Branch," *American Political Science Review*, XXXVIII, 1179-1191. 1189 (December, 1944).

nation thought in terms of coordination of production and prevention of inflation; and after the war the Employment Act directed the President to plan for maximum employment, production, and purchasing power. Irrespective of men's differences on
the degree and methods of government intervention, the relation
of particular steps to broader objective is being recognized.

It will be seen in the subsequent discussion that various means
of coordinating economic policy have been proposed. Some say
that this is a job for Congress. Others suggest coordinative committees or a line of contact between the President and the chairmen of the commissions.

It will be our thesis that a bolder attack must be made on this
problem. It appears to the author that it is now time—high time
—to consider the problem of the unity of the executive branch
in terms of possible future eventualities. It may have been largely
immaterial what form of regulatory organization was devised in
1887 and 1913, but the prosperity and defense of the nation may
depend upon unity within the executive branch in the future. The
proper perspective for consideration of the problem of coordination and unity must be the world of today in which military and
economic considerations, national and international, alike demand
prompt and consistent alignments and adjustments of national
policy.

A related challenge to the commission system is that of democratic control. One essential of democratic government is that
there must be a channel of control over public business by one or
more persons representing the people. It is widely recognized
that regulatory agencies are making policy, and this fact has been
confirmed by an earlier chapter. Fesler has argued that "This dominance of policy considerations in regulatory work means . . . that
it is futile to attempt to isolate the agency from the political
milieu in which it must and should operate." [41] His argument
finds support in the action of presidents toward the commissions.
And, as Fesler indicated, agencies should respond to the political

[41] James W. Fesler, *The Independence of State Regulatory Agencies*, 65 (Chicago, 1942).

climate. A bureaucracy independent from political control on policy matters is a challenge to democracy. Escape from Cushman's conclusion seems impossible: "It is certainly hard to defend on any basis of theory a status of independence for such vast policy-determining functions free from any directing authority to integrate them into the general legislative program of the Nation." [42]

It is natural, of course, that economic groups subject to regulation will desire that the regulatory agency be free from political control. These groups fear politics, they trust their power to obtain friendly commissioners, they share the normal human desire to find stability and certainty in insulated chambers even though the world goes topsy-turvy. Nevertheless, the area of high policy is one in which the claim must and should yield. The only question is the extent to which lacunae will be left in high policy by Congress, thus creating a need for policy leadership in administration by the President.

Fourth, there is need for some corrective for the dangers revealed in the preceding chapters, namely, traditionalism in approach, narrowness of point of view, and weakness in overcoming resistance to public policy. We have noted that agencies, once having achieved a balance among older forces, may then move within the confines of their own developed systems and become unresponsive to new demands in a flexible economy. We have shown also that fragments of government dealing with bits of the economy develop close associations with special clienteles, which constantly threatens their perspective, independence and vigor.[43] We have noted the weakness of administrative agencies in their struggle with special interests when they have lost the support of political

[42] *Report with Special Studies,* 220. Cushman was referring to the Interstate Commerce Commission.
[43] Fesler has concluded: "As a matter of fact, the freeing of a policy-determining agency from intimate contact with the politicians in the governor's mansion and in the legislative halls often throws the agency into the hands of the special interests it is supposed to regulate." *Op. cit.,* 65. Compare also David Truman's conclusion: "The political survival of an independent commission depends upon its reaching a *modus vivendi* with the regulated. Because other interests may have a larger voice in the arrangements made by an executive agency, 'independence' for the regulators has a defensive advantage for the regulated." *The Governmental Process,* 420.

power. The remedy for these things must come from the top political structure, which is inevitably responsive to new demands and responsible for the larger results of government. Politics must freshen, broaden, and invigorate, and serve as the link between the bureaucrat and the public.

Fifth, the deficiencies of boards, particularly if not subject to outside correctives, are well-known. Deep-seated cleavages sometimes develop among the members. Boards seem incapable of dispatch and energy. They seem more fitted to conserve than to advance. The novel idea of the new member is lost in the face of numbers, and his initial enthusiasm and drive may disappear in the sharing of responsibility. To the usual effort of staff experts to absorb a new chief is added the lateral absorption by older members. Thus, plurality makes for independence from the outer urge and for a truly bureaucratic government.

In the case of the commissions, a major defect of group action is delay. The staff reports to the Hoover Commission's task force on regulatory commissions gave plenty of evidence to support the task force's conclusion that group deliberation in commissions is time consuming.[44] Decisions are sometimes held up because members are in disagreement; more significant, however, is the fact that the time required for the members to have their studies made and for their deliberations adds to the other factors causing delay. Commission deliberation and study contributes to that lack of sensitiveness on time passage which seems to prevail on some of the commissions.

Sixth, the commission system may weaken the position of regulatory agencies and rob the nation of the benefits of agency experience and aid. The staff report for the Hoover Commission on the Federal Reserve Board emphasized that one factor which placed the Board in a weak position vis-à-vis the Treasury was the latter's close connection with the President.[45] Independence created

[44] *Task Force Report on Regulatory Commissions*, 21-22.
[45] George L. Bach, *Staff Report on the Federal Reserve System*, III, 5-7 and 18. See further IV, 6 ff and IV, 11-15. At III, 5: "Treasury rather than Federal Reserve leadership in the resolution of conflicting views apparently arises, anomalously, in substantial part from the very 'independence' with which

dependence, for power in government rests where political force is. Other staff reports pointed out the weakness of agencies which have lost a pipe line to the White House.[46] The independence of isolation carries with it the penalty of independence from support of political power. Also, in times of crisis or pressure for forceful and expeditious action the independent board is not likely to be too useful; plurality, primarily, but perhaps independence also, will limit the utility of the independent board.

Finally, the commission idea is too simple for sophisticated modern regulation. It assumes too easy a distinction between politics and administration. It fails to discriminate between the proper areas for independence and dependence. It does not take account of the internal safeguards in the administrative process. It overlooks the associative tendencies of the commissions as respects the interest groups. As a concept, it has been too absolute to square with the realities of presidential power and responsibility. It misdirects our hopes toward independence rather than toward planning

---

the Board is vested." "Federal Reserve stress on its 'independence' from the ordinary executive branch of the government has placed it in strong contrast to the close operating responsibility of the Treasury in executive affairs." It should be noted, however, that the Federal Reserve Board did win in a controversy with the Treasury in the spring of 1951.

[46] From the *Staff Report on the United States Maritime Commission:* "The Commission as a unit does not feel in a position to request White House support. As a result, it seems that it often is acting in a vacuum when important national policy is concerned. The Commission feels the absence of White House support in disputes with other departments or with Congress." Chapter III, 9.

"It is not surprising that a recent Commissioner describes the Commission's plight as that of a 'lost sheep.' Many members and officials of the Maritime Commission have been struck by the disadvantages of 'independence' far more than by its advantages." Chapter IV, 7.

From Irene Till, *Staff Report on the Federal Trade Commission* (Mimeographed for Hoover Commission):

"It has been suggested that, as an independent agency, the Commission should remain in formal isolation and conduct its work on its own. Whatever advantages this may have for other administrative agencies, it has none for the Federal Trade Commission. The reason has already been indicated. The Commission is one of the two agencies operating in the field of antitrust enforcement; it should make its influence felt as widely as possible in all branches of the government." Chapter II, 9. And compare Chapter IV, 9, where it is said that the Commission should have "close and intimate contact with the White House."

internal operations, quality of staff, and the relations between political and permanent officials.

THE ISSUE OF ORGANIZATIONAL CHANGE

Can a balance be found between the advantages claimed for the commission by the task force of the Hoover Commission and the deficiencies of the commission system which have been noted? This has been tried and has led to more than a decade of discussion.

The Report of the President's Committee on Administrative Management

In 1937 the President's Committee on Administrative Management, composed of Louis Brownlow, Charles E. Merriam, and Luther Gulick, presented its report to the President. In this report the issue of independence was joined with that of the union of functions. A search for the answer to the former was sought by an attack upon the latter.

The Brownlow Committee described the independent commissions as "miniature independent governments," constituting "a headless 'fourth branch' of the Government, a haphazard deposit of irresponsible agencies and uncoordinated powers." They exercise powers "under conditions of virtual irresponsibility," "produce confusion, conflict, and incoherence in the formulation and in the execution of the President's policies," and "whittle away" his leadership. Also, merging the discretionary work of the administrator with that of the judge created "an unwholesome atmosphere in which to adjudicate private rights"; and requiring the same men "to serve both as prosecutors and judges," "undermines judicial fairness" and "weakens public confidence in that fairness."

The Committee "put forward as a possible solution" a transfer of the functions of the commissions to executive departments where "all the purely administrative or sublegislative work" and certain preliminary work in judicial proceedings would be placed in an administrative section, constituting a regular bureau "headed by a chief with career tenure" but responsible to a departmental secretary and through him to the President, and where, on the other hand, all judicial work would be placed in a judicial section, headed by persons appointed by the President with the consent of the Senate for long, staggered terms and subject to removal only for causes stated in the statute, and independent except that it would be in the department for purposes of administrative house-keeping. The Committee declared that "The division of work between the two sections would be relatively simple," but recognized the need of adaptations in the division to meet the requirements of particular commissions. This could be effected by executive order.[47]

The Committee's recommendations were based on the special report by Professor Cushman. His report lacked the rhetorical phrases and the dogmatism which characterized the Committee's report. He recognized greater difficulties in the division of work between two sections and doubted the applicability of any single solution to all the existing commissions. He was concerned chiefly with the multiplication of commissions and sought a principle which could be adjusted in a flexible manner to "newly emerging regulatory functions." [48]

Cushman's analysis was made with unusual skill. He argued, on the one hand, that the independence of the commissions impaired "the aggressiveness and effectiveness of the President's general law enforcement program" and obstructed "coordination of national administrative policy," and on the other, that the merging of functions threatened the impartiality of judicial decisions.[49] He found, therefore, that the regulatory commission "suffers from a sort of internal inconsistency" in that it has administrative and policy-determining functions for which it should be politically responsible, judicial tasks which should be exercised with independence, and mixed functions (which constituted the "vast bulk" of their work) "with respect to which it ought to be at the same time both *politically responsible* and *judicially independent*." [50]

Against this background of imperatives he sought a way of di-

[47] *Report of the President's Committee on Administrative Management,* 39-42.
[48] *Report with Special Studies,* 205-243, particularly pages 207, 229, 234.
[49] *Ibid.,* 221-3.
[50] *Ibid.,* 219. The emphasis is Cushman's.

viding functions. The problem was to state the functions which should go to a judicial section. "Clearly judicial functions" (such as decision in reparation cases) would, of course, go to the judicial section; but Cushman recognized that they "do not make a very impressive list." For a second type of functions, called "mixed" functions, Cushman proposed a bifurcated procedure. After stating that "Perhaps the most important part of the job of the regulatory commissions is the 'mixed' function of applying 'standards' to the conduct of individuals and businesses," he offered a plan for handling one type of mixed function, that performed by the Federal Trade Commission. He suggested that an administrative section could make the preliminary investigation, issue the complaint, prosecute the case, take the testimony and prepare findings of fact; then the case would go to the judicial section for consideration of briefs, final argument, and decision.[51] A third function of the judicial section would be to act as an appellate body "where this bifurcated procedure is too slow and clumsy." Examples were the issuance of certificates of convenience to motor carriers, the granting of radio licenses, the registration of securities and probably of exchanges. The judicial section would review on "questions of law, at least" or "on all legal questions involved."

The Separation of Functions

The Brownlow Committee's concern over the union of functions has been shared by many persons. The union of functions has been widely condemned by many in the legal profession since about 1933 when the Committee on Administrative Law of the American Bar Association was appointed. Particularly condemned has been the union of complaint and prosecution with that of decision. A veritable proliferation of condemnation came in law journals, congressional committees, and public addresses. Usually there was concern only with impartiality in judicial decisions, not with the enervating effects on government in the combination of

---

[51] Cushman called this a "horizontal procedural cleavage" in contrast to the "vertical classification of duties that are rule-making, administrative, or judicial." *Ibid.*, 231.

functions. The discussion has ranged wide. To the practical arguments on threat of impartiality have been added arguments based upon the separation of powers, appeal to the tradition that a man should not be judge in his own case, and the contention that the union of functions contributes to administrative absolutism.

The Committee on Administrative Law itself went through an interesting history. In 1934 it made a preliminary report in which it declared that

In principle and with certain exceptions, the judicial functions of federal administrative tribunals should be divorced from their legislative and executive functions

and placed either in an administrative court or in one or more "independent tribunals," analogous to the legislative courts, and that

Subject to the successful accomplishment of a segregation of their judicial functions, existing independent administrative boards and commissions exercising executive and legislative powers should, in principle and with certain exceptions, be abolished and their executive and legislative functions should be transferred to the several executive departments . . . responsible to the president.[52]

In advance of investigation the committee committed itself to a principle, but its subsequent studies failed to reveal a plan for applying the principle. It never fully defined the exceptions or attempted a segregation of the judicial functions. It soon renewed its proposal for an administrative court,[53] but it recommended the transfer of only one function now performed by administrative regulatory organs to this court, namely, the revocation and suspension of licenses, permits, and other grants.[54] The Committee expected that other functions would be transferred to the court in succeeding years,[55] but before the Logan Bill for establishment of the administrative court had been considered on the floor of either

[52] *American Bar Association Report,* LIX, 539, at pages 539-540.
[53] "Report of the Special Committee on Administrative Law," *American Bar Association Report,* LXI, 720 (1936).
[54] *Ibid.,* 746ff.
[55] *Ibid.,* 748.

house of Congress the Committee withdrew its advocacy of the plan and proceeded on another line.[56] Its later proposal, resulting in the Logan-Walter Bill,[57] did not provide for any division of the functions of the existing regulatory organs. Finally the Bar Association threw its influence behind the Administrative Procedure Bill, which sought an answer in an internal division of functions within the agencies.

In spite of the widespread attack on the union of functions, the Brownlow Committee-Cushman proposal for solution of the problem of the independent commission by separation of functions was opposed by respected authorities.[58] One argument was emphasized by the Brookings Institution in a report submitted to committees of Congress several months after the Brownlow Committee Report.[59] It alleged that the proposal to separate functions "assumes a simplicity in the regulatory process which does not exist," the process being "an inseparable mixture of policy-determination, fact-finding, and decision." It concluded that "It is impossible to effect any clear-cut division of the functions of these commissions into administrative on the one hand and judicial on the other." [60]

Noteworthy is the fact that Cushman's report did not provide any satisfactory answer to this attack. He offered only one example of how a procedural cleavage could be drawn in "mixed" func-

[56] Because of hostility of members of the bar who practiced before existing legislative courts which would be absorbed in an administrative court. "Report of the Special Committee on Administrative Law" (1937), *American Bar Association Advance Program*, 185.

[57] Seventy-sixth Congress, third session, H. R. 6324.

[58] For a concise summary and overall criticism of the then current proposals for reform of the regulatory system see Ralph Fuchs, "Current Proposals for the Reorganization of the Federal Regulatory Agencies," *Texas Law Review*, XVI, 335-358 (1938).

[59] Senate Report No. 1275, *Investigation of Executive Agencies of the Government* (1937). The report was prepared for the Select Committee to Investigate the Executive Agencies of the Government and the Committee on Reorganization of the House of Representatives. The primary report on regulatory activities is at 709-815.

[60] Pages 799-800, 808. For the same view, see Frederick F. Blachly and Miriam E. Oatman, *Federal Regulatory Action and Control* (Washington, 1940), 177; O. R. McGuire in *Hearings Before a Subcommittee of the Senate Committee on the Judiciary on S. 3676*, Seventy-fifth Congress, third session, 148 (1938).

tions and this was a relatively simple example. The complaint-prosecution-hearing-decision sequence is only one of many types of mixed functions. It would have been helpful if Cushman had applied his proposal for bifurcation to the work of agencies which are regulating industries. In the absence of this, it may be wondered whether the regulatory egg has a separable white and yellow, or whether, from the standpoint of the traditional notions of types of powers, it is not hopelessly scrambled.

Another argument against the division of functions stressed the desirability of organizational unity. Landis emphasized the need for coordination between policy making and enforcement and believed that placing "adjudication outside the administrative process would tend to threaten the carrying through of those policies whose formulation was so deliberately given to the administrative." [61] He urged especially the need for unity in those cases where government regulates an industry. He said that no private industrial organization had been conceived along the "triadic contours" outlined by Montesquieu and that "when government concerns itself with the stability of an industry it is only intelligent realism for it to follow the industrial rather than the political analogue." [62] The Attorney General's Committee on Administrative Procedure also feared "the loss of consistency of action as a whole." It noted that agencies exercise "interrelated powers." [63] Similar to these arguments is the contention that "Administrative abjudication is an integral part of the administrative process," [64] and that "each part of their [the regulatory agencies'] work now strengthens each other part." [65]

Beyond this, the critics even attacked the ideal of separation in cases like those in Cushman's example, namely, where there was a combination of prosecuting and deciding. Landis argued that sep-

---

[61] James M. Landis, *The Administrative Process*, 98. Copyright 1938 by Yale University Press.
[62] *Ibid.*, 10-12.
[63] *Final Report*, 57-58.
[64] Frederick F. Blachly, *Working Papers on Administrative Adjudication*, 2. Reprinted in K. C. Sears, *Cases on Administrative Law* (1938) as Appendix I.
[65] Blachly and Oatman, *Federal Regulatory Action and Control*, 182.

aration of these functions could not be the answer to the problem of arbitrariness. Government often achieves its aims as prosecutor rather than as judge. In securities regulation, for example, cases do not go to trial; issuers change prospectuses to meet the requirements of regulators. Also, the fact that complaints receive publicity may make the issuance of a complaint more significant than the ultimate decision.[66] The Attorney General's Committee saw practical objections to the separation of functions of the various agencies, including those like the Federal Trade Commission and the National Labor Relations Board. "Of prime importance among these objections is the danger of friction and of a break-down of responsibility as between the two complementary agencies." And whereas at present prosecuting agencies are restrained by the "added responsibility of deciding," "a special body whose single function is to prosecute will almost inevitably increase litigation and with it harassment to respondents." The prosecuting agency will be intent upon "making a record" by prosecuting "as often and successfully as possible." It will have to guess what the deciding agency will think and hence may "explore the periphery." Particularly where statutes are general, there will be danger of "a series of litigations in which the enforcing branch endeavors to ascertain the mind of the deciding branch." Also,

the separation of functions would seriously militate against what this Committee has already noted as being, numerically and otherwise, the lifeblood of the administrative process—negotiations and informal settlements. Clearly, amicable disposition of cases is far less likely where negotiations are with officials devoted solely to prosecution and where the prosecuting officials cannot turn to the deciding branch to discover the law and the applicable policies.[67]

A minority of the Attorney General's Committee agreed only in part. It thought that as long as statutory delegations were so general a separation of functions would result in two agencies deter-

[66] *The Administrative Process*, 106-110.
[67] *Final Report*, 57-59.

mining policy. It believed, however, that where government acted
both as prosecutor and decider, "complete separation, with adjudication by wholly independent agencies, is normally to be preferred." [68]

Separation of prosecution and decision between agencies independent of each other was provided in the Labor Management Relations Act. The power to issue and prosecute complaints is vested
in a General Counsel, who is a presidential appointee for a definite term but without restrictions on the power of removal. Decisional power remains in the Board, whose independence is confirmed by the usual limitations on presidential removal.

The results have not been such as to commend the separation.
A confused situation resulted from statutory provisions concerning
regional offices, which were to serve the Board on representation
cases and the General Council on complaint cases, and whose
personnel was to be appointed by the Board but subject to the
supervision of the General Counsel. Also, the Board needed the
services of the General Counsel on certain functions, such as representation of the Board before the courts. An effort to solve the difficulties resulting from split jurisdiction was made through delegation
of certain powers by the Board to the General Counsel in August
1947; but the delegation did not prevent controversy between the
two and an amended delegation was issued February 25, 1950.
Opportunities for discord remain. Moreover, Dean Landis' argument on the futility of the search for protection in the deciding
organ alone is confirmed, for the General Counsel has broad discretionary powers on issuance of complaints and there is no appeal
from a negative decision by him. The first incumbent of the office
has said that his powers "are broad and absolute and his authority

[68] Additional views of Messrs. McFarland, Stason, and Vanderbilt, *Final
Report*, 207-208. This group also thought a special problem was posed as to
whether adjudication between private parties, as in reparation cases, should not
be vested in the courts. For the additional views of Mr. D. Lawrence Groner,
Chief Justice of the Court of Appeals of the District of Columbia, who thought
neither the majority nor the minority of three went far enough, see *Final
Report*, 248-250.

final to an outstanding degree seldom accorded a single officer in a peacetime agency." [69]

Except for the Taft-Hartley Act attention since the report of the Attorney General's Committee has shifted from the Brownlow Committee proposal for division of work between separate sections to proposals for strengthening the tendencies toward division of duties within the subordinate staff. These proposals leave intact the unified control of the agency heads, no separation being attempted at that level.

The most significant effort of the Attorney General's Committee and of the Administrative Procedure Act was to strengthen, dignify, and increase the independence of, the position of the officers of the commissions or departments who conduct hearings. The Attorney General's Committee desired to rename them hearing commissioners, but the older name of examiners has prevailed in usage.

Additional ways of separating functions internally have been developed. Notable is the use of the internal appeals board. Numerous boards and committees in the Department of Agriculture hear appeals from determinations of "standards, grades, inspections, qualities, etc."; and similar authorities exist in a number of other agencies. [70] One of the most notable examples was the Appeals Board set up within the War Production Board during the war to make final decisions on individual appeals under Board orders.

Internal appeals need not be limited to questions of law, as is the tendency for external bodies of review or as was suggested by Cushman in his outline of functions for a separate judicial section. They deal with questions of fact. They have a more comprehensive and a more intimate effect on the quality and content of regulation than is contemplated through organs of judicial review. Technical appeals boards may safeguard against arbitrariness, but they also tend to confirm standards of competence and rigorousness in the

[69] Quoted in *Task Force Report on Regulatory Commissions*, 139. The Task Force recommended that the Office of General Counsel should be integrated more closely with the Board or the executive departments according to the functions to be performed. See their report at pages 134-141.

[70] See Frederick F. Blachly, *Working Papers on Administrative Adjudication*. Blachly gives a list of appeals boards in national agencies.

subordinate staff. The Appeals Board in W.P.B., with its flexible assignment of mitigating the severity of regulations in particular cases, was not a judicial organ applying law to facts but exercised a discretionary authority which placed it among the policy organs of the agency.[71]

The appeals board system may go further than the examiner system in that the agency heads may lose control over the making of particular decisions. The same is true where an agency delegates its complete jurisdiction—original as well as appellate. The outstanding example of the complete delegation of a judicial function is the Office of Administrative Hearings in O.P.A. Its functions were strictly and solely judicial. It provided a "system of courts" within an administrative agency. Cases were heard in original jurisdiction by hearing commissioners located in field offices; appellate jurisdiction was vested in the Hearing Administrator in Washington. What is significant is that these officers were completely independent of the enforcement staff and of overhead controls; the functions of administrative officers with respect to their work was limited to housekeeping services.[72]

The feature that distinguishes the recent trends in administration from the Brownlow Committee proposal in that of limited independence. Examiners, appeals boards, and hearing commissioners have been located within the agencies. As a result, disassociative tendencies can be checked. The authorities exercising delegated jurisdiction are subject to agency directions on policy. They can be kept continuously informed on the objectives and the intricacies of agency policy.[73] In appropriate cases closer links can be established with

---

[71] See Civilian Production Administration, *Industrial Mobilization for War* (Washington, 1947), 311-313, and John Lord O'Brian and Manly Fleischmann, "The War Production Board Administrative Policies and Procedures," *The George Washington Law Review*, XIII, 1-60, at pages 40-44 (December, 1944).

[72] See Chapter VII, footnote 109, for a list of references on the Office of Administrative Hearings.

[73] In 1945 the head of the Office of Administrative Hearings in O.P.A. discussed with the Assistant Deputy Administrator for Rationing ways of communicating general information on rationing to hearing commissioners and requested, among other things, that the weekly rationing letters sent by the Deputy Administrator for Rationing to regional rationing executives be made

responsible operating divisions, as in W.P.B. where the Appeals Board had representatives from such divisions. Except for examiners under the Administrative Procedure Act, no crystallization of an idea of irremovability has threatened to generate independent views of policy in the segregated unit.

It is suggested that it is these limitations on independence of status which make it possible, in most cases, to allow independence in decision. Independence in decision is possible because of the removal of the threat of impairment of program through friction and cleavage between those having responsibility for total results and those having responsibility for given particulars. The danger in independence of examiners is that it will limit their utility as organs of initial decision.[74] The weakness of the Cushman proposal was that the utility of the judicial section was limited by the completeness of its independence. An independent body may review on points of law; it may sometimes have utility for clearly separable and distinctly judicial functions; but a fully independent body cannot be a corrective on policy and factual analysis, or even in the application of law to facts where this function is so closely related to the total program that separation threatens the degree of unity required in program development and application.

The idea of independence, nevertheless, is so alluring that it reappears frequently. A recent instance is the proposal of the Hoover Commission's task force on *Agriculture Activities*. It was recommended that

responsibility for all adjudication, including licensing, and for all rule making in proceedings conducted by the Department where opportunity for hearing is made mandatory by act of Congress or regulations thereunder be placed in the Judicial Division, save for exceptions of the same character as those recognized by section 5 of the Administrative Procedure Act involving solely inspections and tests, or matters subject to court trial de novo, or relating to selection and tenure of officers and employees of Government.

---

available for distribution to the hearing commissioners. He believed that it was desirable for the hearing commissioners to be kept informed on the general developments in the rationing program.

[74] For fuller discussion see pages 208-209, 212, and 216.

Moreover, it was suggested that the judicial officers in the Judicial Division "be appointed by the Director of the Administrative Office of the United States Courts subject to removal by him only for cause after hearing, nominations for appointment to be made by the Secretary." In this way they would be made "completely independent from the administrative officers." [75]

The startling nature of this proposal is partially hidden in the fact that, to a considerable extent, it confirms trends in regulation in the Department of Agriculture. The Schwellenbach Act sought the answer to the problem of delegation raised by the Morgan Case by authorizing the Secretary to delegate his power to make regulatory decisions based upon hearings,[76] and such delegations have been made to the Judicial Officer; several acts of Congress have required that departmental rule making be made on the basis of the record; and the Administrative Procedure Act defined adjudication to include licensing. Independence for a judicial section takes on new meaning with this kind of background. Independent commissions to regulate rates, make rules, and exercise licensing powers is one thing; but to vest all power of decision in independent lawyer-appointed lawyers would be quite a new capstone in national regulatory experience.

Coordination and Direction

The proposal of the Brownlow Committee for executive control was also attacked. Moreover, in contrast to the success of critics and the Congress in finding substitute means for separating functions, little progress has been made toward a solution of the problems of coordination and aggressiveness presented in Cushman's analysis.

One attack came from Dean Landis. He argued that "Efficiency in the processes of government is best served by the creation of more rather than less agencies." [77] He was doubtful of the "eugenic possibilities of breeding supermen" to control a variety of func-

[75] *Agriculture Activities*, 17.
[76] 54 *U. S. Stat. at Large* 82 (1940); 5 U.S.C. 516a-516e.
[77] James M. Landis, *The Administrative Process*, 24. Copyright 1938 by Yale University Press.

tions. Expertness could be achieved only through limitation of the sphere of action. Responsibility was dulled by the anonymity of the departmental process. Moreover, new responsibilities could be better met by new agencies. Also, permanence and consistency of policy had been to an extent achieved as a result of having "the fashioning of industrial policy removed to a degree from political influence" and of the professionalism which characterizes the independent commission.[78]

Landis did make advocacy of numbers contingent upon limitation of the area of government and upon means of effecting "appropriate coordination of their policies." [79] The danger, however, of an agency "pursuing a policy that runs counter to the general direction of the executive" was "more apparent than real." For, "Executive policy to be effective needs the support of the legislature and when these two forces combine, their effect is such that the administrative cannot pursue a course of action contradictory to their desires." [80] He also saw the reality of the lack of aggressiveness which Cushman had stressed.[81] He thought, however, this could be met by strengthening the position of the chairman of the commission.

Landis' brilliant exposition put emphasis on the real need for preventing such an overconcentration in the exercise of power as would impair the resourcefulness and responsibility of experts at the center of operations. On the other hand, students of administration may doubt whether executive-legislative cooperation provides a sufficiently intimate, direct, and immediate means of policy coordination.

The same question is left by studies issuing from Brookings Institution. F. F. Blachly and Miriam E. Oatman laboriously dissect the administrative process into its minutiae but conclude, nevertheless, that it is a unity and that that unity is found in the essentially legislative nature of the regulatory process. They seek an answer in the doctrine of the separation of powers. Since regulatory work

[78] *Ibid.*, 23-30, 46, 111-117.
[79] *Ibid.*, 30. See also page 24.
[80] *Ibid.*, 116.
[81] "The real danger to the executive from the independent Commission lies in the possibility of inaction on the part of its members." *Idem.*

"is largely legislative in nature," regulatory authorities "should be responsible directly to Congress and should not be controlled by executive or administrative authorities." [82] This is a conspicuous example of logical legerdemain in inserting the desired conclusion in the premise by using such an ambiguous term as "legislative" in the premise. And, taken literally, the argument proves too much, for it would equally take from the President all rule-making powers, even in the field of foreign affairs.

But admitting the argument for the moment, how then can Congress control the commissions? One answer given by Brookings Institution was that "if sublegislative policy is not in harmony with legislative policy, Congress can easily change the situation by itself laying down more detailed standards and norms, by changing the functions of the commissions, or by diminishing or enlarging their membership." [83] But experience does not indicate that changing congressional directives can include very much of the real content of regulation.[84] Meriam and Schmeckebier, of the staff of Brookings Institution, suggested that the standing committees of Congress should have permanent staffs which could effectively supervise administration.[85] But is there any reason in experience to expect that the permanent staffs provided in the recent legislative reorganization will be able to coordinate and invigorate administration? Can coordination be achieved through a plurality of groups, each attached by association to particular agencies? Would such groups be backed by prompt and effective action from Congress? Would they not be agents of restraint rather than invigoration? Would they be centers of sniping and special pressure? [86] Brookings Institution also suggests that Congress might require submission of rules to it for approval. But this is piecemeal control by a veto power, and wholly negative. Can it be a substitute for over-all coordination and direction?

[82] Blachly and Oatman, *Federal Regulatory Action and Control,* 168-182. Quotations from pages 170 and 182.

[83] *Investigation of Executive Agencies of the Government,* 802-803.

[84] See Chapter IV.

[85] L. Meriam and L. F. Schmeckebier, *Reorganization of the National Government* (Washington, 1939), 155ff.

[86] See Cushman's comments in *The Independent Regulatory Commissions,* 679.

It is admitted—it will in fact be argued subsequently—that an effort should be made to provide for more effective congressional oversight of administration. Irrespective, however, of success in this effort, it appears that congressional control is too remote, divisive, and sporadic to compensate for the absence of a clearly recognized executive authority of coordination and direction. The tendencies in modern congressional control strongly confirm the judgment of the framers of the Constitution on the need for unity in the executive branch of the government.

Another argument against presidential control dodges the problem of coordination and direction by emphasizing the power and irresponsibility of the presidency. This argument was ably summarized by Schuyler Wallace. He noted that many critics fear the exercise of presidential control for personal and partisan reasons and that these critics emphasize the difference in legislative control over the executive in the United States and Great Britain, where the departments, according to Wallace, are the "obvious place" for quasi-legislative and quasi-judicial functions.[87] But this argument overlooks the fact that in Great Britain a more significant safeguard perhaps than parliamentary control is the delicate balance between the political and the permanent official. In this country we may need to strengthen the safeguards in congressional criticism and a permanent officialdom; but we cannot deny, nevertheless, that the prospectus of future regulation carries a problem of coordination.

There emerged between the reports of the Brownlow Committee in 1937 and of the Hoover Commission in 1949 several ideas for checking the disintegration of the commission system without a thrust at its heart. One was the suggestion of Landis and of Cushman, in his larger treatise, for presidential designation of the chairman. Another was the idea of locating planning, executive, and promotional activities in departments. The planning function had been placed in a separate officer in the creation of the temporary Federal Coordinator of Transportation. Executive functions were separated from "regulatory" functions in civil aviation. The

[87] Schuyler C. Wallace, *Federal Departmentalization: A Critique of Theories of Organization* (New York, 1941), 158-163.

functions of administration and enforcing safety regulations, developing and operating a system of federal airways, and the administration of the Federal Airport Act of 1946 are vested in an Administrator. Other functions, such as granting certificates, making of rates, control of intercorporate arrangements, making of safety regulations, fixing compensation for mail carriage, and investigation of accidents are vested in the Civil Aeronautics Board. At first, the Board and the Administrator were parts of an independent Authority; but in 1940 the President located the Administrator in the Department of Commerce, to which the Board was also attached for housekeeping purposes. Initially also the function of investigating accidents was in a special independent Air Safety Board, but after some experience this board was abolished and its functions transferred to the Civil Aeronautics Board.

Brookings Institution in 1937 contrasted promotional and regulatory activities in regard to transportation. It recommended that the former be placed in a Department of Transportation or a division of the Department of Commerce.[88]

One objective in this proposal was an "articulated national policy" in substitution for the "divergent policies" in promotion of the separate types of transportation. A similar objective of coordination led to suggestions for structural integration of regulatory work in commissions. Brookings Institution recommended centralization of regulatory functions over transportation in the Interstate Commerce Commission.[89] It favored, also, the transfer of functions similar to those of the Federal Trade Commission to it from other agencies, including those of the Department of Agriculture over unfair trade practices [90] and of the Department of Justice over monopolies and restraint of trade, except for prosecution of criminal cases.[91]

A final idea was that of centralized planning. This is now em-

---

[88] *Investigation of Executive Agencies of the Government*, 436-445.

[89] *Ibid.*, 445-452.

[90] This included at that time not only functions relating to packers but also those of the Food and Drug Administration, though Brookings Institution suggested that the Department might retain the functions of investigation and complaint with respect to foods and drugs.

[91] *Ibid.*, 808.

bodied chiefly in the Employment Act of 1946.[92] It asserts central purpose in public economic policy: promotion of maximum employment, production, and purchasing power. It assumes the necessity of over-all economic thinking and provides for its incorporation in an annual economic report by the President. It provides in the Council of Economic Advisors a staff aid to the President, a central organ of thought. It recognizes the interrelations among government's economic activities by providing that the Council of Economic Advisors shall appraise the various programs and activities of the federal government to determine the extent to which they are contributing to the policy of the Act.

Central planning is required not only for domestic economic policies but also for foreign policies. It has been said that "Sound high-level foreign policies . . . can only be formed by placing side by side for comparison a financial outlook, a national resources outlook, a transportation outlook, a manpower outlook, and a security outlook." [93] These foreign policies, in turn, have implications for the domestic economic program. These implications led to the creation of the National Securities Resources Board, which was given responsibility for planning for economic mobilization in wartime; the implications may also call for adjustments in peacetime policy in the various areas of economic regulation.

The work of central planning organs should aid the President and Congress in the development of over-all policy. It should reveal some of the areas where coordination is needed. Further development of staff facilities in the President's office would provide additional means of considering the needs for correlated action among the agencies.[94]

[92] 60 U. S. Stat. at Large, 23.

[93] Hoover Commission, General Management of the Executive Branch (1949), 18.

[94] Ibid., 11-14, and see the following articles in the American Political Science Review: Don K. Price, "Staffing the Presidency," XL, 1154-1168 (1946); Wayne Coy, "Basic Problems," XL, 1124-1137 (1946); John J. Corson, "Organizing Government Staff Services for Full Employment," XXXIX, 1157-1169 (1945); Edwin G. Nourse and Bertram M. Gross, "The Role of the Council of Economic Advisers," XLII, 283-295 (1948); Sidney W. Souers, "Policy Formation for National Security," XLIII, 534-543 (1949); Ralph J. Watkins, "Eco-

Is this and the other measures outlined above enough? How bridge the gap between central policy and separateness and independence of administrative agencies? What, it may be asked, was the answer of the Hoover Commission on this and related issues of organization?

The Hoover Commission's Recommendations and Recent Reorganization Orders

The Hoover Commission and its Task Force on Regulatory Commissions accepted the commission system. Nevertheless, they found serious deficiencies in the system and recommended changes to correct these. The outstanding criticisms and recommendations are summarized.

First, the Commission believed that "Purely executive functions too frequently have been entrusted to these independent regulatory commissions." It gave several arguments against this: a plural executive is not the best device for performance of "operational duties"; these duties commonly call for integration with the executive branch; independence creates obstructions to the handling of executive programs; the necessity for performing them has interfered with performance of "strictly regulatory functions." [95] Accordingly, it recommended transfer (1) of the power planning function of the Federal Power Commission to the Department of Interior; (2) of the functions of ship construction and the operation, charter, and sale of ships from the Maritime Commission to the Department of Commerce; (3) of functions relating to safety and car service from the Interstate Commerce Commission to the Department of Commerce; (4) of promulgation of rules relating to safety of aircraft operation to the Department of Commerce with a right of appeal to the Civil Aeronautics Board; and (5) of certain executive func-

---

nomic Mobilization," XLIII, 555-563 (1949); Fritz Morstein Marx, "The Bureau of the Budget: Its Evolution and Present Role," XXXIX, 653-684, 869-898 (1945). See also John D. Millett, *The Process and Organization of Government Planning* (New York, 1947).

[95] Hoover Commission, *Regulatory Commissions*, 4, 11.

tions relating to transportation to the Department of Commerce.[96]

Second, the Commission said that "The chief criticism that can be made of the regulatory commissions is that they become too engrossed in case-to-case activities and thus fail to plan their roles and to promote the enterprises entrusted to their care." Finding that this was typical of the attitude of the Interstate Commerce Commission and the Civil Aeronautics Board on building a route structure for the nation, it recommended "that the Secretary of Commerce be charged with developing an over-all route pattern for land, sea, and air" and that he be allowed to present views and initiate recommendations on route changes for consideration by the regulatory authorities.[97]

Third, it was found that there had been insufficient delegation to the staffs due to legislative restrictions and poor internal organization. It was recommended that the statutes be amended to permit delegation of routine, preliminary, and less important work.[98]

Fourth, again condemning administration by a plural executive, the Commission recommended that all administrative responsibility be vested in the chairman. The task force found that "Many of the commissions suffer badly from inefficiency and delay in handling their work." Delegation and concentration of administrative responsibilities were the solutions proposed.[99] The Commission said that it should be the responsibility of the chairman "to deploy the work force" and "to see that business is dispatched in an orderly manner." He would be assisted by an executive officer.[100]

Fifth, the Commission gave recognition to the principle of independence by recommending that the general rule of bipartisan representation be extended to all the commissions and that, for the three commissions for which the President's power of removal

[96] *Ibid.*, 12-13. From the last recommendation Commissioner Brown dissented believing that since regulatory functions were predominant in this field separation of executive, promotional, and administrative activities would "create a serious imbalance within the organization of the Government." *Ibid.*, 13.

[97] *Ibid.*, 4, 15.

[98] *Ibid.*, 4, 9-10.

[99] *Task Force on Regulatory Commissions*, 43-51.

[100] Hoover Commission, *Regulatory Commissions*, 5-6.

is not now restricted, there should be a limitation to removal "for cause." [101]

Sixth, the discussion of coordination is marked by its restrictive, if not negative, nature. The Task Force on Regulatory Commissions reached the following conclusion: [102]

The point to be emphasized here is that the study of the separate agencies forces the conclusion that lack of coordination is not an insuperable obstacle with respect to the independent commission. As has already been stated, some problems do exist and should be dealt with. But on the whole, coordination is needed in more limited areas than might be supposed a priori, and has been achieved in most of the major fields through interdepartmental committees or more informal techniques.

The Commission thought also that "the problem has not been too serious in the past," but concluded that "The coordination of policies pursued by these independent regulatory commissions with those of the executive branch as a whole has been generally loose and casual." [103] The majority decided against the recommendation of the task force on transportation for consolidation of regulatory functions in one commission. It thought the problem of lack of coordination in this area would be "greatly minimized by centering executive transportation functions within the Department of Commerce." [104] Also, "coordination can now be easily effected because the above recommendations suggest that the chairman of each commission effect liaison between their commissions and the rest of the Government." [105] But though the task force recommended that the chairman be designated by the President, the Commission did not mention this. Finally, coordination could be further effected "through the proposed machinery of the President's Office," which would include staff aides and cabinet committees. [106]

[101] *Ibid.*, 3-4, 7, 16. Three commissioners dissented from the recommendation on limitation of grounds for removal.

[102] *Task Force on Regulatory Commissions*, 27-28.

[103] Hoover Commission, *Regulatory Commissions*, 15.

[104] *Ibid.*, 14. Commissioners Brown and Pollock gave reasons for their support for a consolidated transportation commission at pages 19-22. Brookings Institution, which had served as the task force on transportation, had recommended a consolidated transportation commission.

[105] *Ibid.*, 15.

[106] *Idem.* See also Hoover Commission, *General Management of the Executive Branch.*

Since the report of the Hoover Commission, reorganization orders, issued under the authority of the Reorganization Act of 1949, have made a number of significant changes in the commissions. First, as recommended by the Hoover Commission, administrative functions were transferred to the chairman in five commissions, namely, the U.S. Maritime Commission (now Federal Maritime Board), Federal Trade Commission, Federal Power Commission, Securities and Exchange Commission, and Civil Aeronautics Board. The functions transferred included appointment and supervision of personnel, distribution of work among personnel and administrative units, and use and expenditure of funds. The chairman is subject, however, to general policies of the commission in the exercise of his administrative functions. Second, as a result of several orders the President can now designate the chairman of all commissions except the Interstate Commerce Commission. Third, the U.S. Maritime Commission was abolished and its functions divided between a three-member Federal Maritime Board and an administrator (who is also the chairman of the Board). Certain regulatory functions and functions in regard to subsidies are vested in the Board, and all other functions are given to the Administrator. The Administrator and the Board are located in the Department of Commerce; the former is subject to supervision from the Secretary of Commerce; the Board and the chairman are independent from the Secretary's control in regulatory functions, but subject to his direction on general policy on subsidy and related functions.[107]

These changes may result in improved operations, but they fall short of correcting the deficiencies of the commission system. The speed and quality of staff work, and its integration with commission work, may be substantially improved under the control of a single individual. But some difficulties of integrating staff work and commission decision will still remain, and time only will show whether conflicts between commissions and their chairmen will develop. Executive direction is provided for a large part of the program of maritime control and service, but the major regulatory decisions

[107] For the reorganization orders, see *Federal Code Annotated*, Title 5, Section 133z.

are still left in a board with independent status. A novel method of reconciling the rival claims of independence and control which may furnish the clue for regulatory operations in the future is contained in the provision subjecting the Federal Maritime Board in its subsidy activities to the control of the Secretary of Commerce on *general policies*. Further discussion of this technique will follow in the conclusion of this chapter.

Hyneman's Conclusions

The most recent analysis of the problem of organization for regulatory activities has come from Charles Hyneman, political scientist and former executive officer of the Federal Communications Commission.[108]

Hyneman strikes at the contrast in thought about commissions and departments, in which it is assumed that "the President will keep his hands off the regulatory commissions altogether" and "that he will direct the work of the great executive departments in any way that he pleases." [109] He believes that within departments "there is a considerable area of policy determination that should be made by subordinate officials" and offers for illustration the work of granting patents in the Department of Commerce.[110] He recognizes, also, the many practical limitations on what a department head can achieve in control of the policy of subordinate units. On the other hand, he believes that the ideals of democratic government require that the President have some control over the policy of the commissions. He concludes: "Surely we want the chief executive of the nation to give some direction to the commissions that are charged with making and enforcing policy. And just as surely we want all political influence removed from certain aspects of the work of the departments that are headed by cabinet members." [111]

[108] For the full presentation of his views, see *Bureaucracy in a Democracy*, Chapters 16, 21, 22, 23. Chapter 23 contains a most illuminating analysis of the internal operations of commissions, which should be read in connection with the Hoover Commission's recommendations concerning the chairman's position.

[109] From page 309 of Charles S. Hyneman, *Bureaucracy in a Democracy*. Copyright 1950 by Harper & Brothers.

[110] *Ibid.*, 449, 462-466.

[111] *Ibid.*, 309.

How determine the areas in which departmental or presidential control is proper? Hyneman questions the feasibility of placing "the policy making and the law applying" functions in two separate organizations, as was suggested in the 1937 study. He notes, however, that the Administrative Procedure Act has gone far in the segregation and safeguarding of judicial acts. He urges, also, that there has been a "deficiency in our theory and our practice" in that "we have not fully analyzed the administrative job, differentiated the components of the administrative process, and indicated the points at which the President may and at which he may not intervene."[112]

Hyneman suggests, therefore, that Congress could "specify by law his [the President's] relation to specific actions or categories of actions."[112] Ordinarily, presidential conference with members of commissions would be sufficient for him to carry out his authority; but where it was believed that "voluntary response" would not be sufficient, Congress could require that the President sign the document authenticating the government action, or that the decision should not be effective without his approval, or that the President should have authority to modify, suspend, or set aside the decision.[114]

CONCLUSIONS

Facing the mixture of views through fifteen years of discussion, an author could choose the course of caution and confine his conclusions to eclectic summation. Yet the import of many a segment of the preceding pages would be lost if the author did not venture the more dangerous, but more hopeful, path of search for guiding principle. We believe the answer on regulatory organization must be sought in the principles normally applicable in public administration.

In beginning, it may be said that a problem of unity is presented

[112] *Ibid.*, 316.
[113] *Ibit.*, 319.
[114] *Ibid.*, 316-317.

at two levels. Landis emphasized the unity of the regulatory process at the agency level; Cushman stressed the unity of a part of the process at the executive level. We submit that there is a problem of unity at both levels—the operative or agency level and the coordinative and directive or executive level.

The basic purpose in administrative organization is to link together the separate activities which have a joint relation to the attainment of a common goal. It is often difficult to choose the appropriate centers for integration, but it is believed that the guide is normally to be found *in the total job to be done rather than in the nature of process and function*. In regulation, it appears to be necessary to guard against the misleading effects of overmagnification of process and functional distinctions.

The unity of regulatory operations has been threatened by attack from two sides. The first argues for separation of judicial functions, the second for separation of executive, promotional, and planning functions. Each has its value and each has its limitations.

Clearly separable judicial functions do not form a large part of regulation. More significant than application of law to facts is expansion of policy through case-to-case administration. It is submitted that the argument for independent placement breaks down where policy cannot be made specific in advance of the exercise of the judicial function. Even where it appears that policy is specific, there may be a threat to unity in placement of judicial functions in a separate agency, for disassociation may bring differences in point of view, and—equally significant—decision on sanction in particular cases can make or destroy policy.

No one has outlined a way of separating the judicial and quasi-judicial in industry regulation from other functions. Even in the enforcement of standards, the limited independence inherent in differentiation of function within the staff of an agency has been the more accepted answer in governmental practice. Occasionally, segregation of judicial functions in a separate agency may be desirable; but the step should be taken cautiously after decision that unity in control is not threatened. Moreover, it should be recognized that the segregable judicial work would be, at the most, so small a part of control that it would fall short of providing the safeguards against arbitrary power and political influence which those who advocate separation believe are needed.

The placing of executive, promotional, and planning functions in separate agencies, on any large scale, may also destroy the unity of control. If executive functions include only routines of application, their significance, though real, is after all, like housekeeping functions, a stage removed from the vital issues in control. But if they include such executory functions as prosecution and inspection, their disconnection from the rest of the task may create cleavages and a lack of functioning unity. Promotion and regulatory action are often separate functions, but they may be so closely related that organization in separate agencies is undesirable or even infeasible. How separate the promotive from the restrictive function in regulation of civil aeronautics? Grant or denial of certificates are part of a pattern in which promotion and restriction are combined. As for planning, it may sometimes be done by external, lateral organs, particularly if organized for temporary purposes; but the most fruitful organization for continuous planning will be that which is geared to the hierarchy of operations. Planning must derive some substance from the experience of those engaged in the process of administration. And plans made in disassociation from deciding organs have diminished chances of adoption by such organs. Furthermore, planning is an essential part of any meaningful effort of administrators responsible for operations.

The center of unity in economic control is the unfolding of policy. This unfolding has executory, facilitative, judicial, and planning aspects. Policy is unfolded in the course of policing, prosecution, and compromise of cases; in application of sanctions; in case-to-case administration; and in advance planning embodied in rules governing individuals or in policy standards governing the administrators. Unity in the result must be the objective. The central need, therefore, in administrative organization at the operative or agency level is to correlate all types of function with the policy objectives of government. In this respect, economic control does not differ from

administration in general. There can, of course, be allocations, sepa-
rations, and internal checks within the unified structure.

More troublesome has been the issue of unity at the higher level.
Here three aspects of normal administrative practice furnish guides
for the future. These are planning, direction, and structural integration.

Real progress has been made toward central planning. The term
"planning" has been under suspicion because of association with
the idea of a single economic blueprint; but the concept of planning
in the sense of study, thought, and coordinated policy has gained
acceptance. Progress has been made in implementing the idea of
planning both in the office of the President and in some agencies.

*What is lacking is a recognized transmission line from central
purpose to centers of decision and action.* The line from President
to Congress and from there to agency is sufficient where change
reaches the high and general level of policy which can be embodied
in congressional directive; but, in the opinion of the author, a
recognized direct line is needed for policy developments of smaller
scope. Moreover, the link with the chairman may be insufficient
where he is only one of a group which regards itself as independent.

It is suggested that the answer may lie in the written directive.
Robson has proposed that ministers in England might send open
letters of instruction to quasi-judicial tribunals which were indirectly accountable to them. The instructions would not be mandatory and would deal with policy.[115] The suggestion has greater value
for the American commission whose functions extend beyond that of
adjudication and encompass the unfolding of the policy of the nation.
Cushman gave some consideration to the potential values in Robson's proposal as applied to this broader area. He pointed out that,
even if it were assumed that the President could not or ought not
to enforce his policies on the commissions, there is no reason why
he should not "openly and frankly state his policies" in a "published
letter or statement" to the commissions. He thought that if sanctioned by tradition the directive would lose its "present superficial

---

[115] For comments on the proposal, see Cushman, *The Independent Regulatory
Commissions,* 643.

aspect of being a type of unauthorized interference," and that public opinion would tend to prevent the use of the method for control of "strictly quasi-judicial work." [116]

The authoritative, as contrasted to the suggestive, directive was used extensively in this country during World War II. It was an outstanding feature of the supervisory and directory controls exercised by the Director of Economic Stabilization and by the head of the Office of War Mobilization. It has been said that these coordinators "developed the 'directive' into what is almost a new tool of coordination." [117] The President also used the authoritative directive as a means of allocating functions among agencies and prescribing policy guides for them to follow.

The written directive would have advantages as a regular tool of executive direction. It would substitute open, public statement for influence and pressure by the President on commissions, whether through the chairman or on other members. It would, as Cushman indicated, provide its own safeguards against interference in matters on which presidential influence would be inappropriate. It could also be used in combination with any or all kinds of agencies— single- or plural-headed, within or outside departments—which Congress might desire to use.

We suggest, however, that it would be desirable for Congress to authorize the use of the directive. It could thus be a true mandatory directive, not a mere statement of presidential desires. A congressional enactment authorizing the use of the directive on matters of policy only would confirm the idea that the President should not use his influence on particular applications of policy. The power to issue the authoritative directive would destroy all justifications for presidential use of subterranean and circuitous methods. And if our views are correct that policy development is the center of regulation and that the prospectus of future regulation indicates the need for greater coordination and direction than in the past, then it would follow that we should not pussyfoot on this matter of central

---

[116] Robert E. Cushman, *The Independent Regulatory Commissions,* 689. Copyright 1941 by Oxford University Press, Inc.

[117] Gulick, "War Organization of the Federal Government," *op. cit.,* 1174.

direction but should recognize frankly the necessity for coordination, freshness, and democratic control.

The step would, of course, delimit the effect of the limitations on presidential removal. If these remained, failure to follow a presidential directive would become "neglect of duty" and cause for removal. On the other hand, the clarification by statute of the President's function as one of policy direction only would lay the basis for a stronger tradition of independence, freedom, and irremovability on matters left within the discretion of those at the operative or agency level.

It would not be realistic to suggest that mere legalization of the written directive would result in its full substitution for other methods used in the working processes of government. During the war, consultation and agreement on a common course of action often made the use of the directive by the coordinators unnecessary. The same would be true of presidential coordination and leadership, particularly if the power to use the written, authoritative directive lay in the background. Nevertheless, the legalization of the directive or written instruction, along with the rules and traditions being built around the Federal Register, would be the anchor point around which new traditions could be developed. The essence of these traditions would be that the President should act through known rules or declarations of policy and at the level of policy which lay between congressional mandates and the level which was appropriate for agency determination alone. The authorization of the written directive would tend to focus attention on these imperatives.

It is believed that the written directive on policy has advantages over the techniques suggested by Hyneman. The danger in requirements for presidential signature, approval, or veto is that this may load the President's office with repeated routine calls on its time, or bring politics into the decision of particular applications of law or smaller issues of policy, and diminish the responsibility of operating executives and overenlarge the influence of presidential assistants. The techniques may be necessary in some instances, particularly where conflicts among agencies must be resolved; but even where conflicts exist, the embodiment of the solution in a policy directive, leaving the formal issuance of documents to the agencies concerned, may be the preferable technique.

Congressional authorization to use the directive could be limited and safeguarded, if Congress desired. Presidential authority could be limited, as Hyneman suggests, to "specific actions or categories of actions." It is suggested, however, that it would be impossible to anticipate the cases where need for policy directives would arise and hence that it would be desirable to give a blanket grant of authority to issue directives on general policy. The recent executive order subjecting the Federal Maritime Board on subsidy functions to the direction of the Secretary of Commerce on general policy sets the pattern which should be followed. Congress could also subject presidential directives on policy to congressional veto, as in the case of reorganization plans under recent acts; but the wisdom of such a limitation would be debatable.

If planning and direction are two components of unity at the upper level, structural integration may be the third. The advantages Landis asserted for the small agency with restricted jurisdiction, though substantial, must be measured against other needs. The distribution of functions among many unlinked agencies ultimately must result in overconcentration of planning and direction at the presidential level. Intermediary centers of unity are the means of relieving the burden and congestion at that point. At the same time, intermediary centers provide a continuing view of related things and thus set up a counterpoise to specialized viewpoint in the agencies.

If the need for some measure of central coordination and direction be admitted, the principle of the span of control, that is, the number of units one man can deal with directly, has some weight in determining the subordinate structure.[118] Also, there is need for not overlooking the larger areas of relatedness in government. Is it important that the nation have someone take a view of the whole problem of

[118] But note the conclusion of H. Struve Hensel and John D. Millett in *Task Force Report on Departmental Management* (Prepared for the Hoover Commission), page 4: "We believe it makes little difference whether the number of executive departments is 10 or 20."

transportation? Of trade regulation? Of fiscal policy? Are each of these needs sufficiently continuing to call for an intermediate level of planning, coordination, and direction?

Of the many problems posed by structural integration, two deserve comment. One is the need for organs of unification which will be sympathetic to the purpose of legislation. Where there is probability of conflict between the public interest expressed in statute and regulated groups, the Departments of Agriculture, Commerce, and Labor seem to be inappropriate for regulatory work. But a dilemma is presented: Modern governmental programs tend to fuse promotion and control; yet the identities of interest between promotional agency and private groups reveal dangers in the combination of the two functions. There is no universal answer. It appears that the proper units for integration of the work of existing regulatory commissions would lie outside the three departments named above, but any principle of separate location of activities where work was predominantly regulatory in character would be subject to qualification in special cases because of the force of the more general test of relatedness.

The other problem is that of relationships within the structurally integrated organization. This is the problem of degree of unification. Three possibilities exist. One is the unitary department which is operated as a cohesive, closely-knit organ. Another is the federal or holding company department, in which primary centers of unity, and therefore the primary rights of decision, are at operating units below the departmental level. The third is another type of federal structure in which unification is achieved by coordinators. This was the system used in World War II, where agencies carried primary responsibility for their tasks but were subject to the coordinative and directive functions of the Office of Economic Stabilization and the Office of War Mobilization. The "federal" department and the coordinator are definitely part of the coordinative and directive level, and are distinct from the operative level. Such structures would provide opportunities for the crystallization of the idea that the department head or coordinator should act only on matters of general policy, as was provided recently with respect to the control of the Secretary of Commerce over certain functions of the Federal Maritime Board.

It is surprising that the possibilities of other systems between the unified department and the commission system have received so little attention. Large business enterprises show many examples of middle arrangements: the holding company, the lease within the department store, and the franchise dealer being a few. With the increase in and the centralization of government functions, the national government may find its answer in some fields in something less concentrated than the unified department and less deconcentrated than the independent commission.[119]

This brings us to a point which is much broader in its implications. The thesis is submitted that discussion of this problem of responsibility versus independence in regulatory work has been plagued with absolute concepts. It is further suggested that study should turn to the types of relationship which are appropriate between men at different levels of organization and how these can be implemented in organization and practice. It would be seen there are levels of particularity in policy elaboration. Moreover, it would be recognized that policy application and some bottom part of policy elaboration should be immunized from political influence and reserved entirely for the permanent official. It would be seen that there are operational centers, and that above these the relationship was one of planning, coordination, and general direction.

The danger in any hierarchical relationship in government is the movement of detail to the top center. This is the result of external pressures. Men affected by government, their national associations, and their representatives in Congress want to get to the top men. These, in turn, seek protection against attack by pulling the strings of administration tighter to the center. This is not reason for denying

---

[119] But see the criticism of holding company departments, Hoover Commission, *Task Force Report on Departmental Management* (1949), 5. We have referred to the system of organization which existed in OPA as a "multi-level federalized structure." See our *Field Administration of Wartime Administration* (Washington, 1947), 34. The Government Corporation Control Act of 1945 goes far in providing a middle solution for the government-operated enterprise for which arguments for autonomy had been advanced, similar to those for independence for the regulatory commission.

the real need for coordination but only for balancing concepts and techniques. The written directive and the varieties of organization for structural integration may give opportunities for the middle term between operating independence and central direction, between the area of impartiality and that of politics, between expertness in specialized areas and planning for broader purposes, between the continuity that comes from administration's protection of its evolved patterns and the urge to change that comes when movements of opinion agitate the public. If these seem too uncertain in result, it is perhaps because we have not fully grasped the fact that all government is the result of the relationships of men. And at least these guides might be more useful than this double talk about the supremacy of political organs and the independence of policy-making commissions, and about a theory of independence at the same time that there are unregularized methods of presidential intervention.

The issue of plurality remains. The question loses much of its significance if disassociated from the idea of independence. The board can be used in a function similar to that of an appellate court if its function is circumscribed, or its position is set within the agency lines of communication of purpose, so as to prevent frustration and disunity in the operation of government. The regulatory board can also be used in the channel of policy formation IF ITS SUBORDINATION TO OVERHEAD DIRECTIVE IS CLARIFIED AND ITS OPERATING CUMBERSOME-NESS CAN BE ELIMINATED. But the latter is difficult and can probably only be achieved by bold delegation of day-to-day decisions similar to that which would be made by a corporate board to a general manager. But can boards do this if they stick to case-to-case administration as the means of evolving policy? For it is not housekeeping functions but day-to-day decisions on substantive issues which bog the commissions in detail and freeze them in their own delays.

It is submitted that if (along with the demise of the idea of independence) the nature of the institutional process were understood, the argument for the regulatory board would lose force in most situations. The complementary contribution of cooperating groups of staff experts provides the expertness, impartiality, stability, and group decision which have been sought in the commissions. What is needed from the top of the agency is clarity in the communication of purpose to the staff below; then and then only can a staff make its best contribution. But boards normally fail to supply this—in part, because of lethargy; in part, because of divisions; in part, because they often delay their collective thought on problems until after the staff has done all of its work. Plurality undoubtedly is justified at places in the complex of government regulation, but it requires very strong special justification in a day when men can see that the problem of administration is the simultaneous accommodation of the flow of purpose from above and of staff expertness and collaboration from below.

Chapter XI

The Problem of Safeguards

The span of administration has been shown. It fashions the content of program; chooses among methods of application; opens or closes the regulatory valve with initiative, prosecution, and settlement; makes decisions having legal effect; applies sanctions, and constructs its defenses in Congress, with interest groups, and in public opinion. Inevitably, and justifiably, the question follows: in the presence of this array of powers, what safeguards does the nation have?

Safeguards for what? For four things. First, that the exercise of power shall be confined within the limits of the delegations. Action should not be ultra vires. Second, that power shall be exercised in a reasonable or non-arbitrary manner. This means that decisions should be made on the basis of data, in accord with proper purpose, and in an even-handed manner. Third, that power shall be exercised effectively. This means success in doing jobs assigned in directives. Fourth, that power shall be exercised under conditions of democratic responsibility. This calls for accountability to the public and its representatives.[1]

[1] A fifth could be mentioned separately: that power shall be exercised in accord with constitutional provisions. But (1) the import of the due process clause so far as administration is concerned is to prevent *arbitrary exercise* of power; and (2) including more in delegations than is constitutionally valid is a problem of safeguard against the legislature rather than the administrative authority. If the legislative delegation is valid, holding the administration within the delegation prevents unconstitutionality in the scope of power.

Safeguards against what? Against unenlightened decision and incompetent action. Against particularistic politics and pressures. Against institutional inertia, delay, and lack of vision.

What safeguards does the nation have? They may be discussed under the following divisions: those exercised through the courts to ensure the rule of law; those exercised through Congress and the President to insure democratic responsibility; those which may exist for various ends within the administration itself; and those existing within the society of which administration is a part.

JUDICIAL REVIEW

The ideal of the rule of law, which has had so many manifestations in Anglo-American history, has been strongly intrenched in administrative-judicial relations. The abolition of the prerogative courts in England and the growth of the jurisdiction of the courts of law and equity—through which the courts in various ways could control official action—led to the view that all controverted questions concerning the application of law should be finally determined in the courts. Summarizing this development, an eminent English constitutional historian compounded, near the end of the nineteenth century, a definition of the "supremacy of law:" "We mean, in the first place, that no man is punishable or can be lawfully made to suffer in body or goods except for a distinct breach of law established in the *ordinary legal manner* before the *ordinary courts* of the land. . . ." [2]

Obviously, this is not an accurate description of twentieth-century government. It assumes a political society in which men "suffer in . . . goods" only for *breaches of law,* not one in which the conditions under which men produce and distribute goods are regulated by *policy decisions.* Even for the application of law in an adjudicatory manner the definition is outmoded for it requires trial de novo in courts.[3]

The inescapable reality of administrative decision has led men

[2] A. V. Dicey, *Law of the Constitution* (8th ed. 1915), 183-184. My emphasis.

[3] See Landis, *The Administrative Process,* 124, and John Dickinson, *Administrative Justice and the Supremacy of Law,* 35-36.

in our time to seek for the maintenance of the "supremacy of law" in a different way, namely, through judicial review of administrative decisions. Administrators could decide, but the courts would correct; in this way "law" would still be supreme.[4]

But how far would review go? Justice Brandeis said it should include two things: "The supremacy of law," he wrote, "demands that there shall be opportunity to have some court decide whether an *erroneous rule of law was applied;* and whether the proceeding in which facts were adjudicated was *conducted regularly.*"[5] This, however, is narrower than the general view. The following language of the Supreme Court puts in a third element which is generally included: "The determination whether a rate is unreasonable or discriminatory is a question on which the finding of the Commission is conclusive if supported by *substantial evidence,* unless there was some irregularity in the proceeding or some error in the application of the rules of law." [6] This statement recognizes three elements which enter discussions of judicial review: procedure, law, and facts. Were the proceedings "conducted regularly"? Was there error in the application of law? Was there adequate basis in fact for the decision? [7]

The courts have been able to establish basic safeguards on administrative procedure. This they have done primarily under the constitutional provisions for due process of law and by interpretation of statutes. Statutes so frequently require hearings that it is often difficult to tell whether the decision of the courts on what is necessary in an administrative hearing rests on statutory requirement or on constitutional provision. The courts, nevertheless, have gone far in defining the cases in which due process of law requires notice and hearing for affected parties, and have indicated strongly that

---

[4] Dickinson, *op. cit.*, 37-38.

[5] Dissenting in St. Joseph Stock Yards Co. *v.* U. S., 298 U. S. 38, 84 (1936). My emphasis.

[6] Western Paper Makers' Chemical Co. *v.* United States, 271 U. S. 268, 271 (1926). My emphasis.

[7] Oftentimes, as the subsequent discussion shows, other explanations may be given for judicial decisions. And yet the three elements in the text appear recurringly and are again emphasized in the Administrative Procedure Act, Section 11 (e) on "Scope of Review."

in certain other cases the requirement may rest on something more fundamental than the statutory requirement. The courts have also established the basic essentials of an adequate judicial hearing.[8] In this way the judiciary has evolved standards of "fair play" for administration.

Some have thought that the procedural safeguards required by the courts under due process and existing statutes did not go far enough. Thus, some felt that the safeguards of adjudicatory process should be extended to rule making or uncovered aspects of licensing, or that independence for deciding officers was a basic requisite for fairness,[9] or that institutional decisions should be further restricted,[10] or that the rules of evidence should be the same as those in the courts.[11] The result was the movement for statutory prescription of procedure, which, of course, would give the courts new standards to enforce through judicial review.

On the other hand, the Morgan cases illustrate dangers in the judicial safeguard. The effort to fix rates was stymied for nearly a decade while the process of marching upward to Mahomet and back again was repeated.[12] Moreover, the requirement for the judicial pattern, with personalized decision and adversary proceedings, may have been overextended. However, the case did involve interpretation of a statutory requirement for "full hearing" and the special

[8] As to the nature of these, see pages 188-189.

[9] See pages 211, 292 ff.

[10] See pages 205-206.

[11] Evidenced in the Labor Management Relations Act, in which it is provided that the National Labor Relations Board shall in unfair labor practice proceedings follow "so far as practicable . . . the rules of evidence applicable in the district courts of the United States under the rules of civil procedure for the district courts of the United States, adopted by the Supreme Court of the United States pursuant to the Act of June 19, 1934." Title I, Section 10 (b).

[12] The administrative proceedings in these cases were instituted by the Secretary of Agriculture in 1930. The order fixing rates was made in June, 1933. Decision I in Morgan v. U.S. was made in 1936 (298 U.S. 468). Decision II was made in 1938 (304 U.S. 1). An opinion on denial of the Solicitor General's petition for rehearing came also in 1938 (304 U.S. 23). Decision III came in 1939 (307 U.S. 183) and Decision IV in 1941 (313 U.S. 409). In Decision IV Justice Frankfurter began the opinion of the Court as follows: "This case originated eleven years ago." (p. 413) Though substantive issues intruded in the later stages, the primary cause of delay was the procedural issues. For discussion of the first two decisions of the Supreme Court see pages 194-195, 200-201.

function of rate making, in which administrative-judicial relations have been more uncongenial than in most other fields.

Controversy over particulars should not lead us too far away from two sets of facts about the judicial safeguard on procedure. First, the courts have made a material contribution in enunciating and clarifying certain minimum essentials of fair and adequate adjudicatory procedure. They have given substance to the requirements of due process and the general provisions of statutes regarding hearings. Morcover, judicial control must be counted on as one line of safeguard against uninformed and unprotected decision. On the other hand, the limits on the safeguard are great. So large a proportion of the task of government is not conducted under formal processes, or fails to reach the courts for review, that much of the hope for fair, as well as effective, administration must be based upon other safeguards.

The other issues about the function of judicial review relate to the scope of review on decisions made by administrative agencies. To what extent can—or should—judicial review on questions of "law" and "fact" be a safeguard for administration of economic controls under law and according to high standards of judgment?

There are limits on the safeguard which reveal the impossibility of maintaining, except in limited part, the ideal of the "supremacy of law" through judicial review. First, most men will accept the day-to-day decisions of government, either as just or inevitable, or because they want to avoid the courthouse. They may seek correction of what they regard as improper or too severe through their Congressman or trade association, or they may exhaust the processes of appeal within an agency; but few of the decisions of administrative agencies are carried to the courts.[13] Statistics, of course, do not tell the whole story, for while some appealed cases are merely the big, the minor, or the unusual, some lead to judicial precedents which govern a broad category of future administrative decisions.

Second, there are many types of decisions in economic control which obviously lie outside the purview of the courts. The courts

[13] See the figures given by Col. O. R. McGuire in "Judicial Reviews of Administrative Decisions," *Georgetown Law Review*, XXVI, 574-605 (1938).

cannot determine which cases will be prosecuted and which will not, nor can they reach a multitude of cases where men choose to compromise with government agencies in order to avoid punitive action or loss of benefit.[14] They cannot adequately prevent adverse effect on men's rights and interests from administrative delay. They cannot affect decisions of Federal Reserve or Treasury policy, such as those on open-market negotiations, the level of margins for trading on stock exchanges, and the timing and manner of distribution of government bonds. They cannot force the President to make or not to make a trade agreement. They cannot force constructive planning, such as a sound route pattern for air transportation. They cannot force a decision to make a marketing agreement. They cannot correct laxness in bank examinations or in the granting of bank charters. Nor can they force competence in the development of techniques of wage, price, and production control.

It is not justiciable questions only which affect men's welfare. In each of the above examples of administrative immunity men may suffer or gain in goods. But judicially applied law does not reach the decision; these are areas of policy and performance and are part of the government of men working in institutions.

Third, within the area where judicial review might conceivably take hold, the courts have had to yield a large measure of finality to the agencies to which responsibility has been delegated by the legislative power. They have been impelled to this end by one of the same necessities which led them to recognize the right of initial decision in administrative agencies, namely, the need for an informed judgment on intricate and technical economic data.[15] Other factors, such as the desire to avoid the crippling of government, and the need of protecting the courts from too large a volume of cases, have undoubtedly influenced the judges also. Beginning with a faith in judicial operations and a distrust of administrative government, and with a ready identification of the former as a government of law and of the latter as a government of men, the courts have

---

[14] See Kenneth C. Davis, "Administrative Powers of Supervising, Prosecuting, Advising, Declaring, and Informally Adjudicating," *Harvard Law Review,* LXIII, 194-240 (1949) for many examples.

[15] On initial decision, see pages 140-148.

nevertheless found that, whatever the scope of the review might be on some other types of cases, economic legislation required a reappraisal of the function of the courts vis-à-vis administration.

The adjustment between the courts and administrative agencies has not been easy and has left much uncertainty as to the precise field for each. The courts, with whom the decision on scope of review has rested, have found it difficult to evolve satisfactory guides as to the proper scope of their review authority.

The most common rationalization of judicial decision has been from the conceptual approach, in which the traditional distinction between law and fact, familiar to all as the basis of the judge-jury relationship, has been regarded as the knife of judicial policy. It has been assumed generally that courts would review on questions of law, including the meaning of constitutional terms, the extent of delegated power, and the interpretation of statutes. On the other hand, the trend of opinion has favored much judicial deference to administrative decisions on questions of fact.

Yet law and fact have not been clearly separable things. First, decisions on fact, if made without the support of evidence, are arbitrary and hence, according to courts, have no standing in law. Thus, as for issues of fact, the federal courts have in general adopted for review of administrative action the test used in appeals from jury decisions, under which the decision of the administrative agency would be upheld if based upon substantial evidence.[16] For the

---

[16] The substantial evidence rule is a middle course. A court could (1) weigh the facts to determine on which side there was a preponderance of evidence, or differently stated, make its own independent judgment on the facts; (2) accept the administrative findings as prima facie correct, that is, on their face correct but subject to rebuttal; (3) accept such findings if based upon substantial evidence; (4) accept such findings as conclusive unless fraudulent; or (5) accept such findings as absolutely conclusive. There are obviously other possibilities. The Supreme Court has said, "Substantial evidence is more than a scintilla. It means such relevant evidence as a reasonable mind might accept as adequate to support a conclusion." Consolidated Edison Co. v. National Labor Relations Board, 305 U.S. 197, 229 (1938). The courts sometimes use alternate terms, such as "rational basis," as in Miss. Valley Barge Co. v. U.S., 292 U.S. 282, 286-7 (1934); Rochester Telephone Corporation v. U.S., 307 U.S. 125, 146 (1939). As to some of the various possibilities in judicial review see the chart in J. Roland Pennock, *Administration and the Rule of Law* (New York, 1941), 208.

Interstate Commerce Commission this rule was one of judicial origin solely. The Hepburn Act provided that rates fixed by the railroads could be set aside if after a hearing the "Commission is of the opinion that the charge was unreasonable"; and the government argued in Interstate Commerce Commission v. Louisville & Nashville R. Co. that a rate order of the I.C.C. could not be set aside by the courts even if without evidence to support it. The Supreme Court rejected this argument, saying: "But the legal effect of evidence is a question of law. . . . It is therefore necessary to examine the record with a view of determining whether there was substantial evidence to support the order." [17] This was in 1913 and many of the regulatory statutes passed since that time have specifically authorized judicial review on questions of fact. Both the Federal Trade Commission Act and the Clayton Act provided that administrative findings "as to the facts, if supported by testimony, shall be conclusive." A number of statutes specifically require that the findings of fact must be supported by "substantial evidence." [18] The inclusion or noninclusion of the word "substantial" seems not to be significant, for the Supreme Court held that the National Labor Relations "statute in providing that 'the findings of the Board as to the facts, if supported by evidence, shall be conclusive,' means supported by substantial evidence." [19]

The rule that courts shall review to determine if there is "substantial evidence" to support an order has been subject to attack from two sides. Those who feared the administrative process have often quoted the words put by Chief Justice Hughes in the mouth of a hypothetical unscrupulous administrator: "Let me find the facts for the people of my country, and I care little who lays down the general principles." [20] They have feared, moreover, that the reviewing court would look only for a scintilla of evidence rather than for substantial

[17] Interstate Commerce Commission v. Louisville & Nashville R. Co., 227 U.S. 88 (1913). See also the earlier case, Interstate Commerce Commission v. Union Pacific R. Co., 222 U.S. 541 (1912).

[18] Including the Securities Exchange Act, the Federal Power Act, the Fair Labor Standards Act, and perhaps others.

[19] Consolidated Edison Co. v. N.L.R.B., 305 U.S. 197, 229 (1938).

[20] Address to Federal Bar Association, New York Times, February 13, 1931, p. 18.

evidence, or would rule that the evidence supporting an administrative decision was substantial without looking at parts of the record which contained opposing evidence. On the other hand, the substantial evidence rule provides an opportunity for the courts to ease over to the position where they weigh the evidence to determine on which side there is a preponderance of facts.[21] Moreover, some have doubted whether the courts, in the area of application of standards to intricate economic facts, can make a useful contribution to government through review of administrative determinations of fact.

Second, law and fact are not clearly separable because there is a vast area in which the issues are mixed questions of law and fact. At one end of a scale are pure issues of legal interpretation, at the other are decisions on basic or evidentiary facts, but in the middle where a decision must be made on whether the law applies to a particular state of facts issues of legal determination and determinations of the ultimate conclusions to be drawn from the facts become fused. Thus, on the question of whether the application of law to particular states of fact raises an issue of law or fact, good authorities have said that it was one of law,[22] or that it was not,[23] or that it was only so if the decision would establish a standard applicable generally,[24] or that it was capable of being made either depending

---

[21] McFarland's conclusion in 1933 concerning judicial review of the cases coming from the Federal Trade Commission was: "From the beginning the courts have determined the weight of the evidence and have substituted their judgment for the conclusions of the commissioners." From page 32 of Carl McFarland, *Judicial Control of the Federal Trade Commission and the Interstate Commerce Commission: 1920-1930.* Copyright 1933 by the President and Fellows of Harvard College. The Federal Trade Commission Act does not, of course, contain the word "substantial."

For discussion of the various meanings of "substantial evidence," see E. Blythe Stason, "'Substantial Evidence' in Administrative Law," *University of Pennsylvania Law Review,* LXXXIX, 1026-1051, at pp. 1035-1039 (1941).

[22] Holmes, *The Common Law* (1881), 122, 129, and recently Clarence Morris, "Law and Fact," *Harvard Law Review,* LV, 1303, 1312-1313 (June, 1942).

[23] Thayer, *A Preliminary Treatise on Evidence* (1898), 226, 229, et seq.

[24] "Where the ground of difference between court and fact-finding body can be isolated and expressed as a general proposition applicable beyond the particular case to all similar cases, the court, if it holds the proposition one of sound law, must enforce it by overruling the administrative determination." Page 168 of John Dickinson, *Administrative Justice and the Supremacy of Law.* Copyright 1927 by the President and Fellows of Harvard College.

on practical considerations or legislative intent.[25] In the most complete analysis it has been concluded:[26]

> In truth, the distinction between "questions of law" and "questions of fact" really gives little help in determining how far the courts will review; and for the good reason that there is no fixed distinction. . . . Matters of law grow downward into roots of fact, and matters of fact reach upward, without a break, into matters of law. . . . It would seem that when the courts are unwilling to review, they are tempted to explain by the easy device of calling the question one of "fact"; and when otherwise disposed, they say that it is a question of "law."

The conclusion is buttressed by that of McFarland after an exhaustive comparative analysis of judicial review of two agencies. He concluded that "separation of functions into 'fact-finding' and 'law-making' does not explain the relations of the courts to the Federal Trade Commission and the Interstate Commerce Commission." [27]

Gerald C. Henderson has shown some of the practical insufficiencies of the fact-law criterion. When railroad rates are set for the future he thought it was not sensible to regard what might happen six months later as either a question of fact or law. In this instance, "The commission is merely doing what every board of directors of a business corporation must do—exercise its best judgment, in the light of existing facts and past experience, in determining what is likely to happen in the future, and what is likely to be the practical consequence of one course of action or another." And where a decision must be made on whether a bridge is an unreasonable obstruction to commerce, whether a person has a communicable disease, or whether a rate will yield six per cent,

---

[25] As to the bearing of legislative intent, see Robert L. Stern, "Review of Findings of Administrators, Judges and Juries: A Comparative Analysis," *Harvard Law Review*, LVIII, 70-124, at pages 106-109 (Nov. 1944).

[26] From page 55 of John Dickinson, *Administrative Justice and the Supremacy of Law.* Copyright 1927 by the President and Fellows of Harvard College.

[27] From page 33 of Carl McFarland, *Judicial Control of the Federal Trade Commission and the Interstate Commerce Commission: 1920-1930.* Copyright 1933 by the President and Fellows of Harvard College. For McFarland's explanation of court action toward these commissions, see above, p. 86.

the legislative intent to create an expert tribunal to handle the matter was more relevant than whether it was an issue of fact or law.[28]

For more than a decade the trend in Supreme Court opinions has been toward judicial deference to administrative judgment on mixed questions of law and fact, i.e., the application of legal concepts to facts.[29] But cases in which administrative judgment on such issues has been accepted can be matched by cases in which the Supreme Court has substituted its judgment for that of administrators. A competent scholar, after analysis of the apparent inconsistencies, concludes that the challenge of the cases is for a wider search for guides for decision.[30]

It appears that the fact-law distinction, drawn from the jury system and the common law, is insufficient as a measure for judicial review of administrative action in economic regulation. There is little resemblance between use of a jury to pass upon physical facts or motives in a single case under the direction of a judge and the committal to specialized administrative agencies of the undivided responsibility for making a series of interrelated decisions on the proper course of future economic behavior. Fact-law is only a part of the kit of conceptual tools used by the courts to maintain their control over a new social development, under the assumption that law and reason will not prevail unless courts hold an umbrella over government.

There are, however, other concepts to be considered. The doctrine of constitutional fact has been raised in utility cases.[31] Under this doctrine the courts must make their own independent judgment on both law and facts when the claim of violation of due process through confiscation of property is made. The doctrine has not been

[28] *The Federal Trade Commission* (Yale University Press, New Haven, 1924), 9.

[29] In line with the leading case of Gray *v. Powell*, discussed at pages 338-339.

[30] Kenneth Culp Davis, "Scope of Review of Federal Administrative Action," *Columbia Law Review*, L, 559-612 (May, 1950).

[31] Ohio Valley Water Co. *v.* Ben Avon Borough, 253 U.S. 287 (1920); St. Joseph Stock Yards Co. *v.* United States, 298 U.S. 38 (1936).

reasserted in recent years,[32] but the cases have not been expressly overruled and the doctrine could be revived. The doctrine of jurisdictional fact, under which the courts must make their own independent conclusions on facts affecting the issues of administrative jurisdiction, or even, as in Crowell v. Benson, build their own record, has been used to widen the scope of review.[33]

In recent years a new approach, which might be called the functional approach, has been evolving. In this approach an answer to the proper scope for judicial review is sought by reference to the functions which administrators and judges are each equipped to perform. Landis finds a good reason for the past emphasis on "the issue of 'law' as being the dividing line of judicial review":[34]

OUR DESIRE TO HAVE COURTS DETERMINE QUESTIONS OF LAW IS RELATED TO A BELIEF IN THEIR POSSESSION OF EXPERTNESS WITH REGARD TO SUCH QUESTIONS. IT IS FROM THAT VERY DESIRE THAT THE NATURE OF QUESTIONS OF LAW EMERGES. FOR, IN THE LAST ANALYSIS, THEY SEEM TO ME TO BE THOSE QUESTIONS THAT LAWYERS ARE EQUIPPED TO DECIDE.

But if the reason justifies, it also limits. He thought administrative agencies might in some areas have a superior competence to determine questions of law:[35]

The interesting problem as to the future of judicial review over administrative action is the extent to which judges will withdraw, not from reviewing findings of fact, but conclusions upon law. If the withdrawal is due to the belief that these issues of fact are best handled by experts, a similar impulse to withdraw should become manifest in the field of law.

Expertness could justify, he believed, differentiation between types of cases. Thus, in immigration cases no special administrative ex-

---

[32] It appears to be inconsistent with Railroad Commission v. Rowan & Nichols Co., 310 U.S. 573 (1940), 311 U.S. 570 (1941). But see John Dickinson's argument that the two cases can be distinguished. "Judicial Review of Administrative Determinations, A Summary and Evaluation," *Minnesota Law Review*, XXV, 588-612, at p. 598 (1941).

[33] See pages 151-152 for discussion of the doctrine of jurisdictional fact.

[34] James M. Landis, *The Administrative Process*, 152. Copyright 1938 by Yale University Press. Emphasis by Landis.

[35] James M. Landis, *The Administrative Process*, 144. Copyright 1938 by Yale University Press.

pertness might be required, while in utility cases the administration might be expected to have more of the required expertness than judge or jury.[36]

This factor of expertness has undoubtedly had a great influence on courts in leading them to defer to administrative agencies. Brandeis' oft-quoted reference to an administrative agency as being "informed by experience" has emphasized this fact. It has been emphasized also in recent opinions of the Supreme Court.[37]

In applying the functional test the courts may only *presume* the expertness of the administrative agency. This is exemplified in the Rowan and Nichols cases,[38] where the Supreme Court took a limited view of the review function of federal courts as to proration orders issued by a state regulatory agency. In proration for the East Texas oil field the Court found that judgment was "necessarily beset by the necessity of inferences bordering on conjecture," that claims were "enmeshed in a conflict of expertise," that sound foundations were "only to be achieved through the fruitful empiricism of a continuous administrative process," that the "accommodation of conflicting private interests" is "beset with perplexities, both geological and economic." The Court took note of "the limiting conditions of litigation—the adaptability of the judicial process only to issues definitely circumscribed and susceptible of being judged by the techniques and criteria within the special competence of lawyers." But on the other side of the competence comparison, the Court, though referring to "expert conclusions" which were made, said of the state agency that "Presumably that body . . . possesses an insight and aptitude. . . ."

A purely pragmatic approach has also been suggested. Courts, it has been said, should be influenced by a variety of practical considerations such as "quality of administrative personnel, procedural safeguards and political susceptibilities of administrative bodies, nature of subject matter, specialization of judges and of adminis-

[36] *Ibid.*, 142-144.
[37] Illustrative are the Rowan and Nichols cases and Gray *v.* Powell, discussed below.
[38] Railroad Commission *v.* Rowan & Nichols Co., 310 U.S. 573 (1940), 311 U.S. 570 (1941).

trators, and relative judicial and administrative biases." [39] Undoubtedly, courts are influenced by this wide variety of factors. Thus, in Dobson *v.* Commissioner of Internal Revenue the Supreme Court, in extending to the Tax Court the more liberal rules of review applicable to "administrative" agencies generally, took note of the Tax Court's independence, neutrality, fair procedures, freedom from bias and pressures, staffing, experience, and other factors. The Court concluded, "Tested by every theoretical and practical reason for administrative finality, no administrative decisions are entitled to higher credit in the courts." [40]

Still another suggestion is that the courts should look for their guides in the statutes. Justice Frankfurter has said: "Apart from the text and texture of a particular law in relation to which judicial review is sought 'judicial review' is a mischievous abstraction." [41]

The Justice would have us believe that, in this particular, too much mischief had not been done. For he argues: "Judicial review when recognized—its scope and its incidence—was derived from the materials furnished by the particular statute in regard to which the opportunity for judicial review was asserted." [42] Statutes are, in theory, authoritative on issues not touching constitutional right. But very often statutes are silent on the scope of review, as was the Hepburn Act except for reparations orders. The legislative history may contain no helpful materials. Words like "final" or "final and conclusive" convey different meanings to different judges, or even to the same judges in different situations. The decisions give ample evidence that judges are influenced by a variety of extra-statutory materials, such as the law-fact concept, the jurisdictional fact concept, the deference or lack of deference to the "expert," and the reputation of the agency.

The fact is that the various tests for review get intermingled in difficult cases. Gray *v.* Powell illustrates this. [43] Where Congress

---

[39] Kenneth C. Davis, "To What Extent Should the Decisions of Administrative Bodies be Reviewable by the Courts," *A.B.A. Journal,* XXV, 770.

[40] 320 U.S. 489 (1943).

[41] Stark *v.* Wickard, 321 U.S. 288, 312 (1944).

[42] *Ibid.,* 314.

[43] 314 U.S. 402 (1941).

had vested in the Director of the Bituminous Coal Division the function of determining on application whether a person was a producer of coal within the meaning of the Bituminous Coal Act, the Supreme Court held that it was the Court's duty to uphold the administrative decision unless it was "so unrelated to the tasks entrusted by Congress . . . as in effect to deny a sensible exercise of judgment." The minority of three thought the issue was a bare question of statutory construction, which would be a question of law. The majority thought the decision was one "for the expert, experienced judgment of those familiar with the industry," and a competent scholar has thought that the case gave support to the measurement-of-competence approach suggested by Landis.[44] At the same time, however, the Court stressed that the matter had been left by Congress to administrative judgment, and another commentator has thought that the significance of the case was the opportunity afforded in statutory construction for determining which horn of the law-fact dilemma should be followed.[45]

What has happened is that the courts have evolved a varied set of doctrines under which they can allow the administrative decision to stand. They can call it a matter of discretion or of fact rather than of law, or one requiring expert judgment, or can find a statutory intent for administrative finality. The judicial yielding to administrative government may even extend these days to deference to administrative judgment on the meaning or coverage of statutory terms[46] or to interpretation of statutes in such a way as to make decisions of administrative agencies nonreviewable.[47]

[44] Ray A. Brown, "Fact and Law in Judicial Review," *Harvard Law Review*, LVI, 899-928, at pages 921-926 (May, 1943).

[45] Robert L. Stern, *op. cit.*, 103, 106-108, 122-124.

[46] Illustrative are *Gray v. Powell*, 314 U.S. 402 (1941), where on the issue of whether a company was a producer within the meaning of the Bituminous Coal Act the Supreme Court said: "Unless we can say that a set of circumstances deemed by the Commission to bring them within the concept 'producer' is so unrelated to the tasks entrusted by Congress to the Commission as in effect to deny a sensible exercise of judgment, it is the Court's duty to leave the Commission's judgment undisturbed"; and *National Labor Relations Board v. Hearst Publications, Inc.*, 322 U.S. 111 (1944), where the Court said that "the Board's determination that specified persons are 'employees' under this Act is to be accepted if it has 'warrant in the record' and a reasonable basis in law."

[47] For full discussion of cases see Kenneth Culp Davis, "Nonreviewable Ad-

On the other hand, the courts can reassert their power in a given instance through holding that the question is one of law, that there is lack of evidence to support a conclusion, or that the facts are jurisdictional, or on other bases. The courts may still regard the definition of general statutory standards applied through case-to-case administration as a question of law,[48] and thus repeat the history of interpretation of the Federal Trade Commission Act, in which the Commission was reduced by judicial interpretation to a minor role. Any one who sought to predict the operation of public utility regulation in the future would have to take account of the possibility that judicial review would again stultify the process.[49] Moreover, the courts can still impair the public faith in administration by overextended "denunciatory fervor," repeating situations in the past where administrative decisions or procedures were called "wholly unreasonable and arbitrary,"[50] or likened to Star Chamber invasions of human liberty,[51] or found to result in lack of "fair play,"[52] or "to sweep all our traditions into the fire."[53] Judicial review, though a safeguard against illegal or arbitrary administration, can also be the most serious threat to the effectiveness of regulation.

Some, wanting more certainty, have felt the need for a formula on judicial review of administrative action.[54] Others have wanted

---

ministrative Action," *University of Pennsylvania Law Review*, LXXXXVI, 749-792 (June, 1948).

[48] Though S.E.C. *v.* Chenery Corp., 332 U.S. 194 (1947), points the other way.

[49] For one of the most effective explanations on how judicial review on valuation has hampered regulation see Felix Frankfurter, *The Public and Its Government* (1930), Chap. 3. But in Federal Power Commission *v.* Hope Natural Gas Co., 320 U. S. 591 (1944), Justice Frankfurter, dissenting, believed that the case should be returned to the Commission because "the range of its vision was too narrow."

[50] Jones *v.* Securities & Exchange Commission, 298 U. S. 1, 23 (1936).

[51] *Ibid.*, 28. Protesting the reference of the Court, Justice Cardozo said, "Historians may find hyperbole in the sanguinary simile." P. 33.

[52] Morgan *v.* U. S., 304 U. S. 1, 22 (1938).

[53] Federal Trade Commission *v.* American Tobacco Co., 264 U. S. 298, 306 (1924).

[54] "The need of a formula to define the areas of administrative immunity and judicial superiority is one of the most pressing problems with which the government is faced today." Robert M. Cooper, "The Proposed United States Ad-

only a "creative philosophy."[55] The Administrative Procedure Act evinces the former view in its statement of rules of review.

The section of the Act dealing with judicial review (Section 10) is complicated. First, the applicability of the entire section is limited by the following introductory statement: "Except so far as (1) statutes preclude judicial review or (2) agency action is by law committed to agency discretion." This provision excludes from the coverage of the section entirely or partially ("so far as") two categories of cases.[56] Second, the section contains provisions as to the availability of review. It seeks to define "reviewable acts" and persons having the "right of review." Third, it defines the scope of review in a long statement which will leave many points for construction.[57]

Probably the most significant wording in the statement on scope of review is that requiring the reviewing court to "review the whole record or such portions thereof as may be cited by any party." The effect of this language in connection with a preceding require-

---

ministrative Court," *Michigan Law Review*, XXXV, 565-596, at p. 586 (1936-1937). This was also the attitude of the Committee on Administrative Law of the American Bar Association in the years preceding the enactment of the Administrative Procedure Act.

[55] See Davis, *A.B.A. Journal*, XXV, 770-780, p. 780. This was Landis' effort in *The Administrative Process*. See above, pp. 336-337.

[56] As to the effects of the provision see Kenneth Culp Davis, "Nonreviewable Administrative Action," *University of Pennsylvania Law Review*, LXXXXVI, 749-792 (June, 1948).

[57] "So far as necessary to decision and where presented the reviewing court shall decide all relevant questions of law, interpret constitutional and statutory provisions, and determine the meaning or applicability of the terms of any agency action. It shall (A) compel agency action unlawfully withheld or unreasonably delayed; and (B) hold unlawful and set aside agency action, findings, and conclusions found to be (1) arbitrary, capricious, an abuse of discretion, or otherwise not in accordance with law; (2) contrary to constitutional right, power, privilege, or immunity; (3) in excess of statutory jurisdiction, authority, or limitations, or short of statutory right; (4) without observance of procedure required by law; (5) unsupported by substantial evidence in any case subject to the requirements of sections 7 and 8 or otherwise reviewed on the record of an agency hearing provided by statute; or (6) unwarranted by the facts to the extent that the facts are subject to trial de novo by the reviewing court. In making the foregoing determinations the court shall review the whole record or such portions thereof as may be cited by any party, and due account shall be taken of the rule of prejudicial error."

For other provisions the reader should see the text of the act.

ment that the reviewing court pass on the substantiality of evidence, and of a similar provision in the Taft-Hartley Act making the findings of the National Labor Relations Board conclusive on "questions of fact, if supported by substantial evidence on the record considered as a whole," was before the Supreme Court in February 1951 in Universal Camera Corporation v. National Labor Relations Board[58] and a companion case, National Labor Relations Board v. Pittsburgh Steamship Co. [59]

In the Camera Case, Justice Frankfurter, speaking for a unanimous court, noted that the Court's language in regard to the word "substantial" in earlier National Labor Relations Board cases "readily lent itself to the notion that it was enough that the evidence supporting the Board's result was 'substantial' *when considered by itself*," or "*when viewed in isolation*" (author's italics). He showed that dissatisfaction with this "restricted application of the 'substantial evidence' test" had led to the provisions in the two governing statutes requiring that substantiality be determined from the record as a whole, and added that in using the new language "Congress expressed a mood." He concluded that Congress had "made it clear that a reviewing court is not barred from setting aside a Board decision when it cannot conscientiously find that the evidence supporting that decision is substantial, when viewed in the light that the record *in its entirety furnishes, including the body of evidence opposed to the Board's view*" (author's italics).

To what extent does the Camera Case rebroaden the scope of judicial review in the circuit courts of appeals? Justice Frankfurter, mindful of the difference in practice in these courts in the past, concludes "that courts must now assume more responsibility for the reasonableness and fairness of Labor Board decisions than some courts have shown in the past." He indicates that the new formula involves some measure of duty to weigh the facts. "The substantiality of evidence must take into account whatever in the record fairly detracts from its weight." In the Pittsburgh Steamship Case he notes the possibility that "fair-minded judges could find it [the evidence]

[58] 340 U. S. 474.
[59] 340 U. S. 498.

tilting either way." On the other hand, he states in the Camera Case that "Retention of the familiar 'substantial evidence' terminology indicates that no drastic reversal of attitude was intended;" that the new statutory language was not "intended to negative the function of the Labor Board as one of those agencies presumably equipped or informed by experience to deal with a specialized field of knowledge, whose findings within that field carry the authority of an expertness which courts do not possess and therefore must respect," nor was it intended that even on "matters not requiring expertise a court may displace the Board's choice between two conflicting views, even though the court would justifiably have made a different choice had the matter been before it *de novo.*"

Against the backdrop of these varied statements, can one say that the Administrative Procedure Act has achieved a single formula for review? This would be saying too much. Justice Frankfurter, in the Camera Case, makes this clear: "Since the precise way in which courts interfere with agency findings cannot be imprisoned within any form of words, new formulas attempting to rephrase the old are not likely to be more helpful than the old." Undoubtedly, there has been a choice, by legislative enactment and judicial interpretation, in favor of the broader of contending views on the proper scope of review, and this has been encased in a formula. But the expertness, or the reviewing court's view of the expertness, of the National Labor Relations Board may still carry weight.

And will the courts of appeals act in the same way with respect to all types of cases coming to them under the standard set in the Administrative Procedure Act? The extent to which the facts are weighed and the deference shown for administrative judgment may vary, depending upon all the factors which have hitherto affected review, such as the need for special competence in analysis of facts, the legislative history behind the agency, and the judicial estimate of the quality of its work.

The attempt to encase in a formula cannot prevent the continued search for a "creative philosophy." Some elements of an adequate philosophy, growing in this case out of the compulsions of circumstance, may be suggested. First, the process of government must go on. Review action which only delays or which can yield no constructive aids to future decision will be more of a threat than a safeguard in the intricate business of economic control. Second, the differences between the judicial function and the administrative function in economic control are great. Only in part does the latter operate through adjudication of rights under specific law. More largely, it is policy and managerial; it involves predictions of future economic effects; it often includes discretionary judgment among many alternatives, no one of which could be adjudged "right" in any absolute sense. Third, the test of competence supplies one useful guide for legislatures and judges in determining the scope of review. It should help separate such areas as alien and selective service cases and application of specific economic regulations to particular parties, in which courts have developed skills, from the areas of policy and managerial controls, where skilled judgment can be expected only from those who are immersed in the analysis of the factual interrelationships. Application of this test may ultimately result in recognition that in policy and managerial regulation[60] the substantial evidence rule and the rule that courts should determine the content of general statutory language draw the courts into areas where economic considerations, economic research, and skilled judgment of those with specialized experience are more helpful than legal concepts, legal techniques, and the judgment of the occasional intervenor. It is suggested that the courts should presume the expertness of the constituted administrative authority, as in the Rowan and Nichols cases, rather than follow the purely pragmatic course of judging whether the expertness really exists. The latter throws an audit function on the courts which they are ill-equipped to handle; the former recognizes that "responsibility is the great developer of men" and forces the Congress, the administrative agencies, and the public to assume responsibility for administrative performance.

Finally, an adequate philosophy will recognize that the noble ideal of the "supremacy of law" may be attained in various ways.

[60] See Chapter II for analysis of types of economic control.

Two of these deserve special mention. One is the influence of the lawyer within the administrative agency. Through him the agency constantly shares the "received ideals of the law." Through him it is kept close to its statutory directives and is constantly reminded that action must not be discriminatory or arbitrary. The author has seen an outstanding example of this in a wartime agency. Thousands of men were recruited from business or other pursuits where they had been unaccustomed to operating with continuous attention to legality and the need for nondiscriminatory action, but the decisions of these were confined by the ever-present necessity for lawyer clearance or advice. Occasionally action was taken over lawyer objection, but very frequently contemplated action was changed as a result of the objection. The strength of the lawyer's influence was indisputable, and it was on the side of the concepts of the "law."

Admittedly, the lawyer's position in administration raises problems. We have noted the danger of delegating too much to an independent legal staff.[61] One commentator has noted the possibility of "a miniature judicial review within the agency whereby the legal staff exercises a veto power over proposed actions and procedures."[62] These dangers can ordinarily be best avoided by organizational arrangements which recognize the supremacy of the policy-operating executive but which make the legal assistant a constant and intimate staff aid of the executive. In this setting the legal specialist would have an opportunity "for the infusion of a sense of law into

[61] See pages 302-303.

[62] Vincent M. Barnett, Jr., "Modern Constitutional Development: A Challenge to Administration," *Public Administration Review*, IV, 159-164, 161 (1944). Barnett saw "serious dangers" in the kind of situation which existed in O.P.A. where initially "the legal department became an almost complete duplicate of the price department, with staffs of lawyers attached to most sections, branches, and divisions" and where these lawyers, responsible not to the operating chiefs at the various levels but to the General Counsel, had a virtual veto over policy. He admits that the lawyers "were generally on the right side so far as basic policy in the public interest was concerned." Nevertheless, he argues, and this could hardly be denied, that there was "organizational absurdity" which confused the lines of responsibility and caused delays. It may be added that the organizational arrangements were changed in 1943 but that the deep antagonisms between operating executives and attorneys produced by the faulty organization of the early period were never fully overcome.

the entire organization" without producing the conflicts which result from overcompartmentalization of functional specialties.[63]

The other factor is the diversity in methods of reviewing administrative action. We have previously referred to internal appeals boards.[64] These have in some fields practically supplanted court adjudications.[65] There are also many internal devices for administrative review of action of subordinates which serve to check aberrant action. Thus, for example, in O.P.A. the decisions of field offices on price adjustments were audited at higher levels—sometimes a preaudit and sometimes a postaudit. In addition to administrative review and internal appeals, there is the possibility of specialized courts of review, such as the Tax Court and the Court of Customs and Patents Appeals, and the Emergency Court of Appeals during World War II.

Our several comments concerning philosophy and method and the inevitable limitations on judicial review may be followed by a few concluding remarks. Judicial review is too occasional and cursory, and is exercised from too remote a point, to supply an adequate corrective for arbitrary administration of economic controls. Moreover, unless applied only at the periphery it runs counter to the basic idea of delegation of responsibility to administrative agents. In the opinion of the author, we were led down the wrong road initially by two judicial assumptions. One is the idea that courts should determine whether administrative decisions on complicated economic issues are based on substantial evidence, and the other

[63] The quoted words are from the excellent and comprehensive discussion by Fritz Morstein Marx, "The Lawyer's Role in Public Administration," *Yale Law Journal*, LV, 498-526, 510 (1946). Note the following statement by Marx at the same place: "Precisely because the innate drives of public administration exert themselves in the direction of ultimate results in a very generalized sense, a counterinfluence toward justice in the individual case would be most welcome."

[64] See pages 300-302. Col. O. R. McGuire concluded that the statistics he had gathered "demonstrate that the number of cases arising in the administrative departments would swamp any court system unless the number be greatly reduced by some method of interdepartmental review." "Judicial Reviews of Administrative Decisions," *Georgetown Law Journal*, XXVI, 580 (1938).

[65] Dimock, "Control over Administrative Action," in Charles G. Haines and Marshall E. Dimock, *Essays on the Law and Practice of Governmental Administration* (1935), 303, 321.

is the notion that judges should determine the content of general statutory provisions if these are developed through case-to-case administration.[66] The first was the legacy of the vaunted but doubtful liberality of the courts toward the Interstate Commerce Commission; the second was exhibited in Federal Trade Commission experience. A more satisfactory statement of the proper area for the courts, at least in economic control, was, in the opinion of the author, given years ago by McFarland:[67]

Rule of law must be formulated for no other purpose than to express the judicial estimation of the limits of delegated authority—a process of outlining the scope of the statutes under which administrative agencies operate; the courts ought not to intervene to lay down what the judiciary believes the proper rule for the particular case or for all similar cases, for to do so is to usurp the task of administrators who act under broadly delegated authority. Similarly, judicial review of the administrative ascertainment of facts should involve no more than an inquiry into the sufficiency of the evidence to bring the matter within the range of administrative competence (that is, there must be sufficient evidence to identify the particular subject matter with the statutory authority of the administrative tribunal).

This would confine the courts, except for questions of procedure, to the issue of jurisdiction of the agency to act.

The statutes, lately the Administrative Procedure Act, have not usually gone this far. Nevertheless, the method of judicial review is futile, in large measure, in economic regulation. Fuller safeguards against acts which are arbitrary or which extend too far under the delegations must be provided by something closer to the centers of operation. This "closeness" might be achieved by continuous absorption in an aspect of the same task, as in special agencies of

[66] There is a contrast between the scope of judicial review over rules issued to carry out general statutory provisions and over adjudicatory decisions which elaborate statutes as in the case of the Federal Trade Commission. Landis says, however, that "the problem seems essentially to have the same core" in that both "require appreciation and evaluation of a wide variety of business facts." See pages 149-151 of James M. Landis, *The Administrative Process.* Copyright 1938 by Yale University Press.

[67] From page 29 of Carl McFarland, *Judicial Control of the Federal Trade Commission and the Interstate Commerce Commission: 1920-1930.* Copyright 1933 by the President and Fellows of Harvard College.

review.[68] Really adequate safeguards must come, however, by such techniques of procedure and use of technical personnel as will infuse a proper respect for the best ideals of the law at the point where policy is made or the initial decision on application of policy is reached. This is a matter of internal safeguards.

CONGRESSIONAL CONTROL

It is not surprising that near the end of World War II, Leonard D. White, after a quarter-century of writing on public administration, should have chosen for the topic of his presidential address to the American Political Science Association: "Congressional Control of the Public Service." [69] Depression and wartime government had magnified administration into a leviathan beyond contemplation in any earlier period. In the Yakus decision, upholding wartime price controls, the Supreme Court had accepted what it had seemed to deny in the Schechter case.[70] Men had argued that the governance of society was passing to managerial classes.[71] Two eminent political scientists had argued over the extent to which the responsibility of the public official should rest on a "sense of responsibility" or on external controls from the representatives of the people.[72] Studies were being made of the ways in which Congress might be equipped for more adequate discharge of its functions.[73] Universally, men were interested in the issue: could representative organs control the government?

Professor White asserted "that congressional control of the administration is not only democratically essential but also technically

[68] This would be particularly true if the special agencies were composed, in part, of persons who had administrative experience, as has been the practice in the filling of positions in administrative courts in some European countries.

[69] *American Political Science Review*, XXXIX, 1-11 (Feb., 1945).

[70] See pages 53-54, 57, 61.

[71] See James Burnham, *The Managerial Revolution* (New York, 1941).

[72] *Supra*, 233-234, footnote 36.

[73] *The Reorganization of Congress; A Report of the Committee on Congress of the American Political Science Association* (Washington, D.C., 1945); Joint Committee on the Organization of Congress, *Organization of the Congress*, 79th Cong., 2nd Sess., Sen. Rep. No. 1011 (1946); Robert Heller, *Strengthening the Congress* (Washington, D.C., 1945).

feasible." [74] The democratic necessity of a large measure of congressional control is generally recognized; this discussion moves, therefore, to some significant aspects of present controls and to the ways in which it may be feasible to provide greater control over the *policy* aspects of government.[75]

The Constitution gave Congress four levers for control of administration. These were the legislative power, the appropriations power, the Senate's power of confirmation of appointments, and the impeachment power.

Although the legislative and appropriations powers provide ample power for direction of action to be taken, the Constitution did not provide any effective means for retroactive or current check on administration. Obviously, the historic device of impeachment is not an effective means of legislative oversight of administration.

Inquiry into the conduct of administration has been developed in practice as a means of filling the gap left by the Constitution. The legislative power of inquiry is upheld by the courts as an incident to the power to legislate and to the other powers of the Congress;[76] in practice, however, the power of inquiry has become a power having independent significance as a means of administrative surveillance.

The surveillance is exercised in many ways. Appropriation committees probe into administrative policy and operating detail. Standing committees, ostensibly having only a power of passing upon legislative measures, try to learn how things are being done in administrative agencies. Special committees of investigation are established. A large administrative agency in Washington is at any given moment likely to be working to supply information on its operations to one or more committees; and it knows that this is related to its appropriations, the retention of its functions or its freedom to exercise them as it deems best, or to the continuance in office of some of its personnel.

[74] *Op. cit.*, 2.
[75] A recent and very complete discussion of Congress' relation to administration may be found in Charles Hyneman, *Bureaucracy in a Democracy* (New York, 1950), Chapters 5-10.
[76] See McGrain v. Daugherty, 273 U. S. 135 (1927).

The significance of the power of confirming appointments varies with the type of office. As for appointments of minor officers or those serving locally, our political history shows that upper house approval degenerates into patronage rights for members of legislative bodies or local political organizations. It does not provide an opportunity for the legislature as a whole to control administration; rather, it scatters control over administration to a multitude of points and makes it more difficult to get effective performance of the tasks committed by legislatures to administrative agencies. As for officers of general importance, it is difficult to measure how significant a control senatorial approval provides. Most appointments are approved and this without much contest over them. In the occasional instance in which there is a serious question, considerations irrelevant to the performance of the administrative function are apt to influence decision materially. The formal power of confirmation is limited because it is negative in effect, but sectional or group dissatisfaction with administration may lead to pressure from either or both houses for appointments more satisfactory to the dissentient groups. Moreover, it must be recognized that for major posts the necessity of finding appointees who can win favor in congressional appearances before appropriating and investigating committees has much the same effect as the requirement of confirmation where that exists.[77]

There are three aspects of congressional control which deserve special attention. The first is the informal control or influences. Because they realize the power that can be wielded by Congress, administrative agencies are sensitive to opinions existing within the body and will seek to establish and preserve good relations with committees and individual legislators who are in a position to affect them. Much time and effort may be spent in cultivating friendly relations with important committee members or other members taking a strong interest in the work of an agency. Even the administrative heads of field offices may cultivate Congressmen from their areas. On the other side, committee members gain a continuing

[77] For further discussion of senatorial confirmation see Hyneman, *op. cit.*, Chapter 10, on "Choosing Men for Jobs."

interest in the matters with which they deal year after year. Other legislators also come to have a strong interest in administrative action in particular subject-matter fields. These two factors, the vulnerability of administration and the interests of legislators, lead to a multitude of informal and even personal relationships between administrators and legislators.

Informal means of control and influence develop. The criticism of a committee or its suggestion of a future course of policy, or even the lines of questioning or investigation in committees, may have great weight with an administrative agency. The suggestions of friendly legislators or the pressure of the friendly or unfriendly may be accorded an attentive ear. Appointments of personnel may be cleared, with or without the aid of party committees or chiefs, with members of the two houses.

A second notable feature of congressional control is the extent to which it has extended to details of organization and operation, and even sometimes to details of policy. As to organization, Congress usually prescribes the unit of organization (department, bureau, or commission), indicates its place in the governmental structure, and fixes the method of appointment and removal of the heads of the unit; it may go further and regulate the internal organization, as for example, in the prescription of rules to regulate delegation within the Interstate Commerce Commission.[78] It has often denied executive and administrative heads the authority to fashion organization as they deemed desirable, though in recent years the President has been given extensive power on several occasions to shuffle units of organization. Congress has also regulated administrative methods, particularly the procedure for legislative and judicial tasks. Almost every regulatory statute has contained provisions concerning hearings, appeals within administration, and similar matters of procedure; and the Administrative Procedure Act contains, as has been shown, a considerable amount of prescription. A great mass of legislation concerning housekeeping activities has developed, and appropriations may be loaded with restrictions.

[78] See John A. Fairlie, "The Legislature and the Administration, I," *American Political Science Review*, XXX, 241-256 (April, 1936).

As for policy, the trend has been, of necessity, toward general grants of authority. Sometimes, however, Congress particularizes its directives as a result of pressures from economic groups. Examples are the interchangeable mileage scrip amendment to the Interstate Commerce Act in 1922 and the Hoch-Smith Resolution in 1925,[79] the provisions of the White Act of 1927 concerning sectional allotment of broadcasting licenses,[80] the amendments to the Emergency Price Control Act and the later rent control extension acts,[81] and the changes made in 1951 in the extension of the Defense Production Act of 1950.

The third and most significant feature of congressional control is the "atomization of control." [82] The action of Congress is dissipated among its many parts. Individual members, having particular interests and beset with the importunities of constituents, become channels of influence and coercion on administrative agencies. Pressure groups work through pieces of Congress to weaken administrative programs or to influence the directions of their development. The committee system has dispersed "congressional authority among many working centers" and has put great power in the hands of a few individuals.[83] A dissentient group may shop from one counter to another in Congress in search for a channel through which it can market its desire for influence upon administration.

The informal contacts and the lack of a tradition against action in detail accentuate the atomization of control. The result is that from a multitude of directions the pieces of Congress pick at the administration at many little points.

Toward this result there are many contributing factors. One is the physical and psychological distance between the people and Washington, which leads the former—particularly the small and unor-

---

[79] For a discussion of these see I. L. Sharfman, *The Interstate Commerce Commission*, Vol. II (New York, 1931), 466-472. On the Hoch-Smith Resolution, see above at pages 71-72.

[80] See E. Pendleton Herring, *Public Administration and the Public Interest* (New York and London, 1936), Chapter X.

[81] *Supra*, 68.

[82] V. O. Key, "Legislative Control," in F. Morstein Marx, ed., *Elements of Public Administration* (New York, 1946), 342.

[83] *Ibid.*, 345, 342.

ganized—to turn to their Congressmen as the only channel of information and agency contact which they know how to use. Another is the lack of unity in the American political system. The separation of powers and the lack of integration of the party system create opportunities for the organized groups to use pieces of our political machinery to their advantage. Still another factor is the gap between the administrative and the legislative arms. On the one side, administration shields itself by revealing only what it wants to reveal; on the other side, the committees grope for avenues of information and find, nevertheless, that they have only bits of data but no over-all picture. This is paralleled by a gap in thought. The administrator thinks in terms of over-all results and of the necessity of avoiding discriminatory action; the Congressman is continuously forced by the action of his constituents to think of individual cases, and his political experience makes him think in terms of "human" factors rather than "the needs of the service."

Key has emphasized other factors in the atomization of congressional controls. Noting the particularistic influences within the departments which make it difficult to integrate the action of the bureaus, and the connections which exist between bureau chiefs and members of Congress, he concludes that "The strong centrifugal tendencies in an administrative structure organized to a large extent on a clientele basis are reenforced by the dispersion of congressional authority among many working centers."[84]

It would be wide of the point to condemn all these tendencies in congressional action. Weaknesses in political systems sometimes carry a measure of counterbalancing benefit. If the administrator finds that the pressures of Congressmen are annoying and threaten effective and equal administration under directives, it is also true that the congressional complaint is one of the channels through which the people can make their dissatisfactions known. A sophisticated view of administration will accept it as inevitable and one of the means by which weaknesses in administration may be brought to light. It may be an ever-present reminder to the bureaucrat of the effects of program on people. Moreover, the very dis-

[84] *Ibid.*, 345.

tribution of these complaints among Congressmen safeguards the administration to a considerable extent against the necessity for yielding to the complaint which is without basis.[85]

Moreover, the decentralization of congressional work has real advantages. The committees are centers through which continuity of view may be attained. In spite of the ill effects of the seniority system, the senior members of the committees, along with the bureau chiefs, may sometimes be, as Key says, "the cream of the career crop in the federal government."[86] Buttressed by a staff of expert aides, they may provide on the side of congressional oversight the equivalent of the expert view in administration.

Though full condemnation of the present may be avoided, it is yet true that an adequate system of congressional control cannot be developed until a strong supplement to present tendencies is found. Congress' attention needs to be lifted from the particular to the general. White, in speaking of the inadequacy of private complaint as a means of informing Congress of official incompetence, put emphasis on the basic need: "The problem at this point is to devise institutional means of bringing to the attention of Congress the really important issues of administration, and to aid Congress in finding genuinely effective solutions."[87] This attention of Con-

[85] In Commission on Organization of the Executive Branch of the Government, *Task Force Report on Regulatory Commissions,* 38, it is suggested: "If the members adopted the practice of referring all such complaints and inquiries regarding a commission to the appropriate standing committee charged with its oversight, the committee could use them for investigation. The volume and character of such material would be a rough index of the performance and weaknesses of the commission. At the same time, this method would shield both the Congressman and the commission from the suspicion of influence in direct approaches for constituents." George B. Galloway, *Congress at the Crossroads,* 234: "Criticism of particular agencies or regulations should be referred to the appropriate supervisory committees." (Copyright 1946 by Thomas Y. Crowell Co.) Reference to a committee for information sounds like a good step, but would Congressmen go to the trouble of referring something for information of the committee only? If, as the Task Force Report seems to suggest, committee attention would take the place of action by individual members, then the dangers to administration would be great. Congressmen would desire that committees become their "special pleaders." Pity the poor administrator if the concentrated power of committee pleading should take the place of the dispersed petitions of the Congressmen!

[86] Key, *op. cit.,* 346.

[87] *Op. cit.,* 9.

gress needs to be focussed, not merely on important operating problems of administration, but also on the major problems of *policy and program development*. Congress' primary responsibility is not administrative operations but policy development and policy supervision.

Some ways of achieving this objective are indicated by past experience. First, experience points to the conclusion that Congress can make its most effective contribution to sound administrative development by establishing appropriate organs of central control and planning. The outstanding example is the Bureau of the Budget. Other examples are the Civil Service Commission and the General Accounting Office. Recently, the creation of the Council of Economic Advisors gave expression to Congress' desire for a similar organ in the field of economic policy. Likewise, the establishment of the Executive Office of the President [88] a number of years ago under the Reorganization Act of 1939 facilitated the over-all view of government which Congress and the President are seeking.

Second, the American constitutional system offers no possible center for unified direction of organs of central control and planning except in the presidency.[89] It would be futile to hope that these organs would be self-operating. And yet Congress could not give continuing direction to such agencies. Any attempt to provide for an overview of administration by organs of control reporting to Congress would inevitably lead to conflict with the presidency and to the disappearance of the desired unity before the disunity of Congress.[90]

Congress and the President must have a common purpose for the long run. Both are interested in good budget analysis, good personnel practice, and better administrative management and operating techniques. The interest of both has been in providing central mechanisms to work toward these objectives. Similarly, in

[88] By Executive Order issued September 10, 1939.

[89] Exception may be made of organs, such as a post-audit authority, which check on past action and do not carry responsibilities for future policy and administration.

[90] Compare E. Pendleton Herring, "Executive-Legislative Responsibilities," *American Political Science Review*, XXXVIII, 1153-1166 (1944).

policy development both must be interested in the unified handling of problems common to more than one unit of administration, in planning rather than drift, and in *drawing from the administrative process those basic issues of policy which should have the attention of political officials.*

Assuming that the executive is equipped for oversight and planning, several means of focussing the attention of Congress on the main issues of policy are at hand. One is the report of the President to the Congress, such as the report which accompanies the budget and the report which is required by the Employment Act. Another is consultation of the executive, department heads, and staff aids with the committees and leaders of Congress. A particularly significant example is the close relationship which has existed recently between the executive and the congressional committees on foreign policy, the defense establishment, and atomic energy. Still another is the study of the congressional committees on the report or proposal of the President.

Admittedly, these arrangements for Congressional contact and focussing of attention are inadequate. But other means are dependent upon reform in the Congress itself and upon bold change in the relationships between the executive and legislative branches. Perhaps it is time to consider anew whether cabinet members should have seats without vote in Congress, a preferred status on calendars of the houses be given to proposals emanating from the executive, and time be set aside for questioning executive heads on administrative policies and operations. The various other suggestions for raising the attention of Congress to the large developments and issues in the executive branch also need attention.

The biggest problem of American government is neither administrative nor political, but is both. It concerns the relationships of the Congress and the executive branch. Nevertheless, the basic essential on the administrative side is clear. Executive oversight and planning and arrangements for gearing the work of Congress to that of the President provide the only feasible approach for democratic control of administration.

This may not seem like a satisfactory answer to two groups. The first would accept the need for executive planning and direction but would argue that this must be accompanied by the system of executive responsibility involved in the cabinet system. The second would argue that Congress should by its own efforts coordinate the functions of government.[91] But neither of these answers is feasible, the first because it is too radical a departure from American traditions, the second because it assumes more than Congress can fulfill. In contrast, the answer suggested here is the line on which tendency is set in this country. It is the emerging pattern, though delayed and hampered by the notions of independence which grew with the regulatory commission.[92]

Some have proposed that the provisional order system, long a practice in Britain, should be adopted in this country. Under this system, administrative rules or general orders would be reported to Congress, which would have an opportunity within a specified number of days to veto them. Legislation has, in fact, provided for this system in a limited number of instances, as under four administrative reorganization acts, two of which made the reorganization plans of the President subject to veto by resolution of either house[93] and two providing that such plans could be vetoed by concurrent resolution of the houses.[94]

[91] Galloway gives the following definition: "According to the theory of congressional oversight, on the other hand, the proper function of Congress is to supervise the government; the lines of control and accountability should run horizontally from the administrative agencies directly to Congress; and the agencies of control should be attached to the legislative branch or should exercise independent judgment in dealing with administrative offices." George B. Galloway, *Congress at the Crossroads*, 232. Copyright 1946 by Thomas Y. Crowell Co.

[92] We have not argued the question as to whether executive-legislative relationships should be fundamentally altered by organizing a joint executive-congressional cabinet. The fundamental needs sketched here would remain the same, whether or not this step is ever taken. Keeping within the present framework we have argued for presidential direction. The president would in turn be assisted by his political associates, and serve therefore as the center of an executive directorship. For discussion of the proposal for a joint executive-legislative council see Hyneman, *op. cit.*, Chapter 25, and his references to Professor Corwin's works in which the proposal was apparently first advanced.

[93] Acts of 1932 and 1949, 47 *Stat. at Large*, 414, 63 *Stat. at Large*, 205.

[94] Acts of 1939 and 1945, 53 *Stat. at Large*, 56, 59 *Stat. at Large*, 613. For a discussion of disapproval by concurrent resolution and a view that this kind of process might provide a "nicer balance" between Congress and the executive see

A variation of the provisional order technique is contained in the Atomic Energy Act of 1946 in a provision designed to prevent administrative action which would have significant long-run effects until Congress could have an opportunity to consider the matter. The Act provides that when the Atomic Energy Commission is of the opinion that "any industrial, commercial, or other non-military use of fissionable material or atomic energy has been sufficiently developed to be of practical value" it shall make a report to the President, who shall transmit this report and his recommendations to Congress, and "No license for any manufacture, production, export, or use shall be issued by the Commission under this section until after" the report has been before Congress, while in session, for ninety days.[95]

The limits and dangers of the provisional order technique have sometimes been overlooked in proposals for its use. Obviously, the great mass of rules issued by administration with effect upon the life of the citizen cannot be thrown into Congress. Congress would be drowned under such a flood. Moreover, nothing could be more dangerous than a general practice of referring particulars to congressional consideration. The provisional order technique would be helpful only if held to issues of general policy as basic, or almost as basic, as those contained in the initial delegation of responsibility. The most promising area for its use would seem to be on presidential directives of broad scope. Once again, it appears that executive direction is the condition for effective congressional control.

The issue of congressional control is basically no different from that of hierarchical relations generally. The purpose of organization is to push particulars downward. There is, moreover, no magic clue for differentiation between the general and particular, between what is basic and what is extension of the basic. There are only

---

John D. Millett and Lindsay Rogers, "The Legislative Veto and the Reorganization Act of 1939," *Public Administration Review*, I, 176-189 (Winter, 1941). For discussion of substitution of executive decision subject to congressional veto by concurrent resolution for legislative decision by private bill see Harvey C. Mansfield, "The Legislative Veto and the Deportation of Aliens," *Public Administration Review*, I, 281-286 (Spring, 1941).

[95] Sec. 7(b), 60 *Stat. at Large*, 764.

degrees of generality and significance. In the administration of government's economic programs, some things are basic enough to require the attention of the President, his staff, and immediate subordinates. A more limited group of issues need the attention of the Congress. What needs to be grasped, however, is that the power of Congress cannot be exercised successfully unless there is a sifting process. The executive power of direction, recommended heretofore, and executive planning and report, are, in a sense, sifting techniques; and these are, therefore, preliminaries to any intelligent effort to provide for congressional consent or veto.

What has been said does not prevent an independent check of Congress upon the administration through its own power of inquiry. This power can be used with respect to control of administration under existing law or as a basis for new legislation. With respect to the former, Dimock, who has given much study to this problem, has concluded: "As an effective method of orderly control over administrative conduct, the legislative investigation cannot begin to qualify. Investigations are sporadic and incomplete, and only too frequently are they motivated by callous partisanship and legislative jealousy." He believes that government would lose if they dropped out of the picture completely at this stage, but as advances are made in other controls "the legislative investigation should gradually fade out of the picture." [96] The substantial value of the check has been attested by others.[97] It probably has its greatest value where it is brought to bear on the emerging issues of policy, whether in contemplation of new legislation or with the immediate purpose of being informed on the steps being taken in the administration for resolution of the issues.[98] In our brief analysis

[96] Marshall E. Dimock, "Forms of Control over Administrative Action," in Charles G. Haines and Marshall E. Dimock, *Essays on the Law and Practice of Governmental Administration* (1935), 295.

[97] E.g., Leonard D. White, *Introduction to the Study of Public Administration* (3rd ed., 1948), 596. One may recall the work of the Truman Committee during the war.

[98] A good case study would be the parallel search for constructive solution of the serious meat situation in the spring of 1945 in the House Committee of Agriculture, of which Clinton Anderson was chairman, and in the executive-administrative hierarchy, which included the Director of Economic Stabilization, the War Food Administration, and the Office of Price Administration.

we can only say that *both as a means of checking upon perform-ance and considering the emerging issues of policy and method,* the independent power of inquiry of Congress does provide an additional line of check and action in the areas which Congress has delegated to administration.

Noteworthy, finally, are the various methods being made to im-prove the internal operations of Congress. The limitation of number of committees in the Legislative Reorganization Act of 1946 should, in spite of the necessity of delegations to subcommittees, operate as a counterinfluence to the atomistic tendencies. The growing use of joint committees (as on atomic energy, labor-management rela-tions, and the economic report) should provide more unity in con-gressional consideration of matters which have been referred to the administration. The provision for expert aid to committees should help equip the Congress to deal with the experts in adminis-tration on a more equal basis, and should reduce the feeling of frustration among Congressmen who seem unable to pierce the veil between them and the administrative agencies. The ever-present contest for leadership within the Congress and for effective liaison with the chief executive also aim toward making Congress a more effective instrument for larger participation in government.

Professor White's selection of presidential topic was timely. The "controls on behalf of the people" need strengthening. The piece-meal controls, with all their dangers, are nevertheless one of the means by which insulation from the public is checked. This, how-ever, does not suffice; congressional attention needs better direction toward the main issues of administration and policy. A pattern for movement toward this objective is in the making. But neither the emerging pattern nor the gaps in the weaving are sufficiently under-stood. Perhaps it would be advantageous to have a commission study, not the executive branch or the legislative branch, but the ways in which both may contribute effectively in the areas where the policy of government is being elaborated in the process of administration.

EXECUTIVE DIRECTION

Much that has been said in this volume points toward the need of an executive directorship at the crest of administration, the center of which would be the President, but who would be assisted by staff aides, department heads, and perhaps other officials having directive and coordinative functions. We noted in Chapter IV that administration makes much of the *high policy* of government, and that Congress seems unable to go beyond general directives. We noted in a chapter on organization that the pressure of foreign affairs on the economy, the ramifications of expenditure and fiscal policies, and the demand for maximum production, employment, and purchasing power, added to the older problems of coordination, produced continuing problems of interrelationship in the economic policy of government. And we have noted the need of a check in government on the tendency of the specialists in particular areas of control to move within the confines of their developed systems, particularly when these have come to be identified with the interests of particular groups immediately affected by the action of the specialized units.

Traditionally, an answer has been sought to the problems of economic regulation in ways which seem to the author to be antidemocratic. Powers have been vested in commissions which it was assumed should be independent. Then when their broad policy decisions brought political complaint, commentators have—quite unrealistically—thought there was something evil in the interest of the politician. Unconsciously, men have sought in the commission or board a substitute for a balanced relationship between the political and permanent official. Also, an effort has sometimes been made to immunize the formulation of policy from politics by judicializing the procedure of the delegatee.

We have suggested in this and a preceding chapter that the requirements of unity and democratic control make it necessary to *segregate* some part of this vast delegation of policy-making powers and place it in the President. We have even suggested that

this is the condition precedent to effective congressional control.
Alarmists would fear that this places too much power in the chief
executive, and that "executive absolutism" would be the result.[99] To
this there are several answers. First, is the complexity of regulation
in a democratic society. In a society which is splintered in a thou-
sand ways, in which there is a maze of crosscurrents of opinion
and pressure, where free-acting associations are continuously at
work, the forum of Congress is open, the party system is decentralized, and the strongest beam of publicity ever known is focused
on the presidency, the fear of "executive absolutism" sounds incon-
gruous, to say the least. Second, there are checks and balances
within organization. There are strong disintegrative tendencies in
a large and diversified bureaucracy, connected at numerous points
to powerful organized interests. There is resistance at working centers to the novel and disrupting suggestion from above.[100] Finally,
the democratic objective calls for a continuing channel through
which policy can be considered in terms of the dominant opinions
of the nation.

Many would fear, not the power, but the irresponsibility of the
presidency—the fact that the president is not subject to the control of a majority in the Congress. The choice, however, is between
the measure of responsibility which can be placed on the President
and that which can be placed on independent agencies of administration, and in the area of top policy the principles of democracy
call for the former choice.

Assuming that there will be no radical reorganization of the
presidential-congressional system, along the lines of the parliamentary or cabinet system, or otherwise, the recognition of the
need for an executive directorship is the basic requirement for
definition of the areas of responsibility for fulfillment of the pur-

---

[99] Note the following: "Control of an omnicompetent administrative hierarchy,
accountable only to an ultimate administrative head, will prove as effective a
means of absolute government as was formerly control of an army." Roscoe
Pound, *Administrative Law* (Pittsburgh, 1942), 35-36.

[100] "We need to counteract centrifugal rather than centralizing trends. The
forces supporting coordination are hardly equal to meeting the pressures of
bureaucrats and politicians to go their various ways." Herring, "Executive-
Legislative Responsibilities," *op. cit.,* 1163.

poses which have been assumed by government. At three points clarification might follow. First, the responsibility of the executive directorship would extend, within the confines of Congressional directives and the President's powers in foreign and military affairs and of legislative proposal, *to all questions which were issues of policy of general significance.* Perhaps we could recognize that *anything is the business of politics which can be encompassed in a general directive* and leave it to the judgment of the executive officials and the criticism of professional observers, the Congress and the public to safeguard against too extensive an interpretation of what is "general." The use of the open written directive, as suggested in the preceding chapter, would provide the focus for criticism. Second, the concept of an executive directorship sets the framework for definition of the functions of the permanent and the political official, the expert and the politician, and for a working compromise between continuity and the requirements for change in a society in flux. Third, Congress' responsibility could be better understood if the emerging issues of administration under existing laws or under prospective laws were drawn upward and placed in the spotlight by the action or thought of the executive directorship.

Historically, the President and the cabinet were supposed to be just the kind of directorship which is suggested here. This has not worked, chiefly because of two things. First, Congress has delegated policy functions to independent agencies or has provided for independent exercise of such functions by bureaus or other units within departments. Recent reorganization orders have vested all the powers of several departments in the department head, who can redelegate to his subordinates. A parallel need is to bring the policy functions of commissions under executive direction, either from the President directly or through his department heads. Second, the complexity of government has outrun the simple concept of executive direction through a council of men acting alone. Staff aides of various kinds are needed, and also a proper adjustment of functions between the President, department heads, and special coordinators—if these exist. Executive direction today must be complex, and involve smooth working relationships between a number of constituent elements of the executive directorship which the President heads. The cabinet meeting might be one element, but only one, in the actual operation of the executive directorship.

For a safeguard against the dangers of "administrative absolutism," so far as these relate to policy formation, the answer is the executive directorship and a coactive Congress. The dangers lie not in the overgrowth of the executive directorship, but in the natural limits upon the comprehension and span of action of a central planning and directing mechanism in a structure as large and diversified as the national administration, and in the failure to provide for a proper reorganization of the work of Congress so as to focus its attention on the proposals and decisions of the executive directorship.

SAFEGUARDS WITHIN THE ADMINISTRATIVE SYSTEM

Our discussion has shown three lines of external safeguard and has indicated the limits of each. Judicial review can restrict administration to its jurisdiction, enforce conformance with procedural safeguards which exist for certain types of action, and maintain constitutional guarantees. Beyond this, its reach is limited by circumstance and the boundaries of its own area of expertness. Congress, it is hoped, may be equipped to exert controls over the larger issues of policy and administration. Beyond this, time limits alone should warn against the assumption of more extended functions. The third line of safeguard would lie in the further development of the executive directorship. Its function, too, would be limited to those issues which can rise above the working units of administration.

The task of moving forward with government will still rest largely with the administrative agencies. They will still make policy and execute it straight through to the final application. Neither the Congress, the President, nor the courts can successfully withdraw from the administration its basic functions. In a wide area society's safeguards must exist in the system itself. Some of these safeguards may be listed by way of final summary, others require new discussion.

The primary institutional safeguard lies in the operation of the institutional process. The complementary contribution of men of different competences, the facilities for institutional research and analysis, and the unity and coherence that come from hierarchical control are the central safeguards in the administrative process. Here is the group decision which men have sought in commissions, perhaps because they have not understood the nature of the institutional process. Here are real checks against one-man absolutism. And against the incompetence of the single mind. Here is the answer in methodology for the society which has not been able to find in the developed "materials of the law," nor to embody wholly in statutes, the answers to the economic problems of its day.

The process has its dangers. The greatest of these is not arbitrariness, for the internal checks operate strongly against this. The greatest dangers are institutional sluggishness, failure to delegate, and failure to plan.

A second safeguard might be found in the use of the methods of planning. These are rule making, internal policy standards, and overhead directives. All have the same effect. They are means of search for the larger and the further view. They substitute conscious purpose for drift. Moreover, they safeguard against discrimination in the particulars of government by providing standards of reference against which each particular application of policy must be measured. They help solve the problem of delegation and overhead direction, the former by providing standards under which subordinates, including examiners, can operate, the latter by confining the chief executive and other coordinative and directive authorities to the area of general policy.

A third safeguard rests in the procedural techniques which are available for the different types of public decision and for dispatch of public business. Processes like those of the courts are available for use where these are appropriate. In addition, modern technical processes and research methods provide for the administration a diversity of skills which can be adapted to any type of situation. Also, operating techniques may ensure the dispatch in public affairs which is required both for private and public interest.

Closely connected are the safeguards which can exist in internal organization. Institutional organization offers an opportunity to segregate the tasks of government in units which can bring a proper professional spirit and technique to each type of task and yet be bound to the central purpose of the organization. To the lawyer, the examiner and the appeals board are the most significant examples; but to the professional student of administration, the executive officer, the skilled technician, the automatically operating clerical employee, and the staff officer are equally significant in the total pattern of institutional process.

Fifth, safeguards for a more responsible administration may be found in arrangements for local and lay participation. Advice from interest groups—a form of lay participation—provides information on what is technically feasible and on the probable results in economic trend and industry compliance. Local and lay participation may diminish the strain on the national organization, provide needed sectional adaptations, and insure continued appreciation of the human factors in regulation.

In the use of the various expedients of procedure, internal organization, and local and lay participation the *true safeguard for efficient and fair administration must come from sound and balanced judgments on multiple and often conflicting considerations.* The danger is overextension of meritorious approaches. Safeguard is found in no neat set of guides but only in the overview—from which each mechanism can be considered in relation to the whole problem of efficient, fair, and responsive administration.

A final set of safeguards center around the quality, professional specialization, and attitudes of government's personnel.

There are automatically operating restraints upon the official. Like men generally, the public official wants to do his job well and wants to maintain the kind of record of efficiency, fairness and integrity which will win the respect of the public for himself and the agency for which he works. Moreover, he soon learns that he works behind a glass wall and that if there are any curtains they are likely to be drawn open at any time. He becomes conscious of the scrutiny of associations, Congress, the press, his coworkers, superiors, and subordinates. He learns that national economic action affects so many people in so many diverse ways that he becomes accustomed to looking for all the angles, to consultation with many persons, to cautious decision. He leans on the lawyers and other technicians, he pushes to his superior the problem which may draw criticism to the agency. He finds an enveloping set of agency rules on internal jurisdictions and clearances which limit his sphere of action.

Normally, then, the public official will strive to be circumspect and upright. There is danger, of course, that his official decisions will be compromised by affiliation or entanglement with outside interests. To prevent these evils, and thus to supplement the automatic restraints upon the public official, we urged in Chapter IX that outside affiliations in interest should, so far as possible, be proscribed and that standards of ethics and good administrative practice should be developed for public officials.

The public official, moreover, is not an autocrat. On the contrary, the effect of the system under which he works may be toward timidity, fear, and resignation to things as they are. Such attitudes may have an effect upon the total agency attitude. As a result, inertia rather than aggression becomes the central problem of bureaucracy.

Except, then, for the negative steps needed to prevent affiliation and entanglement with outside interests, the safeguards in personnel should be positive and aim toward competence, vigor, and proper orientation.

The first need is to make public service sufficiently attractive to draw men of competence, vision, and energy. The jobs are certainly big enough to be challenging, and many find them so in spite of the restrictions under which the government official works. One essential for improvement of government's personnel is adequate compensation, particularly for the highest policy-determining officials. Big steps in this direction were taken in two acts in 1949, which provided for increases in salary for heads and assistant heads of departments and independent agencies, and created supergrades in the civil service, which now carry compensation up to $14,800.[101] Another essential is a change in public attitude toward the public official, so as to increase the prestige value of public employment.[102] This may sound like wishful thinking in a society where men of talent have tremendous opportunities for high remuneration and prestige in private pursuits. It must be evident, nevertheless, that society must respect and value its public servants if it is to enlist and retain the high quality personnel required for good administration.

Second, we have already noted the importance of strengthening the professional elements in the staffs of agencies of economic control.[103] All groups in public administration will have a sense of duty, but in the professional employee this inner compulsion is re-enforced by the standards of his profession and the desire that he be well-regarded among his professional associates. The lawyer, engineer, economist, expert in public administration, and other professionals not only bring a standard of professional competence but may help in the maintenance of the proper ideals of public service.[104]

Third, there is need for striking a proper balance between the permanent and the political official. One gives expertness, continuity, and stability; the other gives freshness, new drive, and political responsibility. In departments, tendency has moved toward permanence for the bureau chief and for certain types of managerial officials (budget, personnel, etc.) at higher levels. The main issue of the future will be the extent to which civil service employees can be used as experts in policy planning at departmental and presidential levels. It is our suggestion that the most progress could be

[101] Act of October 15, 1949, 63 *U. S. Stat. at Large*, 880 and "Classification Act of 1949," 63 *U. S. Stat. at Large*, 954, amended late in 1951.

[102] See Leonard D. White, *The Prestige Value of Public Employment in Chicago* (Chicago, 1929), and *Further Contributions to the Prestige Value of Public Employment* (Chicago, 1932), and chapter 31 in his *Introduction to the Study of Public Administration* (3rd ed., 1948).

[103] See pages 250-251.

[104] See John M. Gaus' comments in John M. Gaus, Leonard D. White, and Marshall E. Dimock, *The Frontiers of Public Administration* (Chicago, 1936), 39-42, and C. J. Friedrich's in Friedrich and Mason, *Public Policy* (Cambridge, 1940), 3-24.

made in resolving the conflicting needs in public regulation if by abandonment of the commission system we could transfer discussion of the rival claims of independence and political responsibility to the new plane of the relationship of the permanent and the political official in a hierarchical organization.

Finally, there is the basic problem of training for the public service. Two phases of this problem are of paramount importance. The first is the task of developing a flexible, transferable group of administrative experts for service at the top levels in administration and as staff aids to the political directorate. We are not referring to the expert in strictly administrative processes, such as personnel, budgeting, organization planning, and the handling of administrative routines. These constitute only another speciality. We are thinking rather of the experts in social engineering—the men *who are skilled in the process of finding, within the framework of institutional organization and process, solutions to public problems.*[105] We are not assuming that such a group of men can be trained in any one pattern or that all of them would necessarily be developed in a single class within the career service.[106] We are only saying that within the permanent government service the prime need is for men who by their background of education and experience are equipped to assume new responsibilities in social decision and management as these arise.

The war brought a need for an army of experts in social engineering. Men were needed who could do new jobs, such as allocating materials, controlling wages and prices, conserving transportation facilities, and promoting production toward a defined national objective. In the emergency the government could draw men of creative talents from colleges, business, and the public service. For

---

[105] L. D. White puts the problem somewhat differently: "General administration is understood to mean those duties concerned with the formation of policy, with the coordination and improvement of government machinery, and with the general management and control of the departments of the public service." *Introduction to the Study of Public Administration* (3rd ed., 1948), 344.

[106] On this problem see Leonard D. White, *Government Career Service* (Chicago, 1935); Lewis Meriam, *Public Service and Special Training* (Chicago, 1936); and L. D. White, *Introduction to the Study of Public Administration* (3rd ed., 1948), 344-348.

normal times, however, government needs its own corps of creative experts, and even for emergencies safety demands that government have a corps of experienced personnel ready to move quickly to new tasks.

In public administration, then, there is need for a new type of generalist. In regulatory work he needs, among other things, a background of knowledge of economics, political processes, social organization, institutional technique, and social ethics. Beyond that he would need the steerage of experience.

The second need is for training in the ethics of government service. On the author's last day in war-time government service, he asked a widely respected and successful government administrator for advice on training college students for administrative service. The administrator's reply was, "Teach them the meaning of public responsibility." This is no easy task, for our literature on government has been more on the plane of mechanics than of ethics. However, the educator in college and in the in-service training room could state some basic connotations of the term "public responsibility."

The task would be simplified if, as suggested at other points in our discussion, the basic rules of ethical conduct and good administrative practice were summarized.[107] Dean Pound has said of administration: "It has no well-defined ideals."[108] He contrasts the position of judges who "from their very training are impelled to conform their action to certain known standards and to conform to settled ideals of judicial conduct."[109] Public administration does have its ideals. Some of these could be summarized and set up as protective standards with appropriate sanctions. Others cannot be captured by rule or must rest on a deeper perception of the ideal of public responsibility than can be gained from written rule alone.

This perception of the public service ideal must, inevitably, include recognition of two ethical imperatives. The first is political responsibility, which means that "administration is a subordinate function and that in a democracy it must be responsive to the channels for proper expression of the dominant will of the community."

[107] See pages 255-256, 371-372.
[108] *Administrative Law*, 5.
[109] *Ibid.*, 60.

The other is the "public interest, which assumes that there are areas of generality of interest larger than various particular interests and that this generality of interest should be objectified in administration." To the administrator these two may sometimes appear to be in conflict, as when a political directive carries "some concept of purpose which contradicts or falls short of his view of the general interests of society." In such an event, the overriding supremacy of the political will, if expressed in a proper directive, must be recognized by the administrator. But his directives frequently leave him so wide a scope of discretion that his own perception of the public interest remains as the chief safeguard. It is in the understanding of the implications of the two ethical imperatives that the soundest safeguard for the proper operation of the administrative system is to be found.[110]

THE SAFEGUARDS IN SOCIETY

We are brought close in the above discussion to the safeguards existing within society itself. In the society in which we live, the safeguards are multiple.

First, there are the professional and ethical standards of society and its groups. The professional employees of the public service are members of professional communities and share the standards of competence and objectivity, and the service ideals, of their groups. All employees in the public service share the ideals which are the common heritage of their society. Such ideals as equal treatment under the law, "public office is a public trust," the dignity of man, the service obligations of the public official, the impropriety of private reward for official acts, are commonly accepted by the public employee as well as the private citizen.

In part these are merely standards of personal ethics. The Senate Subcommittee on "Ethical Standards in Government" concluded that the basic integrity of the public service was relatively high and noted that witnesses with long experience in public life believed that the standards of official conduct (though subject to dips) had

[110] The quotations in the paragraph in the text are from my article, "The Value of the Hoover Commission Reports to the Educator," *American Political Science Review,* XLIV, 283-298, at p. 297 (June, 1950).

been rising. Nevertheless, recent revelations of violations of standards of personal ethics show the urgent need for definition and strict enforcement of society's standards. The Senate Subcommittee has outlined the basic needs; and though all of its recommendations will probably not be adopted, one may expect that progress toward definition of standards will result from the present discussion. On the plane of personal ethics, society should be able to find adequate safeguards.

A second safeguard lies in the independence and capacity of the press, radio, and other channels of communication. Information about government cannot be hidden these days. The press conference has become common. The press release, though often suspect as incomplete or one-sided, is nevertheless a safeguard—it is not so much an indication that government wants to influence people as it is that people expect government to give them news about its activities. The press is represented in Washington by able and vigilant men whose business is to ferret out the news. It is likewise in this country free from control by the agencies on which it focuses its searchlight.

The responsibility of the press (radio, etc.) as a safeguard for good administration is tremendous.[111] Safeguard does not come from adverse criticism alone—nor from commendation either; it must come from full and accurate reporting and balanced interpretation. The danger is that the predisposition of the press for or against the Administration in power and the political trends of the day will lead to distortion in reporting and interpretation of particular administrative policies and actions. The danger may be great either when the press is antagonistic or when it is sympathetic to the general trends in politics. Hope for avoidance of the danger rests in part in the professional competence and integrity of the journalistic profession and in part in checks and balances within the media of communication similar to those in government, which in the case of the former can result only from dispersion of ownership and control.

A third safeguard in society lies in the action of groups. These

[111] Compare page 64 of *Ethical Standards in Government,* Report of a Subcommittee of the Committee on Labor and Public Welfare, U. S. Senate, 82nd Cong., 1st Sess., 1951.

will ordinarily be vigilant in bringing their interests to the attention of administrative agencies and in protecting their claims of right against arbitrary governmental acts. They will avail themselves of the checks within government—in courts, Congress, and administration—and of the power resources at their command.

A final safeguard lies in the attitudes of our people. They abhor and resist unnecessary encroachments upon freedom, aggressiveness in administration, and any appearances of arbitrary action.[112] The spirit of administration will inevitably be attuned to these and other basic attitudes of the people.

CONCLUSION

It appears that the negative safeguards against arbitrary, aggressive, or ill-considered action are numerous and adequate. The checks and balances operating upon administrative agencies are far more varied and pervasive than the founding fathers were able to contemplate for any branch of the government. Negative checks to ensure compliance with society's ethical standards should be adopted. Beyond this issue of the moment, the citizen's concern should be over positive safeguards for effective administration. His concern should not arise from any absence of checks from outside parties upon government but from the danger that no inclusive view of the public interest will be achieved; not from any absence of congressional efforts to control administration but from a Balkanization of administration and Congress which prevents timely attention to the vital over-all problems of government; not from any absence of internal checks within administration but from the timidity and lethargy which may accompany institutional activity. For positive safeguards against these dangers the citizen must depend upon the strengthening of executive controls, the strengthening of congressional oversight, the improvement of institutional operations, and the recruitment and proper training of public personnel.

The next chapter summarizes attitudes and circumstances in our society which condition the success of administrative controls and hence will further emphasize the need for positive safeguards for effective government.

[112] The effect of such attitudes is discussed in the next chapter.

Chapter XII

The Effectiveness of

Administrative Control

This book began with the statement of certain facts, namely, that government controls are exerted through administrative machinery and that there has been an expansion over recent years in the number and in the intimacy, normality, and frequency of public administrative controls over economic life. It was noted also that the public's expectancy concerning the functions of these controls has been broadened. It will be appropriate in concluding to extend discussion to some of the factors which may affect the degree of fulfillment of public purposes through administrative control of the economy.

Such a discussion at this stage in a book can at best be cursory, piecemeal, and suggestive only. Moreover, it extends beyond the primary purpose of this book, which was merely to examine the mechanism of control and to consider ways in which it might be made as effective as possible. Whether it would then be strong enough to move mountains or merely to shift a little soil from place to place was no part of our inquiry. Ultimate effectiveness is, after all, a matter of degree and measurement of results under particular objectives. Nevertheless, a general statement of some of the factors which challenge the effectiveness of administrative control of the economy will provide a background for a final conclusion on the need for strength in governmental machinery.

374

INSTITUTIONAL AND IDEOLOGICAL CONFLICTS

Administrative control of economic activities by public instrumentalities conflicts with some habits of thought and tendencies in human reaction which are strongly confirmed by our institutional and ideological heritage.

There is a basic conflict between cosmic and managerial philosophies. The cosmic philosophy assumes that there is an orderliness and regularity in a free-moving economy and that human agency should not interfere with the operation of an assumed natural system, either because it is beneficent or because it is inevitable. On the other hand, managerial "science" and art is based on the assumption that human behavior is governable, that there are areas of pliability which can be manipulated, that men rather than an unseen ghost—institutional framework rather than "economic" forces—may ride in the saddle and at least partially govern the behavior of an unruly steed.

For a time men may reconcile the two philosophies. It has been urged that management in political economy has one legitimate purpose—the removal of human impediments to the natural system. Antitrust, not free contract; government action to maintain a free market, not complete laissez faire; such is the proper course in political economy because it restores the cosmic system. Or management has a second purpose—to refine the processes of nature. The human atoms which play against each other in the economy of nature should not battle beneath the belt line; they should play clean like good sports in an American game. Public management, therefore, may appropriately extend to the prescription and enforcement of rules of clean play.

Inescapable, however, is the conclusion that sovereign man has gone beyond restoration and cleansing. Thus, through government he has made large choices affecting the framework of society—e.g., the substitution of division of estates for the rule of primogeniture, the abolition of slave labor, and the authorization of the pooling of resources and the limitation of liability through use of the corporate form. By law and administration individual and group shares in the product of the economy are modified—by agricultural payments, minimum wages, taxation, social expenditures, etc. By administrative action industries and functional areas are managed in line with prescriptions of law. Furthermore, the ideal of a compensated economy, in which the planning of man supplements the correctives of nature, is repeatedly stated and begins to be translated into action through legislation and administration.

As cosmic "system" yields to sovereign man a new ideal arises. This is the ideal of managerial science and art. It is the ideal of decisions made on the basis of analysis of economic fact and under the guidance of public objective. Ultimately, it becomes the ideal that the expert, working within an institutional framework which is partly political and partly administrative, may find solutions which accord with the purposes of men.

Ideological difficulties arise as the techniques of human management are applied in ever-widening areas of the economy. Faith in cosmic system lingers in the human breast. Man often feels that if he battles only the forces of nature there is a kind of natural or cosmic justice in the verdicts against him. Or perhaps it is only resignation—what is, must be. Faith or resignation is reinforced by "science" and propaganda. Authorities in economics—in colleges or in the world of affairs—teach that under certain assumptions— given this and given that—the economic world will be governed with a certainty comparable to that of Newtonian physics. And all the arts of salesmanship are used to keep alive the ideas that the "laws" of supply and demand, and the "natural" selection of the fit, are the beneficent and final gifts of an "invisible hand."

Different are the instinctive or cultivated reactions to public decision. Men generally have not come to have faith in the processes of administration and politics. They either feel that any decision of man is arbitrary or distrust the claim that the action of distant bureaucrats is not arbitrary because made in accord with facts and under general directive. Bureaucrats are meddlers, they are controlled by improper forces, they are ignorant of the facts of business, their decisions are arbitrary—this is the suspicion of men.

It is true, of course, that men are constantly acting in ways which show that they do not accept the cosmic system. Either through their own joint action or through their demands on government they seek to counteract the effect of "natural" forces. Nevertheless, the alternative of public control is under suspicion. When the administrative shoe pinches regulated man either tries to get a more comfortable shoe, or falls back on the argument that going barefooted accords with the eternal system of providential nature, or concludes that in any case no administrative shoe can be more comfortable than a bare foot.

It is not our purpose to argue that these techniques of resistance do or do not have value; there may be real basis for men's suspicions of regulation or great value in their vigilance against public authority. Our point is merely that the climate of human predispositions will qualify the impact of control mechanisms.

The administrator's difficulty is increased by the fact that he has no universal norm, equivalent to supply and demand, free trade among nations, or natural selection among men, upon which he can confirm the claim of the legitimacy of administrative justice. To be sure, he has the concept of the public interest and the new norms of the legislative-administrative state—"fair," "just," and "reasonable"; but these higher notions are vague and must derive their content from an understructure of fact. Ultimately, *acceptance of administration must be acceptance of a process*. It has to be based upon faith in the ability and will of cooperating groups of men working with facts and under directives in an institutional system to find wise and beneficent answers to pressing public problems.

Ultimately, as this is understood, and as men strive to establish the proper safeguards in the mechanics and morals of administration, there may be more acceptance of the process of administration. Perhaps also, acceptance will come because men will become more accustomed to the thing which does exist.

Nevertheless, administrative controls must be exerted among a confusion of notions. The economic world is a mixed system in which public control shares the field with self-operative forces and private manipulation. In this world, all absolutes in doctrine are under challenge, and conflicting notions battle for supremacy at the points where public policy emerges. Inevitably, the administrative system must run the gauntlet for understanding and acceptance in a world of conflicting notions. And this, to the democrat and to the person who believes that the efficiency of all human mechanisms must be continuously proven, will appear good, even though it here and there limits the effectiveness of government.

Another conflict is that between public control and the traditional notions of the rights of ownership and management. Administrative control creates a dual system in which private management still carries its responsibilities but is subject to overhead limitation and supervision by public management. The public authority may be superimposed in an area where private managers have been accustomed to freedom, or it may occasionally develop contemporaneously with the rise of an industry. In the former case, men who have been free from overhead restraint face the necessity of adjusting to limitations upon their freedom of action. In either case, new potentials for irritation and conflict are created. If the control hangs lightly, is exercised only occasionally, or can be adjusted to quickly and finally, then the irritations and conflicts may not be of serious dimensions; but if it invades deeply the erstwhile independent areas of private prerogative, is exercised continuously or dangles overhead in continuous threat, or if it is a dynamic system to which private management must make frequent adjustments, then the potentialities for irritation and conflict are increased.

Private managers of enterprise in regulated areas of the economy will of necessity become more accustomed to a trinitarian rather than a unitarian system of management. Their responsibilities are shared with a collateral labor power and a presumably superior public power. Thus, the president of a public utility system may find that the bulk of his time is spent with labor and with governments as a result of the limitations which both place upon his freedom. In time, he may become adjusted to the necessities and to a new concept of managerial responsibility.

Yet the seeds of irritation and conflict remain. They are continually sown out of the conflicting purposes of different groups of agents. As for the public management-private management relationship, these seeds of conflict can be fully eliminated only if the position of government is wholly one of service rather than control or if the kinship of objectives or the collaboration of private management in public regulation creates a continuously harmonious relationship. This, however, requires that any conflicting purposes embodied in the directives to administration shall be shelved. Inevitably, public control creates a measure of conflict or a measure of futility, or usually some intermediate measure of both.

Another conflict is the age-old conflict between authority and freedom. It may be true that public controls will operate to increase the freedom and happiness of man. Some may, some may not; the total trend of controls, operating as one factor in a complex system in which the initiative of a multitude of private centers is retained, is one of the uncertainties facing the verdict of future history. Man may set before him, however, the ideal that the controls he exercises through government shall contribute to and complement the forces which sustain and increase the opportunities of men to use their capacities, including that of initiative, in an expansive and self-satisfying way.

Yet the fact remains that government control involves coercion. To the extent that there is control there is restriction. The measures of control may appeal so completely to the conscience of mankind that individuals will not be conscious of coercion. On the other hand, this is not a thoroughly organic society in which the interests of each are always the interest of all or vice versa. Economic controls are in substance coercive. Moreover, as Mill recognized a century ago, there is a psychological as well as a substantive element in freedom. To an extent men are not free if they feel they are not free. Their soul may be cramped, even though their capacity is increased. The man who is angered by a red traffic light is a coerced and frustrated man, and so likewise is the manager of enterprise who has not adjusted his thought reflexes to acceptance of the surrounding system of economic controls.

Men who feel they are coerced often become rebellious men. The administrator of economic controls becomes limited in turn by the potentialities for rebellion by those who feel they are coerced, for rebellion leads to the courthouse, the Congress, the party machinery, and to the administrative hierarchy. In a free society, therefore, the freedom of man to object and seek a change limits the control activities of government.

The real hope for government in a democratic society is that it may find ways of attaining broad and enduring objectives of men generally without overextension of the coercive authority of the state over individuals. The service state is a more alluring vision than the control state. And yet the service state raises antagonism at points, either because it often brings a tax, or because in one area, namely, that where public action must reach deep into the managerial aspects of a particular business, the question is presented as to whether direct government supply of the service to the consumer is not sometimes a more suitable device than overhead regulation for a government interested in effectiveness, freedom, and a harmonious society. Where service (i.e. benefit) can be mixed with control, as in the current agricultural program, the conflict between public authority and the individual affected may be diminished or eliminated. And yet here, dangers of public committal to service or benefit without sufficient control arise. Where control rather than service is the method of government, the administrator will seek to obtain voluntary acceptance through communication of purpose and the marshalling of cooperative opinion among those affected by control. He will seek to avoid the sense of subjection in men because this coincides with his democratic ideals and with his objective of maintaining the solvency of his program. Beyond all this, those who fashion economic policy will need to search for ways in which government policy may contribute to a balanced advance in the economy as a whole, for in such an economy the pressure on government for expansion of controls over particulars is reduced and the sense of coercion in existing areas of controls is also reduced.

THE CONDITIONS AFFECTING PUBLIC ACTION

Ofttimes public administration is given responsibility only after a situation has developed which defies solution by ideal standards. Railroad rate regulation came after a period of rate distortions by competitive urges; the power to approve changes in railroad organization came only after the railroad network had become a complex of weak and strong lines; and the various other powers in the Transportation Act of 1920 for providing an adequate transportation system were granted only after the railroads were disorganized, unplanned, and in financial stress. The biggest weakness in anti-trust enforcement has been that it has had to try to revise industry organizations or practices which have already crystallized. Coal and agriculture were sick industries when the government took action in the thirties. There was an inheritance of a multitude of weak state banks, and traditions of free banking, before the national government began to create and regulate banks. An administrative agency had to try to obtain employer acceptance for the right of labor to choose its representatives for collective bargaining after the struggle between two systems of organization had split labor itself into warring groups. A broad attack on the problem of inflation in World War II came only after wages and agricultural prices had risen and after government spending had reached enormous heights. Like the teacher in a correction home for delinquent children or the social worker working with adults, the administrator often finds that the past limits the future.

In some cases, however, public administration has been able to start with a clean slate. This was true substantially of air commerce, radio, and atomic energy. In such cases the statutes have sought to retain all the elements of public power needed for protection of the public interest. In radio, short licenses and the rule that property rights in wave lengths should not vest in licensees seemed to provide adequate safeguards to the public. In the regulation of air commerce, the various administrative powers which experience had shown should be vested in a body regulating a utility were given to the

Civil Aeronautics Authority and the responsibility for planned development was implicit in the statutory system. In radio regulation, however, the regulatory agency was weak in the formative period; and the evolution of a concept of public interest lagged behind the crystallization of trends in the industry, which soon left the regulatory agency with restricted pliability. In air commerce the present route pattern problem raises doubts as to whether public planning can forge a policy in advance of the growth of complexities comparable to those in the railroad industry. As for atomic energy, time only will tell whether the political attacks which have been made on the regulatory agency are only a prelude to a swarm of influences which will destroy the administrative power to govern the lines of development of a new industry.

These comments point to the difficulty of matching public foresight with the rapid course of events and the diversified situations which arise under private initiative. Experience does not indicate that public regulation stops the course of private initiative (though it may modify or restrict the course); rather, it reveals that the great difficulty is that of obtaining an over-all and forward view in situations which quickly become complex and full of resistances to alterability.

These resistances limit the administrator because interests are centered around each factor in the developed or developing situation. Each interest sets up a claim for consideration. A free society gives to each a variety of avenues for protection of its interests— Congress, the appointive power of the President, the courts, the press and the radio, and the administrative forum itself. It allows to each a variety of approaches, varying from open hostility to infiltration of influence through the medium of cooperation. Given these opportunities, vigilance and versatility will characterize the efforts of interests affected by administrative action.

The administrator's responsibility with respect to these interests may extend no further than the mediation of conflicts. Ordinarily, however, his directive will have been framed with the idea that he shall effect some change. He may be expected to obtain acceptance of a new standard of conduct, or to expand the protection

given to some particular group, or to effect some change in the
organization of industry, or to exercise some continuing manipulative
force of a managerial nature over an industry or a functional segment of the economy.

But the attainment of these objectives is obstructed by the complex of resistances which face the administrator. Those who have
an established position which may be threatened will seek delay,
inaction, or moderation; and those who seek licenses or other government consent or benefit will seek to avoid restrictive conditions.
The resistances of interests will join the complexities of fact situations to tempt the administrator into the easy path of handling the
minutiae of today and leaving for more investigation the hard
answer for the long run. In the course of time the administrator
finds that the initial public drive and congressional sentiment behind
his directive has wilted, and that political support for change from
the existing pattern is lacking. Moderation, temporizing, and resignation to inevitables, not aggressive and forceful action, become,
therefore, for better or worse, the usual attributes of administrative
control over the lives of men who are free to protect and promote
their interests in the multiple ways offered by a democratic society.

The difficulties in administrative control may be increased by the
balance which is struck between public power and private action.
The administrator may find that the power of his agency hangs
lightly over the private interests subject to control. This was the
historical situation in utility regulation where it was long assumed
that regulation of rates could be successful without correlative regulation of utility finance, organization, and corporate interrelationships. It is the situation in anti-trust regulation where intervention
is so occasional and often so tardy. Seldom does an agency have
the plenitude of power over industry organization which is given
to the Securities Exchange Commission in the "death sentence" for
holding companies which do not meet the standards of the holding
company act. Normally, as in railroad organization and in air line
consolidation, the regulatory agency stands at a point removed from
the problem and acts only as the initiative of parties brings proposals
to the agency, which faces limitations against compulsory action.

The veto system over a complex rate structure, as in railroad regulation, means occasional intervention except through broader rate proceedings initiated by the regulatory agency; and the recent act authorizing railroads to fix rates by agreements presents the question as to whether the supervisory power can extend far enough to give protection to interests unrepresented or inadequately represented in the rate-making bureaus. Even in radio regulation, where public powers are broad, the regulatory agency must seek to give meaning to the public interest in a context of private application and private payment of broadcasting costs without public support through subsidy or a levy on listeners.

Normally, regulatory power is broad and deep only after great abuses in private action or deficiencies in public power have been revealed by hard experience. Deeply imbedded in the thought of the people are the ideas that men should be free and have initiative and that public intervention should be exceptional, correctional, and moderate. Moreover, politics fishes only in agitated waters; it grabs at the issues forced by the exigencies of the moment and looks reluctantly at tomorrow's problems.

"Too late and too little" are, therefore, the weaknesses inherent in governmental efforts to influence the course of a complex and rapidly moving economy. Foresight is limited, public power is expected to be moderate in relation to private initiative, and the nature of politics is to give attention to the immediate.

Further factors will affect the performance of government. The administrator wants to be "right." The responsible administrator of economic controls recognizes that he is dealing with a complex structure and that the welfare of millions may be affected by what he does. His diversified staff and the interests regulated will pile before him a multitude of facts, a diversity of angles of the problem which must receive attention, and a mountain of objections and partial views concerning solutions. He must feel that he is right and that he is able to carry the burden of proof before he disturbs the status quo, restricts the freedom of enterprise, or seeks to affect the operation of a delicate economic mechanism.

The administrator will also want to be safe. Will the action stand up in the courts? In the Congress and the public? Can it be "lived with"? Or will it bring that avalanche of criticism, if only from a minority, and that attack from within Congress, which the administrator wants to avoid because he has learned from experience or observation that these are exasperating, frustrating, and make expendables out of administrators?

In addition, the administrator acquires an institutional viewpoint and shrinks from action which threatens the stability and continuity of the evolved system of administrative control. Rarely does an administrator feel that his agency or a stabilized portion of its work should be threatened with expendability by a new advance or a novel approach. Past gains which are stabilized and the safety of institutional program are measured heavily on the scales, against prospective public advantages.

Such factors influence the judgment of men who must plan for the administration even of emergency programs. They seek an organizational vessel which will not be overly concerned with its own perpetuity and they seek men who will not worry as much about the danger of expendability as the government careerists must. Such factors also reflect something of the normal expectancy which men may legitimately hold for administration. Those who fear recklessness in large administration and those who look for quick adjustability in going and established public administrative institutions have small basis for their fears or their hopes, at least when the context is one of regulation of the economic pursuits of free and vigilant men. More realistic is the view which recognizes that the full effects of institutional behavior condition the force and freshness of government program.

In the light of the preceding reflections, it is possible to advance a set of hypotheses concerning the level of expectancy which men may reasonably set for administrative institutions. In an initial period after a new statutory program is created the conditions may be such that society may justifiably place a heavy demand upon administrative agents. There is an initial political force which moves with a directive from Congress, and it may be extended by presidential support for the new program. This may give the agency the opportunity—perhaps the only one it will ever have—to make a material contribution to the shape of things. But very probably, if it is to achieve such results, it must establish its beachheads quickly, and extend and fortify its lines without delay. Standards for conduct of private enterprise, guiding standards for the administrative agency, and the position of the agency may be established before the political force behind the agency's directive is spent and the dissident groups have found ways of moderating or checkmating the new program. Later, there comes a period of maturity, when the agency has lost the original political support, when it has found its position among the contending forces in society, and when it has crystallized its own evolved program. It then becomes part of the status quo and thinks in terms of the protection of its own system and its own existence and power against substantial change. Its primary function in government is to operate the mechanisms which have been developed in its creative stage and adjust these as circumstances change. This is not to say that it may not still initiate constructive changes, for changes, and even leaps, in administrative program are sometimes made as conditions change, and agencies also may go to the Congress for new directive; but it is too much to expect that, after maturity is reached, government will find all the origination and perspective which it needs in its administrative institutions alone.

THE TESTS OF THE FUTURE

The mechanism of control can operate with only limited effectiveness. Yet hard demands have been made of it and tougher demands may be made in the future.

The mere maintenance of standards in a complex economic organism is itself no easy task. Thus, the Wages and Hours Administration has a difficult job in obtaining compliance, the C.A.B. has difficult technical problems in air safety, the F.T.C. has not yet solved the problem of maintaining fair trade practices, and the N.L.R.B. and the General Counsel face many thorny problems in labor and management practices.

Likewise, the limited function of "moderating the strains" among groups is often a difficult one to perform. This has been true in railroad regulation where the function of the I.C.C. has become so largely one of maintaining a "moving balance" between groups and sections. It is especially true at this time in labor relations, where the hope for avoiding government prescription of positive labor standards under a system of compulsory settlement rests on success of government definition of the rights of each party, the spirit of the parties at the bargaining table, and the government's mediatory and fact-finding work.

The public responsibilities in maintaining the economic and social health of regulated industries become increasingly complex and baffling. Agriculture, banking, railroads, natural gas, and others, present their special problems and so likewise do the industries for which the Department of Justice and the courts try to find in anti-trust suits a pattern of competition which is workable. How meet the problem of existent or threatened overexpansion? Can means be found to eliminate the unfit in a regulated industry? Can regulated industries be organized rationally instead of haphazardly? Can guiding principles of positive policy be applied in fuel and transportation? Can standards concerning the proper income of regulated industries be evolved? Can subsidies and benefit payments be used constructively and with proper restraint? Can a balance be struck between private and public power which maintains the initiative of the former and the policy of the latter? Can regulatory mechanisms work with sufficient satisfaction to justify their selection instead of a system of direct public supply of the commodity or service?

Even more difficult problems arise as public administration is given responsibilities concerning the operation of the economy as a whole. Can budgets, public works programs, credit and labor policies, as developed in administration, be geared to the over-all needs of the economy? Can administration be prepared for its tasks in various types of emergencies, such as the threat of a runaway inflation, or of a general depression, or of a serious imbalance in the economy with high unemployment accompanying high returns for employed labor and capital, or of all-out mobilization for an international emergency?

These questions are unanswerable, perhaps even imponderable, unless broken down into particular contexts. Nevertheless, they, along with the preceding discussion, convey an imperative of our day. Whether one accepts willingly or with great reluctance the expansion of public administrative control in the economy, he must nevertheless recognize that there are areas in which it has been or may be inevitable, that public controls in a society which respects the acquired rights of men and their right to present their interests through multiple channels and also values the self-generative forces of human initiative will be only partially successful, and that the responsibilities placed on administration and the limitations on its success require concern over its ability to meet the public requirements upon it. A final brief summary on some of the ways by which the effectiveness of administrative control may be measurably assured must, therefore, follow and conclude this volume.

A SUMMARY ON THE MECHANISM OF CONTROL

Experience has abundantly revealed some essentials for effective and responsible administration. At this stage, some must, indeed, be stated generally, with specific means to be revealed by further experience and analysis.

The central trend has been toward unification in so-called administrative agencies of all parts of the job of moving forward with the business of government. The administrative span now reaches to all types of power or function differentiated in either the tripartite or bipartite theories of government functions.

The basic trend appears to have been inevitable. Elements in the trend have often been condemned, but we believe the advantages of unification are so great that correctives should not strike at the heart of the system. The policy-making function cannot be completed in congressional directives, and legislative science should be directed toward clarity without overspecificity in directives. Functions of planning, promotion, routine performance, and decisions having quasi-judicial aspects, may be differentiated in considerable degree; but usually the differentiations will need to be made within an agency having responsibility for total results so that the unity of the regulatory process may not be impaired.

In the area of methods, there has been a steady expansion of techniques for developing and implementing policy. Time has been prolific in yielding a variety of basic instruments from which choice may be made by legislators or administrators. Experience in the older fields of control has shown the types of facilitative arrangements which are needed in order to make the administrative agency the center of authority in the regulatory process. Experience has revealed to the framer of statutes the essentials of power which must support the administrative agency and to the administrator the need for skill in developing understanding, in adjusting sanctions, and in increasing force by persuasion and conviction. The agencies have gone through the initial period of groping for forms of procedure which were adapted to expertise and dispatch; and although the Administrative Procedure Act creates some uncertainties for the future, it allows much diversity in administrative procedure, and it may be that the agencies will still find ample freedom to work toward informality, simplification, and institutional collaboration in their operating methods.

Although the interrelations between the regulators and the regulated in the operation of control mechanisms create problems which can never be fully solved, some of the basic needs are distinguishable. One is the need for a positive statement of the administrator's function. We have defined this function as one of expertness in finding the ways in which the areas of pliability in the economic organism can be made to yield to community purpose as stated in political directives. The other need is to maintain the concept of the independence of public office from private point of view and to strengthen this concept in the arrangements of organization, personnel, and procedure, and in ethical standards of administration.

Perhaps the most hopeful present tendency is the increased recognition of the needs for planning at all higher levels and for the conversion of plan into general rules of future applicability. These approaches provide opportunities for the larger and the longer view and for the injection of objective thought into policy making in advance of the organization of the forces of resistance.

Experience has indicated some of the lines along which responsibility in administration must be sought. The courts have seen the threat to government (and of their own inundation) involved in the judicial attempt to share administrative discretion, and there is widespread recognition that the main safeguards must come from the character and experience of men and the proper organization and functioning of the institutional process. Perhaps further advance can be made if the attention given to questions of power, mechanism, and operating method is supplemented by greater search for ways of improving the quality of administrative personnel and by an attempt to clarify for administrative personnel the standards of ethics which should govern in the administrative service.

It is in the area of political responsibility that the most difficult problems are presented. In our opinion the most serious present deficiency in the system of administrative control is the particularism of the administrative agencies and the claims made on their behalf for autonomy from overhead controls. On this point there is, of course, much difference of opinion. It would be generally admitted that more effective oversight from the Congress would be desirable. The points of disagreement arise over integration into larger administrative units and over the power of the president. The problem is one of balancing needs. Administration needs to be decentralized in operation and needs some check underneath through contact with those immersed in the details of industries. The more pressing need, however, is to get an inclusive view of public policy and to keep the administrator's activities oriented to the larger objectives of government. We have suggested that these ends might best be met in our political system by clearly vesting responsibility in the President (informed by staff aides and properly limited to general policy and to action insofar as is feasible by open directive) to correlate administrative policies with the larger purposes of government. And we have also suggested that this is the condition precedent to more effective congressional control of administration.

At the higher level of responsibility, where the President and Congress share authority, control over administration is weakened and dissipated by the unresolved riddles of political power. The separation between the executive and Congress, the weakness of party controls within the Congress, the disintegration of the party system in the country, and the organization and persistence of functional and sectional interests, overextend the power of particularistic influences and weaken the ability of Congress and the President, acting together, to evaluate administrative performance and to use the legislative power as a means of giving new directives to administration. This means that the ultimate problem of American government is neither political nor administrative but is both; and that the problems of administration, congressional direction and control, and executive-legislative relationships all merge in one major problem which must challenge the attention of professional political scientists and statesmen.

But on the administrative side alone the problem is simpler and the clues for solution are clearer. The problem there is to strike a balance among three types of administrative centers—operating, planning, and directory. The operating centers—bureaus, boards, and administrations—are the primary units in administration. They carry the responsibility for particular programs. They should have the full responsibility for the application of policy to particular persons and for the normal development of administrative policy. They supply the continuity which comes from the operation of going concerns and the expertness which comes from the familiarity with special facts, the collaboration of groups of specialists, and the acquired experience of responsible men. The planning centers are staff units to aid at the operating and directory levels. Their function is study and recommendation. They should, as part of their task, take another view—a new look, and an over-all look—at the problems which should be met at the administrative levels at which they are working. The directory centers—President, department heads, and coordinators—have responsibility for direction, supervision, and coordination of lower units in the administrative scale. Though the responsibility be continuous, its exercise is occasional with respect to particular operating units. The responsibility is in part political; it is, however, subordinate to the final dual power of the Congress and the President. The function of the directory staff is to deal with new and large issues of policy. Its utility lies in its middle position between the capacity of Congress, able to act only through very broad directives, and the capacity of agencies, limited by the areas of their assignments and their absorption in the operation of their evolved systems.

The directory function is only weakly and partially provided in present arrangements for economic control. The full establishment of the directory power and a clear concept of the appropriate area for its exercise are, in the author's opinion, urgent needs in a nation which must gird itself for an uncertain future.

INDEX